The Right to Family Life in the European Union

Exploring the main developments and challenges for the right to family life in the context of European integration, this book examines the right to family life in the EU Charter of Fundamental Rights and the interplay between family life, citizenship, and free movement; it analyzes the combined impact of the EU and the European Convention on Human Rights on the concept of the family protected by the law in light of recent case law. Considering the broadening understanding of what constitutes family, the challenges for the right to family life in the context of immigration, and the protection of families and social rights, it provides a comprehensive overview of the current state of family life in the European Union.

Maribel González Pascual is Law Professor at Pompeu Fabra University. Her research fields include comparative federalism, fundamental rights and judicial cooperation and welfare rights in Europe.

Aida Torres Pérez is Law Professor at Pompeu Fabra University. Her research interests include European constitutionalism, judicial dialogue, fundamental rights in Europe, and the independence of the international judiciary.

Routledge Research in EU Law

For a full list of titles in this series, please visit www.routledge.com

Available titles in this series include:

Kadi on Trial
A Multifaceted Analysis of the Kadi Trial
Matej Avbelj, Filippo Fontanelli and Giuseppe Martinico

The Judge and the Proportionate Use of Discretion
A Comparative Administrative Law Study
Sofia Ranchordás and Boudewijn de Waard

European Agencies and Risk Governance in EU Financial Market Law
Paul Weismann

EU Health Systems and Distributive Justice
Towards New Paradigms for the Provision of Health Care Services?
Danielle Da Costa Leite Borges

EU Criminal Law and Policy
Values, Principles and Methods
Joanna Beata Banach-Gutierrez and Christopher Harding

The European Union as an Area of Freedom, Security and Justice
Maria Fletcher, Ester Herlin-Karnell and Claudio Matera

The Right to Family Life in the European Union
Edited by Maribel González Pascual and Aida Torres Pérez

Forthcoming in this series:

Retail Investor Protection under EU Law
Constantinos Tokatlides

The Right to Family Life in the European Union

Edited by
Maribel González Pascual and
Aida Torres Pérez

Routledge
Taylor & Francis Group
LONDON AND NEW YORK

First published 2017 by Routledge

2 Park Square, Milton Park, Abingdon, Oxfordshire OX14 4RN
52 Vanderbilt Avenue, New York, NY 10017

Routledge is an imprint of the Taylor & Francis Group, an informa business

First issued in paperback 2018

British Library Cataloguing in Publication Data
A catalogue record for this book is available from the British Library

Library of Congress Cataloging in Publication Data
A catalog record for this book has been requested

ISBN: 978-1-138-18627-9 (hbk)
ISBN: 978-0-367-07552-1 (pbk)

Typeset in NewBaskerville
by Apex CoVantage, LLC

In memory of our friend Kristine Kruma.
She will be sorely missed.

Contents

Notes on contributors

Lucía Alonso Sanz is Lecturer of Constitutional Law at the University Loyola Andalucía. She holds a European PhD from the Complutense University of Madrid and has been a visiting researcher at the European University Institute (Florence); the University of Lisbon; the Max Planck Institute for Comparative Public Law and International Law (Heidelberg); and the Pontifical Catholic University of Peru (Lima). Her research interests include fundamental rights in Europe, constitutional status of immigrants and minors, and democratic regeneration.

Lucia Busatta is Assistant Professor at the University of Trento. She wrote a doctoral dissertation on *Constitutional guarantees for the right to healthcare.* She has been a visiting researcher at King's College London, University of Glasgow, and Pompeu Fabra University. Her main fields of research are the guarantees of the right to healthcare, the principle of equality, human dignity and fundamental rights' protection. She collaborates on the BioLaw project, of the Department of Legal Sciences at the University of Trento and in Firb 2007 Project, on the impact of biotechnological innovations of fundamental rights.

Guillem Cano Palomares has held the position of Lawyer of the Research and Library Division at the European Court of Human Rights since 2005. He is a member of the Board of Directors of the Human Rights Institute of Catalonia. He has taught several courses and seminars on Human Rights. Moreover, he is the author of several articles on the European Court of Human Rights.

Keiva Carr is an administrator-lawyer at the Research and Documentation Directorate, CJEU. She holds a PhD and an LLM from the European University Institute, Florence, Italy. She is a scientific collaborator at the Lider-Lab, Scuola Superiore Sant'Anna, Pisa, Italy. Her research interests include Private Law, Comparative Law, Family Law, European constitutionalism, and fundamental rights in Europe.

Samantha Currie is a Lecturer at the University of Liverpool. Her work covers several aspects of EU law and migration, including: migration in the context of the EU's eastern enlargement; Union citizenship; the cross-border posting of workers in the EU; gender and migration; and the rights of non-EU family members accompanying EU migrant workers. She has published a monograph on *Migration, Work and Citizenship in the Enlarged European Union* (Ashgate 2008).

Ester Farnós Amorós is Law Professor at Pompeu Fabra University, prior to this, she was Assistant Professor of Private Law at Pompeu Fabra University (Barcelona). Her PhD on the *Failure of the parental project and the disposition of pre-embryos* received the Extraordinary Award by Pompeu Fabra University. She has been a visiting researcher at the Oxford Centre for Family Law and Policy and Cornell Law School. Her main fields of research are family law, torts, and contract law.

Maribel González Pascual is Law Professor at Pompeu Fabra University. She was a research scholar at Salamanca University, at the National Institute of Public Administration and at the Max Planck Institut für ausländisches öffentliches Recht und Völkerrecht. In addition, she has been a visiting scholar at the abovementioned Max Planck Institut, the Deutsche Verwaltungs Hochschule, the Maastricht Center for European Law, Bristol University and Bergamo University. She is a member of the international project 'BEUcitizen' (European Union's Seventh Framework Programme). Her research interests are comparative research on Federal States, fundamental rights within Europe, particularly welfare rights, and also the interplay between mutual recognition principle and fundamental rights.

Sara Iglesias Sánchez LL.M. (Yale Law School), PhD (Universidad Complutense of Madrid) is a Référandaire at the European Court of Justice. Prior to this, she was a lawyer in the Research Direction of the CJEU and lecturer at the University of Cádiz. She has been a visiting researcher at the Max Planck Institute for International and Comparative Law, at Radboud University, and the Center of Research and Studies of the Hague Academy of International law, and has been a Schuman Fellow at the legal service of the European Parliament. Her research has mainly focused on EU migration law, citizenship and the protection of fundamental rights in the European Union.

Kristine Kruma was Pro-rector of the Riga Graduate School of Law, Judge of the Constitutional Court of Latvia and Judge ad hoc of the European Court of Human Rights. She obtained her PhD at Lund University, was a visiting lecturer in Public International Law and EU law at the Riga Graduate School of Law and an expert of European Commission against Racism and Intolerance. She was a visiting scholar at the Max Planck Institute of International and Comparative Law in Heidelberg and the Centre for Migration in Nijmegen. Her research was on EU citizenship, migration, integration of third country nationals, and national citizenship regulation.

Luis López Guerra has been a Judge on the European Court of Human Rights since 2008. He holds a Doctorate in Law from the University of Madrid and a Master's degree in Political Science from Michigan State University. He is a former Professor of Constitutional Law at the Universidad Carlos III (Madrid). He was a Judge of the Spanish Constitutional Court (1986–1995), Vice-President of the General Council of the Judiciary, Alternative Representative and Legal Expert for the Venice Commission. He is the author of several articles and books on Constitutional Law.

Anna Lorezentti is a Researcher at the University of Bergamo, where she earned her PhD. She authored several articles and papers particularly on LGBTI rights and also a recent monograph on the legal condition of transgender people. She has been a visiting scholar at the Humboldt Universität zu Berlin. She is a member of the project 'Litigious Love: Same-Sex Couples and Mediation in Europe' (funding from the European Commission). Her fields of interest are antidiscrimination law and equality, gender and the law, and LGBTI rights.

Sílvia Morgades-Gil is a Lecturer of International Public Law at Pompeu Fabra University. Her PhD on human rights and the protection of refugees received a Research Award on Human Rights by the Generalitat de Catalunya. She holds a Diplôme d'Université de Droit des Réfugiés, Etrangers et Apatrides (Université de Montpellier I); and a Master's degree in European Studies (Autonomous University of Barcelona). She is an expert on asylum and her research interests include EU law, immigration and citizenship.

Joan Solanes Mullor is Assistant Professor at Pompeu Fabra University (Barcelona). He earned an LLM at Harvard Law School and a PhD at Pompeu Fabra University. He has been a visiting researcher at Harvard Law School and the University of Leuven (Belgium), and a visiting professor at the University of Trento. His main research interests include administrative agencies, public administrative law, and fundamental rights.

Aida Torres Pérez is Law Professor and Coordinator of the PhD Program at Pompeu Fabra University. She holds an LLM and a JSD from the Yale Law School and has been a visiting scholar at the European University Institute (Florence); the University of Trento; the University of Maastricht; the Max Planck Institute for Comparative Public Law and International Law (Heidelberg); and the Centre of Excellence for International Courts (Copenhagen). Her research interests include European constitutionalism, judicial dialogue, fundamental rights in Europe, and the independence of the international judiciary.

Bruno de Witte is Professor of European Law at the European University Institute and at the Robert Schuman Centre for Advanced Studies and co-director of the EUDO Observatory on Institutional Change and Reforms. He is also a Professor of European Law at the University of Maastricht and co-director of the Maastricht Centre for European Law. His main fields of research are constitutional reform and treaty revision in the European Union; the relationship between international, European and national law; the protection of fundamental rights in Europe; rights of minorities, language law and cultural diversity in Europe; internal market law; decision-making and legal instruments of EU law.

Abbreviations

Area of Freedom, Security and Justice (AFSJ)
Common European Asylum System (CEAS)
Convention on the Rights of the Child (CRC)
Court of Justice of the European Union (CJEU)
EU Charter of Fundamental Rights (Charter)
EU General Court (EUGC)
European Arrest Warrant (EAW)
European Commission of Human Rights (EComHR)
European Committee of Social Rights (ECSR)
European Convention on Human Rights (ECHR)
European Court of Human Rights (ECtHR)
European Social Charter (ESC)
European Union (EU)
International Covenant on Economic, Social and Cultural Rights (ICESCR)
Parliamentary Assembly of the Council of Europe (PACE)
Third Country National (TCN)
Treaty on European Union (TEU)
Treaty on the Functioning of the European Union (TFUE)
United Nations (UN)

Introduction

Maribel González Pascual and Aida Torres Pérez

Family life plays a crucial role in the upbringing of individuals and their personal and social development, and is traditionally linked to cultural and national values. In recent years, changing social attitudes, a broader understanding of what comprises family, increasing mobility, and the economic crisis have greatly affected family-related matters. In this context, the rights attached to family relationships are no longer of limited domestic concern and need to be examined within the framework of the plural system of rights protection in Europe.

The Treaty of Lisbon strengthened the role of EU fundamental rights by rendering the EU Charter of Fundamental Rights legally binding. The Charter enshrines the right to respect for private and family life, home and communications in Article 7. This provision is grounded on Article 8 ECHR, and the ECtHR has produced relevant case law on the interpretation of the right to family life in diverse fields encompassing same-sex couples, transsexuals, parental visiting rights, parental abduction, medically-assisted procreation, immigration, and even social rights. The ECHR shall guide the interpretation of Article 7 of the Charter, since according to Article 52(3) of the Charter, the rights of the Charter that correspond to rights guaranteed by the ECHR should have the same meaning and scope of the rights of the Convention. At the same time, Article 52(3) leaves the door open for a more extensive protection in the EU. Therefore, the inquiry about family life in the EU needs to be conducted within the framework provided by the ECHR and the Strasbourg case law.

In addition, the respect of family life is guaranteed in other international instruments, such as the International Covenant on Civil and Political Rights (Article 17), or the International Covenant on Economic and Social Rights, which includes the right "of everyone to an adequate standard of living for himself and his family, including adequate food, clothing and housing" (Article 11). Furthermore, there are international conventions of specific relevance in this field, such as the Convention on the Rights of the Child.

The goal of this book is to explore the main developments and challenges for the right to family life in the context of European integration.

What is the role and content of the right to family life in EU law? Which are the future challenges to the right to family life posed by the technological and sociological developments? To what extent does the EU contribute to the protection of the right to family life and what are the main shortcomings in key fields, such as immigration and welfare? The book will therefore start by examining the right to family life in the ECHR and the EU Charter. Next, the combined impact of EU law and the ECHR in framing the concept of the family protected by the law will be analyzed. Thereafter, the study will focus on two fields that are both timely and relevant: the right to family life in immigration law and the protection of social rights of particular relevance for families. Accordingly, the contents have been structured in four main parts.

The right to family life in Europe

The first part will approach the right to family life as a fundamental right in Europe. In the opening chapter, the ECtHR Judge López Guerra examines the primary issues in the Strasbourg case law concerning the right to "private and family life" guaranteed under Convention Article 8. An immediate characteristic of this case law involves the evolution of the concept of family, including non-marital and *de facto* relationships, stressing the notion of "life together" as an essential element. From this perspective, and following the Court's general approach, its judgments reflect the idea that this right entails negative as well as positive obligations for the State, i.e., both respecting as well as protecting private and family life. The Court's case law demonstrates that these obligations have impact in many areas, of which the most relevant in quantitative terms may be the right to enter and reside in a country that is party to the Convention based on family ties. The Court's application of Convention Article 8 is likewise relevant in matters concerning the voluntary separation of families due to divorce or other causes, as well as mandatory separation resulting from measures adopted by authorities, such as assuming custody of children. Lastly, the chapter analyzes a new aspect of the protection of private and family life: barring public authorities from depriving citizens of minimally sufficient conditions for family life in the midst of the current crisis.

The following chapters will focus on the right to family life as it is protected by the Charter. At first, given the limited scope of application of the Charter to the Member States, de Witte explores the meaning of Article 51(1). The main issue is ascertaining what is exactly meant by the words "when they are implementing" EU law: when can the action of a national institution be qualified as a measure that implements EU law obligations? In particular, it is questionable whether the Member State institutions are bound by the Charter in cases where EU law provides for minimum harmonization, and where the national legal rules go further than the text of the

EU regulation or directive. The discussion will mainly focus on the Directive on family reunification and the role of Charter Article 7.

Iglesias and Carr seek to analyze the specific content of the right to family life in EU law, focusing on the interpretation of Article 7 of the Charter in recent case law, and through the examination of the impact of relevant acts of secondary law.

In this context, the chapter argues, on the one hand, that whereas the content of Article 7 does not entail the introduction of big innovative elements with regard to the wording of Article 8 ECHR, the interaction of this provision with Article 24 of the Charter and its development through secondary law, are endowing the right to family life with specific and differential contours in EU law. On the other hand, it will be posited that, whereas free movement law fosters the development of new ways of family life and has, in many ways, contributed to render more flexible the family model in the EU, it is sometimes ill-equipped to give a response to the transnational ways of life of EU families. Through a family-life centered reading of the CJEU case law, this chapter discusses some of the challenges and limitations of the protection of family life in EU law.

Finally, González Pascual focuses on the impact upon the right to family life of judicial cooperation based on the principle of mutual recognition in the EU. This principle implies that decisions made in one Member State must be respected and applied automatically in another Member State. However, the parameters shaped to guarantee the right to family life can only be effectively applied by a court with jurisdiction over the place where a family actually lives. Therefore, the court actually equipped to guarantee the right to family life is not always the one empowered by EU law.

Besides, both the CJEU and the ECtHR have shied away from considering the right to family life of a person who will be separated from his or her family for having committed a criminal offence in another State. Regarding parental abduction, the case law of the CJEU and of the ECtHR are contradictory. Domestic courts lack clear guidance in this field.

Ultimately, the aim of this chapter is to strike a new balance between the right to family life and mutual recognition in the EU to enable judicial cooperation without undermining fundamental rights by focusing mainly on the case law related to the EAW and children abduction.

Towards a broader understanding of the family

The second part of the book will examine the impact of the EU and the ECtHR case law in expanding the notion of the family. Over time, the social understanding of what constitutes a family has broadened and, as a result, so has the notion of family life protected by the law. Family life now potentially includes married and unmarried couples, both homosexual and heterosexual, with or without children, whether biological or adoptive, as well as single-parent families. EU law and, more significantly, ECtHR case law, have had major impact on national legal systems in terms of the protection of family life. In particular, this section will reflect upon the strengthening of the right to family life of transsexuals as a consequence of the interplay between the ECtHR and the CJEU; the recent developments regarding the right to family life in connection to medically assisted procreation, and the tensions between biological truth and social parenting in the Strasbourg case law.

Lorenzetti critically examines the ECtHR and CJEU case law regarding the enjoyment of family life by transsexuals vis-à-vis the traditional conception of the family. The central point for transsexual persons is that when they cross genders, they defy binary distinction between male and female.

Since the landmark case *Goodwin v UK*, the ECtHR has recognized the obligation of national authorities to ensure legal recognition of the person's gender reassignment and the absence of any justification for barring the transsexual from enjoying the right to marry. The judicial dialogue with the ECtHR also fostered a number of significant decisions by the CJEU. In fact, the CJEU rejected the idea that "sex" can only mean the biological status of a person that is fixed at birth. In illustrating the arguments used by these European courts, this chapter seeks to determine whether the approach represents reaffirmation of the binary gender system and the traditional idea of family based on marriage between a man and a woman or whether it moves beyond these traditional categories.

Next, Cano Palomares analyses the evolution of the case-law of the ECtHR regarding access to and the consequences of medically-assisted procreation, from the early judgments concerning access to medically-assisted procreation. Although the ECtHR has extended the applicability of Article 8 of the Convention to include the right to become a genetic parent of a child and the right of a couple to conceive a child and to make use of medically assisted procreation, the use of the doctrine of the State's margin of appreciation and the lack of European consensus in these matters have limited the extent of the protection afforded to these rights. The Convention being a "living instrument", the ECtHR may adopt a more liberal approach in the future, taking into account the fast-moving legal and scientific developments in the field of artificial procreation.

In connection with the previous chapter, Farnós reflects upon the challenges of biology-based parentage systems. The different legal positions concerning the exercise of paternity claims highlight the contrasting prevalent values endorsed by European countries in parentage law. Comparative law findings show two main trends moving in opposite directions: biological truth versus family life or legal certainty. The chapter examines the different types of "safety valves" that allow the respect deserved by social parenthood to be reconciled with the identity interests. At the end, the chapter questions whether the legal status derived from the parent–child relationship should be maintained as a unitary status or could be broken up into different parental legal positions.

The right to family life in immigration law

The third part will focus on the challenges for the right to family life in the context of immigration law. The EU has passed relevant legislation applicable to TCNs who are the family members of EU citizens (Directive 2004/38, on the rights of EU citizens and their family members to move and reside freely within the territory of the Member States), or other third country nationals residing lawfully in the EU (Directive 2003/86 on the right to family reunification for third country nationals). In addition, the protection of family life has timidly become a part of the regulatory instruments pertaining to the common European asylum policy. At the same time, in implementing EU legislation, Member States have striven to preserve their policy making power. The law in this area is fragmented along lines following the multiple and partially overlapping statuses of individuals encompassing nationals, EU citizens, TCNs, lawful or unlawful residents. The right to family life cuts across all these categories and becomes relevant in the myriad scenarios that arise when the members of the family move across countries. The chapters in this section will discuss family life in connection to EU citizenship, the expulsion of TCNs, non-accompanied minors, and asylum.

On the basis of the CJEU case law, Kruma argues that the right to family life has furthered a more robust notion of EU citizenship. The chapter first examines the concept of EU citizenship and Directive 2004/38 on the free movement of citizens and their families in light of the right to family life. Next, it discusses the achievements and challenges posed by recent case law regarding dual citizens, the protection of children, and reverse discrimination. The author claims that although the test formulated in Ruiz Zambrano regarding the "genuine enjoyment of the substance of rights" conferred by virtue of EU citizenship might seem unclear and its methodology is poorly explained by the CJEU, it has substantial potential for advancing EU citizenship.

In the following chapter, Torres Pérez will address the following question: to what extent does the right to family life bar the expulsion of third country nationals in the EU? In order to do that, first, the ECHR and the evolution of the Strasbourg case law will be examined, since the ECHR sets a minimum floor for the interpretation of EU Charter rights. While the ECtHR tends to be deferent with national immigration laws and policies, it has developed a set of guidelines for balancing the right to family life and the state power over immigration. Next, the role of the right to family life as a bar to the expulsion of third country nationals in the EU will be analyzed. On account of the right to free movement, the CJEU has given protection against expulsion for TCNs who have family ties with EU citizens in various situations. Moreover, the concern for family life has enhanced a more forceful understanding of citizenship, albeit in limited circumstances. It is argued that a reading of the CJEU case law in light of family life would contribute to unveiling its actual role and potential. In so doing the chapter calls for a robust understanding of residence that cannot be disentangled from family life.

Alonso's chapter addresses the legal treatment granted by the EU to unaccompanied migrant minors. While the special protection imposed by the principle of best interests of the child and by the ECtHR case law on particularly vulnerable groups should neutralize the restrictive influence – regarding the exercise of rights – derived from their immigrant status, European laws are often applied without taking into account that protection requirement. This is partly due to the lack of EU competence in the subject of minors, along with the competence, shared with the Member States, in the field of immigration and asylum. Hence, European regulations affecting the studied group have been developed within the arena of the Migration Law, which has an impact on the spirit and content thereof. Those norms, even if tempered due to the best interest principle and to vulnerability reasons, often surpass the protection tenets granted to minors by the States.

Regarding asylum, Morgades examines the specific mechanisms for the protection of family life that are expressly established in the main instruments that comprise the Common European Asylum Policy, and the prospects for improving the protection of this fundamental right that can be envisaged as a result of the regulatory provisions in the second phase of this policy and recent case law by the European courts. The instruments that will be discussed are: the Dublin II system for determining the Member State responsible for examining applications for asylum presented in the area of free movement; the Directive on minimum standards for the qualification of a person as a refugee or a person eligible for subsidiary protection and its statutes; and the Directive on minimum standards for the reception of asylum seekers.

Social rights and family life

Finally, the fourth part will deal with the combined protection of families and social rights. States should provide a certain level of material conditions in order to preserve family life. Still the effectiveness of social rights under the Charter and the role of the CJEU have been questioned. In this context, the CJEU has refused to apply the Charter to a variety of norms and mechanisms that derive from the economic governance system. At the same time, the ECtHR's record on protecting social rights is fairly thin and generally quite deferent towards the States, Yet, the ECtHR has taken into consideration certain cases that could lead to a new interpretation of social rights, such as the right to housing.

Furthermore, the creation of an integrated and transnational market renders necessary the coordination of social entitlements of migrant workers and their families. The mere existence of this market encourages people to seek better enjoyment of their rights, such as the right to healthcare, which can be crucial to found a family in certain cases. This section will include three chapters dealing respectively with the interplay between the right to family life and the access to healthcare, the right to housing and the reconciliation of work and family life in the frame of an integrated market.

First, Busatta's contribution takes into account the rights of families travelling in Europe for healthcare reasons, the criticalities that might arise and the solutions elaborated at the EU and national levels. Factors that drive families to move across Europe for healthcare might be related to the ban of a specific treatment by the home State and its availability in another one (i.e. abortion or assisted reproduction), or the likelihood to receive a faster or better treatment elsewhere. This phenomenon has called for EU institutions' intervention, in a field (that of setting and organization of social security and health systems), which still remains within States' competences.

In this context, a number of issues concerning the right of patients and their families to obtain medical treatments abroad arise at the intersection between EU and domestic law. The aim of this chapter is to reflect upon the increasing role of the EU in this area and the consequences for the rights of patients and their families. In the end, the possible development of a common European standard for access to healthcare and its framing under a collective, rather than an individual, perspective will be considered.

Solanes will explore the relevance of the right to housing for the development of family life from the perspective of Strasbourg and Luxembourg's case law. The real threat of losing one's own home or the difficulties to have access to housing, are at the core of the economic hardships of European citizens, especially in Spain. Despite this situation, national legislators and governments have been reluctant to change their approach to the right to housing.

The ECtHR, embedded by a long-standing classical conception of the right to housing as an almost non-enforceable fundamental right, appears to have reconsidered its approach. The use of interim measures in this field is an indicator of the pro-active role of the Strasbourg Court. For its part, the CJEU, from the perspective of consumer protection law and refugees' status, has also recognized the importance of the right to housing. Furthermore both courts, and especially Strasbourg, are receptive to link the right to housing to the protection of family and vulnerable groups. As a result, new developments on the judicial recognition of the right to housing are expected to come from the existing case law on the protection to family life.

Lastly, according to Currie, the reconciliation of work and family life remains predominantly framed within the confines of a static worker model. Whilst there is no doubt that the family members of EU migrant workers have been accorded important entitlements under Union secondary legislation, and that the CJEU has further enhanced the available protection in its interpretive role, the distinct body of law on policy that endeavours to facilitate a better balance between work and family life has not, thus far, acknowledged the specific situation of mobile Union citizens.

This chapter articulates the argument that the agenda for reconciliation has failed to take into account the importance of balancing work and family life for migrant workers. Furthermore, it emphasizes the incongruity of such a position, given the importance attached to the status of such workers in the Treaties. The chapter also demonstrates the benefits that a more holistic approach to reconciliation could bring, not only to the workers and families implicated, but also to the economy more broadly.

* * *

The contributions to this book highlight that right to family life has been progressively strengthened in the EU, despite the scarce EU powers on the field. While family life, as a fundamental right, has been shadowed in the CJEU case law, it has a dormant potential that should be explored, in light of the ECtHR case law on Convention Article 8.

In order to further the effective protection of family life, the proposals put forward in this book include from developing an impact assessment upon family life in the design of European policies; striking an adequate balance between the right to family life and other goals, such as judicial cooperation or borders' control; exploring the interaction with other rights to better determine the scope of protection, including the best interest of children and social rights; to eventually promoting a notion of rights-based citizenship. These proposals emerge from an evaluation of the present shortcomings and show potential avenues to enhance the respect of family life in the EU.

This book has been supported by a Jean Monnet Action for Research and Dissemination Activities on "Families and Fundamental Rights after the Lisbon Treaty" (EUFAM); and by the Spanish Ministry of Economy and Competitiveness (Grant DER2014–57116-P).

Part I

The right to family life in Europe

1 European Convention on Human Rights and Family Life. Primary issues

Luis López Guerra[*]

I The extent of the right to respect of family life

When considering the "respect for family life" right of Convention Article 8, the ECtHR has adopted a concept of family that takes into account the effective existence of an affective and personal relationship derived from kinship and life in common, and not only from legally formalized ties. The Court has repeatedly affirmed that the existence of family life in the terms of Article 8 "is essentially a question of fact depending upon the existence of close personal ties".[1] It has reiterated that the notion of "family" in Article 8 is not confined solely to marriage-based relationships and may encompass other *de facto* "family" ties where the parties are living together outside of marriage.[2] The Court accepts, in certain situations, the existence of a *de facto* family life between an adult and a child without their being bound by biological ties or a recognized legal relationship, provided that there are effective personal ties.[3] Among these *de facto* relationships the Court has included not only situations of life in common between persons of different sex, but also situations of same-sex relationship. In *X. v Austria*[4] the Court stated that the relationship of a cohabiting same-sex couple living in a stable *de facto* relationship falls within the notion of "family life" just as the relationship of a different-sex couple in the same situation would. Furthermore, the Court found in its admissibility decision in *Gas and Dubois v France*[5] that the relationship between two women who were living together

* Judge at the European Court of Human Rights and Professor of Constitutional Law, Universidad Carlos III de Madrid.

1 *Marckx v Belgium* App. No. 6833/74 (ECtHR, 13 June 1979), para. 31; *K. and T. v Finland* [GC] App. No. 25702/94 (ECtHR, 12 July 2001), para. 150.

2 *Keegan v Ireland* App. No. 16969/90 (ECtHR, 26 May 1994), para. 44; *Kroon and Others v the Netherlands* App. No. 18535/91 (ECtHR, 27 October 1994), para. 30; *X, Y and Z v The United Kingdom* App. No. 21830/93 (ECtHR, 22 April 1997), para. 36; *Van der Heijden v The Netherlands* App. No. 42857/05 (ECtHR, 3 April 2012), para. 50.

3 *K. and T. v Finland* [GC] App. No. 25702/94 (ECtHR, 12 July 2001), para. 150; *Nazarenko v Russia* App. No. 39438/13 (ECtHR, 16 July 2015), para. 56.

4 *X v Austria* [GC] App. No. 19010/07 (ECtHR, 19 February 2013), para. 95.

5 *Gas and Dubois v France* App. No. 25951/07 (ECtHR Decision, 31 August 2010).

and had entered into a civil partnership, and the child conceived by one of them by means of assisted reproduction but being brought up by both of them, constituted "family life" within the meaning of ECHR Article 8.

This extension of the concept of family to the *de facto* situations (including same-sex relationships) has had relevant effects on the case law on the ECtHR, as it makes possible to apply to them the non-discrimination mandate of Article 14. This article, according to the case law of the Court, only complements the other substantive provisions of the Convention and has no independent existence since it has effect solely in relation to "the enjoyment of the rights and freedoms" safeguarded by those provisions. The application of Article 14 means that the matter brought to the Court falls "within the ambit" of one or more of the articles of the Convention. The affirmation by the Court that the relationship of a cohabiting same-sex couple living in a stable *de facto* relationship falls within the notion of "family life" just as the relationship of a different-sex couple in the same situation represents that same-sex relationship may be considered subject to the mandate of non-discrimination of Article 14 "in the ambit" of ECHR Article 8.[6]

The content of the concept of family life, as developed by the ECtHR is even wider, as it may include potential or intended family life, not yet brought into practice, but derived from the existence of a kinship relationship: "Moreover, the Court has considered that intended family life may, exceptionally, fall within the ambit of Article 8, notably in cases in which the fact that family life has not yet fully been established was not attributable to the applicant. . . . In particular, where the circumstances warrant it, 'family life' must extend to the potential relationship which may develop between a child born out of wedlock and the natural father."[7]

II Negative and positive obligations

From this wide approach, the Court has considered that the essential content of the right to respect of family life is the right of the members of the family to live together.[8] A forced separation of the members of the family from each other appears therefore as the typical attack against family life. But, as in many other cases, the violation by the State authorities of this right may happen in very different circumstances. The Court has appreciated this violation in cases in which there has been a direct action of the State against family life as well as in cases in which the State has not protected adequately this right. As a consequence, a violation of the right may derive both from the direct interference of the State on the person's family

6 *Schalk and Kopf v Austria* App. No. 30141/04 (ECtHR 22 November 2010), para. 97.
7 *Anayo v Germany* App. No. 20578/07 (21 December 2010), para. 55.
8 *Kutzner v Germany* App. No. 46544/99 (26 February 2002), among many others.

life (which means a violation of the State's negative obligation) or from the non-compliance by the State of its positive obligations to protect family life.

With respect to the first type of violations (that is, direct interference on the right to family life), the Court has followed its usual approach to determine whether a State activity represents an illicit encroachment on Convention rights. Taking into account the terms of Convention Article 8, second paragraph, which establishes the possible limits to the right,[9] the first step in the Court reasoning when confronted with an alleged violation, consists in determining whether there has been an effective State interference affecting negatively family life; if that is the case, and in order to verify whether this interference is justified, the Court considers whether the interference was provided by law, and, if this requisite is accomplished, whether the interference had a licit goal, as established in the Convention. If these circumstances are present, the Court examines whether the interference was necessary in a democratic society; this last requisite includes, in the view of the Court, that the interference should be proportional to the pursued goal.

However, as pointed out above, the protection of the right to family life includes not only negative obligations (to abstain from any undue interference on the right) but, according to the Court, also positive obligations, that is, duties for the State authorities to take certain active measures.[10] The concept of positive obligations of the State as recognized in the ECHR implies that a Convention violation may arise not only from the State's active interference, but also from the State's failure to fulfill the obligation to protect that right. If Convention Article 8 has the fundamental goal of protecting the individual against arbitrary interferences of public powers, it may create, furthermore, positive obligations inherent to an effective respect of family life. Anyway, it must be taken into account that, in the words of the Court, "the boundaries between the State's positive and negative obligations under Article 8 do not lend themselves to precise definition".[11]

Both from the point of view of negative and positive obligations, in cases concerning family life, the State must take into account the presence of different rights and interest, sometimes in conflict. In some cases, the interest of the parents must be balanced against the interest of the child; in others, the right of family life must be balanced against public interests, such as the

9 "There shall be no interference by a public authority with the exercise of this right except such as is in accordance with the law and is necessary in a democratic society in the interests of national security, public safety or the economic wellbeing of the country, for the prevention of disorder or crime, for the protection of health or morals, or for the protection of the rights and freedoms of others."

10 *Dcikson v U.K* [GC] App. No. 44362/04 (ECtHR 4 December 2007), para. 70, among many others.

11 *Hristozov and others v Bulgaria* App. No. 47039/11 and 358/12 (ECtHR, 13 November 2012), para. 117.

need to control the entrance of immigrants into the State territory. This balancing exercise implies, in the words of the Court, the presence of a margin of appreciation by State authorities, concerning negative as well as positive obligations. In the words of the Court: "In both cases, it is necessary to take into account the fair balance between the concurrent interests of the individual and of society; anyway, in both cases, the State disposes of a certain margin of appreciation."[12]

III Family life, immigration and rights of aliens

The Court has had ample opportunity to delimit the extent of the right to family life in several contexts. One of them, maybe the most frequent, is the one relating to the effects of this right on the legal situation of foreigners or immigrants. One question repeatedly posed to the Court refers to the right of a foreigner to enter, or to remain in, the territory of a Convention State in which he or she has family ties. In that case, when does the expulsion of the territory, or the prohibition or denial to enter into it suppose interference with family life contrary to Convention Article 8?

It must be remembered that, as the Court has pointed out on many occasions, the Convention does not recognize a right for any person to enter or live in a country different from the one he or she is a national.[13] Also, as a result, the mandates of Convention Article 6 concerning due process of law are not, in principle, applicable to proceedings related to entrance or expulsion of foreigners,[14] as they do not deal with civil rights or with a criminal accusation. However, decisions on expulsion or non-acceptance of foreigners may disrupt in a decisive way the family life of the affected persons[15] and, therefore, the Court must examine whether this interference represents a violation of the Article 8 or it is allowed by the limits to this right established in the second paragraph of the same article.

Some of these limits which may justify the interference on the family life of foreigners most commonly cited by the Court are the ones concerning national or public safety, or the economic well-being of the country. Taking into account these limits, the Court has considered that the establishment of family ties within a country does not imply as a general principle the right to choose it as country of residence, especially if there are reasonable possibilities of living in the country of origin. That is to say that marrying a national or having children with the country nationality does not

12 *Sen v The Netherlands* App. No. 31465/96 (ECtHR, 21 December 2001), para. 31.

13 *Vilvarajah and Others v United Kingdom* App. No. 13163/87, 13164/87, 13165/87, 13447/87, 13448/87 (ECtHR, 30 October 1991), para. 102; *Chahal v U.K* [GC] App. No. 22414/93 (ECtHR, 15 November 1996), para. 73.

14 *Maaouia v France* App. No. 39652/98 (ECtHR Decision, 22 March 2000); *Monedero Angora v Spain* App. No. 41138/05 (ECtHR Decision, 7 October 2008).

15 *Gül v Switzerland* App. No. 23218/94 (ECtHR, 19 February 1996), para. 38.

concede automatically the right, according to the Convention, to reside in that country.[16]

The authorities may impose conditions or restrictions, provided by law, on the entry or residence in a country. But, as pointed out above, the analysis of the Court concerning the right to family life must deal not only with the legality of the restricting or conditioning measure, and the legitimacy of the pursued goals, but also with the necessity of that measure and its proportionality with the goal to be attained. Using these criteria, the Court has had to deal with many different situations.

A Right to entry and family life

A type of cases in which the Court must determine whether there has been an illicit interference by the State authorities in the right to family life is the one in which these authorities deny the entrance to the country to someone having already family ties in it. One element important for the decision of the case in the Court case law is whether the affected person had reasonable possibilities to develop his or her family life without entering the country. For instance, in *Gül v Switzerland*,[17] a Turkish married couple with children residing provisionally in Switzerland asked for permission for entrance and residence in Switzerland for another child. The permission was denied, and the couple asked the Court to declare a violation to their right to family life. The Court considered that there had not been a violation in the case: the son had no previous ties with Switzerland, the family was residing in the country only provisionally, and there were no signs of special difficulties to pursue family life in Turkey. The interference in family life was justified by the goals sought by the Swiss immigration legislation.

However, an example of a case in which the Court found that the right to family life was disrupted contrary to Convention Article 8 by the refusal to allow the entry of a foreigner could be the judgment in *Sen v the Netherlands*.[18] In the case, a Turkish married couple residing legally in the Netherlands in a permanent way, and having a child living in Turkey, and another two children born in the host country, asked for permission for entry and residence of the first one, permission that was denied by the Dutch authorities. In this instance, the Court considered that that denial represented a disproportionate interference in family life. The parents were rooted in the Netherlands in a stable way, their two children born in the country were adjusted to their country of birth, and the applicant son was of an age in which the reunion with his parents and brothers was the more adequate

16 *Abdulaziz, Cabalas and Balkandali v United Kingdom* App. No. 9214/80 9473/81 9474/81 (ECtHR, 28 May 1985), para. 68.

17 *Gül supra* n. 15.

18 *Sen supra* n. 12.

way to get integrated into his family. As a result the Court considered that by the choice imposed by the Dutch authorities to the parents (to abandon their situation in the Netherlands or to renounce to the company of their son) they had not performed a right balance between the interests of the applicants and the interest of the country to control immigration. The criterion of proportionality was in the case the decisive one; the Court expressly[19] made reference to the existing differences with the case posed in the above cited case *Gül v Switzerland*, particularly in the difficulties to establish a new family life in their country of origin, if the parents had to leave their residence in the Netherlands.

B Expulsion and family life

More frequent in the case law of the Court have been the cases in which the claim presented by the applicants referred to an alleged violation to their right to family life due to their expulsion from the country of residence or stay. That expulsion would disrupt or make impossible the maintenance of family ties in a way contrary to Convention Article 8.

In this type of cases, the Court (employing the point of view of negative obligations) also has applied its usual criteria, as pointed out above, to verify whether there were reasons to consider that the expulsion was covered by the limits to the right of the second paragraph of Article 8, that is, whether the measure of expulsion was provided by law, pursued one of the ends specified in the Convention and was necessary and proportional in a democratic society.

Usually, the criterion of proportionality appears as decisive in this type of cases. The Court, to ascertain that proportionality, takes into account a series of factors, such as whether the national authorities have performed an adequate balance of the opposing interests, as well as the level of integration of the affected persons, the intensity of their family ties, how possible (or difficult) would be the integration of these persons in their country of origin after the expulsion, and whether there were specially cogent reasons for that expulsion (such as the existence of a criminal record).

A typical example of this approach could be the judgment in the case *Berrehab v The Netherlands*.[20] In this case, the applicant, a Moroccan national, lost his residence permit as a result of his divorce from a Dutch national, and subsequently the Dutch authorities ordered his expulsion of the country. The Court considered that there had been a violation of the right to family life, as the authorities had not performed an adequate balance of interests; they had not taken into account the strong ties of the applicant with his minor daughter, residing in the Netherlands, nor the difficulty to

19 Ibid. para. 40.
20 *Berrehab v the Netherlands* App. No. 10730/84 (ECtHR, 21 June 1988).

continue a life in common with her if he were expelled to Morocco. Also, the Court pointed out that there was not any special reason for expulsion due to the behaviour of the applicant, who had no criminal record.

Within this general approach, which takes into account the proportionality of the expulsion measure, several types of cases deserve a special attention, as they have originated a particular reasoning by the Court. They refer to measures of expulsion of what might be called second-generation immigrants because of the commission of crimes, or other infractions, declared by judicial sentences.

This type of cases pertaining to "second generation immigrants" show the relevance, for the case law of the Court, of the presence of a particularly intense integration of the affected person in the country of residence to evaluate the extent of the right to family life against eventual expulsions, even in cases of criminal activities. In *Moustaquim v Belgium*[21] and *Beldjoudi v France*,[22] the Court found that expulsion would be a disproportionate measure, due to the fact that the affected person had maintained a lifelong tie with the country of residence (*Moustaquim*) and furthermore, his continuation of family life in his country of origin would be impossible or extremely difficult (*Beldjoudi*) or the low importance of the crime (*Boultif*).[23]

An example of the criteria followed by the Court in these type of "second generation" cases to determine whether the expulsion could represent an undue interference on family life could be the judgment in *Maslov v Austria*.[24] In this case, the applicant, a Bulgarian adolescent of 18 years of age, residing legally with his parents in Austria, was deported to Bulgaria after being sentenced for committing a crime. The Court established a list of points of reference to appreciate the necessity of the measure. These included the nature and gravity of the infraction; the time the person to be expelled has resided in the country; the time passed after the infraction committed by this person, and his posterior behaviour; the strength of his family and social ties with his country of residence and his country of origin. Also, the Court pointed out the relevance of the age of the person at the time he committed the infraction for which he is to be deported.

In the words of the Court in *Maslov*,[25] following previous case law,[26] "Although Article 8 provides no absolute protection against expulsion for any category of aliens . . . , including those who were born in the host country or moved there in their early childhood, the Court has already found that regard is to be had to the special situation of aliens who have spent most, if

21 *Moustaquim v Belgium* App. No. 12313/86 (ECtHR, 18 February 1991).
22 *Beldjoudi v France*, App. No. 12083/86 (ECtHR, 26 March 1992).
23 *Boultif v Switzerland* App. No. 54273/00 (ECtHR, 2 August 2001).
24 *Maslov v Austria* App. No. 1638/03 (ECtHR, 23 June 2008).
25 Ibid. paras. 74–5.
26 For instance, *Üner v the Netherlands* App. No. 46410/99 (ECtHR, 18 October 2003), para. 55.

not all, of their childhood in the host country, were brought up there and received their education there. . . . In short, the Court considers that for a settled migrant who has lawfully spent all or the major part of his or her childhood and youth in the host country very serious reasons are required to justify expulsion. This is all the more so where the person concerned committed the offences underlying the expulsion measure as a juvenile."

Within this line of reasoning, in *Jeunesse v The Netherlands*[27] the Court found a violation of the right to family life due to an expulsion order. In this case, the applicant had lived in the Netherlands, without legal authorization, for more than 20 years, and she had established permanent family relationship with a Dutch national, with whom she had two children of the same nationality.

A further development of this case law may be found in the judgment *Tarakhel v Switzerland*.[28] Here the Court took into account the requisites for expulsion derived from ECHR Articles 3 and 8. The applicants were an Afghan family with two small children, which, according to the so-called Dublin Rules, were going to be returned to Italy by the Swiss authorities. The Court, in view of the painful situation of asylum solicitants in Italy, considered that returning them to that country would represent a grave impairment of the family life of the applicants, as well as (with respect to the minors) a violation of Convention Article 3.

IV Care orders and family life[29]

Another aspect that has been widely dealt with in the case law of the Court refers to the interference in family life caused by measures adopted by the authorities to take a child from the authority of the parents in order to take care of it in a public institution or to place it with a foster or adoptive family. In this type of cases, the Court requires a balancing the rights of the parents to maintain a family life with their children, and the interests of others, mainly the interest of the child, and in some cases, the interest of the foster or adoptive family. It is difficult to separate completely in these cases positive and negative obligations of the authorities, as to the duty of not unduly disrupting family life must be added the positive obligation to make all possible efforts to reunite the parents with their children.[30]

In what concerns the interference caused by care orders, with the goal to separate the child from its family, the Court recognizes, in principle, a wide margin of appreciation in assessing the necessity of taking a child into

27 *Jeunesse v the Netherlands* App. No. 12738/10 (ECtHR, 3 October 2014).
28 *Tarakhel v Switzerland* App. No. 29217/12 (ECtHR, 4 November 2014).
29 See on this matter, Kribeche 2008.
30 Such was the case, for instance, in *Wallowa and Walla v Czech Republic* App. No. 23848/04 (ECtHR, 26 March 2007).

care.[31] But this margin of appreciation may be revised by the Court in the light of the seriousness of the interests at stake. For instance, in what concerns the care orders affecting new-born children and taking them from their mothers, the Court has affirmed that: "The taking of a new-born baby into public care at the moment of its birth is an extremely harsh measure. There must be extraordinarily compelling reasons before a baby can be physically removed from the care of its mother, against her will, immediately after birth as a consequence of a procedure in which neither she nor her partner has been involved. The shock and distress felt by even a perfectly healthy mother are easy to imagine."[32] Also the Court has examined from a strict approach the cases in which the separation of the family was not due to a behaviour of the parents dangerous or harmful to the child but to purely economic reasons; in these cases, the Court considers that the authorities should look for less harsh measures, or, from the point of view of positive obligations, to look for some remedy to the situation of the children different from the separation from their parents (*Wallova and Walla v Czech Republic*).[33] In the case *R.M.S. v Spain*[34] in which a child had been taken into custody by the administration, due to the economic hardships of the parents (Castellote 2013, pp. 272–278), the Court considered that there had been a violation of Article 8 of the Convention, as the order of care of the child has been adopted due to the situation of poverty of her mother in the moment of the decision, without taking account, later of the evolution of her situation. From the point of view of the Court, it was only a question of lack of economic resources of the applicant, which could have been remedied by the authorities by other means different from the total separation of the child from its family; that ultimate measure cannot be apply but in the most grave cases. And the Court extends its reflections on the matter: "The Court considers that the Spanish administrative authorities should have considered other measures less radical than taking care of the child. The Court considers that the role of the authorities in charge of social welfare is precisely to help those persons in difficulties which do not have a sufficient knowledge of the system, to guide them in their proceedings, and to give them advice, among others, on the possibilities to obtain a social shelter or other means to overcome their difficulties, as the applicant had tried initially."[35]

If the Court admits a certain margin of appreciation with respect to this type of decision, concerning the taking into care of children in order to protect their interests, it, however, maintains a stricter scrutiny on additional limitations which may derive from the care order, particularly in what

31 *K and T supra* n. 3, para. 155.
32 Ibid. para. 168.
33 *Wallowa and Walla supra* n. 30.
34 *R.M.S v Spain* App. No. 28775/12 (ECtHR, 18 June 2013).
35 Ibid. para. 86.

refers to the contact between family members: "However, a stricter scrutiny is called for in respect of any further limitations, such as restrictions placed by the authorities on parental rights of access, and of any legal safeguards designed to secure an effective protection of the right of parents and children to respect for their family life. Such further limitations entail the danger that the family relations between the parents and a young child are effectively curtailed."[36]

This is a result from the nature of the right to family life, and its essential content, that is, the living together of the family members. As a consequence, the Court considers that separation measures should be exceptional, and, therefore, of a provisional character: the guiding principle, in these cases, should be that "a care order should be regarded as a temporary measure, to be discontinued as soon as circumstances permit, and that any measures implementing temporary care should be consistent with the ultimate aim of reuniting the natural parents and the child".[37]

The State positive obligations to protect family life in cases of separation from parents and children as a result of care orders are closely connected with the State negative obligations. Particularly, the Court is concerned with the effects of passing of time on the relationships between parents and children when a long separation is the result of the care orders. The obstacles to the access of the parents to their children, or the absence of activity by the authorities to reunite the family may have as an effect that the children become progressively disconnected from their original family, making reunification difficult or even contrary to the best interests of the child. When a considerable period of time has passed since the child was originally taken into public care, the interest of a child not to have his or her *de facto* family situation changed again may override the interests of the parents to have their family reunited.[38] Therefore the Court has stated that "the positive duty to take measures to facilitate family reunification as soon as reasonably feasible will begin to weigh on the competent authorities with progressively increasing force as from the commencement of the period of care, subject always to its being balanced against the duty to consider the best interests of the child".[39]

Separation must be considered as an exceptional measure, and the authorities have the obligation to remedy that situation adopting the necessary measures to promote the reunification of the family. As an example, in *Saleck Bardi v Spain*,[40] the Court found a violation of Convention Article 8 due to the lack of care of Spanish authorities in a case of separation of mother and child. In that case, the child had come from the Saharaui camps in Algeria to Spain to spend the summer holidays with a Spanish

36 *K. and T supra* n. 3, para. 155.
37 Ibid. para. 178.
38 Ibid.
39 Ibid.
40 *Saleck Bardi v Spain* App. No. 66167/09 (ECtHR, 24 May 2011).

family. The child did not return to her family after the end of the holidays, and remained in Spain for many months without the Spanish authorities taking any measure. The mother, as well as some Saharaui organizations, made claims for the child to return, without any success; only four years after the separation was the mother able to come to Spain to present her claims. In the meantime, proceedings to put the child in a foster family and further to give this family the custody of the child were continued. Finally, several years after the separation of the child from her family, the Spanish Courts rejected the demands of the mother to regain the custody of her child. The Court found that the Spanish authorities, by not having taken any action for many months to take care of the child or to give back the child to her family, in spite of the demands for her return, had violated Convention Article 8: "The Court notes in this respect a complete inactivity of the administrative authorities from September 2002 to May 2004, and notes that no satisfactory explanation has been given to justify this delay of almost two years before the administration took the child into custody, when she had no legal title for residing in Spain."[41] But the Court, in spite of finding a violation of Convention Article 8, admits that the Spanish authorities are in a better position to decide on the situation of the child, taking into account that her interest was the primary factor to consider.[42]

A similar ruling was adopted in the judgment on *K.A.B. v Spain*.[43] The mother of a 13 months child was expelled from Spain, without the authorities taking any action concerning her child, in spite of having been warned of his existence. When the father came to the authorities to claim the custody of the child, he was told a DNA analysis should be performed to prove his paternity; the father had not the means to pay for the analysis, and the authorities kept the custody of the child, and placed him in a foster home, and later on adoption with a family. When the father came back with the money to pay for the DNA analysis, the proceedings for adoption were in course, and in spite of having proved his paternity, his claim for recuperating his child were rejected. The Court found a violation of the positive obligations of the State in the lack of intervention of the State to protect the child when the mother was expelled, as well as in the lack of information and support to the father when he tried to prove his paternity. However, as in *Saleck Bardi*, the Court considered that, due to the passing of time, the Spanish authorities should be in a better position to take a decision concerning the situation of the minor taking into account the best interests of the child.

V Parental visiting rights

Other types of applications to the Court deriving from situations of family crisis refer to the denial of parental rights of visit to children in case

41 Ibid. para. 61.
42 Ibid. para. 64.
43 *K.A.B. v Spain* App. No. 59819/08 (ECtHR, 10 April 2012).

of divorce or separation. In these cases, the Court has taken into account the presence of both positive and negative obligations of public authorities derived from Convention Article 8 in order to make possible a continuity of contacts between parents and children. Among the authorities' positive obligations are included the respect for the procedural guarantees of the parents in the proceedings to determine the custody of the child and the regime of visits by the parent not entitled to custody.[44] But these positive obligations go further, and they also include the duty of the authorities to make sure that visiting rights are duly guaranteed and complied with by the other party in an effective manner, guaranteeing the contact between parents and children.[45] These duties may include imposing sanctions in case of non-compliance with the regime of visits by the parents in charge of the custody of the child.[46] The Court has also stressed the principle of the protection of the best interests of the child, which may imply that in some cases the obligation to impose sanctions in case of non-compliance is not absolute: in the words of the Court, "the Court is aware that in different situations as the present one, involving unresolved issues between parents, a certain amount of time has to pass for the parents to be able to overcome emotional hurdles and establish a mature relationship focusing in the best interests of the child . . . However, reestablishing contact with a child in such delicate circumstances requires long time efforts. . . ."[47] The Court considered that, although the regime of visits by one of the parents had not been respected by the one in charge of the custody of the child, there had not been a violation of the Convention by the Romanian authorities, taking into account that these authorities had made all reasonable efforts, having regard to the best interests of the child and of the family as a whole.

Concerning the negative obligations of the authorities, the Court has had ample opportunity to point out that the prohibition of discrimination of Convention Article 14, in connection with the right to family life makes inadmissible any restriction in the regime of visits of parents based on the grounds enumerated in that article: in *Vojnity v Hungary*[48] the Court found a violation of Convention Article 14 in connection with Article 8, due to the total ban on the applicant's access rights to his child on the basis of his religious convictions. The Court considered, however, that no separate issue arose under Article 9 guaranteeing freedom of religion.

VI Parental abduction of children

One aspect of the right to family life repeatedly examined by the Court has been the one concerning cases of child abduction by one of the parents,

44 *Pascal v Romania* App. No. 805/09 (ECtHR, 17 April 2012), para. 71.
45 *Eberhard and M. v Slovenia* App. No. 8673/05 and 9733/05 (ECtHR, 1 December 2009), para. 130.
46 *Kuppinger v Germany* App. No. 62198/11 (ECtHR, 15 January 2015), para. 103.
47 *Pascal supra* n. 44, para. 85.
48 *Vojnity v Hungary* App. No. 29617/07 (ECtHR, 12 February 2013).

from the country of origin or residence of the child (Beaumont 2015). As a general and initial point of view, the Court has considered that the protection of family life in these cases must respond to the provisions of the Hague Convention on the Civil Aspects of International Child Abduction (the Hague Convention), establishing that the authorities of the country to which the child was abducted should provide for a prompt return to the country of origin or residence; the substantive question concerning the right of custody of the child by one or other of the parents must be therefore resolved by the judicial authorities of that country.

The two questions (return of the child on the one side and decision on the custody on the other) appear therefore as different and separate questions. In principle, the decision on the first one (return of the child) would derive from the mandates of the Hague Convention, and following the procedures there established. ECHR Article 8 should be interpreted in that way.

Following this line, the Court, in some cases, has considered as inadmissible the complaints against rulings by Convention country authorities ordering the return of the abducted child to the country of origin, as these rulings, in execution of the Hague Convention, would not represent a violation of Convention Article 8.[49] Conversely, the Court has considered that, if the authorities of the country to which the child had been abducted did not show enough diligence in complying with the rules of the Hague Convention, there would be a violation of Article 8.[50] The same considerations would be applicable in this matter in case of negligence by the authorities of the country of origin or residence.[51]

As said, that represents, in principle, the position of the Court. However, the case law on the matter presents some additional peculiarities, due to the presence, in some cases of a (at least apparent) conflict between two different considerations: on the one side, the obligation, derived from the Hague Convention, of a prompt return of the child; on the other side, the necessity of taking into account the best interests of the child, which could be negatively affected by its return to the country of origin.[52]

These types of problems, of course, arise when it is alleged that, applying the mandates of the Hague Convention concerning a prompt return of the child, would result in damaging its best interests. Certainly, and following the system of the Hague Convention, it must be inferred that, in principle, this best interest will be best served by the return of the child to the country of origin from which it was abducted; furthermore, the Hague Convention itself accepts that in some cases, the return is not required; its Article 13 establishes that an application for return may be rejected by the authorities

49 *Eskinazi v Turkey* App. No. 14600/05 (ECtHR Decision, 6 December 2005); *Paradis v Germany* App. No. 4065/04 (ECtHR Decision, 4 September 2007).

50 *Ignaccolo Zenide v Romania* App. No. 31679/96 (ECtHR, 25 January 2000).

51 *Iglesias Gil v Spain* App. No. 56673/00 (ECtHR, 29 April 2003).

52 See, for instance *X v Latvia* [GC] App. No. 27853/09 (ECtHR, 26 November 2013), para. 95.

of the State if there is a grave risk that the return would expose the child to physical or psychological harm or otherwise place the child in an intolerable situation (Silvis 2015). However, given the characteristics of the Hague Convention (which does not establish any central authority in charge of the interpretation of its mandates), in many cases it is not a simple task to determine the way in which the (apparent?) conflict between the principles of prompt return and of protection of the best interests of the child is to be solved.

In this context, the case law of the Court has evolved from an initial stage of semi-automatic application of the procedural mandates of the Hague Convention to a more nuanced assessment, proclaiming, anyway, that there is no inherent contradiction between the requirements of the Hague Convention and the mandates of Convention Article 8 (as interpreted by the case law of the Court) concerning the protection of family life. In this respect, up to this moment, two main rulings of the Court (both by the Grand Chamber) are particularly relevant, as well as demonstrative of the evolution on the Court's case law on the matter.

The first one, the case *Neulinger and Shuruk v Switzerland*[53] (Rietiker 2012), deals with a ruling of the Swiss courts ordering the return of a child from Switzerland to Israel, in application of the mandates of the Hague Convention. The Grand Chamber (reversing a previous Chamber ruling) found that the application of the Hague Convention by the Swiss authorities, ordering the return of the child to the country of origin, without having conducted an examination in depth of the circumstances related to the substantive best interest of the child, constituted a violation of the right to family life of Article 8. Therefore, the Court seemed to give preference to the substantive mandates of Convention Article 8 over the mostly procedural mandates of the Hague Convention, which established that the child should be returned to the country of residence, while the material aspects concerning the best interests of the child, related to the custody, could and should be solved by the authorities of that country.

This apparent conflict between the mandates of the Hague Convention and ECHR Article 8 was addressed by the Court (also by the Grand Chamber) in its judgment on the *X v Latvia* case.[54] There, again, the applicant complained of an order by the authorities of the country to which the child was abducted (Latvia) for the return of her child to the country of origin (Australia) in application of the Hague Convention. The Court dealt with one of the criticisms formulated on the previous *Neulinger* ruling, interpreted as establishing that the authorities of the country of abduction should perform an in-depth examination of the best interests of the child; namely, that examination should imply a slowing down of the summary

53 *Neulinger and Shuruk v Switzerland* [GC] App. No. 41615/07 (ECtHR, 6 July 2010).
54 *X v Latvia supra* n. 52.

proceedings for prompt return established by the Hague Convention and, as a result, would made the provisions in the latter ineffective. Taking into account these criticisms, the position of the Court in *X v Latvia* was that its judgment in *Neulinger* did not represent a mandate for the domestic courts on how should they apply the Hague Convention, but it meant that these courts should take into account the "arguable" allegations concerning the possibility of a grave risk for the child, in case of return to the country of origin, and that they should give a reasonable response to these allegations.[55] The Court, therefore, imposed a procedural, rather than a substantive obligation to the national authorities in application of the mandates of the Hague Convention.

VII Surrogacy and family life

The development of biotechnologies in the field of human reproduction has had an undeniable impact on the very concept of family, and of filiation relationships. A particular complex situation is to be found in those cases in which the legal relationship between parents and child must be defined when the child has been carried by a surrogate mother. Although the questions posed in this type of situations are (still) relatively new, the Strasbourg Court has had the opportunity to take some initial steps in defining the extent of the protection of family life defined by Convention Article 8 in this matter, as well as the precise obligations of the Member States in this respect (Sosson 2015).

These initial steps may be found, for the time being, in three relevant rulings of the Strasbourg Court: *Mennesson and others v France*,[56] and *Labassee v France*,[57] both of 2014, and *Paradiso and Campanelli v Italy*,[58] of 2015; this last ruling is not definitive, as it is still pending a final decision of the Grand Chamber.

In *Menesson* and *Labossee*, the facts are very similar: a married couple asked recognition in France of parent–child filiation relationship of a child resulting from surrogate motherhood. In both cases the surrogate pregnancy

55 In the terms of the judgment, Ibid. para. 106: "The Court considers that a harmonious interpretation of the European Convention and the Hague Convention (see para. 94 above) can be achieved provided that the following two conditions are observed. Firstly, the factors capable of constituting an exception to the child's immediate return in application of Articles 12, 13 and 20 of the Hague Convention, particularly where they are raised by one of the parties to the proceedings, must genuinely be taken into account by the requested court. That court must then make a decision that is sufficiently reasoned on this point, in order to enable the Court to verify that those questions have been effectively examined. Secondly, these factors must be evaluated in the light of Article 8 of the Convention."

56 *Mennesson v France* App. No. 65192/11 (ECtHR, 26 June 2014).

57 *Labassee v France* App. No. 65941/11 (ECtHR, 26 June 2014).

58 *Paradiso and Campanelli v Italy* App. No. 25358/12 (ECtHR, 27 January 2015).

took place in the United States, employing genetic material from the male member of the couple; in both cases also the parental relationship was recognized by United States judicial authorities. However, also in both cases, the French authorities denied registering the filiation relationship of the child with respect to the couple. In both cases the applicants (the couples and the children) invoked a violation or ECHR Article 8, and their rights to private and family life.

The answer of the Court was twofold, distinguishing the two aspects of the right, concerning family life on the one side, and private life on the other. With respect to family life, and consequently with the Court's wide (and not restricted to legal definitions) concept of family life, the Court found that there was no violation of Article 8, as there was no evidence that the denial of French authorities to the recognition of a filiation relationship had disturbed or prevented the family relations between the couples and the children. The Court considered that in the matter the Member States had a wide margin of appreciation, concerning the legal definition of the position of the surrogate child.

However, the Court did find a violation of Article 8 concerning the right of the child to respect of private life. The denial of the French authorities to recognize the child's filiation had necessarily severe and unfavorable consequences on the insertion of the child in French society. The complete denial of that possibility went further than the margin of appreciation of the State, as affecting very negatively the person of the child.

In contrast, in *Paradiso and Campanelli v Italy*, a Chamber of the Court found a violation of Article 8, in its family life dimension, derived from the placement in social service care of a child born following a surrogacy contract between a couple (parents of intention) and a woman; there was no biological relationship between the couple and the child. The Italian authorities refused to recognize the parent–child relationship of the couple with the child, and ordered for him to be put in foster care.

In spite of the lack of a biological link, the Court found a violation of the right to family life, as the removal of the child from its *de facto* family went against the best interests of the child. According to the Court case law, only in extreme cases, and in the event of immediate danger to the child, that removal was admissible.

In any case, as in other occasions in the case law of the Court, the finding of a violation of the right to family life did not result in a ruling establishing the return of the child to its original family, due to the specific circumstances of the situation of the child, and its relations with the foster family, questions to be appreciated by the domestic courts. The case anyway is pending before the Grand Chamber.

VIII Social rights and family life: A note

At first glance, the European Convention and its Protocols seem to refer only to "first generation" rights, that is, those rights intended to protect the individual against interferences by public powers, without recognizing "social rights" including public provisions or the guarantee of a minimum subsistence level. However, the case law of the Court has recognized, since *Airey v Ireland*, that:

> The Court is aware that the further realisation of social and economic rights is largely dependent on the situation – notably financial – reigning in the State in question. On the other hand, the Convention must be interpreted in the light of present-day conditions . . . and it is designed to safeguard the individual in a real and practical way as regards those areas with which it deals. . . . Whilst the Convention sets forth what are essentially civil and political rights, many of them have implications of a social or economic nature. The Court therefore considers, like the Commission, that the mere fact that an interpretation of the Convention may extend into the sphere of social and economic rights should not be a decisive factor against such an interpretation; there is no water-tight division separating that sphere from the field covered by the Convention.[59]

This approach has led the Court to an interpretation of the Convention rights with relevant social and economic consequences. Such has been the case also concerning family rights. In some cases (as in the already cited *Wallowa and Walla v Czech Republic*, or *Tarakhel v Switzerland*) these consequences have been mostly of an indirect nature; in other cases, however, the case law of the Court has established the obligation of the States to protect a certain level of material conditions in order to preserve family life. Such would be the case, particularly, in what concerns the loss of family home due to an expulsion by the public authorities.

The right to family life, interpreted as the right to maintain family relationships, may be adversely affected by the deprivation of a family home, particularly when such deprivation affects vulnerable groups, such as minorities or children. In some circumstances the Court has considered that the right to a family home is protected under Convention Article 8.

Possibly, the most representative judgment on this matter is *Yordanova v Bulgaria*.[60] In this case, several Roma families had been expelled from their homes of many years (most of them illegally built). The State alleged the necessity to recover land unduly occupied, as well as the presence of building projects. The affected families (which included children) claimed that the expulsion would put them in a situation of complete destitution.

The Court judgment recognizes that the authorities have a wide margin of appreciation concerning urban planning policies. But it also takes into account that the expulsion of illegally occupied land, after an extended

59 *Airey v Ireland* App. No. 6289/73 (ECtHR, 9 October 1979), para. 26.
60 *Yordanova v Bulgaria* App. No. 5126/05 (ECtHR, 2 October 2012).

period of tolerance, represented considerable damage for the applicants, as belonging to an especially vulnerable group, which, deprived of their domiciles, would face grave difficulties to maintain their family life. The invocation of the legality of their orders by the authorities was not sufficient reason to consider that there was an ineludible necessity to justify such a measure. Attending to considerations of proportionality, the dislodgment of the Roma families impaired in an unacceptable way their family life, against the mandates of Convention Article 8.

This type of reasoning is also shown in the judgment in the case *Winterstein v France*,[61] also concerning the eviction of Roma families (*gents du voyage*). In that case, it was stated also that dislodgment constituted a disproportionate measure, taking into account the damage to family life, the vulnerability situation of the applicants and the lack of any resettlement measure to make possible the continuation of family life.

In the same line, in the case *Raji v Spain*,[62] concluded by a Court decision of 2014, the Court asked the Government for observations concerning the planned demolition of the family home of the applicants, illegally built on land of public property, under a regime of tolerance maintained for many years, affecting also many other families. The Government gave notice to the Court that the authorities would cancel the demolition order, and would look for a negotiated solution to the problem. The case was accordingly struck out by the Court.

References

Beaumont, P. (2015). Child abduction: recent jurisprudence of the European Court of Human Rights. *International and comparative law quarterly*, 64(1), pp. 39–63.

Castellote, C. (2013). R.M.S. v. Spain: a mother's economic hardship does not justify permanent separation from her child. *Cyprus Human Rights Review*, 2(2), pp. 272–8.

Kribeche, N. (2008). Le placement des enfants dans la jurisprudente de la Cour Européenne des Droits de l'Homme. In: F. Krenc and M. Puechavy, dirs., *Le droit de la famille à l'epreuve de la Convention Européenne des Droits de l'Homme*. Bruxelles: Bruylant, pp. 113–26.

Rietiker, D. (2012). Un enlèvement d'enfant devant la Grand Chambre de la Cour Européenne des Droits de l'Homme: l'affaire Neulinger et Shuruk c. Suisse analyisée à la lumière des méthodes d'interpretation des traités internationaux. *Revue Trimestrielle des droits de l'homme*, 90, pp. 377–413.

Silvis, J. (2015). Prevention of Child Abduction: Return to the State of Origin. In: *Liber Amicorum Dean Spielmann*. Osterwijk: Wolf, pp. 603–14.

Sosson, J. (2015). La jurisprudence européenne et la gestation pour autrui. *Journal de droit européen*, 15(2), pp. 52–5.

61 *Winterstein and Others v France* App. No. 27013/07 (ECtHR, 10 October 2013).
62 *Mohamed Raji and others v Spain* App. No. 3537/13 (ECtHR Decision, 16 December 2014).

2 The scope of application of the EU Charter of Fundamental Rights

Bruno de Witte[*]

I Introduction

The term "scope of application" can mean several different things. The English language version of the Charter uses the word "scope" in the heading of two different articles: Article 51 (entitled "Scope") and Article 52 (entitled "Scope of guaranteed rights"). In other language versions, though, very different terms are used in both articles. In Spanish, for example, Article 51 is entitled "*Ámbito de aplicación*" and Article 52 is called "*Alcance e interpretación de los derechos y principios.*" In this chapter, I will limit myself to discuss the scope of the Charter as meant by Article 51, and I will not discuss the "scope" of the single rights contained in the Charter which, taken together, form the Charter's subject matter.

Even so, Article 51 does not address all the questions that can arise in relation to the scope of application of a legal document. Nothing is said, neither there nor in other parts of the Charter, about its application *ratione temporis*, a question that the Court of Justice has had to address in a number of a cases (Iglesias Sánchez 2012, pp. 1573–5); nor about its application *ratione loci* (apart from the special rules about its application in Poland and the UK contained in a Protocol to the Treaty of Lisbon).

Article 51 also does not deal with the application *ratione personae* on the "active" side, that is, the question of who are the beneficiaries of the rights contained in the Charter. It is true that many single provisions of the Charter state that a right is recognized to "everyone" or that "no one" shall be denied a particular right, whereas some of the Charter rights are reserved to "every citizen of the Union", but other provisions do not specify their beneficiaries, nor is anything said about whether rights can only be claimed by physical persons or also by legal persons. For example, when Article 16 recognizes the freedom to conduct a business, is that right reserved for private persons or can it also be claimed by companies? This is a question to which the national constitutional law of the member states offers partly

* Professor of European Law at the European University Institute and at the Robert Schuman Centre for Advanced Studies. Professor of European Law at the University of Maastricht.

different answers. However, the CJEU has recently confirmed implicitly the view it had taken earlier on, in its general principles case law, that this freedom could also be invoked by companies.[1]

But the most problematic question concerning the scope of application of the Charter (indeed, the question which most legal writers have in mind when they deal with "the scope of the Charter") is that of its application *ratione personae* on the "passive" side: who are the *addressees* of the obligation to respect or protect the Charter rights? This is the one question that Article 51(1) does indeed deal with, although in a very brief manner, which has left many problems of interpretation:

> The provisions of this Charter are addressed to the institutions, bodies, offices and agencies of the Union with due regard for the principle of subsidiarity and to the Member States only when they are implementing Union law.

It is clear, and uncontroversial, that the Charter is primarily binding on all the EU institutions and bodies and, on this point, there will only be some marginal skirmishes for deciding whether a body should be defined as an "EU body". What is much less clear is when exactly the *Member States* are bound by the Charter and I will devote the rest of this chapter to that question.

II "Only when implementing"

In most scholarly accounts of EU fundamental rights prior to the Charter of Rights' coming into force, it was said that EU fundamental rights (in their traditional form of unwritten general principles of EU law) applied to Member State action in two situations: the first concerns the implementation of European law (implementation situation). The second concerns derogations from European law (derogation situation).[2] The leading early case for the first situation is *Wachauf* and the leading early case for the second situation is *ERT*.[3] In the latter judgment, the Court held that, when Member States take a measure that restricts one of the freedoms of the common market, that restriction must not only be justified by one of the mandatory requirements recognized in the Treaty text or in the Court's case law, but the restriction must also be compatible with the fundamental rights as protected by the general principles of Union law. In such a case, the Member State is not transposing or applying an EU directive or

1 Case C-283/11 *Sky Österreich GmbH v Österreichischer Rundfunk* EU:C:2013:28, para. 41 and ff.
2 For a retrospective look at the evolution of this discussion, see Dougan (2015, pp. 1210 ff.).
3 Case C-5/88 *Wachauf* EU:C:1989:321, and Case C-260/89 *Elliniki Radiophonia Tiléorassi* EU:C:1991:254.

regulation, but is acting autonomously in a way that causes a restriction of a right protected by the Treaty.

So, it could seem that the "second situation" was not recognized and codified in the Charter, since Article 51 includes the Member States "only when they are implementing Union law". Legal authors have scratched their head about this discrepancy between the existing case law of the CJEU, developed with regard to the unwritten general principles of EU law, and the text of the Charter, which seemed more restrictive.[4] The Court of Justice, for several years after the entry into force of the Lisbon Treaty, avoided taking a clear stance on this question. It gave a number of individual judgments in which it either affirmed or denied[5] that a measure of national law came within the scope of the Charter, but it did not give general guidance on how to interpret Article 51. The impatience with the Court's dithering attitude was mounting and was expressed for example in the following passage of the Opinion of Advocate General Cruz Villalón in *Åkerberg Fransson*: "I believe that now is the time for the Union judicature to make an additional effort to rationalise the basic but indeterminate view that the Member States are subject to the Charter 'when they are implementing Union law' ".[6]

Basically, three solutions were available to deal with this problem. The first solution would have been to confine the application of the Charter to the first situation, whereas the general principles of EU law, which continue to be part of primary EU law alongside the Charter (in view of the text of Article 6 TEU), could continue to cover both situations, as before. This solution would have been most unfortunate. Since the material content of the Charter must be held to correspond, almost entirely, to the material content of the Court's unwritten general principles, we would end up with two parallel lists of identical rights with a different scope of application. As Advocate General Trstenjak convincingly argued in his Opinion in the *Dominguez* case, this solution would be unacceptable.[7]

A second solution would have been for the CJEU to accept that its earlier case law dealing with the second situation had been contradicted and overruled by the authors of the Charter, and the Court could therefore have decided to review national measures for compliance with EU fundamental

4 For an early analysis of this question, see Eeckhout (2002, pp. 977–9).

5 There were many judgments in those first post-Lisbon years in which the Court, often in very few words, denies the relevance of the Charter for lack of sufficient connection with EU law, including the cases of *Estov, Chartry, Rossius, Lebrun, Pagnoul, Boncea* and *Vinkov* (Iglesias Sánchez 2012, pp. 1588–90).

6 Opinion of Advocate General Cruz Villalón in Case C-617/10 *Åkerberg Fransson* EU:C:2012:340, para. 39.

7 Opinion of Advocate General Trstenjak in Case C-282/10 *Maribel Dominguez* EU:C:2011:559, paras. 127–31 (the argument was made in the context of a discussion of the horizontal effect of Charter and general principles, but it applies equally to the question of the applicability to Member State action).

rights *only* when they implement EU law in the *Wachauf* sense (Huber 2008). Against this view, one could argue that it does not clearly appear from the preparatory work on the Charter that its authors wanted to overrule the CJEU on this point; certainly, this is not the message conveyed by the Explanations of the Charter (which, as we know, are an obligatory aid to its interpretation) that refer to the existing case law of the Court, citing the *ERT* case as an illustration of what is meant by the text of Article 51.

The third, and most appealing, solution was to interpret the notion of implementation in a broad way so as to incorporate the "derogation" situation.[8] Whereas the term implementation is often used to refer to the action taken by the Member States when transposing EU directives or regulations into national law, this narrow meaning is not necessarily the one intended by the drafters of the Charter. Indeed, if one looks at some other language versions, one finds significantly broader terms being used: "*cuando apliquen el derecho de la Unión*", "*nell'attuazione del diritto dell'Unione*", and "*lorsqu'ils mettent en oeuvre le droit de l'Union*". So, one could argue that what Article 51 actually refers to are all the situations in which the Member States apply EU law (or should be applying EU law), whether that EU legal norm is contained in a directive, in a regulation, in the founding treaties or in another binding norm. Seen in this light, the typical "derogation situation", as exemplified by the *ERT* case is also a case in which the Member State is called to *apply* EU law, namely the norm of primary EU law that prohibits restrictions of the free movement of goods, persons, services or capital, and that situation would hence be covered by the terms of Article 51.

The controversy about this question was decided by the CJEU in the *Pfleger* judgment of 2014 when it clearly and expressly confirmed that the *ERT* line of cases had not been displaced by Article 51 of the Charter. It stated that the "use by a Member State of exceptions provided for by EU law in order to justify an obstruction of a fundamental freedom guaranteed by the Treaty must . . . be regarded . . . as 'implementing Union law' within the meaning of Article 51(1) of the Charter".[9]

This particular question having been settled, there is still considerable uncertainty on when exactly the Member States should be considered to act for the "implementation" of EU law. Nowadays, the CJEU often uses a very general formula, which it first coined in the *Åkerberg Fransson* judgment of 2013, namely that "the fundamental rights guaranteed in the legal order of the European Union are applicable in all situations governed by EU law, but not outside such situations".[10] This "Fransson formula" is adequate for

8 This solution was proposed, for example, by judge Lenaerts (2012, p. 385) writing in an extra-judicial capacity.

9 Case C-390/12 *Robert Pfleger* EU:C:2014:281, para. 36.

10 Case C-617/10 *Åkerberg Fransson* EU:C:2012:340, para. 19. For examples of use of this "Fransson formula", see *Pfleger, supra* n. 11, para. 33, and Case C-56/13 *Érsekcsanádi Mezőgazdasági Zrt*, EU:C:2014:332, para. 54.

excluding the application of the Charter in cases where national laws have really no connection with EU law obligations;[11] but it still leaves considerable uncertainty in cases that are to some extent "governed by EU law". We will discuss two typical borderline situations in the next two sections of this chapter.[12]

III The problem of discretionary choice and of incomplete harmonization

A first difficulty in assessing whether a situation is "governed by EU law" results from the fact that, when adopting measures to implement EU law, the national parliaments and governments often add legal norms that are not strictly required by the EU directive or regulation. EU acts often leave to the Member States' discretion to adopt certain measures or not, or to choose between different legal solutions (the *discretionary choice* hypothesis); and EU acts may require certain measures but leave it to the Member States whether or not to adopt accompanying or more far-reaching measures (the *incomplete harmonization* hypothesis). In both these situations, the question arises whether Member States, when going beyond the strict obligations imposed on them by the EU act, are still acting within the scope of application of the Charter or not.

In the first hypothesis, that of *discretionary choice*, the Charter will normally be applicable. Since the EU act explicitly leaves a choice between different courses of action, each course of action will count as "implementation" and will therefore be subject to the Charter. The "Dublin Regulation" judgment *N.S. et al.* is a good example of this. The Regulation[13] organized the allocation of asylum seekers between the Member States on the basis of several criteria, the main one being the country of first entry in the EU territory. However, Article 3(2) of the Regulation added that "by way of derogation" each Member State may decide to examine applications for asylum even if they would normally not be its responsibility according to the criteria of the Regulation. This is a fine example of a purely discretionary choice; still, when making that choice, the Member State concerned becomes the "responsible State" in the sense of the regulation and must comply with the

11 For example, in a case involving the application of an Italian law for the protection of the cultural heritage and landscapes, a subject matter on which there is no EU legislation. Case C-206/13 *Cruciano Siragusa* EU:C:2014:126.

12 For some more detailed arguments as to why the question of the scope of the Charter remains unclear even after the ruling in *Åkerberg Fransson*, see Fontanelli (2014) and Dougan (2015).

13 The version in force at the time of the judgment was that of 2003: Council Regulation 343/2003 of 18 February 2003, establishing the criteria and mechanisms for determining the Member State responsible for examining an asylum application lodged in one of the Member States by a third-country national. [2003] OJ 2003, L 50/1.

substantive clauses of the regulation and with all other provisions of EU asylum law. Therefore, as the CJEU rightly decided in the *N.S.* judgment, the Member State that makes use of the derogation clause contributes to the "implementation" of the regulation and of EU asylum legislation more generally. The Charter should therefore apply to this situation and may turn the discretionary choice into an obligation – namely, when not exercising that discretion would lead to a serious violation of the asylum seeker's fundamental rights in another EU country.[14]

The second hypothesis, that of *incomplete harmonization*, is more problematic, and the position taken by the CJEU not entirely consistent. In one case, *Zoi Chatzi*, it held that the national authorities, even when going beyond the requirements of a directive, must still respect EU fundamental rights, but without explaining why this was the case. That case dealt with the implementation of the parental leave directive in Greece. Ms Chatzi, who had given birth to twins, requested two separate and additional periods of parental leave. The CJEU found that the directive did not contain any special rules for twins, so that there was no obligation for Greece to grant two periods of parental leave in the case of twins. Nevertheless, the Court added, the general principle of equality in EU law imposes an obligation on Greece to take the special situation of the parents of twins in due consideration, in one way or the other.[15] In a number of other cases, the Court has taken the opposite, and more logical, view, namely that when national authorities decide to enact legal rules of their own that are not required as an EU law obligation, they will be subject to compliance with their national constitutional law (and the ECHR), but not with the Charter. This can be illustrated by the *Hernández* case.[16] Directive 2008/94 on the protection of employees in the event of the insolvency of their employer lays down a number of norms that the Member States must implement, but also (as many directives do) leaves open "the option of Member States to apply or introduce laws, regulations or administrative provisions which are more favourable to employees".[17] A Spanish law containing such more favourable rules was challenged for violation of the equality provision of the Charter, but the Court found this situation to be outside the scope of the directive and therefore also outside the scope of the Charter. The Court's reasoning about the scope of the Charter was quite elaborate in this case. It is therefore safe to assume that the *Chatzi* judgment, which reached a different conclusion but without detailed reasoning, was an isolated mistake.

14 Joined Cases *N.S. v Secretary of State for the Home Department et al.* C-411/10 and C-493/10 EU:C:2011:865.

15 Case C-149/10 *Zoi Chatzi*:EU:C:2010:534, para. 62 ff.

16 Case C-198/13 *Victor Manuel Julian Hernández et al.* EU:C:2014:2055.

17 Article 11 Directive 2008/94, of the European Parliament and of the Council of 22 October 2008 on the protection of employees in the event of the insolvency of their employer [2008] OJ L 283/36.

Given the continuing uncertainty about the scope of application of the EU Charter, national authorities and national courts may be forgiven for not always being clear about the matter. In particular, national courts may be led to pose questions of interpretation of the Charter rights in situations that are not obviously within the scope of the Charter. In such cases, the Court of Justice sternly refuses to answer the question. It tends to put the burden on the national court to explain why they think that the Charter applies to the facts of the case, and in the absence of convincing arguments, the Court declares the question inadmissible. It dismisses the reference on the ground that "there is nothing specific in the order for reference demonstrating that the legal situation at issue in the main proceedings comes within the scope of EU law".[18] The Court adopts this approach even when the facts of the case clearly show some connection with EU law but the national court fails to articulate that connection; it did so most controversially in a series of references challenging national austerity measures for violation of fundamental social rights, despite the fact that those austerity measures had been adopted in connection with budget reform programmes imposed by the European institutions. (Kilpatrick 2015, pp. 348–50).

IV Allocating responsibility for fundamental rights compliance between the EU and the Member State

Assuming that we find ourselves in a situation where a Member State "implements Union law" in the sense of Article 51, and is therefore bound to apply and respect the EU Charter, the question can still arise whether the Member State authorities should be held responsible for a violation of the Charter, or whether that violation is mainly or exclusively caused by the underlying norm of EU law, so that the European Union should be held responsible. In terms of the activity of a national court faced with a dispute, the reply to that question will make a huge difference: if the EU is responsible for the alleged breach of the Charter, the national court must ask the CJEU whether the act is invalid as a matter of EU law; if the Member State is responsible, then the national court can decide the case itself or, if necessary, ask a preliminary question to the CJEU about the interpretation of the Charter.

More specifically, the question will be whether the (possible) violation is committed by the EU legislator when adopting a directive or regulation or by the states when using their policy discretion in implementing the directive or regulation.

18 Case C-483/12 *Pelckmans Turnhout* EU:C:2014:304, para. 22. See, similarly, Case C-23/12 *Mohamad Zakaria* EU:C:2013:24, para. 39; and Case C-497/12 *Davide Gullotta* EU:C:2015:436, paras. 19–21.

That question was implicit in the Court's judgment of 2006 on the validity of the family reunification directive.[19] The European Parliament had argued that the directive was invalid for, among other reasons, violating the right to family life of migrants due to the fact that it allowed the Member States to impose quite drastic conditions for family unification. The Court held that the Directive itself complied with fundamental rights and that any violations that could occur when Member States made use of the discretion given to them by the directive would have to be addressed at that level. The Court added that "while the Directive leaves the Member States a margin of appreciation, it is sufficiently wide to enable them to apply the Directive's rules in a manner consistent with the requirements flowing from the protection of fundamental rights".[20] As was rightly observed by Loïc Azoulai, the Court's approach "has the effect of protecting EU acts. These acts are sheltered from censure by the sole fact of their incompleteness. Any flexibility in the EU legislation is thus interpreted as an implicit commitment to respect fundamental rights and it is the national measure which shall be blamed and must be set aside" (Azoulai 2012, p. 209).

The CJEU took a rather different approach to the question of allocation of responsibility in its judgment of 2014 finding the EU data retention directive to be invalid for violation of the right to privacy and to data protection. Earlier on, three constitutional courts, those of Germany, Romania and the Czech Republic, had held that the national laws implementing the directive infringed the right of privacy protected by their respective national constitutions. None of them referred a question on the validity of the underlying EU directive, as they considered that the fundamental rights violation had occurred at the implementation stage, when the national legislature adopted rules on the conditions for the use of retained personal data. An Irish and an Austrian court, on the other hand, when faced with a legal action against the implementation of the same directive in Ireland and Austria, declared to have doubts about whether the directive itself was compatible with the right to privacy as protected by the EU Charter and put that question to the CJEU, thus giving rise to the judgment in the joined cases *Digital Rights Ireland* and *Kärtner Landesregierung*, in which the CJEU found that the EU legislator had, indeed, breached the fundamental rights of the Charter by leaving too much discretion to the Member States and thereby "facilitating" the commission of human rights violations at the national level.[21] In other words, the CJEU here took an approach that contrasted with its ruling in the family reunification case. Whereas, in the latter case, it had taken the incompleteness of the directive

19 Council Directive 2003/86/EC of 22 September 2003 on the right to family reunification. [2003] OJ L251/12.

20 Case C-540/03 *Parliament v Council* EU:C:2006:429, para. 104.

21 Joined Cases C-293/12 and C-594/12 *Digital Rights Ireland* and *Kärtner Landesregierung* EU:C:2014:238.

as a reason for putting the burden to comply with fundamental rights on the Member States rather than on the EU legislator, in the data retention case the Court held that the EU legislator should have put in place a legal regime guaranteeing that no fundamental rights violations would occur at the national level, and the failure to do so caused the invalidation of the directive.

V Some implications for the right to family life

In this final section, the issue mentioned in the previous section will be illustrated by referring to judicial practice in respect of the Directive on family reunification and the role played therein by Article 7 of the Charter. This practice is mentioned here only by way of example, since a complete discussion of the Charter right is proposed in other chapters of this volume.[22]

As was mentioned above, the CJEU had rejected in 2006 the claim made by the European Parliament that some provisions of the Directive violated the right to family life, but at the same time the Court had recognized that questions of (non-)respect of that right could arise in the context of the transposition and application of the directive at the national level, and the CJEU would then help the national courts in ensuring the observance of EU fundamental rights. In its *Chakroun* ruling of March 2010, made upon a reference by a Dutch court, and decided only a few months after the entry into force of the Lisbon Treaty and of the Charter, the CJEU repeated that the provisions of the directive must be interpreted in the light of the right to family life. The Court concluded in this case that some Dutch administrative measures restricting family unification were incompatible with the directive.[23] It is not entirely clear whether the Court would not have come to the same conclusion on the basis of the *effet utile* of the Directive itself, without reference to the Charter, but the judgment certainly seemed to signal a willingness to check national implementing legislation against a European fundamental rights standard. In later cases, the Court specified that the same Directive must not only be *interpreted* but also *applied* (by the national authorities) in the light of Article 7 of the Charter.[24] The Court declared this on its own initiative, as the national courts referring those cases had not, in fact, referred to the Charter when formulating their preliminary questions. Yet, in each of those cases, the CJEU left it to the national courts and administrative authorities to draw the appropriate conclusions from this reference to the Charter; it did not decide itself whether the concrete national measures at stake were in breach of the Charter.

22 See in particular the chapter by Iglesias and Carr also in this book.
23 Case C-578/08 *Rhimou Chakroun* EU:C:2010:117, para. 44.
24 Joined Cases C-356/11 and C-357/11, *O & S* EU:C:2012:776, paras. 77 to 80; Case C-558/14 *Mimoun Khachab* EU:C:2016:285, para. 28.

Yet, in other cases concerning the domestic application of the directive on family reunification, the Court forgets to mention the right to family life of the Charter. A recent striking example is the Court's ruling on the Dutch pre-entry language and civic integration tests.[25] Dutch immigration law requires TCNs to successfully take a language and civic integration test in their country of origin, prior to exercising their right to family unification.[26] Whereas the Court examined the Dutch regime in the light of the Directive's generic reference to the acceptability of "integration measures", and in the light of the general principle of proportionality, it does not refer at all to the Charter and the right to family life, even though the pre-entry language tests act as a major barrier to entry for family unification purposes, and therefore constitute a serious interference with family life. This lack of reference to the Charter helps the Court in reaching a conclusion that finds the Dutch regime acceptable in its broad outline, even though not in all its detailed provisions. The Court repeats its finding from *Chakroun* that the Directive 2003/86 grants "clearly defined rights" to family unification,[27] but it views those rights as "statutory rights" granted by EU legislation rather than fundamental rights protected by the Charter.[28] This may therefore seem like a missed opportunity for the Court to "give teeth" to the right to family life in a context of multilevel governance. One could argue that in the present case the Dutch legislator had made use of the discretion granted to it by the directive to defeat the purpose of the directive and, beyond this, to interfere quite radically with the right to family life. The failure to discuss this situation in fundamental rights terms seems to indicate that, in this area of EU law, the Charter of Rights is not exercising a meaningful limit on Member State action. This is a sobering counterpoint to the heated doctrinal discussions on the scope of application of the Charter in relation to Member State action.

References

Azoulai, L. (2012). The Case of Fundamental Rights: A State of Ambivalence. In: H.W. Micklitz and B. de Witte (eds.). *The European Court of Justice and the Autonomy of the Member States*. Antwerp: Intersentia, pp. 207–17.

Dougan, M. (2015). Judicial Review of Member State Action under the General Principles and the Charter: Defining the "Scope of EU Law." *Common Market Law Review*, 52, pp. 1201–45.

25 Case C-153/14 *Minister van Buitenlandse Zaken v K & A* EU:C:2015:453.

26 On the Dutch regime, see de Vries (2013); and see also, situating the Dutch regime in the context of the overall evolution of immigration policy, Wallace Goodman (2011).

27 Case C-153/14, *supra* n.26, para. 46.

28 The approach of the Court of Justice in this case to privilege statutory interpretation rather than human rights-based interpretation is noted by Thym (2016, pp.100–4).

Eeckhout, P. (2002). The EU Charter of Fundamental Rights and the Federal Question. *Common Market Law Review*, 39, pp. 945–54.

Fontanelli, F. (2014). National Measures and the Application of the EU Charter of Fundamental Rights – Does *curia.eu* Know *iura.eu*? *Human Rights Law Review*, 14, pp 231–65.

Huber, P.M. (2008). The Unitary Effect of the Community's Fundamental Rights: The *ERT*-Doctrine Needs to Be Reviewed. *European Public Law*, 14, pp. 323–33.

Iglesias Sánchez, S. (2012). The Court and the Charter: The Impact of the Entry into Force of the Lisbon Treaty on the ECJ's Approach to Fundamental Rights. *Common Market Law Review*, 49, pp. 1565–612.

Kilpatrick, C. (2015). On the Rule of Law and Economic Emergency: The Degradation of Basic Legal Values in Europe's Bailouts. *Oxford Journal of Legal Studies*, 35, pp 325–53.

Lenaerts, K. (2012). Exploring the Limits of the EU Charter of Fundamental Rights. *European Constitutional Law Review*, 8, pp. 375–403.

Thym, D. (2016). Towards a Contextual Conception of Social Integration in EU Immigration Law. Comments on *P & S* and *K & A*. *European Journal of Migration and Law*, 18, pp. 89–111.

de Vries, K.M. (2013). *Integration at the Border: The Dutch Act on Integration Abroad and International Immigration Law*. Oxford: Hart Publishing.

Wallace Goodman, S. (2011). Controlling Immigration through Language and Country Knowledge Requirements. *West European Politics*, 34, pp. 235–55.

3 The right to family life in the EU Charter of Fundamental Rights

*Sara Iglesias Sánchez and Keiva Carr**

I Introduction

Family life in the EU is protected, amongst other provisions, by Article 7 of the Charter, which also guarantees the right to respect for private life, home and communications. Together with Article 8 of the Charter, Article 7 is directly linked to Article 8 ECHR, which inspired the drafting of the Charter and which should inspire its interpretation.

Despite the limited scope of application of the Charter,[1] and despite of the fact that the EU has not been endowed with competences to regulate substantive family law, since the earlier times of European integration, it has been clear that EU law has an important impact on the protection of the right to family life. Indeed, the lack of material competences in the specific field of substantive family law – coupled with the reticence of some Member States to see EU law involved in this field[2] – has not precluded that some of the most relevant spheres in which the fundamental right to family life is called upon to deploy its protection fall, to various degrees, under the scope of EU law.

The most important fields in which the fundamental right to family life has played a relevant role in the interpretation of primary and secondary law are those in which the movement of people is involved. Furthermore, with the introduction of new competences in the AFSJ, new instruments in the field of private international law and cooperation in judicial civil and criminal matters, new areas in which the right to family life often comes into play, either concerning the standard of legality of EU acts or as a vital element for their interpretation, have been brought within the realm of EU law.

* Sara Iglesias Sanchez is Référendaire at the CJEU. Keiva Carr is administrator-lawyer at the Research and Documentation Directorate, CJEU. The views expressed in this chapter are purely personal to the authors.

1 See Bruno de Witte in this book.

2 See, in particular, the Declaration by the Republic of Poland on the Charter, which reads as follows: "[t]he Charter does not affect in any way the right of Member States to legislate in the sphere of public morality, family law, as well as the protection of human dignity and respect for human physical and moral integrity."

Against this background, this chapter will first explore the structure of the right to family life under the framework of Article 7 of the Charter and its interaction with other Charter provisions. Further, this chapter seeks to offer an account of the practical application of the right to family life through the case law of the CJEU. Particular attention will be paid in this regard to the role of the right to family life in the case law of the Court in the fields of citizenship of the Union, immigration and asylum law, and judicial cooperation. The chapter will conclude with some general reflections on the different functions that the right to family life deploys in EU law at the jurisprudential level and on the current challenges of the interpretation and legal construction of this right to meet the needs of protection of a supranational right to family life.

II The right to family life according to Article 7 of the Charter

Family life is one of the objects of protection of Article 7 of the Charter. As such, the right to family life is one of the fundamental rights that had already been recognized by the Court as a general principle, respect of which was guaranteed by EU law before the drafting and the subsequent entry into force of the Charter.[3]

The scope, material content and level of protection offered by the right to family life enshrined in Article 7 of the Charter are marked by three important factors that we will examine in turn: the general scope of application of the Charter, its relationship with Article 8 of the ECHR and the interaction between the several elements that this provision covers and with other Charter provisions.

A Scope of application

The scope of application of every Charter right is limited by Article 51 of the Charter, according to which, Charter rights are addressed to the institutions, bodies, offices and agencies of the Union, and to the Member States, only when they implement Union law (Spaventa 2016).

In this regard, the obligation of EU institutions to respect Article 7 of the Charter has been made manifest through several annulment procedures, where the Court of Justice has annulled certain provisions and instruments of secondary law for being contrary to the private life prong of this Article, together with the specific right to data protection contained in Article 8 of the Charter.[4] However, when it comes to the family life prong of Article 7, no annulment actions have succeeded to date.[5]

3 See, for example, Case C-249/86 *Commission v Germany* EU:C:1989:204; Case C-60/00 *Carpenter* EU:C:2002:434 and Case C-459/99 *MRAX* EU:C:2002:461.

4 See judgments in Joined Cases C-92/09 and C-93/09 *Volker* EU:C:2010:662; C-362/14 *Schrems* EU:C:2015:650, and Joined Cases C-293/12 and C-594/12 *Digital Rights Ireland* EU:C:2014:238.

5 See, in particular, the judgment in Case C-540/03, *Parliament v Council* EU:C:2006:429.

According to the case law of the Court, Charter rights can only be invoked, with regard to Member States, when the factual specificities pertaining to the case have a sufficient connection with EU law.[6] The case law of the CJEU, in the particular field of citizenship and family life, has been of great relevance to the general discussion on the limits of the application of the Charter to the Member States. Even before the entry into force of the Charter, the impact of the right to family life on the issue of the scope of EU fundamental rights and freedoms was broadly discussed in the aftermath of the judgment of the Court in *Carpenter*.[7] In that case, the right to family life played a very important role in permitting the Court to find that the freedom to provide services precluded the UK from refusing a residence right to the spouse of an EU citizen that provided services to clients established in other Member States (Editorial Comments 2003; Acierno 2003).

The role and scope of the protection afforded by the status of the citizenship of the Union has also been extended by way of the protection of family life, particularly through the recognition of residence rights for parents of EU minor citizens.[8] However, the limited scope of fundamental rights might explain the absence of explicit considerations regarding the fundamental right to family life, for example in the *Ruiz Zambrano* case,[9] despite its obvious links. Instead, a very innovative interpretation of the right to citizenship has come into being. This case law will be commented upon in the following section. Here, it suffices to highlight that family life related considerations, even if not made explicit, have been at the basis of a very innovative reading of the notion of citizenship of the Union (Kaesling 2014; Hailbronner and Iglesias Sánchez 2011).

The subsequent case law of the CJEU has clarified the limits to the far-reaching considerations in the *Ruiz Zambrano* case,[10] positing a strict interpretation of the relationship between fundamental rights and citizenship of the Union: only in cases where "the essence" of citizenship rights is affected can the protection of the fundamental right to family life be triggered. In other words, if we are not in a citizenship-protected situation, then the situation falls outside the scope of the Charter and therefore the questions

6 With regard to Article 24, for example, the Court has declared its incompetence, according to Article 51 of the Charter, to rule on cases concerning child benefits that had no connection with EU law. See orders in C-608/14 *Pondiche* EU:C:2015:313 and in C-496/14 *Statul Român* EU:C:2015:312.

7 *Carpenter supra* n. 3.

8 See judgment in Case C-200/02 *Zhu and Chen* EU:C:2004:639.

9 Case C-34/09 *Ruiz Zambrano* EU:C:2011:124.

10 See judgments in Case C-434/09, *McCarthy*, EU:C:2011:277; Case C-256/11, *Dereci and Others* EU:C:2011:734; Case C-86/12, *Alokpa and Moudoulou* EU:C:2013:645 and Case C-87/12, *Ymeraga and Others* EU:C:2013:291. Indeed, the result in the *Ruiz Zambrano* case has remained exceptional. Advocate General Szpunar has proposed to follow the line of the Ruiz Zambrano case in his Opinion in Cases C-165/14, *Rendón Marin* and C-304/14, *CS*, EU:C:2016:75.

remains one for national courts to decide, in light of Article 8 ECHR.[11] Therefore, in this line of cases, the protection of the right to family life under Article 7 of the Charter has to a significant extent been made redundant with regard to the protection guaranteed by Article 21 TFUE.

B The relationship with Article 8 ECHR

The Charter right contained in Article 7 corresponds, as noted in the introduction, to Article 8 ECHR. By mandate of Article 52(3) of the Charter, the meaning and scope of the rights of the Charter corresponding to Convention rights shall be the same as those laid down by the Convention, notwithstanding the possibility that Union law provides for more extensive protection.[12] As a consequence, the Charter's right to family life is significantly substantiated by a vast body of jurisprudence defining and interpreting the implications of the right to family life. Nonetheless, Article 7 of the Charter is autonomous in scope. Indeed, as opposed to Article 8 ECHR, it does not cover the particular contents of data protection, which receive a particularized treatment in the Charter, with a new article devoted specifically to data protection (Article 8 of the Charter). Furthermore, even if the Convention level of protection works as the minimum threshold, the Charter can offer a heightened level of protection (Choudhry 2014, p. 207).

Pre-Charter case law very often had recourse to the Strasbourg case law, playing an important role in cases such as *Commission v Germany*.[13] Indeed, in annulment proceedings, the Court relied heavily on the framework put in place by the ECtHR by carefully considering the requirements of the Convention system and subsequently concluding that the family reunification directive[14] in fact provided for higher standards of protection in terms of the right to family life. Therefore, it was held not to be contrary to fundamental rights.[15]

Moreover, the case law of the ECtHR has been particularly relevant in determining what constitutes family life given that it has already established the minimum level of protection to be afforded to several collectives such as gay, lesbian and transsexual relationships. In this regard, the evolution of the Strasbourg case law has had a very strong impact on the approach to be taken in the interpretation of EU law affecting the rights, particularly of same-sex partnerships, by the CJEU.

11 See judgment in Case C-256/11, *Dereci and Others* EU:C:2011:734, para. 71 et seq.

12 Case C-400/10 PPU *McB.* EU:C:2010: 582, para. 53. See, on the interpretation of this provision, Case C-601/15PPU, *N.* EU:C:2016:84, para. 77 et seq.

13 Case C-441/02, *Commission v Germany* EU:C:2006:253, para. 109.

14 Council Directive 2003/86/EC of 22 September 2003 on the right to family reunification, [2003] OJ 2003 L251/12.

15 Case C-540/03, *Parliament v Council*, EU:C:2006:429.

The first cases that arrived before the Court came at a time where the Strasbourg case law had not yet acknowledged the application of the right to family life to same-sex partnerships.[16] Notably then, the CJEU initially took a restrictive stance towards the issue of non-discrimination.[17] In the same vein, the Court found that the denial of certain benefits with regard to same-sex partnerships could not entail an interference with the right to family and private life.[18] However, the evolution of the case law of the ECtHR,[19] together with the development of EU secondary law in the field of non-discrimination, meant that the right to family life weighed significantly on the legal situation of same-sex partnerships and their protection according to EU law. Even though the fundamental right to family life is not often implicitly mentioned in this case law,[20] which relies mostly on the prohibition of discrimination on grounds of sexual orientation under Directive 2000/78,[21] it is clear that an important evolution regarding the conception of family life, parallel to the one that occurred in Strasbourg, underlies this case law (Wintermute 2015, pp. 179–200).

Particularly, the Civil Service Tribunal has put forward the relevance of the right to family life in cases concerning access to allowances. That jurisdiction has established that

> the extension of entitlement to the household allowance to officials registered as stable, non-marital partners, including those of the same sex, reflects the need to protect officials against the administration's interference in the exercise of their right to respect for their family and private life, as recognized in Article 7 of the Charter and Article 8 of the ECHR.

In this connection, the Civil Service Tribunal has found inspiration in the Strasbourg case law, declaring that when investigating if a same-sex couple has access to legal marriage under the legislation of a Member State, the administration cannot disregard the law of another State connected to the situation (for example, because of the nationality of the persons concerned) where that law could render access to marriage and therefore the

16 See, e.g., *X and Y v UK* App. No. 9369/81 (ECtHR 3 May 1983); *S v UK* App. No. 11716/85 (ECtHR 14 May 1986) or *Röösli v Germany* App. No. 28318/95(ECtHR 15 May 1996).

17 Case *Grant*, C-249/96, EU:C:1998:63.

18 Joined Cases C-122/99 and C-125/99, *P – D and Sweden v Council* EU:C:2001:304, para. 59 and seq.

19 The ECtHR has held that homosexual unions fall within the scope of family life in the sense of Article 8 ECHR *Schalk and Kopf v Austria* App. No. 30141/04 (ECtHR 22 November 2010), *Vallianatos and Others v Greece* App. Nos. 29381/09 and 32684/09 (ECtHR 7 November 2013). See, going beyond, *Oliari and Others v Italy*, App. Nos. 18766/11 and 36030/11 (ECtHR 21 July 2015).

20 See judgments in cases C-267/06, *Maruko*EU:C:2008:179; C-147/08, *Römer* EU:C:2011:286; C-267/12, *Hay* EU:C:2013:823 or C-81/12, *Asociaţia Accept* EU:C:2013:275.

21 Council Directive 2000/78/EC of 27 November 2000 establishing a general framework for equal treatment in employment and occupation, [2000] OJ L303/16.

right to the household allowance theoretical and illusory (as is the case with a national law that criminalizes homosexual acts).[22]

The powerful effect of the Strasbourg case law in the interpretation and determination of the standard of protection afforded by Article 7 of the Charter has been put forward in the *McB* case, where the Court made extensive reference to the case law of the ECtHR in order to determine the "essence" of the right of a father with no custody rights, where the children had been removed by their mother. This case, which will be commented on below, provides a significant example of how even though, under the system of the Charter, EU law can provide for a higher level of protection than the one provided for under Article 8 ECHR, this minimum protection standard will be also accepted at the EU level when other fundamental rights (or EU fundamental freedoms, such as the mother's free movement right) collide with the right to family life.

C The material scope of protection: Family and privacy

Article 7 of the Charter, as well as Article 8 ECHR, brings together several aspects: privacy and family life. This furthers mutual enrichment and reinforcement of these interrelated elements. Admittedly, several cases make apparent the independent contents of the right to family life on the one hand, and of the right to private life, on the other.[23] The autonomous concept of the right to family life, which could be understood as covering the existence of the family and the right to be together (Marauhn 2006, p. 538), can however greatly be fostered by the joint protection awarded by the rights to family and private life. This is clear from the case law in which the CJEU has drawn from Strasbourg case law[24] in order to conclude, in a case concerning unfair contract terms in mortgage loans, that "[u]nder EU law, the right to accommodation is a fundamental right guaranteed under Article 7 of the Charter that the referring court must take into consideration when implementing Directive 93/13".[25]

22 F-86/09, *W. v European Commission* EU:F:2010:125, para. 48.

23 The "private life" prong of Article 7 of the Charter has paved the way for important and far reaching developments. See, e.g., judgments in Case C-199/12 to C-201/12, *X and Others* EU:C:2013:720; C-148/13 to C-150/13*A*, EU:C:2014:2406. In the judgment in Case C-208/09 *Sayn-Wittgenstein*, EU:C:2010:806, para. 52 the Court noted, referring to the Strasbourg case law, that "a person's name is a constituent element of his identity and of his private life, the protection of which is enshrined in Article 7 of the Charter and in Article 8 ECHR. Even though Article 8 ECHR does not refer to it explicitly, a person's name, as a means of personal identification and a link to a family, none the less concerns his or her private and family life." See also, judgment in C-391/09, *P – D and Sweden v Council Runevič-Vardyn and Wardyn* EU:C:2011:291, para. 66.

24 Citing the judgments *McCann v United Kingdom* App No.19009/04 (ECtHR 27 September 1995) para. 50, and *Rousk v Sweden*, App. No.27183/04, (ECtHR 25 July 2013) para. 137.

25 See judgment in C-34/13, *Kušionová*, EU:C:2014:2189, para. 65. See also Order in C-539/14, *Sánchez Morcillo and Abril García*, EU:C:2015:508, para. 46.

The Charter has not only enhanced the place of family life in the European legal order but also its legal protection, as an institution in itself and for its individual members, through primary law. Beyond the right to family life of Article 7 of the Charter, this instrument also proclaims the right to marry and the right to found a family (Article 9) as well as the right of every child to maintain on a regular basis a personal relationship and direct contact with his parents (Article 24(3)). The Charter also establishes the mandate of legal, economic and social protection of the family (Article 33(1)) and the right to protection from dismissal connected with maternity, maternity leave and parental leave (Article 33(2)).[26]

Notwithstanding the potential mutual enrichment of all these provisions, they conserve their autonomous contents and scopes of protection. On the one hand, whereas Article 33 of the Charter is more focused on the promotional role of the State towards the protection of the family, in Article 7, the focus is on the "*abwerrechtliche*" dimension (Marauhn 2006, p. 590), even if this does not preclude in any case the emergence of positive obligations in this field. On the other hand, Article 24, regarding the interests of the child, has already had an important bearing in the case law of the Court concerning the interpretation of different instruments of secondary law in the AFSJ, such as Regulation 343/2003,[27] Regulation 2201/2003[28] and Regulation 4/2009.[29] Admittedly, this provision has not yet been the object of a jurisprudential development as wide as that pertaining to Article 7 of the Charter. However, it is to be expected that its effects may be more visible in the future, not only through its self-standing application, but also

26 Only few cases have interpreted these provisions. See judgments in Case C-222/14, *Maïstrellis* EU:C:2015:473 and in Case C-149/10, *Chatzi*, EU:C:2010:534. In the field of social law, family related fundamental rights were not mentioned in the recent cases concerning the rights of a commissioning mother as regards the grant of maternity leave. See judgments in Cases C-167/12, *D.* EU:C:2014:169 and in C-363/12, *Z.* EU:C:2014:159. These cases have been rather examined through the perspective of non-discrimination, particularly with regard to Directive 2006/54/EC of the European Parliament and of the Council of 5 July 2006 on the implementation of the principle of equal opportunities and equal treatment of men and women in matters of employment and occupation, [2006] OJ L204/23.

27 Council Regulation (EC) No 343/2003 of 18 February 2003 establishing the criteria and mechanisms for determining the Member State responsible for examining an asylum application lodged in one of the Member States by a third-country national. [2003] OJ L50/1. See judgment in Case C-648/11, *MA and Others*, EU:C:2013:367.

28 Council Regulation (EC) No 2201/2003 of 27 November 2003 concerning jurisdiction and the recognition and enforcement of judgments in matrimonial matters and the matters of parental responsibility [2003] OJ L 338/1. See judgments in CasesC-498/14PPU *Bradbrooke* EU:C:2015:3; C-4/14 *Bohez* EU:C:2015:563; C-92/12PPU *Health Service Executive* EU:C:2012:255; C-491/10PPU *Aguirre Zarraga* EU:C:2010:828 and *McB*, *supra* n. 12.

29 Council Regulation (EC) No 4/2009 of 18 December 2008 on jurisdiction, applicable law, recognition and enforcement of decisions and cooperation in matters relating to maintenance obligations. [2009] OJ L7/1. See judgment in C-184/14*A* EU:C:2015:479.

and mostly, though the interconnected development of its effects, together with Article 7 of the Charter.[30]

III Family life in the case law of the CJEU

As previously mentioned, the EU has traditionally enjoyed very limited competences in the field of substantive family law (McEleavey 2002; Martiny 2002). The important influence of EU law in family law derives from the incidental effects of integration: it could be said to be linked to "the very success of the free movement project [that] has promoted international integration, leading to a greater degree of international relationships and family formation and, in some cases, dissolution" (Stalford 2007, p. 107).

Therefore, it may not come as a surprise that the most important jurisprudential developments regarding the right to family life have, without any doubt, occurred in the field of free movement of persons and, subsequently, in the field of citizenship of the Union with regard to the rights of family members of Union citizens.

A second influential EU law prong in the field of family law has been incited by the competences, introduced by the Treaty of Amsterdam, in the field of the AFSJ, which necessitated various secondary law instruments significantly bearing on the right to family life. For instance, the right to family reunification has been enacted in the field of immigration and asylum law through different instruments. In the field of asylum, particularly, the interests of the child and family life are fundamental in the application of the rules of the CEAS (particularly, in the framework of the Dublin system). EU law in the field of civil cooperation is also of great importance, in particular, with regard to the Brussels II Regulation. Today, in the field of judicial cooperation in civil matters, according to Article 81(3) TFEU, the EU has the competence to adopt "measures concerning family law with cross-border implications". These measures shall be established by the Council, acting in accordance with a special legislative procedure.[31] Judicial coopera-

30 Indeed, the parties and national courts often have recourse to several of these provisions. See, e.g. judgments in Cases, F-79/14, *EG v Parliament* EU:F:2015:63; *Alokpa supra* n. 10; C-40/11 *Iida* EU:C:2012:691. Arts. 7 and 24 have already deployed their interpretative effects jointly. See, judgments in Cases C-356/11 and C-357/11 *O and Others* EU:C:2012:776, and *McB, supra* n. 12.

31 [See former Article 67 (5) TCE.] This procedure requires unanimity in the Council and mere consultation by the European Parliament. However, according to Article 81(3) TFUE, "The Council, on a proposal from the Commission, may adopt a decision determining those aspects of family law with cross-border implications which may be the subject of acts adopted by the ordinary legislative procedure. The Council shall act unanimously after consulting the European Parliament." Moreover, "The proposal referred to in the second subparagraph shall be notified to the national Parliaments. If a national Parliament makes known its opposition within six months of the date of such notification, the decision shall not be adopted. In the absence of opposition, the Council may adopt the decision."

tion in criminal matters can moreover have an impact on family life in all those cases where a person is sent to another Member State in application of the different instruments that rely on the principle of mutual trust.

These quite astonishing developmental prongs, and their interpretation by the Court, will be examined in turn below.

A From free movement to union citizenship

The underlying premise of establishing a common, internal market meant that market actors were required to ensure the functioning and growth of an economic forum. These actors, otherwise known as *homo economicus* (Everson 1995, p. 71), were characterized as holders of economic rights enjoyed via the exercise of economic activity and supported by the right to free movement, the right to seek employment[32] and the right to provide and receive services in other Member States.[33] According to Ipsen, (as cited by Everson 1995, p. 71):

> whilst market citizens or Marktbürger were drawn from amongst the ranks of the nationals of the EC member states, such nationals were only to be regarded as fully fledged market citizens when 'acting as participants in or as beneficiaries of the common market'
>
> (See also Micklitz 2010).

Based on this logic, family considerations came to be evermore prominent in the field of free movement of workers. This economic premise, however, fundamentally shifted with the recognition that free movement entailed more than protection for individuals availing of their market freedoms. This shift permitted the carving out of a space for fundamental rights considerations, principally through EU citizenship, when interpreting issues concerning migrating families.

a Family life prior to EU citizenship

In the pre-Charter case law, the Court often referred to the right to family life accentuating its very important functional role. The field of free movement of workers and, particularly, interpretation of Regulation 1612/68,[34] rendered clear the need to interpret provisions concerning the free movement of workers in light of the right to family life enshrined in Article 8

32 Case C-344/87, *Bettray v Staatssecretaris van Justice*, EU:C:1989:226; Case C-292/89, *The Queen v Immigration Appeal Tribunal ex parte Antonissen* EU:C:1991:80.

33 Joined cases C-286/82 and C-26/83 *Luisi and Carbone* EU:C:1984:35; Case C-33/74 *Van Binsbergen* EU:C:1974:131.

34 Regulation (EEC) No 1612/68 of the Council of 15 October 1968 on freedom of movement for workers within the Community (OJ, English Special Edition, 1968 (II), p. 475).

ECHR. A holistic interpretation of secondary law led the Court to recognize the humane side of the free movement of workers, and to highlight the importance of family life for integration.[35] The top priority, however, remained functionalism, that is, the proper functioning of the fundamental freedoms in the establishment of a functioning internal market. According to the Court, the EU legislature "recognised the importance of ensuring protection for the family life of nationals of the Member States *in order to eliminate obstacles to the exercise of the fundamental freedoms* guaranteed by the Treaty".[36] Protection of the family therefore was an important vehicle to promote free movement within Europe's external borders. The pro-family legislation focused on permitting the market player to bring his/her family to the host member state so as to avoid that family considerations would be detrimental to migration within the internal market. However, even though various Advocates General grounded their Opinions on detailed analyses of the right to respect for life, the reticence of the Court precluded any open recognition.[37]

The case law related to free movement, in conjunction with its limited, sporadic reference to fundamental rights, permitted the carving out of a legal space within which families were finally afforded substantive protection. The carving of this path to, what we might term, "European justice", began with the renowned *Carpenter*[38] case, which arguably represents an intriguing melting pot of fundamental rights considerations masked by the market based reasoning of the Court. The case concerned the TCN spouse of a British national who applied for a permit to stay in the UK, an application that was rejected. Since Mrs Carpenter was unable to rely on Directive 73/148,[39] the Court was forced to explore other avenues through which the case could be interpreted. The Court chose to decide the case in consideration of Mr Carpenter and in particular his exercise of rights conferred on him by Article 49 EC Treaty. More specifically, the Court considered his economic activities including his occasional provision of services in other Member States. In so doing, the Court held that EC law recognizes the right to family life to those providing services in the EU and that to deport Mrs Carpenter would essentially cause a breach of that right and would also constitute a barrier to his freedom to provide services since Mrs Carpenter

35 Judgment in Case C-249/86 *Commission v Germany* EU:C:1989:204, para. 10. See also Case 413/99*Baumbast and R* C-EU:C:2002:493, para. 68.

36 Cases *Carpenter, supra* n. 3, para. 38 (emphasis added); C-459/99, *MRAX*EU:C:2002:461, para. 53; C-441/02, *Commission v Germany* EU:C:2006:253, para. 109 and C-291/05, *Eind* EU:C:2007:771, para. 44.

37 See for instance the Opinion of Advocate General La Pergola in C-65/98*Eyüp*EU:C:1999:561 paras. 17 and 23.

38 *Carpenter supra* n. 3.

39 Council Directive 73/148/EEC of 21 May 1973 on the abolition of restrictions on movement and residence within the Community for nationals of Member States with regard to establishment and the provision of services. [1973] OJ L 172/14.

maintained care-giving functions to Mr Carpenter's children while he exercised his freedom to provide services. The Court made an important reference to the respect for family life provided for by the ECHR stating that to deport Mrs Carpenter would cause

> an interference with the exercise by Mr. Carpenter of his right to respect for his family life within the meaning of Article 8 of the Convention for the Protection of Human Rights and Fundamental Freedoms, . . . which is among the fundamental rights which, according to the Court's settled case-law, restated by the Preamble to the Single European Act and by Article 6(2) EU, are protected in Community law.[40]

In other words, the Court maintained that if Mrs Carpenter were deported this would effectively result in an infringement in Mr Carpenter's right to provide services, which, in turn, would be contrary to EU law. Effectively then, the unity of this family was upheld not in consideration of its importance *per se* but rather in consideration of Mr Carpenter's market rights. Therefore, even though the Court demonstrated a certain willingness to expressly consider fundamental rights, Carpenter still conjures a very concise example of the functionalist approach tightly bound to the fundamental freedoms.

Surreptitious protection of the family by the Court via its market-based interpretation flourished until EU Citizenship, "destined to be the fundamental status of nationals of the Member States"[41], marked a watershed in the interpretive processes of the Court.

b Family life post EU citizenship[42]

Eventual recognition that a truly integrated market depends on the interdependence of all involved actors led to a change in ideology and, more importantly for our purposes, a shift from market-based to a more socially constructive reasoning by the Court. It became clear that the functionalist approach had reached a deadlock and a new approach was required. That new approach was influenced by the recognition that the common market needed to engage not only with Member States but also with the demos so as to construct a common identity both horizontally amongst the people within Europe's borders and in turn, in a vertical fashion, strengthening the relationship between the people and Europe and its institutions (Weiler 1998). As convoluted as it may appear, citizenship, in conjuring both political and social rights, was meant to allow the growth of the Union beyond

40 Para. 41.
41 C-184/99 *Grzelczyk* EU:C:2001:458 para. 31.
42 See generally, for a more in-depth analysis, the chapter by Kristine Kruma in this volume.

the market while simultaneously strengthening the market itself through protection of its actors. Initially, it was heavily criticized, branded as redundant, derived (Shaw 1997), and a mere symbolic move by the Union in that the new provisions did not extend any new rights to the people of Europe but rather simply congregated existing entitlements under the umbrella of the new concept. It was met with a certain degree of scepticism on the basis that its main value lay in its rhetoric (Lyons 1996; D'Oliveria 1994; contrasted with Comandé 2014) and it would not essentially confer many substantive rights on its intended addressees.[43]

It is argued here however that EU citizenship has paved the way to a real right to family life, quite independent of Mr Carpenter's right to provide services, for instance. The first shift towards a true EU citizenship came with the judgment in *Zhu and Chen*,[44] which illustrates a clean break away from derivative rights based on free movement. In fact, prior to this judgment, the rights and privileges of children could only be triggered by the free movement of their parents (Stalford 2000, p. 110; McGlynn 2006, p. 56). Through Union Citizenship, however, the Court held that a child can, as an independent person, avail of the rights accorded by Directive 90/364,[45] that is, to move and take up residence in other Member States so long as sufficient financial resources and medical insurance are in place. The Court not only moved away from its integrationist market logic but it also, although not expressly, moved towards a more "family life" logic given that it held that a child's right of residence would be yielded ineffective if his/her parent was denied a right of residence. Union Citizenship therefore was established as an independent source of rights that, for the first time, enveloped the right of the family to remain together for motives other than market integration. Contrasted with the *Carpenter* case a clear shift is appreciable.

The scene was set then for a progressive interpretation of the importance of the right to family life in various aspects of EU law, following in the footsteps of the Strasbourg court. With regard to the protection against expulsion and measures related to public policy, for instance, the Court, in the case of *Orfanopoulos and Oliveri*[46] instructed, via a direct reference to the Strasbourg case law, the Member States to take account of the importance of ensuring the protection of family life in assessing proportionality. Expressly, the Court indicated that any expulsion measures should be juxtaposed with "the family circumstances of the person concerned and the seriousness of

43 With this said, the Treaty did specifically confer some substantive rights on those eligible for Union citizenship, such as the right to vote in Parliament elections, the right to petition and the right to a reply in the language of a request.

44 C-200/02, *Zhu and Chen* EU:C:2004:639.

45 Council Directive 90/364/EEC of 28 June 1990 on the right of residence. [190] OJ L 180/26.

46 C-482/01 and C 493/01 *Orfanopoulos and Oliveri* EU:C:2004:262.

the difficulties which the spouse and any of their children risk facing in the country of origin of the person concerned".[47]

In going even further, the well-renowned *Metock* case,[48] expressly reversing *Akrich*,[49] proved to be an important advance in striking a balance between national law, European law and the right to family life (Fahey 2009; Cambien 2009). Through the vehicle of Union Citizenship, the main issue in the case, concerning the reconciliation of residence rights and immigration control, came to be decided (Costello 2009).[50] Particularly interesting in this case is the Court's clarification that the citizens' Directive in question does not specify on issues of family formation.[51] In effect, it held that the Directive does not require that the Union citizen have founded a family at the time when s/he moves in order for his family members, who are nationals of non-member countries, to enjoy the rights established by the Directive. In other words, the Directive has become "an instrument for both family formation and family reunification" (Costello 2009). The reasoning of the Court proves very interesting and a comprehensive tool in protecting the unity of the family. It stated that "if Union citizens were not allowed to lead a normal family life in the host Member State, the exercise of the freedoms they are granted by the Treaty would be seriously obstructed". However, at this juncture of the jurisprudential path to recognizing a real right to family life, again we note a certain functionalist interpretation of the Treaty freedoms so as to accord the right to "lead a normal family life".

c Family life and genuine enjoyment

The protection of the family, both as an institution and of the individual members of it, came to the fore in the notable judgment in *Ruiz Zambrano*.[52]It exposes how the primary law of the Union can grant more comprehensive protection to families in Europe as opposed to national legislation. In *Ruiz*

47 Ibid. paras. 98 and 99 referring to the judgment of the ECHR, *Boultif v Switzerland* App. No. 54273/00 (ECtHR, 2 August 2001) para. 48. See also in this regard the judgment in *Commission v Germany* C-441/02, EU:C:2006:253. In that case, the Commission failed to demonstrate that the administrative practice existing in Germany regarding expulsion was contrary to the requirements regarding protection of the right to respect for family life.

48 C-127/08, *Metock* EU:C:2008:449. The case concerned a refusal by the Irish Minister for Justice to grant residence cards to the non-EU spouses of EU nationals based on the European Communities (Free Movement of Persons) Regulation 2006 (S.I. No. 2) ("2006 Regulations"), which transposes Directive 2004/38 into Irish law. Under Regulation 3(2) of the 2006 Regulations, the spouses of EU citizens were only entitled to a right of residence in Ireland if they had previously been lawfully resident in another Member State.

49 C-109/01, *Akrich* EU:C:2003:491.

50 For an analysis of this case, see the chapter by Kristine Kruma in the present volume.

51 For a development in this sense in the field of immigration law see C-578/08, *Chakroun* EU:C:2010:117, commented below.

52 *Zambrano supra* n. 9.

Zambrano, the Grand Chamber of the Court introduced the genuine enjoyment test stipulating that national measures that effectively exclude EU citizens of the genuine enjoyment of the substance of their rights pertaining to their citizenship status must be held to be contrary to EU law. Although the Court did not make reference to Article 7 of the Charter, and Advocate General Sharpston was of the opinion that

> at the material time of the main proceedings, the fundamental right to family life under EU law could not be invoked as a free-standing right, independently of any other link with EU law, either by a non-Member State national or by a citizen of the Union, whether in the territory of the Member State of which that citizen was a national or elsewhere in the territory of the Member States.

The Court, nevertheless, derived a right, for the father of the Union citizen, a TCN, to reside and work in Belgium. This right was derived from Article 20, with the Court insisting, despite the written submissions of various Member States and indeed the Commission, arguing that the case arose in a wholly internal situation, that "citizenship of the Union is intended to be the fundamental status of nationals of the Member States".[53]

Caution must be adhered to when attempting to draw precise conclusions from the remarkably brief judgment of the Court. However, we might say that *Ruiz Zambrano* is a clear-cut example of the shift in logic we have already made reference to. The economic goals of the EU essentially require the free movement of goods, services and people, which in turn has developed into a social understanding of the internal market. As pointed out by Advocate General Sharpston, "when citizens move, they do so as human beings, not as robots. They fall in love, marry and have families".[54] To this end, the primary law of the EU and its scope of application has had to adjust to provide protection not only for the factors of production migrating in Europe but also for the humanistic aspect that is inherent in the free movement of persons. It is within this realm that *Ruiz Zambrano* takes a significant step essentially recognizing that movement is not a necessary prerequisite to trigger the scope of EU citizenship rules therefore expanding its scope to wholly internal situations. And even further, that EU citizenship not only recognises individuals but also social groups, like the family.

The genuine enjoyment formula was nuanced in the following wave of citizenship case law and, in fact, another type of EU citizen was introduced: the static citizen. In the *McCarthy* case,[55] the Grand Chamber reasoned, again without reference to the Charter, that in contrast to *Ruiz Zambrano*,

53 Para. 41.
54 Opinion of Advocate General Sharpston Case C-34/09 *Zambrano* EU:C:2010:560, para. 128. For further analysis, see the chapter by Kristine Kruma in the present volume.
55 *McCarthy supra* n. 10.

the national measure at issue in the proceedings did not have the effect of obliging Mrs McCarthy to leave the territory of the EU in that, even if her husband were to be expelled, she could choose to remain in the UK. Therefore, the genuine enjoyment of the substance of her rights pertaining to EU citizenship would not be undermined. It would seem that the existence of children in the Ruiz Zambrano family was a decisive factor in distinguishing Mrs McCarthy's case, in that upholding the national decision did not "oblige her to leave the territory of the EU" as would have occurred if the negative decision had been upheld in the *Ruiz Zambrano* case. Thus, whereas *Zambrano* gave effect to EU rights based on citizenship of the Union even though no movement had taken place, the same citizenship logic was not engaged to enforce the rights of Mrs McCarthy. One might question here whether this construction does not indicate a regressive approach to the family, one that considers procreation as fundamental to the very status itself.

It was hoped that *Dereci and Others*[56] would provide some clarification to the confusion that ensued from these two seemingly conflicting cases. Even though the Court did propose an eventual engagement of Article 7 of the Charter, it finally decided that Union citizens, who have never exercised free movement rights, cannot, for that reason alone, be assimilated to a purely internal situation. Following this, the Court in *Iida*[57] decided to maintain its post *Ruiz Zambrano* construction of genuine enjoyment in deciding that the Japanese father of a German child who lived in Austria with her mother could not invoke a right of residence in Germany since his eventual departure from within Europe's borders would not deprive his daughter of the genuine enjoyment of her rights nor would it impede her from moving freely within the EU.

Thus far, therefore, it would seem that the Court took one step forward with *Zambrano*, even reaching the outer limits of EU law. However, in its attempt to proceed with caution, it ended up taking two steps backwards (Carr 2014). Most importantly, in none of the above cases[58] did the Court engage in any serious discussion of the right to family life. It was not until *O and S*[59] that the Court seized the opportunity to address the fundamental right to family life. The case concerned the right of a TCN to derive a right of residence from the Union citizen child of his spouse. The referring Court asked whether EU citizenship precluded the refusal of a residence permit to the stepfathers of Union citizen children given that there was no biological link between them and the stepfather was not a legal custodian. In response, the Court reiterated its genuine enjoyment test as diluted by

56 *Dereci and Others supra* n. 10.

57 *Iida, supra* n. 30.

58 See also *Alokpa supra* n. 10,Case C-83/11 *Rahman and Others* EU:C:2012:519; Case C-423/12 *Reyes* EU:C:2014:16; Case C-145/09 *Tsakouridis* EU:C:2010:708.

59 C-356/11 and C-357/11, *O and S* EU:C:2012:776.

Dereci and followed the view of the Advocate General who had stated that in the case the Union children were forced to leave the territory of the EU, it would only be because of the deliberate decision of their mother based on "the whims and vagaries of his mother's married life rather than a constraint imposed by the implementation of the national legislation". In this way, the Court remained in line with the dependency aspect that underlined the *Ruiz Zambrano* judgment. Furthermore, the Court reiterated that the desirability of keeping a family together was not sufficient in itself to conclude that the Union citizen children would be forced to leave. With that qualification made, the Court furthered the discussion by linking the situation at hand to the Family Reunification Directive.[60] In taking this approach, the Court was permitted to build in the long-awaited fundamental rights arguments in recognizing that the right to family life was a vital consideration to be measured outside the genuine enjoyment test. Essentially, the Court held that national courts must interpret and apply EU law, in this case the provisions of the Family Reunification Directive, in light of Articles 7 and 24(2) and (3) of the Charter with a view to making "a balanced and reasonable assessment of all the interests in play, taking particular account of the interests of the children concerned".

The Charter therefore finally came to play an even more important role than the citizenship provisions, which had, until that point, been used as a vehicle to grant protection to families and family life in Europe. The principal point after having analyzed the main cases is that after the entry into force of the Charter, the right to family life has been detached from this functional purpose with regard to the fundamental freedoms. This detachment is also due to the fact that EU citizenship is not so much dependent on the exercise of an economic freedom. The humanization of free movement has come together with the reconsideration of family life regardless of its promotional role towards the exercise of the fundamental freedoms.

Further developments in this field will prove interesting. Will the Court follow the opinion of Advocate General Szpunar in that a non-EU national having sole care and control of a minor child who is a citizen of the EU may not be expelled from a Member State or be refused a residence permit simply because he has a criminal record?[61] Will the Court pay respect to the Advocate General's mindfulness of the Charter, particularly Article 7?[62] What will the Court respond to the Court of Appeal (England and Wales) (Civil Division) in C-115/15?[63] Must a TCN ex-spouse of a Union citizen be able to show that their former spouse was exercising Treaty rights in the

60 Council Directive on the right to family reunification, *supra* 14

61 C-165/14 *Rendón Marín* and C-304/14, *CS* EU:C:2016:75.

62 Para. 101.

63 [2015] OJ C 171/20. Reference for a preliminary ruling from Court of Appeal (England and Wales) (Civil Division) (United Kingdom) made on 6 March 2015 — *Secretary of State for the Home Department v NA*.

host Member state at the time of their divorce in order to retain a right of residence under Article 13(2) of Directive 2004/38/EC? How will the genuine enjoyment test be applied by the Court and to what extent will Article 7 feature in the Court's decision? It is hoped that the Court will continue on its "clarification march" all the while attributing a correct importance to the Charter and the promotion of family life in Europe.

B The area of freedom, security and justice

Given the particular content of the instruments in fields covered by the AFSJ – where the European project has overcome economic integration – the protection of fundamental rights is situated clearly in the spotlight. In this connection, the right to family life is one of the fundamental rights that can be affected in the various material fields of EU competence in the AFSJ, be that with regard to the positive obligations to be drawn in immigration and asylum law,[64] or with regard to the potential interferences that may arise from the application of the EU instruments of judicial cooperation in civil and criminal matters, based on the principle of mutual trust.[65]

Beside these issues, which will be addressed in what follows, the relevance of the right to family life in the AFSJ is particularly reflected in the very specific procedural consequences that are triggered in the preliminary ruling procedure before the CJEU. The fact that the fields of the AFSJ may have an important effect on the fundamental rights of individuals led the Court of Justice to adopt a modification of its rules of procedure in 2008 with the aim to establish an urgent preliminary ruling procedure. This procedure is exceptionally applied in very restricted cases in the field of AFSJ. Besides the cases in which the person at issue is deprived of liberty (by mandate of the Treaty), the application of this procedure has also been invoked when the outcome of the case at issue risks the relationship between children and their parents. As can be imagined, this happens mostly in the realm of judicial cooperation in civil matters when it comes to the application of the Brussels II bis Regulation.[66] However, the paramount importance of family life, particularly when the relationship between children and their parents is affected, has also lead to the application of the urgent procedure in cases regarding immigration law, particularly with regards to the family

64 For a detailed analysis see the chapter of Morgades in this book.

65 See in particular the chapter of González Pascual in this book.

66 See judgments in C-195/08PPU, *Rinau* EU:C:2008:406; C-211/10PPU, *Povse,* EU:C:2010:344; C-403/09PPU, *Deticek* EU:C:2009:810; *McB., supra* n. 12; C-497/10, *Mercredi* EU:C:2010:829; C-491/10PPU, *Aguirre Zarraga.* EU:C:2010:828 (in this case, ex officio); C-376/14PPU, *C.* EU:C:2014:2268; C-498/14PPU, *Bradbrooke* EU:C:2015:3 and C-455/15PPU, *P.* EU:C:2015:763. The case C-296/10, *Purrucker,* EU:C:2010:446 was dealt with through the accelerated procedure.

reunification directive.[67] Outside the field of the AFSJ, the Court has taken into account elements of family life in the application of the accelerated procedure.[68]

a Borders and immigration

Many of the legal issues concerning the right to family life that have been presented in the field of EU citizenship and free movement of persons will find a parallel in the field of immigration, particularly when it comes to the right of family reunification.

In the general context of modern international law, the possibilities of states to apply certain migration measures have been curtailed by the right to family life, which has strongly shaped the ways in which Member States can control their borders. This was already clear with regard to TCNs who are members of the family consisting of Union citizens, as commented in the previous section. In the framework of the rights derived from the association agreement for TCN and members of their family, several Opinions of Advocates General highlighted the relevance of Article 8 ECHR and of the case law of the ECtHR for the interpretation of the provisions that had a strong connection with family life.[69]

With the new competences in the field of migration and asylum, the protection of family life of TCNs has become more and more central. Proof of this is the fact that the first major piece of legislation in the field of legal migration was precisely the family reunification directive.[70] This directive was challenged by the European Parliament who precisely questioned its compatibility with the fundamental right to family life.[71] Moreover, this case was the first one in which the CJEU ever mentioned the Charter.

The fundamental right of family life has shaped EU law in the field of immigration and asylum. In the case law interpreting secondary law, one of the most important impacts of the fundamental right to family life has been to preclude the possibility to apply with automaticity certain restrictive immigration provisions. This effect was already prefigured in the case law concerning migration-related provisions of EU association agreements. For

67 See case C-155/11 PPU *Imran* EU:C:2011:387.

68 See order in C-300/11, *ZZ* EU:C:2011:646 and order in C-127/08, *Metock*, EU:C:2008:235.

69 Particularly, Advocate General Léger put forward in his Opinion in C-210/97, *Akman*, EU:C:1998:344, para. 26, that since the judgment in C-351/95, *Kadiman* EU:C:1997:205 it had been established that first paragraph of the Art 7 of Decision 1/80 aims to create favourable conditions for family reunification. The Opinion of Advocate General La Pergola in C-65/98, *Eyüp* EU:C:1999:561, building up on this consideration, examined at length the impact of the case-law of the ECtHR on the interpretation of that provision. With regard to the cooperation agreement with Morocco, see Opinion of Advocate General Alber in C-179/98, *Mesbah*, EU:C:1999:249, para. 80.

70 Council Directive on the right to family reunification, *supra* 14.

71 C-540/03, *Parliament v Council*, EU:C:2006:429.

example, in *Gloszczuk*, the Court stated that the decision of a Member State to reject an application for establishment of a Polish national because of false representations or the failure to comply with entry conditions could never have the effect of preventing the full examination of his situation at a later time, in connection with a new application. In this regard, the Court highlighted that such measures "must be adopted without prejudice to the obligation to respect that national's fundamental rights, such as the right to respect for his family life".[72]

Member States have also been prevented from automatically rejecting TCN deprived of visas at the border. In *MRAX*, the Court declared that "[i]n view of the importance which the Community legislature has attached to the protection of family life, it is in any event disproportionate and, therefore, prohibited to send back a TCN married to a national of a Member State where he is able to prove his identity and the conjugal ties and there is no evidence to establish that he represents a risk to the requirements of public policy, public security or public health".[73] In the same vein, having due regard to the importance of the right to family life, States cannot refuse entry for the sole ground that there exists an alert in the Schengen Information System without first verifying whether the persons concerned constituted a genuine, present and sufficiently serious threat affecting one of the fundamental interests of society.[74] However, even if relying on the fundamental right to family life, these judgments have been pronounced in the context of the rights of family members of EU citizens, who derived, purely from their family connection, the rights to enter into and reside in the territory of the Member States. Similar considerations are therefore not easily transposable to the interpretation of immigration and asylum acts of secondary law, since the right of residence under the immigration directives does not purely rest on the existence of family links, but is dependent upon fulfilment of the conditions set out in those instruments.

In this regard, the Court has already established parallels between the legal interpretation of specific provisions regarding the rights of EU citizens and those governing the status of TCN. The judgment in *Chakroun*[75]

72 C-63/99, *Gloszczuk* EU:C:2001:488, para. 85. See also C-235/99, *Kondova*EU:C:2001:489, para. 90. In the field of association agreements the fundamental right to family life of the Charter has also been an important element to support the conclusion that the rights that family members of Turkish workers derive from Decision 1/80 are also applicable with regard to nationals of third countries others than Turkey. See C 451/11, *Dülger*EU:C:2012:504, para. 53.

73 C-459/99 *MRAX*, EU:C:2002:461, para. 61. Also, on this basis, the Court declared the infringement of Spain for refusing to issue residence permit to TCN, members of the family of Union citizens, on the ground that they should first have applied for a residence visa at the Spanish consulate in their last place of domicile. See also, judgment in C-503/03, *Commission v Spain*, EU:C:2006:74.

74 *Commission v Spain*, Ibid.

75 *Chakroun supra* n. 53.

dealt with the interpretation of the transposition of Council Directive 2003/86 on the right to family reunification and in particular Articles 2(d) and 7(1) of it. The Raad van State asked whether the directive allows a distinction to be made between a family relationship that arose before the resident's entry into the Member State and that of a family relationship formed after entry. Advocate General Sharpston asserted that "it might seem foolhardy to assert that the difference between a family relationship which arose before the sponsor's entry into the Member State and one which arose later can never justify difference in some regard" in effect precluding the notion brought forward by the Netherlands legislation. The Netherlands government argued that families that were formed previous to the entry of the sponsor to the Member State are more deserving of favourable conditions in relation to the social assistance requirement as opposed to those families not yet constituted at the time of entry. Here, importantly, the Advocate General again made reference to the principle of non-discrimination in refuting this claim. The Court referred by way of analogy to its judgment in *Metock and Others*, and agreed with the Advocate General in stating that:

> Article 2(d) of the Directive defines family reunification without drawing any distinction based on the time of marriage of the spouses, since it states that reunification must be understood as meaning the entry into and residence in the host Member State by family members of a third-country national residing lawfully in that Member State in order to preserve the family unit, whether the family relationship arose before or after the resident's entry.

The importance of the directive on the right to family reunification as an instrument that actively enhances the protection of family life is also to be highlighted. Admittedly, this directive provides for a regime that is not as favourable and flexible as the one concerning the right of family members of EU citizens to accompany them and reside with them. However, the limited scope of Directive 2004/38 and the limitations of the status of EU citizenship to serve as an alternative path granting residence rights to family members points to the family reunification directive as an important legal instrument aimed at filling the lacunae of the protection of family unit across the divide of EU citizens and immigrants. Despite the fact that in the judgment in *Dereci* the Court had stated that the family reunification directive was not applicable to TCNs who were family members of EU citizens, a more flexible approach was taken in *O and Others*.[76] That case concerned TCNs who where parents of EU citizens and who wanted to be joined in their EU Member State of residence by their spouses, also TCNs. Here the

76 C-356/11 and C-357/11, *O and Others* EU:C:2012:776.

Court, after analyzing the cases from the point of view of EU citizenship, emphasized the fact that the family reunification directive could in fact provide a more straightforward path for the protection of family life, making explicit reference to Articles 7 and 24 of the Charter.

This important role of the rules in the field of immigration law has also been put forward in *Iida*,[77] this time with regard to the directive concerning long-term residents.[78] In this case the Court declared that, in light of the purpose of the derived rights for family members of Union citizens according to Directive 2004/38 – to avoid interference with the freedom of movement of EU citizens by discouraging them from exercising the rights of entry into and residence in the host Member State – the right of a TCN family member can be relied on only in the host Member State in which the EU citizen resides.[79] This interpretation led to the conclusion that a Japanese father of a German daughter, who resided and worked in Germany with his family, did not derive any kind of rights from EU citizenship law to continue residing in Germany once his German wife and daughter have moved to Austria. However, the Court insinuated that Mr Iida could in principle benefit from the status of long-term resident within the meaning of Directive 2003/109.

These judgments confirm the role of EU immigration law as the fallback regime under which family members of EU citizens may be subjected due to the lack of a comprehensive regime of EU law regarding the protection of family reunification. This is not without consequences given that the conditions and requirements pertaining to this instrument are stricter (Cholewinski 2002) and that the definition of family member differs.[80]

b Judicial cooperation in civil matters

In the field of judicial cooperation in civil matters, the Brussels II bis Regulation, concerning jurisdiction and the recognition and enforcement of judgments in matrimonial matters and the matters of parental responsibility,[81] contains rules concerning the restitution of children who have been wrongfully removed from the Member State of their previous residence. In this

77 *Iida supra* n. 30.

78 Council Directive 2003/109/EC of 25 November 2003 concerning the status of third country nationals who are long-term residents, [2003] OJ L 16/44.

79 *Iida supra* n. 30, para. 64.

80 For example, under Directive 2004/38, C-83/11, *Rahman and Others* EU:C:2012:519, even if not making explicit reference to the Charter in interpreting the obligation to facilitate, in accordance with national legislation, entry and residence for "any other family members" who are dependents of a Union citizen. Similarly, non-explicit reference to Article 7 of the Charter was made in the important case C-245/11, *K*, EU:C:2012:685, in the field of asylum law.

81 Cited *supra* 34.

field, the best interest of children, according to Article 24 of the Charter, should be of paramount importance.[82]

However, Article 7 of the Charter is also destined to significantly imprint in this field. One of the first cases concerning family law issues that the Court relied on the Charter, interpreting the horizontal provision regarding its scope of application, was the *McB* case.[83] In this case, the Court was asked, by the Supreme Court of Ireland, whether Article 7 of the Charter influenced in any way the interpretation of the Brussels II bis Regulation. The question was focused on the actions of a mother who removed her children from the country in which the father of the children was living without his consent. The parents of the children were not married when the children were born, and under Irish law the father did not have the right to custody of the children. Based on Irish custody law therefore, formally, the mother had the right to choose the place of residence of the children and, when she removed them, the father could not obtain a court judgment declaring the wrongfulness of her conduct. The father argued that the peculiarity of Irish law disproportionately affected his parental rights and that the Regulation should have been interpreted in light of the Charter (and of Article 8 ECHR), so as to afford the natural father with custody rights *de jure*. This would have allowed him to seek a court declaration of the wrongfulness of the removal of his children by the mother.

The Court confirmed that the Regulation must be construed to allow a parent with custody to invoke the wrongfulness of removal without his consent. However, custody rights are conferred exclusively according to domestic law; a subject matter that, under Article 51(2) of the Charter, is outside the competence of the EU and therefore outside the reach of the Charter. The Court extensively relied on the case law of the ECtHR, according to which national legislation conferring custody rights on only one of the natural parents was legitimate, provided that the other had the right to seek a court order reversing this initial allocation. The Court adopted this minimum standard of protection and rejected the extensive interpretation of the Regulation advocated by the father in the main proceedings, and arguably made clear that, for the time being, it would not abuse any incorporation doctrine in order to expand the competence of the EU. The "essence" of family life, for the purposes of determining the lawfulness of

82 See for example *Detiček*, *supra* n. 68; C-491/10PPU, *Aguirre Zarraga* EU:C:2010:828; C-92/12PPU, *Health Service Executive*, EU:C:2012:255; C-4/14, *Bohez*, EU:C:2015:563 or C-455/15PPU, *P.*EU:C:2015:763. See, on this case-law (Lenaerts, 2013). The case law of the court regarding the restitution of children has however been criticized for not taking sufficient account of the role played by the best interest of the child, particularly in judgment in Povse, *supra* n. 68 (see, e.g. González Pascual, 2014). See, generally, in the issue of "automaticity" entailed by the principle of mutual trust (Mitsilegas, 2012).

83 *McB. supra* n. 12

removal, was defined by the Court by reference to the ECtHR's minimum standard:

> [The] child's natural father must have the right to apply to the national court with jurisdiction, before the removal, in order to request that rights of custody in respect of his child be awarded to him, which, in such a context, constitutes the very essence of the right of a natural father to a private and family life.[84]
>
> (see also Jiménez Blanco 2012)

c Judicial cooperation in criminal matters

The field of judicial cooperation in criminal matters, undoubtedly connected with the use of repressive powers and procedural guarantees, is one of the fields where fundamental rights clearly gain in relevance and visibility. Due to the limitations imposed on the role of the CJEU until the end of the transitional period provided for by the Treaty of Lisbon, the number of preliminary requests has been relatively few. The relevance of the right to family life in this field is however evident at first sight, particularly given the very relevant impact of EU instruments that may entail the transfer of persons under the application of mutual trust mechanisms,[85] in addition to cases where EU instruments concerning procedural rights are at issue.[86]

Among the cases that have already come before the Court, litigation related to the implementation of the Framework Decision on EAW[87] occupies a paramount place. Even considering the relevant differences with extradition, from the point of view of human relations, it cannot be ignored that the effects of surrender under the regime of the EAW entail the same consequences as extradition when it comes to physical separation from members of the family. In this regard, the ECtHR has repeatedly stated that even if extradition can be considered an interference with family life,

84 Ibid. para. 55.

85 Not only the European arrest warrant, commented below, but also Council Framework Decision 2008/947/JHA of 27 November 2008 on the application of the principle of mutual recognition to judgments and probation decisions with a view to the supervision of probation measures and alternative sanctions. [2008] OJ L 327/27.

86 See judgment in C-483/09 and C-1/10 *Gueye and Salmerón Sánchez* EU:C:2011:583. The Court confirmed its case-law stating that Council Framework Decision 2001/220/JHA of 15 March 2001 on the standing of victims in criminal proceedings [2001] OJ 2001 L 82/1 had to be interpreted in such a way that fundamental rights, including in particular the right to respect for family and private life, as stated in Article 7 of the Charter, are respected (para. 55). However, the obligation to ensure the participation of the victim in criminal proceedings did not imply that mandatory injunctions to stay away cannot be imposed contrary to the wishes of the victim (para. 56). In this case, victims of domestic violence opposed the application of such injunctions, affecting their husbands.

87 Council Framework Decision 2002/584/JHA on the European arrest warrant and the surrender procedures between Member States [2002] OJL190/1.

"it is only in exceptional circumstances that the extradition of a person to face trial on charges of serious offences committed in the requesting State would be held to be an unjustified or disproportionate interference with the right to respect for family life".[88] In this regard, the issue of proportionality, that has already come to the fore with regard to the application of the EAW in relation to other fundamental rights, can also be expected in relation to the right to family life.[89]

The very relevant role of the right of family life can be seen in case I.B., particularly, through the interpretation of the objective of "reinsertion" by the Court. In this case, Romania requested the Belgian authorities to surrender I.B., a Romanian national, for the purposes of the execution of a four-year custodial sentence imposed by a decision rendered *in absentia*. I.B's wife and two children were living in Belgium. Due to the fact that the decision *rendered in absentia* could not be considered as definitive, the national court could not apply the provision, which allows for the refusal of the execution if the EAW, issued for the purposes of execution of a custodial sentence, where the person concerned resides in Belgium and the competent authorities undertake to execute that sentence in accordance with Belgian law. The Framework Decision provided for the possibility for the executing national authority to subject surrender to the condition that the person is returned to the executing Member State in order to serve there the custodial sentence. However, according to Article 5(3) of the Framework Decision, this possibility was only available when the warrant was issued for the purposes of prosecution. The Court, considering the importance of the objective of reintegration, interpreted flexibly this provision and concluded that:

> [g]iven that the situation of a person who was sentenced in absentia and to whom it is still open to apply for a retrial is comparable to that of a person who is the subject of a European arrest warrant for the purposes of prosecution, there is no objective reason precluding an executing judicial authority which has applied Article 5(1) of Framework Decision 2002/584 from applying the condition contained in Article 5(3) of that framework decision.[90]

Even though this judgment does not explicitly refer, in any way, to the fundamental right to family life, it is apparent from the order of reference

88 Decision of the EComHR *Launder v the United Kingdom* (Application No. 27279/95). The ECtHR has stated in a similar way in its decision *King v United Kingdom* Application No. 9472/07 (26 ECtHR January 2010) para. 29.

89 See, in this regard, the Third Party Intervention of AIRE Centre and Fair Trials before the ECtHR in case *E.B. v the United Kingdom*, application no 63019/10, available at http://www.airecentre.org/data/files/EB_v._UK_-_Third_Party_Intervention.pdf.

90 C 306/09, *I.B.*EU:C:2010:626, para. 57.

of the Belgian Constitutional Court, and from the Opinion of Advocate General Cruz Villalón,[91] that concerns related to this right underlie the solution arrived at by the Court. Indeed, family life can be understood as being subsumed in the objective of reintegration.

IV Concluding thoughts: On the current challenges to the EU protection of family life

The previous considerations demonstrate the relevant presence of the fundamental right to family life of Article 7 of the Charter – although not exclusively – in the fields of citizenship, free movement of persons, immigration, asylum, and judicial cooperation in criminal and civil matters. In all these material spheres of EU competence, this fundamental right deploys the traditional functions of fundamental rights: it constitutes a parameter of legality of EU rules and determines the possible incompatibility of national laws with EU law within its scope of application; it is an obliged reference in the interpretation of EU law and should also inspire the interpretation of national law that comes within the realm of EU law. In channelling the performance of these functions, EU institutions and EU courts are often and rightly inspired by the case law of the ECtHR on Article 8 ECHR, which constitutes the minimum protection standard to be observed by the Union.

It can be argued that an EU autonomous higher standard of protection for family life is emerging thanks to the action of the EU legislator (for example, in the field of immigration, through the family reunification directive, and in the field of citizenship, through Directive 2004/38), as well as through the jurisprudential construction of the citizenship of the Union (particularly, with the *Ruiz Zambrano* saga) and through the interpretation of judicial cooperation instruments (for example, the relevant role of reinsertion considerations). In these last two cases, the considerations regarding the right family life have not been expressly inserted in the reasoning of the Court, even if they are underlying the discussions and the outcome of the cases.

However, despite these developments, the cases that are often brought to the Court reveal that EU law is not always in the position to give families the legal protection that would be expected, particularly when mobility rights have been exercised. Cases such as *Iida*, where the residence rights of TCN family members are lost because of the exercise of the right to free movement of the EU citizen sponsor, or *O and S*, where family members are not covered by the provisions of the Directive because of the limited duration

91 Opinion of Advocate General Cruz Villalón in C 306/09, *I.B.* EU:C:2010:404, stating that "… [t]he need to interpret the Framework Decision in the light of fundamental rights has become more imperative since the entry into force of the Charter, Article 7 of which covers the right to private and family life."

of the trips of the EU citizen, reveal the deficient design of the configuration of the fundamental right to family life through secondary legislation.

As a result, the right to family life through the operation of migration and citizenship law is legally conceived from a point of view that does not always live up to the expectations and ways of life of EU citizens and the members of their families. On the one hand, the legal evolution in the field judicial cooperation in civil and criminal matters, by operation of mutual trust and mutual recognition, is progressively leading to a situation in which individuals are subject to the law of different Member States as if they were different provinces of a State when it comes to surrender under the EAW or to the restitution of children under Brussels II bis. On the other hand, this reality strongly contrasts with the situation of the protection of the family unit through free movement and citizenship law: the rigidity of Directive 2004/38 and the limitation of the EU regulation of family reunification to the exercise of free movement (in contrast to Directive 2003/86), leaves the exercise of the right to family life anchored to a Member State, and not in the Union as a whole.

References

Acierno, S. (2003). The Carpenter judgment: fundamental rights and the limits of the Community legal order. *European Law Review*, pp. 398–407.

Cambien, N. (2009). Case C-127/08 Blaise Baheten Metock and Others v Minister for Justice, Equality and Law Reform. *Columbia Journal of European Law*,15, pp. 321–41.

Carr, K. (2014). *Deconstructing and Reconstructing Family Law through the European Legal Order.* CADMUS. Florence: EUI.

Cholewinski, R. (2002). Family Reunification and Conditions Placed on Family Members: Dismantling a Fundamental Right. *European Journal of Migration and Law* 4, pp. 271–90.

Choudhry, S. (2014). Article 7 – Family Life Aspects, In: Peers S. et al. *The EU Charter of Fundamental Rights. A Commentary.* Oxford: Hart, pp. 183–221.

Comandé, G. (2014). The Fifth European Union Freedom: Aggregating Citizenship . . . around Private Law in: Micklitz H.W. *The Constitutionalization of European Private Law.* Oxford: Oxford University Press, pp. 61–101.

Costello, C. (2009). Metock: Free movement and "Normal Family Life" in the Union. *Common Market Law Review*, 46, pp. 587–622.

D'Oliveria, H.U.J. (1994). European Citizenship: Its Meaning, Its Potential. In: Dehousse, R. (ed.). *Europe after Maastricht.* Beck: Munich, pp. 126–48.

Editorial comments (2003). Freedoms Unlimited? Reflections on Mary Carpenter v Secretary of State. *Common Market Law Review* 40, p. 537–43.

Fahey, E. (2009). Going Back to Basics: Re-Embracing the Fundamentals of the Free Movement of Persons in Metock. *Legal Issues of Economic Integration*, 36(1), available online at SSRN: http://papers.ssrn.com/sol3/papers.cfm?abstract_id=2096149 (viewed 3 June 2016).

González Pascual, M. (2014). Secreto profesional de los abogados y blanqueo de capitales: La normativa de la Unión ante el TEDH. *Revista Española de Derecho Constitucional*,101, pp. 381–404.

Hailbronner, M. and Iglesias Sánchez, S. (2011) The European Court of Justice and Citizenship of the Union: New Developments Towards a Truly Fundamental Status. *Vienna Journal on International Constitutional Law*, 5 (4), pp. 498–537.

Jiménez Blanco, P. (2012). Unmarried Fathers and Child Abduction in European Union Law. *Journal of Private International Law*, 8(1), pp. 135–57.

Kaesling, K. (2014). Family life and EU citizenship. The discovery of the Substance of the EU Citizens' Rights and its Genuine Enjoyment. In: Boele-Woelki K., Dethloff N. & Gephart W. (eds.) *Family law and culture in Europe. Developments, Challenges and Opportunities*, Antwerp: Intersentia, pp. 291–304.

Lenaerts, K. (2013). The Best Interests of the Child Always Come First: The Brussels II bis Regulation and the European Court of Justice. *Jurisprudence* 20(4), pp. 1–13.

Lyons, C. (1996). Citizenship in the Constitution of the European Union: Rhetoric or Reality? In: Bellamy, R. (ed.) *Constitutionalism, Democracy and Sovereignty: American and European Perspectives* Aldershot: Avebury, pp. 96–110.

Marauhn, T. (2006). Recht auf Achtung des Privat- und Familienslebens. In: Heselhaus, F. S. M. &Nowak, C, *Handbuch der Europäischen Grundrechte*. München: Beck, pp. 573–91.

Martiny, D. (2002). The Harmonization of Family Law in the European Community: Pros and Contra. In: Faure, M., Smits, J. and Schneider H (eds.). *Towards a European Ius Commune in the Legal Education and Research*. Antwerp: Intersentia. pp. 191–201.

McEleavey, P. (2002). The Brussels II regulation: How the European Community has moved into Family Law. *International and Comparative Law Quarterly*, 51(4), pp. 883–908.

McGlynn, C. (2006). *Families and the European Union*. Cambridge: Cambridge University Press.

Micklitz, H.W. (2010). Judicial Activism of the European Court of Justice and the Development of the European Social Model in Anti-Discrimination and Consumer Law. In: Neergaard, U., Nielsen R., and Roseberry L.M. (eds.). *The Role of Courts in Developing a European Social Model*. Copenhagen: DFO, pp. 25–61.

Mitsilegas, V. (2012). The Limits of Mutual Trust in Europe's Area of Freedom, Security and Justice: From Automatic Inter-State Cooperation to the Slow Emergence of the Individual. *Yearbook of European Law*, 31(1), pp. 319–72.

Shaw, J. (1997). European Citizenship: The IGC and Beyond European Integration. *European Integration online Papers*, 1(3).

Spaventa, E. (2016). *The interpretation of Article 51 of the EU Charter of Fundamental Rights: the dilemma of stricter or broader application of the Charter to national measures*. Study for the PETI Committee (European Parliament).

Stalford, H. (2000). Citizenship Status of Children. *The International Journal of Children's Rights*, 8(2), pp. 101–31.

Stalford, H. (2007). EU Family Law: A Human Rights Perspective. In: Meeusen, J. et al. (eds.). *International Family Law for the European Union*. Antwerpen: Intersentia, pp. 101–28.

Weiler, J. (1998). To be a European Citizen – Eros and Civilisation. *Madision Working Paper Series in European Studies*.

Wintermute, R. (2015). In Extending Human Rights, which European Court is Substantively 'Braver' and Procedurally 'Fitter'? The Example of Sexual Orientation and Gender Identity Discrimination. In:Morano-Foadi S. and Vickers L. *Fundamental Rights in the EU: A Matter for Two Courts*. Oxford; Hart Publishing, pp.179–200.

4 Mutual recognition of judicial decisions and the right to family life

*Maribel González Pascual**

I Mutual recognition of judicial decisions and fundamental rights: The challenge of protecting the right to family life

Mutual recognition has been a classic principle of EU law since the *Cassis de Dijon* decision in which the Court of Justice stated that "there is no valid reason why, provided that they have been lawfully produced and marketed in one of the Member States, alcoholic beverages should not be introduced into any other Member State".[1] This reasoning was developed in the frame of the freedom of movement of goods and was applied to other economic free movement categories shortly afterwards (Janssens 2013).This principle allowed for the strengthening of the fundamental freedoms in Europe without requiring legislative harmonization, which made the principle very appealing in the AFSJ.

The mutual recognition principle permits differences within a system of mutual trust and cooperation, whereas harmonization creates a homogeneous system with a common normative code (Fichera 2009, pp. 74–5). Thus, the commitment to mutual recognition reflects a desire to preserve broad decision-making powers for the Member States, as it seeks to facilitate judicial cooperation with minimal changes to national legal systems.

For the mutual recognition principle to be effective, national courts must recognize the validity of judicial decisions in other Member States without questioning their grounds or the proper respect of procedural guarantees by the judge presenting the request. The membership of all Member States of the EU to the same system of values makes it unnecessary to examine whether they have complied with the fundamental rights and basic principles of law. As all Member States comply with these principles and the decisions of the judges respect them, these decisions are fully effective in other Member States.

* Law Professor at Pompeu Fabra University, Barcelona. This chapter has been supported by the research project *BEUCitizen*. FP7/2007–2013, (Grant agreement no. 320294).

1 Case C-120/78, *Rewe*, EU:C:1979:42, para. 19.

Still, the use of this principle when courts from different countries cooperate does pose several problems. In fact, the market analogy for judicial cooperation is far from simple. In the domestic market, mutual recognition usually fosters greater freedom, whereas in transnational judicial cooperation it can have the opposite effect. Moreover, while judgments that create greater freedom require no clearly articulated justification, ones that restrict freedom most certainly do (Nettesheim 2009, pp. 40–1). Whether a common fundamental rights standard shared by all the Member States exists in practice is also debatable and, even if one does exist, the domestic guarantees of fundamental rights are not always effective in transnational scenarios (González 2016, p. 36).

The right to family life is not immune to this dilemma, for its protection is particularly intricate in transnational cases governed by the mutual recognition principle. Firstly, judicial cooperation relies on the swift execution of the decision taken by the judge of the requesting State, yet the actual protection of the right might depend on how active a role is taken by the judge who must execute the decision. In other words, only the judge with jurisdiction over the territory where the person affected by the judicial decision develops their personal life can really ascertain whether the right to family life is being infringed. That judge is normally the one who must surrender the person without questioning the request.

Secondly, domestic courts must often choose between following the guidance provided by the CJEU or the guidance of the ECtHR when deciding on the right to family life in the frame of judicial cooperation as the case law of each seems to differ in certain cases. This dual dilemma must be managed by cooperating courts in both criminal and civil matters.

The controversial cases regarding family life mainly involve the surrender of persons in the context of the EAW and the return of minors in application of the Brussels II bis Regulation. There are similarities between the criminal and civil cases dealing with the right to family life; however, a distinction must be drawn between them. In this regard, even though the protection of the right to family life is linked with the protection of the minor in criminal cases as in civil cases, in most criminal cases the resocialization of the person condemned is generally the most relevant criterion considered. Moreover, the ultimate aim of the judicial decision is the same: preventing crime and maintaining public order. Still, in criminal cases the protection of right to family life does not necessarily require the non-execution of a judicial decision whereas in civil cases such refusal often seems unavoidable.

II Judicial cooperation in criminal matters and family life: The EAW

The Framework Decision on the EAW was the "first concrete measure in the field of criminal law implementing the principle of mutual recognition",[2]

2 Recital 6 Council Framework Decision 2002/584/JHA on the European arrest warrant and the surrender procedures between Member States [2002] OJ L 190/ 1.

and, even today, it is the most emblematic decision in the field of criminal law (Mitsilegas 2012, p. 323). The EAW has given rise to numerous cases that have come before the CJEU since its inception. However, the right to family life has only been indirectly raised in cases where Member States display certain resistance towards EAWs that affect their citizens.

The core of the controversy lies in Article 4(6) of the Framework Decision, according to which "the executing judicial authority may refuse to execute the EAW: if the EAW has been issued for the purposes of execution of a custodial sentence or detention order, where the requested person is staying in, or is a national or a resident of the executing Member State and that State undertakes to execute the sentence or detention order in accordance with its domestic law".

This provision has been understood by several Member States as a mechanism to prevent the surrender of their citizens to courts in other countries (Deen-Racsmány and Blekxtonn). Several domestic laws transposing this provision thus adopted it not only as an automatic protection of their own citizens, who could only be surrendered on condition of remaining in custody in their own country, but also limited its scope or even neglected to apply it when the person to be surrendered was foreign. These national provisions gave rise to three preliminary rulings before the CJEU, the well-known *Kozłowski*, *Wolzenburg*, *IB* and *Lopes Da Silva* judgments.[3]

The General Advocates severely criticized these domestic legal provisions in those preliminary rulings. In their view, privileged treatment of nationals is not supported by the Framework Decision whose addressees are domestic judges, not legislators.[4] Judges must consider the family and social ties that bind a requested person to a State regardless of their nationality. As a matter of fact, "the line of argument put forward by certain governments to the effect that, in such circumstances, nationals are not in a situation comparable to that of the nationals of other Member States is untenable. [I]f this type of argument had held sway, European Union law would certainly not have developed in the extraordinary way in which it has to date."[5]

The CJEU, however, then took a slightly different approach. It did apply the non-discrimination principle among EU citizens enshrined in Article 18 TFEU observing that the goal of Article 4(6) of the Framework Decision was the resocialization of the person condemned, but went further by autonomously crafting an interpretation of the terms "staying" and "resident" of Article 4(6) of the Framework Decision to be applied homogeneously throughout the EU.

A person requested for surrender is thus, according to the CJEU's interpretation, to be considered a "resident" if they have established actual residence in a Member State. The person is "staying" when, "following a stable

3 Case C-66/08, *Kozłowski*, EU:C:2008:437, Case C-123/08, *Wolzenburg*, EU:C:2009:616; Case C-306/09, *I.B.*, EU:C:2010:626; Case C-42/11, *Da Silva*, EU:C:2012:517.

4 Opinion of Advocate General Bot, Case C-66/08 *Kozłowski*, ECLI:EU:C:2008:253, para. 47.

5 Opinion of Advocate General *Mengozzi*, Case C-42/11, *Da Silva*, EU:C:2012:151, para. 50.

period of presence in that State, he has acquired connections with that State which are of a similar degree to those resulting from residence". Such connections must be ascertained by the judge who assesses "the length, nature and conditions of his presence and the family and economic connections which he has with the executing Member State"[6]. However, the CJEU also considered the surrender of nationals to be proportionately conditioned in that further requirements could be demanded if the person requested is a national of another Member State.

Briefly put, the CJEU allows Member States to protect their own nationals but not to disregard the rights of other Members' citizens. The CJEU is aware of the resistance of the Member States towards the extradition of their nationals, so it prefers to rely on the non-discrimination principle on the basis of nationality rather than on the right to family life, since the former is founded in a well-settled case law.

It should not be forgotten that several national laws transposing the EAW were challenged before Constitutional Courts precisely by providing the surrender of their own nationals (Mitsilegas 2009). In fact, the first judgment of the CJEU related to Article 4(6) of the Framework Decision, the *Kozłowski* case, concerned the German law transposing the EAW, which was approved following a German Federal Constitutional Court judgment calling for better legislative protection of German nationals.[7]

However, although the CJEU's cautious approach is understandable, it raises three problematic issues. First, the General Advocates' reasoning is rooted in the protection of fundamental rights as the crucial element of EU citizenship, whereas Member States seem to advance nationality as the essence of EU citizenship. Their understanding is reinforced by the CJEU through its acceptance of nationality as a privileged parameter in the framework of the EAW. As Advocate General Cruz Villalón pointed out, the use of the right to free movement of people, instead of the right to private and family life, was relevant before the entry into force of the Lisbon Treaty. Today, however, it appears that the CJEU needs specify the scope of Charter Article 7.[8]

Second, since the protection afforded to the non-nationals seems to be limited to EU citizens, it might leave the TCNs unprotected. Third, the non-discrimination principle does not imply protection of the right to family life *per se*. Therefore, if a Member State decides not to condition the surrender of any person subject to an EAW, the non-discrimination principle is not violated yet the right to family life might be. Such is the case of the British Extradition Act approved in 2003 that does not implement Article 4(6) of the Framework Decision.

6 *Kozłowski, supra* n. 3 para. 54.
7 *European Arrest Warrant*, German Federal Constitutional Court Judgment, 18 July 2005.
8 Opinion of Advocate General Cruz Villalón Case C 306/09, *I.B.*, EU:C:2010:404, para. 44.

Unsurprisingly, British Courts have inquired whether the EAW might violate the right to family life in cases involving minors. In this regard, the decision in the case of *F-K (FC) v Polish Judicial Authority* handed down by the UK Supreme Court on 20 June 2012 must be mentioned.[9]

MF-K, and AF-K, are a married Polish couple with five children, the eldest of 21 years of age and the youngest three years and ten months at the time of the Supreme Court's judgment. The father worked in construction and the mother looked after the family. They were granted permanent residence in the UK in 2010.

Two EAWs were issued for the mother. The first one, dated 10 January 2006, alleged that she misappropriated clothing entrusted to her for sale in 2001. The second, dated 9 July 2007, alleged two offences: (i) falsifying customs documents in relation to a car imported between 1997 and 1999; (ii) eight instances of minor fraud in 2000. The request for the first EAW was made in December 2004 and the second in April 2007. The District Court and the Administrative Court ordered her surrender. The couple appealed the warrant before the British Supreme Court.

Throughout the proceedings a clinical psychology consultant drafted two reports on the family that concluded that the welfare of the family would be jeopardized should the mother be extradited. The reports observed that the father had been forced to cease work because of an accident and that the children were particularly attached to their mother. Separating the younger children from her was seen as particularly risky. That risk was one of the decisive factors in the decision.

The Supreme Court followed criteria developed by the ECtHR regarding the compatibility of expelling foreigners who have committed a crime with ECHR Article 8.[10] According to the ECtHR, judges have to take into account the gravity of the crime committed, the time elapsed since the crime was committed, the behaviour of the person to be expelled since the crime committed, the nationality of the people affected by the expulsion, the strength of their family and social ties with both the country of residence and the country of origin, and the impact on minors that the expulsion might have.[11]

Still, the application of criteria developed in the framework of expulsion of foreigners due to extradition or because of an EAW is not uncontroversial, given that the criteria regarding the severity of a crime substantially differs in the second case. "In the immigration process [a] country is exercising control over the presence of aliens. This is a purely domestic decision made subject to domestic considerations."[12] However, when applied to

9 [2012] UKSC 25.

10 On this case law see López Guerra in this book.

11 *Üner v The Netherlands*, App. No. 46410/99 (ECtHR, 18 October 2006) para. 58.

12 *Supra* n. 9 (Lord Judge) para. 120.

the EAW, having a judge assess the severity of the crime implies evaluating the criminal process carried out in another State. The ECtHR has actually quoted the criteria referred to above in decisions regarding extradition, but it has yet to deploy them.[13]

If courts are to ponder the seriousness of crimes committed in other Member States, they could jeopardize cooperation between national courts within the EU. Notwithstanding, the UK Supreme Court considered that the best interests of the children were not outweighed by any countervailing interest, and that therefore the EAW had to be rejected. Regarding the countervailing interests, the offences for which the EAWs had been issued were described by the UK Supreme Court as "of no great gravity".[14] Furthermore, the lapse of time between the offences and the issue of the warrant had been considerable in this case, reducing the relevance of the public interest in maintaining an effective system of judicial cooperation.

The emphasis on the lapse of time means that it was not only the best interest of the children, but also the assessment of a foreign legal system that played key roles in the decision. Illustrative is the *HH and PH v Deputy Prosecutor of the Italian Republic*, Genoa case, decided by the UK Supreme Court on the same day as *F-K (FC)*. This case involved the surrender of a couple who had three children, the youngest of whom was 15 months old. In this second case, the Court dismissed the appeal challenging the EAW because the couple had been convicted of trafficking narcotics, which is considered a serious offence.

The nature of the crime committed determined the outcome of each case, severely contradicting the prohibition of double incrimination behind the EAW. In fact, the UK Supreme Court's decision in *F-K (FC)* is not compatible with EU law. The CJEU has insisted that the EAW cannot be rejected, the only admitted exception in the cases specified by the Framework Decision[15] being, as yet, inhumane treatment.[16]

Furthermore, this indicates that the right to family life in EAW cases falls short of having significant impact, given that only in quite radical and scarce situations does it condition surrender of nationals to foreign jurisdictions.[17] Only if children are involved and the offence is considered to be "of no great gravity" is the right to family life actually considered applicable. Two concerns thus rise from the case law described: firstly, neither the right to family life of the adults affected by the EAW nor the resocialization of the person convicted is taken into account. Secondly, the best interests of the children trump the warrant only if the criminal offence is not considered serious.

13 *King v United Kingdom* Application No. 9472/07 (26 ECtHR January 2010) para. 29.
14 Supra n. 9 (Lady Hale), para. 45.
15 Case C-399/11, *Melloni*, EU:C:2013:107, para. 63.
16 Case C-404/15 *Aranyosi*, and Case C-696/15PPU *Căldăraru*, EU:C:2016:198, para. 98.
17 In fact, in most cases, British courts do not reject surrender on the basis of the right to family life (Dickson 2013).

This limited nature of the case law could have been avoided if the CJEU had interpreted the Framework Decision in light of the right to family life, as the General Advocates recommended. So interpreting the Framework Decision would have better delimited the scope of Article 7 of the Charter in a field where the guidance provided by the ECtHR is clearly insufficient. Moreover, such an interpretation would have been in line with the right to family life, which requires the active role of the judges. Finally, it would avoid the existence of a two-faced approach to the protection of the right to family life that results when courts only rely on the principle of non-discrimination among EU citizens.

III Judicial cooperation in civil matters and family life; Brussels II bis Regulation and parental child abduction

Attaining mutual recognition of judicial decisions in civil matters within the EU has been an on-going process since the European Council in Tampere. That said, automaticity in the enforcement of judicial decisions has been particularly pronounced in the field of family law (Mitsilegas 2012, p. 330). Especially noticeable are the provisions regarding parental child abduction.[18]

The Brussels II bis Regulation[19] strengthened the provisions of the Hague Convention on the Civil Aspects of International Child Abduction (the Hague Convention), by speeding the return of the children involved and drastically reducing the possibility of blocking an enforceable judgment. The Brussels II bis Regulation aims at deterring parental child abduction and ensuring the prompt return of the child to the Member State where they resided before the abduction. These goals are to be achieved by establishing clear rules for jurisdiction and expeditious procedures and for decreasing the judicial orders of non-return.

Regarding the rules established by the Brussels II bis Regulation, the courts of the State where the child resided before abduction retain jurisdiction.[20] The courts responsible for return are to issue their judgments no later than six weeks after the application is lodged. Furthermore, according to Article 11(4) Brussels II bis Regulation the return cannot be refused on

18 Child abduction embodies both wrongful removal and wrongful retention, whose definition is provided in Article 2(11) of the Regulation. According to that article, the removal or retention is wrongful when it is carried out in breach of the rights of custody provided that such rights were actually exercised at the moment of abduction, or would have been exercised if it had not been hindered by the removal or retention.

19 Council Regulation (EC) No. 2201/2003of 27 November 2003concerning jurisdiction and the recognition and enforcement of judgments in matrimonial matters and the matters of parental responsibility, repealing Regulation (EC) No 1347/2000 [2013] OJ L 338/29.

20 The only exceptions to this rule are the ones foreseen by Article 10 Brussels II bis Regulation.

the basis of Hague Convention Article 13(b)[21] if adequate arrangements have been made to secure the child's protection on their return. This last provision is particularly controversial because Hague Convention Article 13(b) allows judges to reject return if there exists great risk for the well-being of the child.

Hague Convention Article 13(b) therefore entitles the courts of the State where the children reside at the moment of the application for return to determine, in exceptional cases, whether the return is in the best interests of the child. However, the Brussels II bis Regulation assumes that the best interests of the child are achieved by executing the return order no matter the circumstances. The case law of the CJEU has been consistent with these aims. It has disregarded any exception to the return order on the basis of concerns for fundamental rights.

In fact, the CJEU has elaborated the concept of habitual residence of the child in line with their right to family life in cases where there has been no unlawful removal of the child (Lenaerts, 2013).[22] The CJEU has been inflexible, however, when there has been an unlawful removal or retention: the courts requested to execute the return order are not to analyze the circumstances surrounding the case and must promptly enforce the return order. Again, the CJEU has been clear: the courts of the country where the child resided before the abduction retain jurisdiction.

A case in point from the perspective of the right to family life is the *Povse* case.[23] Ms Povse and Mr Alpago lived in Italy with their daughter. In January 2008 they separated and were given joint custody of the child. Two months later Ms Povse travelled to Austria with her daughter. There Ms Povse requested sole custody before an Austrian court, whereas Mr Alpago also requested sole custody and lodged a complaint for child abduction before an Italian court. The Italian courts assumed jurisdiction on the basis of the Brussels II bis Regulation and requested the return of the child. However, the Leoben District Court refused return on the basis of Hague Convention Article 13(b). In the view of the Austrian court, the return posed a risk for the child because of the aggressive behaviour of the father, the close relationship between the child and her mother, and the expert's reports. The Leoben Regional Court reversed the lower court's decision, however, and ordered the return of the child to Italy on the basis of the Brussels II bis Regulation. This decision was appealed to the Austrian Supreme Court, which gave rise to a request for a preliminary ruling by the CJEU.

21 Article 13(b) Hague Convention "The judicial or administrative authority of the requested State is not bound to order the return of the child if . . . there is a grave risk that his or her return would expose the child to physical or psychological harm or otherwise place the child in an intolerable situation".

22 E.g. Case C-523/07, *A.*, EU:C:2009:225; Case C-497/10, *Mercredi*, EU:C:2010:829.

23 Case C-211/10PPU, *Povse*, EU:C:2010:344.

The CJEU strictly interpreted the Brussels II bis Regulation. The courts of the residence of the child before the abduction were to have the jurisdiction over the case, not those of the State to which the child had been wrongfully taken. The requested court had to enforce the return order. The circumstances, even those involving the best interests of the child, were also to be resolved by the court issuing the return order, which may or not consider it necessary to suspend the enforcement of its judgment.[24] The Austrian Supreme Court thus ordered the return of the child to Italy.

Ms Povse and her daughter, however, took their case to the ECtHR, arguing that there was a strong tie between them and they had settled into a new family; there were criminal proceedings pending against the mother in Italy for parental abduction; the child did not speak Italian; and the father did not speak German and had not seen his daughter during the last three years. The child's return, they argued, would therefore violate the right to family life as enshrined in ECHR Article 8.

The case was challenging because ECtHR case law on child abduction is a world apart from the case law of the CJEU, for the interest of the minor involved in the case is the primary consideration for the ECtHR.[25] According to the ECtHR, national courts are to strike a proper balance between the competing interests at stake but those of the child must take precedence over the rest. The child's interests involve, on the one hand, maintaining their family ties unless those ties are profoundly inadequate and, on the other hand, providing the child a proper environment for their well-being and development. Thus, an order for the return of the child is not to be automatically applied on the sole basis of the legal provisions of the Hague Convention. Judges are to analyse the proper conditions for the child's well-being.[26]

In this regard, the ECtHR considered that the return of a child who had been brought to Switzerland by his mother in breach of the guardianship agreement did not have to be enforced in the case *Neulinger and Shuruk v Suiza*. According to the ECtHR in that case, the return of the child would have amounted to a violation of his mother's right to family life and was not in conformity with the best interests of the child. The child had settled in Switzerland. He had no roots in Israel apart from his father, with whom he had not been in touch. The mother could not accompany her child to Israel without the risk of criminal sanction. Thus, the child would probably lose contact with his mother and be uprooted again. In addition, the behaviour of the father was found unsatisfactory.

24 Supra n. 23 para. 81.

25 For a more detailed analysis of the ECtHR's case law on parental child abduction see López Guerra in this book.

26 *Raban v Romania* App. No. 25437/08 (ECtHR, 26 October 2010), *Sneersone and Kampanella v Italy App. No.* 14737/09, (ECtHR, 12 July 2011), *X. v Latvia* App No 27853/09 (ECtHR, 13 December 2011,), *M. R and L.R v Estonia* App. No 13420/12 (ECtHR, 15 May 2012), *Neulinger and Shuruk v Switzerland* App. No 41615/07 (ECtHR, 6 July 2010).

The similarity between this case and the factual circumstances surrounding the *Povse* case is clear. Yet in the *Neulinger* and *Shuruk* case the Hague Convention was applicable, whereas in the *Povse* case the Brussels II bis Regulation was followed.

The ECtHR showed considerable deference towards EU law in the *Povse* case.[27] Considering that, firstly, the Austrian Courts did not have any discretion as to whether or not enforce the return order, secondly, that the Austrian Supreme Court raised a preliminary ruling, and thirdly, that the presumption of the equivalent protection afforded by the EU legal system had not been rebutted, the application was manifestly ill-founded. In the ECtHR's view the applicants could make their case on the basis of ECHR Article 8 before the Italian Courts and, if necessary, later appeal that decision before the ECtHR. Still, this decision remains controversial for two main reasons.

First, it seems inconsistent with the case law regarding the Hague Convention. The ECtHR considers the Hague Convention an instrument of procedural nature, not a human rights treaty that can exclude the application of ECHR Article 8,[28] but it does not follow this stance with regards the Brussels II bis Regulation, thereby creating a double standard for fundamental rights' protection within Europe.[29] Procedural rules take precedence in cases within the scope of the Brussels II bis Regulation, whereas in the other case ECHR Article 8 is to apply.

The second controversial aspect has to do with the failure of the ECtHR to examine the circumstances of the case in clear opposition to its own case law regarding child abduction. Some may wonder if the ECtHR was trying to ease the EU into adherence to the ECHR by showing so much deference towards the mutual recognition principle. Indeed, the ECtHR seems to have changed its approach since the opinion of the CJEU on EU adherence to the ECHR, requiring an assessment of the fundamental rights' protection in a recent case to rebut the presumption of equivalent protection.[30]

Therefore, on one hand, there are two different legal schemes regarding child abduction within the EU, depending on the States involved in the case. On the other hand, we could witness a clash between the case law of the CJEU and the case law of the ECtHR in the near future. This scenario "may create an appearance of inconsistency in administration of justice in Europe" (Lazic 2015). Moreover, the divergence between the European courts could invite long, drawn-out proceedings in cases of child abduction since the judicial decisions based on CJEU case law might be challenged before the ECtHR if parents can reasonably expect different outcomes.

27 *Sofia Povse and Doris Povse v Austria* App. No 3890/11 (ECtHR 18 June 2013) para. 81.

28 *Neulinger, supra* n. 26, para. 145.

29 The introduction of double standards in Europe by limiting the ECtHR's scrutiny in cases concerning EU law is one of the main criticisms arising from the Bosphorus doctrine. (Eckes 2007).

30 *Avontins v Latvia* App. No. 17502/07 (ECtHR, 23 May 2016) para. 121.

The conflict, however, reflects the competing interests underlying the legal rules on the abduction of children; the need to deter the abductions by frustrating the goals of the parent breaching the law and the right to family life of all the people involved in the case, particularly that of the children.

The drafting of Article 11(4) of the Brussels II bis Regulation was motivated by the conviction that abducting parents were using the Hague Convention to their advantage by successfully invoking the best interests of the child (McEleavy 2005, p. 9). A different legal scheme was thus established to minimize the rejection of orders of return. Such a scheme might not be the most beneficial to the child in certain cases but, all in all, it seems to represent a sound scheme for the prevention of international child abductions (Silberman 2011, p. 749), and, undoubtedly, the reduction of international parental abduction does benefit children's interests.

However, the EU rulings on parental abduction are rooted in the presumption of the children's summary, speedy return and that the return will play out in an orderly manner following expectations. The reality of return orders is, however, more disappointing and it is quite optimistic to believe that one can be swiftly executed in less than six weeks (McEleavy 2005, p. 34). In cases when several years have elapsed since the child's removal, it is difficult to argue that the judge with jurisdiction in the child's former residence is best suited to assess the child's best interests, as required by the CJEU.[31] Furthermore, the passage of time passes affects young children differently than adults, and this must be taken into account. Moreover, the abducting parent might be the caregiver to whom the child relates the most. Last but not least, once the child has returned to their former country of residence, there is no guarantee that the foreseeable proceedings regarding child custody will be resolved quickly. The child might have to endure a return to the second country after waiting a long time, which would also affect their well-being and development.

The need to maintain the jurisdiction of the courts in the child's original first country of residence and the compulsory execution of return orders responds first and foremost to prevent the strengthening of the procedural position of the abducting parent. It is a reasonable objective, but children should not be punished for their parents' deeds so the actual intention of the parents should play a minor role when dealing with their children's rights.

Lastly, the presumption justifying the Brussels II bis Regulation has been questioned, since judges rarely make use of the exceptions granted in Hague Convention Article 13(b). The Commission and several Member States were of the opinion that Hague Convention Article 13(b) was being used by abductors to avoid jurisdiction in the child's habitual country

31 Case C-403/09PPU, *Deticěk*, EU:C:2009:810, para. 36.

of residence, but that opinion did not have a basis in the empirical data available (Ripley 2008, p. 477). Paradoxically, Member States devised a legal scheme that was based on mutual trust that, at least in the case of the respective judiciary systems, did not exist. Unsurprisingly, the scheme fails without trust. In point of fact, proposals to improve the Brussels II bis Regulation recommend that cooperation among judges be enhanced through the channel of the European Judicial Network (McEleavy 2005, p. 34).

The right to family life thus seems poorly protected in Europe in cases of parental child abduction. The coexistence of two legal schemes, and the potential clash between the case law of the CJEU and the ECtHR, warrant a review of the Brussels II bis Regulation. The political will needed to make the necessary reform could be fostered by the CJEU either by allowing the non-execution of return orders on the basis of fundamental rights or by declaring Brussels II bis Regulation Article 11(4) incompatible with Charter Articles 7 and 24. Even though the CJEU does not seem willing to make either of these decisions, the ECtHR could force the CJEU to change its view on the matter. Until then, the right to family life in cases of judicial cooperation in civil matters will remain hobbled by ambiguous European case law and the limited capacity of ordinary courts to guarantee it.

IV Concluding remarks

Judicial cooperation is essential within the EU in both civil and criminal matters and the mutual recognition principle has proven to be a useful legal fiction although, just as any legal fiction, it has its limitations (Weller 2015). The limitations of this particular principle involve the impairment of fundamental rights protection when courts are asked to cooperate without putting proper safeguards in place. Scholars have identified real risk of weaker fundamental rights protection in Europe. Similarly, scholars also agree that the best way to solve this problem is by approving EU rules for judicial cooperation when fundamental rights are at stake. Judicial cooperation would be strengthened by more solid CJEU case law (González 2013, p. 174). This is indeed the case with regards the right to family life.

Still, Member States do not appear to be very concerned over the right to family life, the Framework Decision on the transfer of sentenced persons[32] being a telling example. This Framework Decision stipulates automatic transfer of convicted persons to the State of their nationality without their consent. The right to family life is completely disregarded (Mitsilegas 2012, p. 329).

Notwithstanding this lack of concern, the CJEU would rather defer to national legislatures to protect the right to family life than to the judges,

32 Council Framework Decision 2008/909/JHA of 27 November 2008 on the application of the principle of mutual recognition to judgments in criminal matters imposing custodial sentences or measures involving deprivation of liberty for the purpose of their enforcement in the European Union. [2008] OJ L 327/ 27.

as is shown by the case law on Article 4(6) of the EAW Framework Decision. Experience, however, shows that Member States vigorously resist any encroachment on their sovereignty unless security and public order is endangered, when they tend to respect such orders (Sieber 2009, p. 45). If courts defended rights more actively, then States could be forced to change their approach.

In this regard, the CJEU could encourage political institutions to improve fundamental rights' protection by declaring null EU rules that do not comply with fundamental rights or by promoting interpretations of the EU rules that Member States might not yet fully support. In the field of the mutual recognition the CJEU could play a key policy-shaping role (Canor 2013, p. 416).

The Court, however, has fiercely upheld the effectiveness of the mutual recognition principle in the AFSJ. It has clearly stated that Member States have, "save in exceptional circumstances, to consider all the other Member States to be complying with EU law and particularly with the fundamental rights recognised by EU law".[33] In fact, until now, only in the very extreme case of inhumane treatment has the CJEU taken a clear stance on prioritizing fundamental rights over the effectiveness of the EU legal instrument. The pertinent case law will not be easily adopted for other fundamental rights because the CJEU implies that the prohibition of inhumane treatment is an absolute right that represents a crucial pillar in the architecture of the EU fundamental rights system.[34] The right to family life in cases requiring judicial cooperation, however, sorely wants determinant case law from the CJEU to guarantee it.

Presently, courts lack clear guidance regarding the EAW, since both the CJEU and the ECtHR have shied away from considering the right to family life of a person who will be separated from his family for having committed a criminal offence in another State. Regarding parental abduction, the situation is even worse for ordinary courts, given that the case law of the CJEU and of the ECtHR are deeply contradictory. The correspondence between Article 7 of the Charter and ECHR Article 8(1)[35] is thus of little use.

Only courts can protect the right to family life and the best interests of the child because of the flexibility that is necessary to deal with the myriad individual facts involved in such cases (Ifezue & Rajabali 2013). Still, the court actually equipped to guarantee it is not always the one empowered by EU law. In fact, the EU does not appear to trust courts, as even the discretion allowed to courts by the Hague Convention has been eliminated. Yet courts are being asked to trust each other. This paradox is shocking and

33 Case 2/13, *Opinion*, EU:C:2014:2454, para. 191.
34 Supra n. 16, para. 85.
35 Case C-400/10PPU, *MCB*, EU:C:2010:582, para. 53.

dangerous. It is not only troublesome from a fundamental rights perspective but also for the prospects of developing productive judicial cooperation in Europe.

References

Canor, I. (2013). My brother's keeper? Horizontal Solange; An ever closer distrust among the peoples of Europe. *Common Market Law Review*, 50, pp. 382–442.

Deen-Racsmány, Z. and Blekxtonn, R. (2005). The decline of the nationality exception in European Extradition? *European Journal of Crime, Criminal Law and Criminal Justice*, 13(3), pp. 317–63.

Dickson, D.J. (2013). The proportionate application of Article 8 of the ECHR on execution of a request for surrender of a person with children. *New Journal of European Criminal Law*, 4(I–II), pp. 20–45.

Ecke, C. (2009). Does the ECtHR provide protection from the European Community? The case of Bosphorus Airways. *European Public Law*, 13(1), pp. 47–67.

Fichera, M (2009) The European Arrest Warrant and the Sovereign State: A Marriage of Convenience? *European Law Journal*, 15 (1), pp. 70–97.

González, M. (2013). Criminal Law as an Essential Function of the State: Last Line of Resistance? In: Saiz Arnaiz, A. and Alcoberro Llivina, C. *National Constitutional Identity and European Integration*, Antwerp: Intersentia, pp. 159–76.

González, M. (2016). Cooperación judicial penal y Derechos Fundamentales: ¿Hacia un estándar mínimo europeo? In: Ugartemendía, J. and Labyle, H. *La tutela judicial de los Derechos Fundamentales en el Espacio de Libertad, Seguridad y Justicia de la Unión Europea*. Oñati:IVAP, pp. 34–60.

Ifezue, G. and Rajabali, M. (2013). Protection the Interests of the Child. *Cambridge Journal of International and Comparative Law*, 2, pp. 77–85.

Janssens, C. (2013). *The Principle of Mutual Recognition in EU Law*, Oxford: Oxford University Press.

Lazic, V. (2015). Legal Framework for International Child Abduction in the European Union – the Need for Changes in the Light of Povse, v. Austria. In: Zupan, M. *Private International Law in the jurisprudence of European Courts – Family at Focus*, Osijek: Faculty of Law Osijek, pp. 295–316.

Lenaerts, K. (2013). The Best Interests of the Child Always Come First: The Brussels II bis Regulation and the European Court of Justice. *Jurisprudence* 20(4), pp. 1–13.

McEleavey, P. (2005). The new child abduction regime in the European Union; symbiotic relationship or forced partnership? *Journal of Private International Law*, 1, pp. 5–34.

Mitsilegas, V. (2009). *EU Criminal Law*, Oxford: Hart Publishing.

Mitsilegas, V. (2012). The Limits of Mutual Trust in Europe's Area of Freedom, Security and Justice: From Automatic Inter-State Cooperation to the Slow Emergence of the Individual. *Yearbook of European Law*, 31(1), pp. 319–72.

Nettesheim, M. (2009). Grundrecthskonzeptionen des EuGH im Raum der Freiheit, der Sicherheit und des Rechts. *Europarecht*, 24, pp. 24–43.

Ripley, P. (2008). A defence of the established approach to the grave risk exception in the Hague child abduction convention. *Journal of Private International Law*, 4(3), pp. 443–77.

Sieber, U. (2009). Die Zukunft des Europäischen Strafrechts. *Zeitschrift für die gesamte Strafrechtswissenschaft*, 121(1), p. 1–67.

Silbermann, L.J. (2011). The Hague Convention on child abduction and unilateral relocations by custodial parents: a perspective from the United States and Europe – Abbot, Neulinger, Zagarra. *Oklahoma Law Review*, 63, pp. 733–49.
Weller, M. (2015). Mutual trust: in search of the future of the European Union private international law. *Journal of Private International Law*, 11(1), pp. 64–102.

Part II

Towards a broader understanding of the family

5 The European courts and transsexuals. The binary distinction and the pattern of family

Anna Lorenzetti[*]

I Introduction

This study analyses selected issues surrounding the legal protection of transsexual persons[1] in the European Union and States that have ratified the ECHR through an examination of the approach followed by the ECtHR and the CJEU. In illustrating the arguments used by these European courts, the chapter seeks to determine whether the approach represents reaffirmation of the binary gender system and the traditional idea of family based on marriage between a man and a woman or whether it moves beyond these traditional categories. The reading of the case law suggests that the approach of the European Courts simply confirms the binary gender system and the mainstream idea of family as founded on marriage between men and women. The approach of the ECtHR and the CJEU follows a typical "heteronormative approach" to the family realm, leaving most transgender persons in a sort of legal limbo without full guarantee of their constitutional rights and freedoms.

Over the last three decades there has been an unprecedented wave of decisions by the European Courts regarding transgender persons and the recognition of their rights, in particular regarding the family (transparentality and the right of trans persons to marry). The rights of transgender persons have been upheld both by the ECtHR and CJEU in the context of broadening recognition of rights and freedoms. Generally speaking, several decisions of the European Courts represent important steps towards full recognition of trans rights and freedoms (Sharpe 2007, pp. 50–2, 148–9).

* Temporary Lecturer in Gender Analysis and Anti-discrimination law, University of Bergamo (Law Department).

1 The expression "transsexual" refers to a person who lives in a gender role consistent with his/her inner gender identity but in contrast with social expectations associated with his/her biological sex. The word "transgender" is an umbrella term referring to anyone whose behaviour, thoughts, or traits differ from the societal expectations for his/her biological sex. Trans is an abbreviation used to designate persons whose self-perception of gender, gender identity and/or gender expression differs from the gender assigned to them at birth. The exact content of this concept varies from author to author but, in any event, it covers a wide range of sub-categories.

From these considerations the chapter moves to the following questions: what family model emerges from the decisions? Can we detect any evolution in them from the traditional idea of family founded on the marriage between a man and a woman?

Answering these questions requires reflecting on the manner in which the two European courts engage the idea of family and, consequently, of marriage as traditionally interpreted as the union of one man and one woman. The recognition of the right of trans persons to marry and to create (or maintain) families requires an analysis of the engagement of these two courts with the "sex/gender system" in the construction of family as legal institution. Access to marriage for trans persons is a delicate issue, as it challenges the definitions of gender that operate throughout the legal realm and reveals the implicit role played by gender norms that qualify the family as only possible when founded upon the marriage of a man and a woman.

If on one side the European Courts recognized the right to marry for transsexual persons, on the other side, the recognition was applicable under certain circumstances and (only) went as far as emphasizing the illegality of restricting "postoperative" transsexuals from enjoying their right to marry.[2] The European Courts, therefore, do not overcome the binary dimorphism of sex and gender and the traditional idea of family. The European Court of Human Rights stated that Member States are free to decide legal rules determining the sex of transsexual persons for the purpose of marriage and the requirements to marry.[3] Then, the ECtHR confirmed that the automatic conversion of a marriage into a registered partnership as a precondition to the legal recognition of an acquired gender when the trans person is married does not violate the ECHR.[4] Regarding the CJEU case law, the leading case, *K.B. v NHS*,[5] recognized pension rights to the female partner of a female-to-male transman who could not marry her because he was not legally considered a man and the national legislation barred marriage between same-sex partners. While on the surface the CJEU decision advances trans rights, it also intrinsically recognized and confirmed the traditional idea of family as based on heterosexual marriage.

Through analysis of the decisions and arguments of the European courts, this chapter further evaluates the complexity of the relation between

2 *Christine Goodwin v United Kingdom*App. No. 28957/95 (ECtHR, 11 July 2002) and *I. v United Kingdom* App. no. 25680/94 (ECtHR, 11 July 2002).

3 See, for instance, *Rees v United Kingdom* App. No. 9532/81 (ECtHR, 17 October 1986) and *Cossey v United Kingdom* App. No. 10843/84 (ECtHR, 27 September 1990).

4 *Parry v United Kingdom* App. No. 42971/05 (ECtHR, 28 November 2006); *R. and F. v United Kingdom* App. No. 35748/05 (ECtHR, 28 November 2006); *Hämäläinen v Finland* App. No. 37359/09 (ECtHR, 16 July 2014).

5 Case C-117/01 *K.B. v National Health Service Pensions Agency and Secretary of State for Health* EU:C:2004:7.

transgender persons and the traditional idea of family and marriage. It will first analyze the series of the ECtHR decisions regarding the transsexual condition and estimate the extent to which the decisions reaffirm or move beyond the heteronormative idea of marriage and family.

Secondly, this chapter will examine the case law of the Court of Justice regarding transsexual persons and their family life that also confirms the implicit heteronormative approach to the family realm, i.e., the approach that constructs family as founded upon the marriage of one man and one woman. Finally, the last part of the analysis teases out the meaning implicit in the European courts' decisions and the connections to the pattern of family emerging from them.

II The European Court of Human Rights regarding transgender persons

Over the last three decades, transsexuals have argued that the Contracting States are responsible for a significant number of violations of the ECHR (Choudhry & Herring 2010, p. 142 ff.). In particular, they have argued that the provisions of the Convention that guarantee the right to respect for private and family life (Article 8) and the right to marry and found a family were violated (Article 12) (Lee 2015, p. 133 and ff.).[6] Looking at the case

6 The European Court of Human Rights has dealt with several issues regarding transgender persons. For instance, in *B. v France* App. No. 13343/87 (ECtHR, 25 March 1992), the French refusal to rectify the birth certificate and the name of a post-operative transsexual was considered a violation of Article 8 (right to respect for private and family life). In *Sheffield & Horsham v The United Kingdom* App. No. 22985/93, 23390/94 (ECtHR, 30 July 1998), two MtF trans women claimed that the UK government's refusal to correct their birth certificates violated the ECtHR; the application was rejected. *Van Kück v Germany* App. No. 35968/97 (ECTHR, 12 June 2003), involved the reimbursement of gender reassignment measures against a private health insurance company; *Grant v The United Kingdom* App. No. 32570/03 (ECtHR, 23 May 2006), involved the refusal to pay a retirement pension at the age applicable to other women to a MtF transwoman; *L. v Lithuania* App. No. 27527/03) (ECtHR, 11 September 2007), involved the possibility to undergo gender-reassignment surgery and change gender identification in official documents; *Schlumpf v Switzerland* App. No. 29002/06 (ECTHR, 9 January 2009) focused on the refusal by the applicant's health insurers to pay the costs of her sex-change operation on the ground that she had not complied with a two-year waiting period before gender reassignment surgery; *P. v Portugal* App. No. 56027/09 (ECtHR, 6 September 2011) and *Cassar v Malta* App. No. 35810/09 (ECtHR, 9 July 2013 (strike out decision), involved the lack of legal recognition; *Y.Y. v Turkey* App. No. 14793/08 (ECtHR, 10 March 2015) concerned the refusal by the Turkish authorities to grant authorization for gender reassignment surgery on the grounds that the person requesting it, a transsexual, was not permanently unable to procreate. Finally, in *Identoba and Others v Georgia* App. No. 73235/12 (ECtHR, 12May 2015), the ECtHR stated that trans people are protected against discrimination on grounds of gender identity under Article 14 ECtHR. However, more than 20 years earlier, the ECtHR had already addressed the issue of transgender people. In *Van Oosterwijck v Belgium* App. No. 7654/87 (ECtHR, 6 November 1980), the ECtHR declined to consider the merit (Evain 1997; Mowbray 2004, pp. 130 and ff.; Sudre 2015).

law, it is possible to distinguish two phases in the Court's approach to these lawsuits.

A first phase begins with the refusal of the ECtHR to recognize transgender claims to marry or to found a family (Article 12) according to the national laws, or to exercise the right of familial life (Article 8). In *Rees v UK* and *Cossey v UK* transgender persons challenged the adoption of biological criteria in determining a person's sex for marriage purposes, affirming that Article 12 of the Convention was silent on the criteria to be applied (Sharpe 2007, p. 56 and ff.; Johnson 2015, p. 151 and ff.). At issue in the case was the desire of a female-to-male transman to marry a woman in a country where same-sex marriage was banned and the marriage law used as the legal criterion for a marriage licence the sex of the applicant as registered in the birth certificate. The ECtHR denied that there was any violation of the European Convention, and in so doing reaffirmed the belief that biology determines a person's sex for marriage purposes. In fact, in the Court's opinion, "the right to marry guaranteed by Article 12 refers to the traditional marriage between persons of opposite biological sex", which, following the wording of Article 12, is "mainly concerned to protect marriage as the basis of the family".[7] Despite the possibility that "the exercise of this right shall be subject to the national laws of the Contracting States" and although "the limitations thereby introduced must not restrict or reduce the right in such a way or to such an extent that the very essence of the right is impaired . . . the legal impediment in the United Kingdom on the marriage of persons who are not of the opposite biological sex cannot be said to have an effect of this kind".[8]

In *Cossey*,[9] the ECtHR confirmed the legitimacy of adopting biological criteria to determine a person's sex for the purposes of marriage. The applicant (Miss Cossey) did not dispute that she had not acquired "all the biological characteristics of a woman" (such as, for instance, the ability to procreate).[10] The applicant argued, however, that "she could not marry at all: as a woman, she could not realistically marry another woman and English law prevented her from marrying a man".[11] Despite the fact that

7 *Rees supra* n. 3, para. 49.
8 Ibid. para. 50.
9 *Cossey supra* n. 3.
10 Actually, the application was based on the fact that UK law did not confer legal status on the applicant corresponding to their actual condition, contrasting with Articles 8 and 12. Regarding Article 8, the ECtHR stated that the changes demanded by the applicant would had involved fundamentally modifying the system for registering births, which would have entailed important administrative consequences and imposed new duties on the rest of the population. However, the Court stressed "the seriousness of the problems affecting transsexuals and of their distress" and recommended "keeping the need for appropriate measures under review, having regard particularly to scientific and societal development". *Cossey supra* n. 3, para. 47.
11 Ibid. para. 44.

National States are free to interpret the concept of "sex" in ways that do not privilege biology, the ECtHR stated that the right to marry referred to "traditional" marriage between persons of the opposite biological sex. In fact, "attachment to the traditional concept of marriage provides sufficient reason for the continued adoption of biological criteria for determining a person's sex for the purposes of marriage, this being a matter encompassed within the power of the Contracting States to regulate by national law the exercise of the right to marry".[12]

In their dissenting opinions, Palm, Foighel, and Pekkanen particularly, stressed their dissatisfaction with the link between the right to marry and the ability to procreate according to the assumed gender:

> Gender reassignment surgery does not change a person's biological sex. It is impossible for Miss Cossey to bear a child. Yet, in all other respects, both psychological and physical, she is a woman and has lived as such for years. The fact that a transsexual is unable to procreate cannot, however, be decisive. There are many men and women who cannot have children but, in spite of this, they unquestionably have the right to marry. Ability to procreate is not and cannot be a prerequisite for marriage.[13]

Yet the dissenting opinions also stressed the traditional interpretation of marriage and family, arguing that the procreation is not the aim of the marriage and cannot be a prerequisite for it. In fact, following the wording of the ECtHR, marriage could be only linked with procreation and parenthood, and family could only be founded on marriage. Judge Martens also challenged the reasoning of the majority "because marriage is far more than a union which legitimates sexual intercourse and aims at procreating: it is a legal institution which creates a fixed legal relationship between both the partners and third parties".[14] In both of these cases, the right to marry was contemplated through a traditional conception of marriage as between persons of opposite biological sex, limiting, in this way, transsexual persons from enjoying the right to marry a person of the opposite gender because they were legally considered the same sex.

Some years later, the Court confirmed the position expressed in *Rees* and *Cossey* and similarly applied a biological test to determine the sex of an individual in *Sheffield and Horsham v UK*.[15] The ECtHR considered the functionality of the reproductive capability of the trans person now belonging to the other sex. The Court stressed the difference between the right to

12 Ibid. para. 46.

13 Ibid. para. 5 of the dissenting opinion.

14 Ibid. para. 4.5.2.

15 *Sheffield & Horsham v The United Kingdom* App. No. 22985/93, 23390/94 (ECtHR, 30 July 1998).

marry and the right to found a family, which were explicitly stated in Article 12 of the Convention. The recourse to biological criteria in domestic law for determining a person's sex for the purpose of marriage was included within the power of Contracting States to regulate the exercise of the right to marry by national law. The Court concluded that the national laws could not be regarded as restricting or reducing the right of a transsexual to marry in such a way or to such an extent that the very essence of the right was impaired.[16] The application of the biological criterion implicitly suggested that the right to marry can only be enjoyed if the two partners have the ability to procreate and found a family.

The biological criterion was rejected in *Eriksson & Goldschmidt v Sweden*,[17] where the request for a marriage licence was rejected for a woman and a male-to-female transwoman who, without surgical treatment, had changed her name and the legal sex on the official documents and on the civil registers. Although the two persons were of opposite biological sex, the Court stated that there was no violation of Article 12 of the Convention because under their national law the applicants were both of female sex and marriage was only possible between opposite-sex couples. In the opinion of the ECtHR, the right to marry under Article 12 only covered the right to marry someone of the opposite (legal) sex and declared the application inadmissible. In this case, the biological criterion for the recognition of the right to marry for same-sex couples was not applied because the partners were for legal purposes the same gender.

The approach to the issue of transsexual access to marriage changed radically change in 2002. In that year, the ECtHR decided the *Goodwin v UK* case,[18] unanimously considered a leading judgment in the Strasbourg Court's case law (Lee 2015, p. 136 and ff.). In *Goodwin* (as in *I. v UK*),[19] the ECtHR held that the United Kingdom's refusal to allow transsexual people to obtain new birth certificates and to marry according to their self-identified gender violated the ECHR. The Court of Strasbourg stated that there was "no justification for barring the transsexual from enjoying the right to marry under any circumstances".[20] In *Goodwin* the Court divided the right to marry and the right to found a family and observed "that Article 12 secures the fundamental right of a man and woman to marry and to found a family. The second aspect is not however a condition of the first and the inability of any couple to conceive or parent a child cannot be regarded as *per se* removing their right to enjoy the first limb of this provision."[21] The ECtHR rejected the previous interpretation followed in *Rees v UK* and *Cossey v UK*

16 Ibid. paras. 66–7.
17 *Eriksson & Goldschmidt v Sweden* App. No. 14573/89 (ECtHR, 9 November 1989).
18 *Goodwin supra* n. 2.
19 *I. supra* n. 2.
20 *Goodwin supra* n. 2.
21 Ibid. para. 98.

and stressed the sophistry of asserting that postoperative transsexuals had not been deprived of the right to marry as, according to law, they remained able to marry a person of their former opposite sex. In the Court's view, the very essence of the right to marry had been infringed because the applicant who lived as a woman could not marry her male partner because the two were of the same biological and legal sex.[22] The Court stated that it is for the Contracting State to determine the conditions to establish that gender reassignment has been properly effected or those under which past marriages of transsexuals cease to be valid and the formalities applicable to future marriages (including, for example, the information to be furnished to intended spouses). However, the Court found no justification for barring the postoperative transsexual from enjoying the right to marry under any circumstances.[23] It is significant to note that following these cases, the United Kingdom passed the Gender Recognition Act in 2004, which allows transsexual people to apply for legal recognition of their new gender, and to obtain new birth certificates. As a consequence, trans persons were allowed to marry a person of the same biological sex but of the opposite gender and legal sex. Here the Court went beyond the biologically-based conception of marriage, yet postoperative at the same time, it reaffirmed the idea of marriage as the union between a legal man and a legal woman, and thus the idea of a marriage as a heteronormative institution.

In a second phase of decisions, despite the progressive recognition of rights for transgender persons, the ECtHR put some limits on the recognition of the right to marry and found a family. For instance, the ECtHR failed to recognize the right for the transgender person to maintain their existing marriage when changing sex and introduced limits concerning the possibility to remain married after gender reassignment surgery.

In *Parry v UK* and *R. and F. v UK* of 2006,[24] the Court declared "manifestly ill-founded" the request of two trans persons, married with children, to remain married after gender reassignment surgery. According to the national law (the UK Gender Recognition Act of 2004), the Gender Recognition Certificate could not be obtained unless they terminated their original marriage. The applicants could enter into a civil partnership that could be considered a substitute for marriage but did not entail identical legal protection to that enshrined in statutes governing marriage. The Court's argument stressed the impact of the recognition of same-sex couples on the national systems and the importance of considering the role of marriage in each society (Section B). The Court recognized that, although the applicants should divorce according to English law, they could continue their relationship and also enter into a civil partnership that guaranteed "almost"

22 Ibid. para. 101.
23 Ibid. para. 103.
24 *Parry supra* n. 4; and *R. and F. supra* n. 4.

all the same legal rights and obligations. The Court thus declared the application inadmissible affirming that the State had not failed to afford legal recognition to gender reassignment because the applicants could continue their relationship through a civil partnership. No violation of the right to respect for private and family life was recognized, nor was any violation with regards the right of marry as only permitted between persons of opposite legal sex, for that determination fell within the margin of appreciation of the Contracting States.

Recently, in *Hämäläinen v Finland*,[25] the ECtHR declared that the automatic conversion of an opposite-sex marriage into a registered partnership as a precondition for the legal recognition of an acquired gender did not violate Articles 8 and 12 of the European Convention in the case of a trans-married person (Lee 2015, p. 137 ff.). Despite the "minor differences" between marriage and registered partnership, the Finnish system, which only allows marriage for opposite-sex couples while admitting registered partnership for same-sex couples, does not violate the ECtHR because the rights of same-sex couples are currently protected by the possibility of contracting a registered partnership.[26] As the possibility of maintaining a marriage after gender reassignment would bring with it the introduction of a recognized same-sex marriage, the Court conceded that the State has a margin of appreciation for no European consensus exists on same-sex marriages. The applicants would thus be able to continue enjoying in essence, and in practice, the same legal protection under a registered partnership as afforded by marriage.

The ECtHR has considered not only access to marriage, but also familial rights. Regarding the possibility of family life for postoperative transsexuals who wished to adopt their partner's child, the ECtHR stated that the right to respect for family life guarantees neither the right to found a family nor the right to adopt. In *X., Y. and Z. v UK*,[27] the first applicant, a female-to-male transman, legally considered a woman, could not marry his female partner. However, the situation was considered indistinguishable from the traditional notion of "family life". In the opinion of the Court, in fact, the definition of family could not be confined to families based on marriage. It encompassed other *de facto* relationships according to a number of relevant factors, including whether the couple shared a domicile, the length of their relationship and whether they demonstrated their commitment

25 *Hämäläinen v Finland* App. No. 37359/09 (ECtHR, 16 July 2014).

26 Ibid. paras. 60–9.

27 *X., Y. and Z. v United Kingdom* App. No. 21830/93 (ECtHR, 22 April 1997). *X*, a female-to-male transsexual, was living in a permanent and stable union with *Y*, a woman. *Z* was born to the second applicant as a result of artificial insemination by donor; the applicants submitted that the lack of legal recognition of the relationship between X and Z, born with IVF (in-vitro fertilization) techniques amounted to a violation of Article 8 of the Convention.

to each other by having children together or by any other means.[28] Given that the female-to-male transman was his partner's child's father figure, the Court considered that they were a family *de facto* and that it was in the best interests of the child to have the social father recognized as such by law.[29] However, the Court stressed the wide margin of appreciation of the Contracting State in relation to the "complex scientific, legal, moral and social issues" raised by transsexuality[30] and reminded of the need that a fair balance be struck between the competing interests of the individual and of the community as a whole.[31] The Court also stressed the absence of a "common European standard" with regard to the legal recognition of parental rights for transsexuals and a "generally shared approach" with regard to the manner in which "the social relationship between a child conceived by AID [artificial insemination by donor] and the person who performs the role of father should be reflected in law".[32] In addition, the Court emphasized the public interest in maintaining a coherent system of family law that places the best interests of the child at the fore. In this respect, the Court weighed the caution of the State regarding family law against the disadvantages suffered by the child as a result of the refusal of legal recognition as the son of the transman.[33] Despite the Court's acknowledgment of the family life between the transman and his partner's child, no violation of the right to respect for private and family life (Article 8 ECHR) was recognized.[34]

In *P.V. v Spain*,[35] which involved the restriction of parental rights for a MtF transsexual woman, the Court declined to recognize any violation of ECHR because it considered the applicant's right to visit her son relative to her temporary emotional instability and to the child's well-being. The Court stressed the importance of an arrangement that would allow the child to become gradually accustomed to his father's gender reassignment.

To wrap up the analysis of these two phases, certain considerations present themselves. In the first phase, the ECtHR judgments appear, at least to some extent, quite innovative, because they progressively recognized rights and freedoms for transgender people. However, a closer look reveals that the Court of Strasbourg remained rather restrictive in its approach to the idea of different models of family and marriage. In fact, even though the Court has, since 2002, moved beyond a biological conception of marriage

28 Ibid. paras. 35–6.
29 Ibid. para. 38.
30 Ibid. para. 39.
31 Ibid. para. 41.
32 Ibid. para. 44.
33 Ibid. paras. 47–8.
34 Ibid. para. 37.
35 *P.V v Spain* App. No. 35159/09 (ECtHR, 30 November 2010).

(*Goodwin* and *I.*), it has also confirmed the idea of marriage as the union between a legal man and a legal woman, thus reaffirming the idea of marriage as a heteronormative institution (*Parry; R. and F.; Hämäläinen*).

It is true that in *Goodwin* the ECtHR stressed that Article 9 of the EU Charter of Fundamental Rights departed from the wording of Article 12 of the ECHR by removing the reference to men and women. However, and following the Charter itself, the ECtHR stated that the right to marry and to found a family "shall be guaranteed in accordance with the national laws governing the exercise of these rights".[36] The ECtHR thus recognized a margin of appreciation for the States in governing sexuality and the conditions for marriage. Regarding the right to found a family, a more restrictive approach can be identified, one that leaves no room for overcoming the biological criteria for fatherhood by excluding it in the case of a transman (i.e. a biological woman).

III The European Court of Justice: Mainstream conceptions of family and marriage as heteronormative institution

Before delving into discussion of the issues related to the supposed necessity of the gender dichotomy, it could be interesting to analyze the positions of the CJEU on transgender issues. Since 1999, the CJEU has recognized discrimination against transsexuals based on gender reassignment as a form of sex discrimination.[37] In the family realm, the milestone decision was *K.B. v NHS*,[38] where the female partner of a female-to-male postoperative transman went to court to secure her right to marry him so that she could leave him her pension at death.[39] The Court of Appeal referred the case to the CJEU, which ruled in favour of the applicant *in principle*. Drawing upon *Goodwin v UK* case, the Court of Luxembourg declared that the UK legislation, which disqualified the couple from fulfilling the marriage requirements, must be regarded, in principle, as incompatible with the requirements of Article 141 TEU (formerly Article 119, now Article 157 TFUE, on the prohibition

36 Article 9 (Right to marry and right to found a family): The right to marry and the right to found a family shall be guaranteed in accordance with the national laws governing the exercise of these rights.

37 Case C-13/94 *P v S and Cornwall County Council* ECLI:EU:C:1996:170; Case C-423/04 *Sarah Margaret Richards v Secretary of State for Work and Pensions* EU:C:2006:256, the applicant was a British transsexual woman treated as a man and refused a state pension (Bell 2002; Ellis & Watson 2013, pp. 27 ff.).

38 *K.B. supra* n. 5.

39 Despite the surgical gender reassignment, the trans man partner of K.B. was not allowed to amend his birth certificate to reflect this change officially. As a result, the couple was not able to marry. When K.B. claimed a widower's pension for her partner, the National Health Service Pensions Agency refused to recognize the partner as a widower, which refers to a person married to the pension scheme member.

of discriminating on the basis of sex).[40] Although Member States have the power to determine whether, when and how change of gender can be recognized, the UK law infringed the prohibition of gender discrimination.

The approach of the Court in *K.B. v NHS* has two major weaknesses. First, it does not provide protection for certain transgender persons, namely preoperative trans persons or trans persons who do not wish to undergo surgical gender reassignment. Secondly, it does not clarify the definition of the margin of appreciation and the point at which Member States no longer possess the power to choose when gender reassignment surgeries are required. Even though, at first glance, the CJEU decision appears to represent greater recognition of the rights of transgender persons, a closer look reveals that the Court bolstered the traditional ideas of marriage and family as legal institutions, protecting trans persons only when (and if) they completed the medical process of gender reassignment.

The Court thus demonstrated a continued and rather restrictive approach to different models of family and couples. Despite the fact that the female-to-male transman completed his sex reassignment in *K.B. v NHS*, the applicant was not legally considered a man so could not marry his female partner. In that way, the CJEU heteronormatively conditioned the institution of marriage, i.e., as the union of one legal man and one legal woman. Both European courts moved from biological to legal criteria, but remain committed to a binary conception of sex and gender.

IV The right to family life for transsexuals: The biological foundations of marriage and the heteronormative character of the family

Access to marriage for trans-persons questions the binary idea of marriage and the traditional idea of family as based on marriage between one man and one woman. As a preliminary observation, it must be remembered that the traditional ideas of marriage and family seems to have been confirmed by the decisions of the Strasbourg and Luxembourg courts.

Despite the European courts' progressive recognition of the right to personal identity for transsexual persons, they also reaffirmed the necessity of completing the gender reassignment by surgery, excluding the possibility of remaining in a transgender condition, leaving transgender persons without full protection.[41] This approach can be considered an effect of the persistent gender binary system that not only distinguishes uniquely in terms of man and woman but also requires and prescribes that every person be either man (and male) or woman (and female). The ECtHR and the CJEU have

40 In fact, the EU antidiscrimination law does not include transgender condition in the protected grounds.

41 *Y.Y. v Turkey* App. No. 14793/08 (ECtHR, 10 March 2015).

also reaffirmed the idea of marriage as a heteronormative institution based on gender dichotomy. In fact, according to the case law analyzed earlier, marriage has only been considered possible between a man and a woman as they are identified in the civil documentation.[42] Regarding the right to found a family, as explained above, the Court of Strasbourg did not recognize a female-to-male transman's petition to be considered the legal father of his partner's child because he was not the biological father (*X., Y. and Z. v UK*). Biology thus remains the basis for the recognition of familial rights.

In conclusion, the courts remain fairly restrictive in their approach to family patterns and couples that diverge from the traditional idea of marriage as an heterosexual institution. Regarding the possibility of recognizing marriage for transgender persons without completed gender reassignment, the European high courts have halted their progressive recognition of rights. It seems that the implications of doing away with the binary construction of society and law (especially family law) could destabilize foundational social conceptions that are built upon the gender dichotomy. The European courts have therefore left the Member States to define the sex of transsexual persons and the legal conditions for marriage,[43] leaning heavily on the doctrine of margin of appreciation.[44]

This argument, however, implies the possibility that, according to national law, the concept of marriage be strictly tied to the sexual (biological or legal) difference of the partners, which affects the full recognition of rights and freedoms for transgender persons, for instance, by barring transsexual from enjoying the right to marry and found a family.

The access to marriage for transgender persons poses significant challenges to the legal construction of family law because it requires a new reading of marriage, traditionally considered a legal institution founded on the union between one man and one woman.

V Conclusions

In addressing transgender issues, this chapter has analyzed several family law decisions of the ECtHR and CJEU. The analysis has verified their failure to overcome the gender dichotomy as a basis for marriage and family in order to widen the recognition of rights and freedoms for trans persons. Particular attention was then devoted to the interrelation between the gender dichotomy and the traditional idea of marriage and the impact on individual rights and freedoms in accessing marriage and the right to found a family.

Regarding the conceptions of marriage and family, the case law of the two courts advances a traditional idea of both institutions. In particular, as

42 *Goodwin supra* n. 2; *I supra* n. 2, for the ECtHR; Case C-117/01 *K.B. supra* n. 5, for the CJEU.
43 *Rees supra* n. 3; *Cossey supra* n. 3.
44 *Hämäläinen supra* n. 24.

explained earlier, both courts have emphasized that marrying a person of the same biological sex, as long as they possess a different gender and legal sex, is guaranteed by EU law,[45] but that being recognized as father to your partner's child without a biological link,[46] or maintaining a marriage after gender reassignment because your legal sex becomes identical to that of your spouse, are not guaranteed.[47] In this scenario, this study has offered an analysis of how the traditional conceptions of marriage and family as heteronormative institutions affect the full recognition of rights and freedoms for transgender persons.

Far from attempting a systematic analysis of the theme of transsexuality in the European courts, this chapter sought to examine the ways in which the European courts decisions might offer a perspective to envision overcoming the traditional ideas of family and marriage. The chapter has sought to place in a broader context the decisions of ECtHR and of CJEU that are part of a progressive widening in the recognition of a right to a family and to marry for trans persons. In this regard, it can easily be argued that the European courts have steadily progressed in their recognition of rights and freedom for trans persons.

However, although both courts held that Member States could not deny transsexuals the right to marry altogether, they have stressed that denying it is only illegal under any circumstances regarding postoperative transsexuals. Far from deconstructing the concept of marriage as an heteronormative institution, this action represents its reaffirmation. Member States can define the legal sex for transgender persons, and thus the necessity to be operated or not in order to complete the path to gender reassignment and, in turn, to marry and found a family according to the national system. In fact, Member States can still limit the access to marriage for two persons who are considered by the law to be of the same legal sex.

In sketching a path to full recognition of rights and freedom for trans persons, this piece has underscored how the traditional model of family has been in some ways reinforced by the decisions of the ECtHR and CJEU. Most significantly, the idea of marriage as solely the union of one man and one woman was reinforced without questioning the reasons for considering gender and sex in only two categories. In fact, the institution of marriage remains almost untouched after the courts' decisions. They leave no possibility for EU or international law to push the national legislations in the direction of a more open approach to the institution of marriage. It is true that in *Goodwin v UK*, the ECtHR stressed that Article 9 of the EU Charter of Fundamental Rights departed from the wording of Article 12 of the ECHR in removing the reference to men and women. However, and following the

45 *Goodwin supra* n. 2; *I supra* n. 2.
46 *X., Y. and Z. supra* n. 26.
47 *Parry supra* n. 4; *R. and F. supra* n. 4; *Hämäläinen supra* n. 24.

Charter itself, the ECtHR stated that the right to marry and to found a family "shall be guaranteed in accordance with the national laws governing the exercise of these rights".[48]

According to the margin of appreciation doctrine, the ECtHR recognized a general limit on family law and in the civil status regulation that was followed by the CJEU. In the other direction, there may be potential for the recognition of the right of transgender people to maintain marriages contracted prior to sex and gender changes,[49] which in turn may provide an avenue to challenge the traditional ideas of marriage and family as heteronormative institutions. Similarly, the chapter has suggested that full recognition of rights and freedoms for transgender persons could be a useful tool to overcome the idea of the necessity of sexual dichotomy.

References

Bell, M. (2002). *Anti-discrimination Law and the European Union.* Oxford: Oxford University Press.

Choudhry, S. and Herring, J. (2010). *European Human Rights and Family Law.* Oxford: Hart Publishing.

Ellis, E. and Watson, P. (2013). *EU Anti-discrimination Law.* Oxford: Oxford University Press.

Evain, S. (1997). Le Juge Européen, le Transsexualisme et le Droits de l'Homme. *La Semaine Juridique,* 71(51), pp. 523–8.

Johnson, P. (2015). Marriage, Heteronormativity, and the European Court of Human Rights: A Reappraisal. *International Journal of Law, Policy and the Family,* 29(1), pp. 56–77.

Lee, R. (2015). Forced Sterilization and Mandatory Divorce: How a Majority of Council of Europe Member States' Laws regarding Gender Identity Violate the Internationally and Regionally Established Human Rights of Trans People. *Berkeley Journal of International Law,* 33(1), pp. 113–52.

Mowbray, A. (2004). *The development of Positive Obligations under the European Convention on Human Rights by the European Court of Human Rights.* Oxford: Hart Publishing.

Sharpe, A. (2007). *Transgender Jurisprudence.* London: Routledge-Cavendish.

Sudre, F. (2015). *Droit Européen et International des Droits de l'Homme.* Paris: PUF.

48 Article 9 (Right to marry and right to found a family): The right to marry and the right to found a family shall be guaranteed in accordance with the national laws governing the exercise of these rights.

49 *Parry supra* n. 4; *R. and F. supra* n. 4; *Hämäläinen supra* n. 24.

6 Right to family life and access to medically assisted procreation in the case law of the European Court of Human Rights

Guillem Cano Palomares[*]

I The increasing recognition of the right to have access to medically assisted procreation under the right to respect for family life

In its judgment *Evans v the United Kingdom*, the ECtHR recognized for the first time that the right to respect for the decision to become a parent in the genetic sense fell within the scope of the right to respect for "private life" under Article 8 ECHR.[1] The applicant was a woman who wished to have the embryos created through in-vitro fertilization (using her eggs and the sperm of her ex-partner) implanted, notwithstanding her ex-partner's withdrawal of consent to their use by her.[2] The ECtHR reiterated this finding in another judgment delivered some months after, in the case of *Dickson v the United Kingdom*, extending it, by relying this time not only on the right to respect for "private life" but also on the right to respect for "family life", guaranteed as well by Article 8 ECHR.[3] The reference to family life can be explained by the fact that the applicants in this second case were a couple and they both wanted to conceive a child through artificial insemination.

* Research Division and Department of the Jurisconsult ECtHR. The author expresses himself in a strictly personal capacity.

1 *Evans v the United Kingdom*, App. No. 6339/05 (ECtRH 10 April 2007) para. 72.

2 The applicant, who was suffering from ovarian cancer, underwent in-vitro fertilization with her then partner before having her ovaries removed. Six embryos were created and placed in storage. When the couple's relationship ended, her ex-partner withdrew his consent for the embryos to be used, not wanting to be the genetic parent of the applicant's child. National law consequently required that the eggs be destroyed. The applicant complained that domestic law permitted her former partner effectively to withdraw his consent to the storage and the use by her of embryos created jointly by them, preventing her from ever having a child to whom she would be genetically related.

3 *Dickson v the United Kingdom* App. No. 44362/04 (ECtHR 4 December 2012), para. 66. The applicant, a prisoner with a minimum 15-year sentence to serve for murder, was refused access to artificial insemination facilities to enable him to have a child with his wife (second applicant), who, born in 1958, had little chance of conceiving after his release.

Irrespective of the outcome and the extent of States' obligations flowing from Article 8 in each case, the ECtHR affirmed the existence under the ECHR of a right to become a parent in the genetic sense, which may include access to medically assisted procreation. By doing so it seemed to depart from its previous case law, according to which the right to respect for family life presupposed the existence of a family life[4] and could not be interpreted so broadly as to cover the right to procreate or the right to create a family.[5]

In its judgment *S.H. and Others v Austria*, the ECtHR went a step further and found that the right of two couples to conceive a child and to make use of medically assisted procreation for that purpose was protected by Article 8, as such a choice was an expression of private and family life.[6] Similarly, in *Costa and Pavan v Italy*, the ECtHR held that the applicants' desire to resort to medically assisted procreation and pre-implantation genetic diagnosis[7] in order to have a baby that did not suffer from the genetic disease of which they were carriers fell within the scope of Article 8 (private and family life).[8]

These four judgments, delivered by the Grand Chamber of the ECtHR except for the last one, show how the ECtHR has increasingly incorporated the right to become parent in the genetic sense and the right to have access to medically assisted procreation within the scope of Article 8 ECHR. In the first two cases, *Evans* and *Dickson*, the issue of applicability of Article 8 was perhaps less controversial, since access to medically assisted procreation was provided for under domestic law. The legal or practical impediments hindering the applicants' access to medically assisted procreation were linked to the particular circumstances of each case (the withdrawal

4 See, for instance, *Wagner and J.M.W.L. v Luxembourg* App. No. 76240/01 (ECtHR, 28 June 2007), para. 117. The only exception was the potential relationship between biological parents and their children when no cohabitation or *de facto* ties had been established (see *Keegan v Ireland*, 26 May 1994, paras. 42–5, Series A no. 290; *a contrario Ahrens v Germany* App. No. 45071/09 (ECtHR, 22 March 2012) para. 59).

5 Similarly, the Court has always considered that Article 12 ECHR does not protect the right to procreate.

6 *S.H. and Others v Austria* App. No. 57813/00 (ECtHR 3 November 2011), para. 82.

7 Identification of genetic abnormalities, by means of molecular biology techniques, in embryos conceived by in-vitro fertilization. Source *Larousse Medical Dictionary*.

8 *Costa and Pavan v Italy* App. No. 54270/10 (ECtHR, 28 August 2012), para. 57. The applicants were an Italian couple who were healthy carriers of cystic fibrosis and wanted, with the help of medically assisted procreation and genetic screening prior to implantation, to avoid transmitting the disease to their child. The Italian legislation prohibited pre-implantation diagnosis. It however allowed in-vitro fertilization for sterile couples or couples where the man had a sexually transmissible disease, such as HIV or hepatitis B and C, to avoid the risk of transmitting the infection. Although the Court used the term "desire" when it concluded that Article 8 was applicable, in § 65 of its judgment, at the same time it referred to the applicants' "right to have a child unaffected by the disease of which they are healthy carriers". See Gentile-Brown 2013, p. 189.

of consent by one of the parties to in-vitro fertilization in *Evans*, and the refusal by public authorities of artificial insemination facilities to a prisoner in *Dickson*). By contrast, in the cases of *S.H.* and *Costa and Pavan*, domestic law prohibited in general terms the techniques that the applicants wanted to use (heterologous techniques in *S.H.*, and pre-implantation genetic diagnosis in *Costa and Pavan*). Notwithstanding the complete ban in domestic law, the ECtHR accepted, on the sole basis of Article 8 ECHR, the right of those couples to have access to medically assisted procreation, thereby creating an "autonomous" Convention-based right.[9] Following this reasoning, the ECtHR should in principle reach the same conclusion with regard to those States that prohibit or do not provide for access to medically assisted procreation in general, since the right of couples living in those States to conceive a child would equally fall within the scope of their conventional right to respect for family life.[10]

In the case of *Knecht v Romania*, the ECtHR decided to examine the applicant's complaints from the standpoint of private life only. The case concerned the temporary seizure by the authorities of frozen embryos that the applicant had deposited with a private clinic, preventing her from using them to become a parent.[11] The fact that the ECtHR did not refer to "family life", which the applicant was invoking, can perhaps be explained by the circumstance that the embryos were obtained as a result of an in-vitro fertilization procedure with donated gametes, and that it did not transpire from the facts that the applicant was in a couple.

In any event, the ECtHR will have to clarify in the future whether single persons can assert their right of access to medically assisted procreation by invoking their right to family life and not only their right to private life.

9 For criticisms, see Puppinck, G. (2013, p. 229–32). The author considers that the case *Costa and Pavan* should have been decided by the Grand Chamber of the Court. Although the Italian Government asked for referral of the case to the Grand Chamber on the basis of Article 43 ECHR, the 5-judge panel of the Grand Chamber did not accept that request. Compare with the case-law of the Court in the field of adoption; the question of whether the right to adopt a child should or should not fall within the ambit of Article 8 alone (and not in conjunction with the principle of non-discrimination enshrined in Article 14 ECHR) has not yet been decided by the Court (see *E.B. v France*, no. 43546/02, para. 46, 22 January 2008).

10 According to the materials available to the Court in 2011 in the case of *S.H. and Others*, in-vitro fertilization treatment was regulated in 25 Member States, while in eight Member States such treatment was governed by clinical practice, guidelines or general constitutional principles. This means that in-vitro fertilization treatment was allowed in 33 Member States of the Council of Europe, which represents a majority of those States (there are 47 Member States of the Council of Europe).

11 *Knecht v Romania*, App. No. 10048/10 (ECtHR, 2 October 2012). The embryos had been seized in the context of criminal proceedings concerning the private clinic with which she had deposited her embryos, due to concerns about the clinic's credentials. See also the pending case *Nedescu v Romania*, App. No. 70035/10, communicated to the Government on 6 November 2012.

According to its broad notion of family life, which covers all types of family ties not necessarily falling within the notion of traditional family,[12] and having regard to its well-established principle that the ECHR must be interpreted "in the light of present day conditions", the ECtHR should have no difficulties with applying the right to family life in the context of medically assisted procreation to single persons.

Finally, the ECtHR has recently dealt with cases concerning access to surrogacy abroad and its legal consequences for the parents and the children so conceived. In the cases of *Mennesson* and *Labassee v France, D. and Others v Belgium,* and *Paradiso and Campanelli v Italy,*[13] the ECtHR has had to adjudicate on the rights of couples who resorted to surrogacy arrangements abroad and the rights of the children so conceived. Since the ECtHR's examination was limited to the legal and practical consequences for the private and family life of the persons concerned (the children and intended parents), the ECtHR did not have to assess whether access to surrogacy as such was protected or fell within the ambit of Article 8. However, in the light of *S.H. and Others,*[14] the right to respect for family life should in principle also apply to cases concerning access to surrogacy, especially where the use of this technique is the only means for a couple to conceive a child with whom at least one of its members would be genetically linked.

II The extent of the obligations of states flowing from Article 8 ECHR in the field of medically assisted procreation

Once the ECtHR has recognized the applicability of Article 8 ECHR to access to medically assisted procreation, the next question that arises is the content of the obligations imposed by that provision on States. The ECtHR has considered as a matter of principle that since the use of in-vitro fertilization treatment gives rise to sensitive moral and ethical issues, and since the questions raised by these cases touch on areas where there is not yet clear European consensus, States should have a wide margin of appreciation.[15] The State's margin in principle extends both to its decision to intervene in the area and, once having intervened, to the detailed rules it lays down in order to achieve a balance between the competing public and private

12 For single-parent families, see *Wagner, supra.* For homosexual couples and families, see *Schalk and Kopf v Austria,* App. No. 30141/04, (ECtHR 24 June 2010), and *X and Others v Austria* App. No. 19010/07, (ECtHR 19 February 2013).

13 *Mennesson v France,* App. No. 65192/11, (ECtHR 26 June 2014); *Labasseev. France,* App. No. 65941/11 (ECtHR, 26 June 2014); *D. and Others v Belgium* App. No. 29176/13 (ECtHR, decision of 8 July 2014); and *Paradiso and Campanelli v Italy,* App. No. 25358/12 (ECtHR, 27 January 2015). The *Paradiso and Campanelli* case has been referred to the Grand Chamber and is still pending.

14 See in this regard Puppinck, G (2014, p. 78).

15 *S.H. and Others, supra,* para. 97.

interests.[16] Notwithstanding this wide margin of appreciation, the relevant legal framework must be shaped in a coherent manner allowing the different legitimate interests involved to be adequately taken into account.[17] The ECtHR must examine whether a fair balance has been struck between the competing interests of the State and those directly affected by the legislation at issue.[18]

A *Decision to authorize or not to authorize certain medically assisted procreation techniques*

The ECtHR has had the opportunity to assess the obligations of States when it comes to the authorization of certain medically assisted procreation techniques, such as heterologous techniques (using gametes from a third person), pre-implantation genetic diagnosis, and surrogacy arrangements.

In respect of *heterologous techniques*, the ECtHR held in the case of *S.H. and Others* that the absolute ban on ova donation for artificial procreation and of sperm donation for in-vitro fertilization did not exceed the margin of appreciation accorded to the Austrian legislature at the relevant time.

16 *S.H. and Others, supra*, para. 97. Although the Court seemed to confine its examination to the prohibition of sperm and ova donation at the time it was considered by the Austrian Constitutional Court (1999, following the applicants' request for a review of constitutionality), there are some references in the judgment to subsequent developments and to the present, which support the idea that the margin of appreciation was still considered wide in 2011, when the Court adopted its judgment (see also, for a similarly wide margin of appreciation, the field of surrogacy in 2014, *Mennesson, supra*, para. 79, and the question of the donation of embryos to scientific research in 2015, *Parrillo v Italy* App. No. 46470/11 (ECtHR 27 August 2015), paras. 175–6. See in this regard the criticisms formulated by Judges Tulkens, Hirvelä, Lazarova Trajkovska and Tsotsoria in their joint dissenting opinion in *S.H.*: they expressed the view that through the combined effect of the European consensus and the margin of appreciation, the majority of the Grand Chamber had chosen a minimalist approach that could hardly be of any guidance to national courts. The dissenting judges rightly pointed out that even at the time of the Constitutional Court's judgment in 1999, ova donation was prohibited in only eight countries and sperm donation for in-vitro fertilization in five countries. Although the majority recognised the existence of a clear trend in the legislation of the Contracting States towards allowing gamete donation for in-vitro fertilization, it limited the effects of that trend by saying that "that emerging consensus is not, however, based on settled and long-standing principles established in the law of the member States but rather reflects a stage of development within a particularly dynamic field of law and does not decisively narrow the margin of appreciation of the State" (para. 96 of the judgment). As suggested by the dissenting judges, this seems to be a new and dangerous approach to the European consensus doctrine, which diminishes the value of any emerging or dynamic consensus resulting from recent legislative developments, contrary to the Court's approach in other cases (see, for instance, on homosexual civil unions, *Oliari and Others v Italy*, App nos 18766/11 and 36030/11 (ECtHR, 21 July 2015), para. 178. This approach is even more problematic in an area where law often lags behind medical and scientific developments.

17 *S.H. and Others, supra*, para. 100.

18 *S.H. and Others, supra*, para. 97.

This was so because the legislature had sought to reconcile the wish to make medically assisted procreation available and the unease among large sections of society as to the role and possibilities of modern reproductive medicine, which raised issues of a morally and ethically sensitive nature.[19] In its assessment of the proportionality of the interference, the ECtHR took into consideration in particular the following elements: the legislature had allowed the use of homologous medically assisted procreation techniques, there was no established European consensus on the issue of ova donation, and, in any event, Austrian couples could go abroad to use the techniques prohibited in Austria to conceive a child and in the event of a successful treatment they could establish their paternity according to the Civil Code.[20]

After having found that Austria had not breached Article 8 ECHR, the ECtHR added as an *obiter dictum* that this area, in which the law appeared to be continuously evolving and which was subject to the developments in science, needed to be kept under review by the Contracting States.[21] This warning left the door open for the ECtHR to change its position and find a violation, in the future, in respect of Austria or of any other State still prohibiting the use of heterologous techniques.[22]

19 *S.H. and Others, supra*, para. 104. As reflected in the Austrian legislation, which was guided by the idea that medically assisted procreation should take place similarly to natural procreation, and by the principle of civil law "mater semper certa est", avoiding the possibility that two persons (one carrying the child and the other being the genetic mother) could claim to be the biological mother of one and the same child. The Court accepted that the prohibitions at issue pursued the protection of health or morals and the protection of the rights and freedoms of others (Article 8(2) ECHR). Although the Court conceded that the prohibition of sperm donation for in-vitro fertilization did not raise the same ethical issues as ovum donation, it examined it taking account of the legislative framework as a whole and of the same concerns relied on by the Government (social acceptability, human dignity, well-being of children and prevention of potential misuse; see para. 113).

20 See in this regard Gallus, N (2012, pp. 222–4).

21 *S.H. and Others, supra*, para. 118. This type of warning in a judgment where the Court has found no violation of the ECHR has been used in the past to anticipate changes in the Court's case law concerning sensitive social and ethical issues (see, for instance, the evolution of the case-law regarding transsexuals from *Sheffield and Horsham v the United Kingdom*, 30 July 1998, *Reports of Judgments and Decisions* 1998-V, to *Christine Goodwin v the United Kingdom* App. No. 28957/95 (ECtHR 11 July 2002).

22 In the case of *S.H. and Others*, two other Contracting States (Italy and Germany) intervened as third parties in the proceedings before the Grand Chamber of the Court, defending the bans on heterologous techniques existing in their own legislations (blanket ban in Italy and ban on ovum donation in Germany). Following the Court's warning, Austria modified its legislation in 2014, authorizing sperm donation for in-vitro fertilization and ova donation under certain conditions. In Italy, the Constitutional Court ruled in its judgment of 10 June 2014 that the blanket ban on access to heterologous fertilization in the event of medically established sterility or infertility was unconstitutional. It based its findings on the right to become parent and found a family, the right to self-determination, and the right to protection of health, all guaranteed by the Italian Constitution (judgment no. 162/2014).

In the case of *Costa and Pavan*, without calling into question the margin of appreciation afforded to States in this domain,[23] the ECtHR held that the absolute ban on pre-implantation genetic diagnosis, while pursuing the legitimate aims of protecting morals and the rights and freedoms of others (within the meaning of Article 8(2) ECHR), was disproportionate, "having regard to the . . . inconsistency in Italian legislation on pre-implantation genetic diagnosis".[24] The reason for this inconsistency was that on the one hand the legislation prohibited access to pre-implantation genetic diagnosis, which would have allowed the implantation of those embryos unaffected by the disease of which the applicants were healthy carriers, while on the other hand it allowed the applicants to abort a foetus affected by the same disease.[25] In the view of the ECtHR, the consequences of an abortion, both for the foetus, which is clearly far further developed than an embryo, and for the parents, in particular the woman, would be more serious than those of having recourse to pre-implantation genetic diagnosis.[26] Therefore it concluded that the prohibition at issue had breached the applicants' right to respect for their private and family life.[27]

As regards the Italian Government's argument that the prohibition pursued the aim of protecting the health of "the child", the ECtHR stressed that the concept of "child" could not be put in the same category as that of "embryo".[28] The ECtHR followed in this regard the approach taken by the Irish Supreme Court in the case of *Roche v Roche and Others*, where that court had established that the concept of the unborn child protected by the Irish Constitution (recognizing its right to life) did not apply to embryos created through in-vitro insemination.[29] This consideration appears to somehow contradict the established case law of the ECtHR according to which the issue of the applicability of the right to life to the embryo and/or foetus

23 See however Puppinck, G. (2013, p. 237), who considers that the Court narrowed *de facto* the margin of appreciation of Italy in this case. One can wonder whether the Court narrowed this margin of appreciation in the light of the fact that the case concerned access to homologous and not to heterologous insemination techniques (as noted by para. 69 of the judgment).

24 *Costa and Pavan, supra*, para. 71.

25 *Costa and Pavan, supra*, para. 64.

26 *Costa and Pavan, supra*, para. 62.

27 In its judgment of 5 June 2015, the Italian Constitutional Court declared the unconstitutionality of the legislation which prohibited couples who were neither sterile nor infertile but who were carriers of genetic diseases from using medically assisted procreation (judgment No. 96/2015).

28 *Costa and Pavan, supra*, para. 62.

29 The Court referred to this decision in the comparative law materials of its judgment. See § 33: [2009] IESC 82 (2009). This is a good example of how the case law of the supreme courts of the Contracting States may influence the interpretation of the ECHR by the Court.

is not for the ECtHR to decide, but for each Contracting State within its margin of appreciation.[30]

With regard to *surrogacy arrangements abroad*, although the ECtHR has mainly focused on the practical and legal consequences of those arrangements in Contracting States where surrogacy is prohibited, it has also examined whether those States could actually prohibit surrogacy as such in their territory. In the light of the comparative law study prepared by its Research Division, the ECtHR concluded that there was no consensus in Europe both on the lawfulness of surrogacy arrangements as such and on the legal recognition of the relationship between intended parents and children conceived abroad. Consequently, it accepted that States should in principle be afforded a wide margin of appreciation, regarding the decision, not only whether or not to authorize this method of medically assisted procreation in their legal order, but also whether or not to recognize a legal parent–child relationship between the children conceived and the intended parents.[31] However, and here lies the main difference with the previous cases concerning medically assisted procreation, the ECtHR modulated the margin of appreciation of the State, having regard to the fact that an essential aspect of the identity of individuals was at stake where the legal parent–child relationship was concerned, and that the best interests of the children concerned had to be the guiding principle.[32]

In the light of these principles, the ECtHR held in its judgments *Mennesson* and *Labassee* that by totally prohibiting the recognition and establishment of their legal relationship with their biological father under French law, France had breached Article 8 ECHR with regard to the children's right to respect for their private life.[33] The ECtHR mainly relied on the

30 *Evans, supra*, para. 56; *Vo v France* App. No. 53924/00, (ECtHR 8 July 2004), paras. 84–5; and *A, B and C v Ireland* App. No. 25579/05 (ECtHR 16 December 2010), paras. 227–8, concerning the issue of the protection of the unborn child in the legislation restricting abortion. In *Parrillo, supra*, para. 167, the Grand Chamber of the Court reiterated its reluctance to assess whether the word "others" within the meaning of Article 8(2) ECHR ("protection of the rights and freedoms of others") extends to human embryos, while admitting that the "protection of the embryo's potential for life" relied on by the Government could be linked to the aim of protecting morals and "the rights and freedoms of others".

31 *Mennesson, supra*, paras. 78–9; *Labassee v France, supra*, paras. 57–8. Out of the 35 Member States taken into consideration by the Court, surrogacy was authorized or tolerated in 11 States. In 24 States it was possible to obtain legal recognition of the parent–child relationship between the intended parents and the children conceived through a surrogacy agreement legally performed abroad.

32 *Mennesson, supra*, paras. 80–1.

33 These cases concerned the refusal to grant legal recognition in France to parent–child relationships that had been legally established in the United States between children born as a result of surrogacy treatment and the French couples who had undergone the treatment. In both cases the embryos had been obtained using the gametes of the husband and an egg from a donor and they had been implanted in the uterus of another woman. The intended parents/couples had obtained a birth certificate in the United States, which

principle of the best interests of the child and found a violation only in relation to the children's right to respect for private life, which included the right to establish their identity, notably their legal parent–child relationships (including their inheritance rights) but also their nationality.[34] While it accepted that France could wish to deter its nationals from going abroad to resort to methods of medically assisted procreation prohibited on its own territory (aiming at the protection of health and the rights and freedoms of the children and the surrogate mother[35]), it stressed that the effects of the non-recognition in French law of the legal parent–child relationship between the children conceived and the intended parents were not limited to the parents alone, but also affected the children themselves.[36]

What was crucial for the ECtHR in these cases was the fact that the refusal by the French authorities to establish the legal parent–child relationship concerned the children's biological parent, who was one of the intended parents (the husband). According to the ECtHR, it was not in the interests of the child to deprive him or her of a legal relationship of this nature where the biological reality of that relationship had been established and the child and parent concerned demanded full recognition thereof.[37] Since France prohibited not only the recognition but also any other alternative means of establishing the paternity (such as a declaration of paternity or an adoption), the ECtHR concluded that the respondent State had overstepped its margin of appreciation.[38]

---

stated that they were the father and the mother of the children, but the French national authorities had refused to register those certificates in the French register of births. The Court of Cassation had held that the American decisions giving effect to the surrogacy arrangements conflicted with the French concept of international public policy. The two couples had travelled with their children to France after the birth of the children and had lived there since.

34 However, the ECtHR did not find a violation of the right of the applicants (intended parents and children) to respect for their family life, since the difficulties resulting from the non-recognition of the legal parent–child relationship had not prevented them from settling altogether in France shortly after the birth of the children and there was no risk of being separated by the authorities (see paras. 92–4 of the *Mennesson* judgment).

35 The issue of the protection of the rights of the surrogate mother, and the need to fight against the exploitation of women, will be particularly relevant in cases where the surrogate mother comes from a developing country (see, for instance, *Foulon v France*, App. No. 9063/14, communicated to the Government on 15 January 2015, concerning a surrogacy treatment in India).

36 *Mennesson, supra*, para. 99.

37 *Mennesson, supra*, para. 100; *Labassee, supra*, para. 79.

38 Compare with the situation in Spain, where it appears that the establishment of legal paternity in respect of children born following surrogacy arrangements abroad is possible not only for a biological parent but also for an intended parent with no biological links with the child, for instance through adoption. See the decision of the Spanish Supreme Court of 2 February 2015, in which a distinction was drawn between the Spanish legislation and the legal situation at issue in *Mennesson* and *Labassee*. See, for a description of the Spanish legislative framework prior to that decision, Vaquero López, C 2015, pp. 291–332. Following the

It does not follow from these landmark judgments on surrogacy that Contracting States have an obligation under the ECHR to recognise foreign birth certificates that give effect to surrogacy agreements recording both intended parents as the legal parents of the child. Article 8 only imposes the obligation to provide for the possibility of legally establishing the parent–child relationship with the biological parent, given the importance of biological parentage for the child's identity. While the ECtHR mentioned in its judgments some of the difficulties resulting from the lack of legal recognition of the relationship with the intended mother (notably in terms of inheritance rights), the only reason supporting the violation of the children's rights under the ECHR was the failure by the French authorities to establish a legal relationship between the children and their biological father. However, it may be regretted that the ECtHR did not seize the opportunity to clarify the obligations of States under Article 8 when it comes to the relationship between surrogate children and their non-biological intended parents (in these two cases it was the mother).

The ECtHR had a new opportunity to examine the situation of children born following surrogacy arrangements in the case of *Paradiso and Campanelli v Italy*. This time the surrogate child had no genetic or biological link with the intended parents, who had entered into a gestational surrogacy arrangement with a company in Russia, and discovered on their return to Italy that the husband's gametes had not been used for the in-vitro fertilization treatment and that the child was not the biological offspring of either of them. The ECtHR was precluded from examining the merits of the complaint concerning the Italian authorities' refusal to register the birth certificate of the child issued in Russia.[39] It only addressed the complaint relating to the measures taken by the Italian authorities to remove the child (when he was only nine months) from the applicants and place him under guardianship, which ended any possibility of contact

---

Mennesson/Labassee judgments, the French *Consei ld'État* held on 12 December 2014 that the circular issued in January 2013 by the Minister of Justice inviting the administration to deliver certificates of French nationality (*Certificat de nationalité française*) to children born through surrogacy arrangements abroad if they had biological links with the father was legal. Furthermore, on 3 July 2015 the Court of Cassation, sitting as a plenary, rendered two judgments holding that the transcription of a foreign birth certificate of a child born through surrogacy who had at least a French parent (the father) could not be rejected for the sole reason that the birth had been the result of surrogate motherhood (see Court of Cassation, judgments Nos. 619 and 620). The Court judgments in the *Mennesson/Labassee* cases have had a significant impact on jurisprudential developments in other Contracting States such as Germany (Federal Court of Justice,10 December 2014, XII ZVB 463/13, concerning the recognition of a Californian judgment naming two intended fathers as the legal parents of a child born through surrogacy) and Switzerland (Federal Tribunal, 5A_ 748/2014, 21 May 2015, regarding the recognition of a Californian judgment following surrogacy only in respect of the biological father).

39 For failure to exhaust the relevant domestic remedies (see *Paradiso and Campanelli, supra*, para. 62).

with him. The ECtHR found that these extreme measures had breached the applicants' right to respect for their family life,[40] noting that the sole ground for removing the child was that they had circumvented the Italian legislation on medically assisted procreation,[41] and reiterating that the removal of a child from the family setting can only be justified in the event of violence or immediate danger to the child. The ECtHR noted however that these conclusions were not to be understood as obliging Italy, in executing this judgment, to return the child to the applicants, as he had undoubtedly developed emotional ties with the foster family with whom he had been living since 2013.[42]

If we read together *Mennesson, Labassee* and *Paradiso and Campanelli*, we can draw the following conclusions as regards State obligations under Article 8 ECHR. Firstly, the right of intended parents to respect for their family life with surrogate children places an obligation on national authorities to respect the *de facto* family ties created between the parents and the child, irrespective of whether biological or genetic links exist. This obligation precludes in principle the national authorities from removing the child from the intended parents for the only reason that surrogacy and its consequences are illegal under domestic law. This applies not only to long-term family units (as in the French cases) but also to short periods of family life after the birth of the child (like in the Italian case).[43] Secondly, once the *de facto* family life between the intended parents and the child has been created and tolerated by the authorities, States must guarantee the child's right to identity and to nationality, allowing at least the establishment of the legal parent–child relationship between the child and his or her intended biological parent. The question of the legal status of the non-biological intended parent/s vis-à-vis the child remains to be clarified by the ECtHR in the future, under both the notion of "private life" of the child and the parent/s and that of "family life".

40 *De facto* family life was considered to exist in spite of the short period of time shared by the applicants with the child (six months in Italy from the child's third month of life and prior to that some weeks spent by the first applicant in Russia). Judges Raimondi and Spano rightly pointed out, in their partly dissenting opinion, that the Chamber judgment amounted in substance to denying the legitimacy of the State's choice not to recognize surrogacy, since it implied that for the national authorities to be obliged to recognize the existence of "family life", it sufficed to create, illegally, a link with the surrogate child abroad.

41 On the prohibition of surrogacy arrangements and the use of heterologous medically assisted procreation techniques, but also the legislation governing international adoption.

42 *Paradiso and Campanelli, supra*, para. 88.

43 Nevertheless, short periods of separation between the child and the intended parents can be justified for carrying out legal checks before allowing the surrogate child to enter the territory of the State (see, for instance, a period of three months and twelve days during which the authorities refused to issue the applicants with a travel document to enable the arrival of the child to Belgium, in *D. and Others v Belgium, supra*, where the Court declared the applicants' complaint under Article 8 inadmissible as being manifestly ill-founded).

B Exclusion of certain categories of persons from access to medically assisted procreation

In *Costa and Pavan*, although the main issue before the ECtHR was the absolute ban on the use of pre-implantation genetic diagnosis in Italian law, the case indirectly raised the issue of exclusion from medically assisted procreation of couples who carry a genetic disease. Under Italian law medically assisted procreation was only available to sterile or infertile couples, and to couples in which the man suffered from a sexually transmissible viral disease (such as the HIV virus). In holding Italy responsible for not allowing the applicants to make use of pre-implantation genetic diagnosis in the exercise of their right to respect for private and family life, the ECtHR ultimately called into question the general exclusion of couples such as that of the applicants from access to the benefits of medically assisted procreation.

As regards access of same-sex couples to medically assisted procreation, the ECtHR considered in the case of *Gas and Dubois v France*, that in the area of anonymous donor insemination, the situation of same-sex couples could not be compared to that of infertile heterosexual couples. Therefore, the legislation barring same-sex couples from having access to that medically assisted procreation technique could not amount to a difference in treatment in breach of the principle of non-discrimination guaranteed by Article 14 ECHR.[44] It will be interesting to see if the ECtHR will change its position on this subject, and whether it will take a more protective approach, more in line with recent developments in other areas of its case law regarding same-sex families.[45]

Another category of persons touched by restrictions on access to medically assisted procreation is that of prisoners. The case of *Dickson v the United Kingdom* illustrates well this problematic area. The ECtHR found that the United Kingdom had breached the ECHR for having refused to provide a couple – a prisoner and his wife – with facilities for artificial insemination.

44 *Gas and Dubois v France*, App. No. 25951/07, (ECtHR 15 March 2012), para. 63. The case concerned the consequences of the use by a lesbian of artificial insemination by a donor in Belgium and the right to second-parent adoption by her partner in France. For the consequences in terms of parent–child relationships of the use of artificial insemination by donor insemination by a couple of a woman and a female-to-male transsexual, see *X, Y and Z v the United Kingdom*, App. No. 21830/93 (ECtHR 22 April 1997).

45 See, for instance in terms of second-parent adoption, *X v Austria, supra*. However, the Court has also accepted that States enjoy a certain margin of appreciation as regards the exact statute conferred by the legislation on civil unions or registered partnerships to same-sex couples, implying that the exclusion of some of the rights afforded to heterosexual couples could still fall within that margin (see, for instance, *Schalk and Kopf, supra*, para. 109, on restrictions concerning artificial insemination and adoption, although the applicants were not directly affected by those restrictions). The recent case of *Oliari, supra*, while concerning solely the general need for legal recognition of same-sex couples, confirms that States still enjoy a certain margin of appreciation as regards the exact statute and rights conferred to those couples by civil unions (para. 177).

In doing so, the ECtHR established as a matter of principle the obligation on States, when implementing their penal policy, to balance the competing public (the aim of maintaining public confidence in the penal system[46]) and private (the importance of access to medically assisted procreation for the prisoners' right to become parents[47]) interests, allowing for a proportionality assessment in each individual case. While the violation found by the ECtHR was more of a procedural nature, in the sense that the United Kingdom's procedure and policy had not allowed for a proportionality test in the particular circumstances of the case, it can be inferred from the ECtHR's reasoning that an automatic forfeiture of reproductive rights by prisoners is not acceptable under the Convention.[48]

C Conflicts arising during the medically assisted procreation procedure

The ECtHR has also ruled on certain conflicts that may arise during medically assisted procreation procedures, that is to say, before the insemination or the implantation of the embryo. In this domain the ECtHR has exercised a certain self-judicial restraint, affording States a wide margin of appreciation to reconcile in their respective legislations the different competing public and private interests. In the well-known case of *Evans*, the ECtHR had to examine the irreconcilable conflict between, on the one hand, the withdrawal of the ex-partner's consent for the embryos to be used, and on the other hand, the wish of the applicant to have the embryos implanted. This conflict was particularly dramatic in the circumstances of the case because the applicant had had her ovaries removed after the in-vitro fertilization treatment and the implantation of the embryos already created was the only means for her becoming a genetic mother. Notwithstanding these extreme circumstances, the ECtHR found that the clear rules contained in the UK's legislation, allowing the male gamete provider to withdraw his consent at any time before the implantation of the embryos created, had not breached the applicant's right to respect for her private life. In this respect, it did not consider that the applicant's right to become a genetic parent should override her ex-partner's right to respect for his decision not to have a genetically related child with her. The ECtHR had regard to the different interests at stake, including the principles of legal certainty and

46 *Dickson, supra*, paras. 72–6. The Court however seemed to reject the punitive objective of imprisonment raised by the Government for justifying the restriction, in that it highlighted the evolution in European penal policy towards the increasing relative importance of the rehabilitative aim of imprisonment.

47 The Court emphasized that where a particularly important facet of an individual's existence or identity was at stake (such as the choice to become a genetic parent), the margin of appreciation accorded to a State would in general be restricted (para. 78).

48 For further developments in the Court's case-law regarding family life of prisoners, in particular family visits, see *Khoroshenko v Russia* App. No. 41418/04 (ECtHR 30 June 2015).

free consent in the field of medically assisted procreation, as well as to the absence of a European consensus on the subject.[49] All these factors militated in favour of a wide margin of appreciation of the State, allowing for different legal regulations in each country. It is interesting to note that the ECtHR's finding in this case was not unanimous.[50]

In the case of *Knecht v Romania*, the ECtHR examined whether Article 8 of the ECHR required the national authorities to transfer the applicant's frozen embryos to the clinic of her choice, following the seizure of the embryos ordered in the context of a criminal investigation against a private clinic. The ECtHR held that Article 8 had not been breached, since the embryos had ultimately been transferred in a relatively short time to a specialized clinic where she could now initiate an in-vitro fertilization procedure.[51]

Finally, the last decision concerning medically assisted procreation taken by the ECtHR was delivered in the case of *Parrillo v Italy*. The case concerned a ban under Italian legislation, preventing the applicant from donating, to scientific research, embryos obtained from an in-vitro fertilization treatment and that were not destined for a pregnancy.[52] She complained that she was obliged to keep them in a state of cryopreservation until their death. The ECtHR, ruling for the first time on this issue, held that Article 8 (private life) was applicable in that the applicant's ability to exercise a conscious and considered choice regarding the fate of her embryos concerned an intimate aspect of her personal life and accordingly related to her right to self-determination.[53] It went on to find however that Article 8 had not been breached, having regard to the wide margin of appreciation of the State, the lack of a European consensus on the subject, and the fact that the Italian legislature had already taken account of the different interests at stake, particularly the State's interest in protecting the embryo[54] and that of the persons concerned in exercising their right to self-determination.[55]

49 *Evans, supra*, paras. 83–92. As regards the absence of a European consensus on the specific question raised by the case, the Court noted that other countries (Denmark, France, Greece, the Netherlands and Switzerland) had regulated the consent issue in the same manner as the United Kingdom had, while others had regulated it differently (for instance, Hungary, Austria, Estonia, Spain, Germany and Italy).

50 See the joint dissenting opinion of Judges Türmen, Tsatsa-Nikolovska, Spielmann and Ziemele, who interestingly considered that there had been a violation of Article 8, alone and in conjunction with Article 14 ECHR, since the applicant should have been treated differently given her condition as a woman and her particular situation.

51 It is interesting to note that in both tin the *Evans* and *Knecht* cases the Court had indicated a Rule 39 provisional measure ordering the respondent States not to destroy the embryos created.

52 She decided not to have the embryos implanted after her partner's death.

53 *Parrillo, supra*, para. 159. This was disputed by the Italian Government.

54 The protection of the embryo was accepted as falling under the legitimate aims justifying the ban under Article 8(2) ECHR (see para. 167 of the judgment, see n. 31 above).

55 *Parrillo, supra*, paras. 175–6, and 188. The Court drew a distinction with the other medically assisted procreation cases that concerned "prospective parenthood", noting that the

As to the applicant's argument that the Italian legislation was inconsistent (following the *Costa and Pavan* approach), the ECtHR was of the view that the fact that Italy permitted research on cell lines obtained from embryos destroyed abroad did not directly affect the applicant, and that the destruction of a human embryo could not be compared with the use of cell lines from already destroyed embryos.[56] As regards the applicant's claim that she had a right of ownership over her embryos under Article 1 of Protocol No.1, the ECtHR categorically rejected the idea that human embryos could be reduced to "possessions" within the meaning of that provision.[57]

III Closing remarks

Since the cases of *Evans* and *Dickson* delivered in 2007, the ECtHR has increasingly had to deal with applications concerning medically assisted procreation, raising new and sensitive issues such as the use of heterologous techniques, the consequences of surrogacy arrangements in family law and the donation of embryos to scientific research. It has gradually expanded the notion of "family life" under Article 8 ECHR, by including a new autonomous right to become a parent in the genetic sense and the right of couples to conceive a child and to make use of medically assisted procreation. This has indisputably been an important step for the recognition of reproductive rights, as it has opened the way for recognizing that States can be subject to obligations under the ECHR in order to respect and guarantee the effective and concrete exercise of those rights. However, the case law as it stands still offers a rather limited protection to these rights, since the ECtHR has preferred to take a cautious approach using its well-known doctrine of the margin of appreciation of States. Indeed, the ECtHR has afforded in this field a wide margin of appreciation to Contracting States, particularly with regard to their decision whether or not to authorize certain medically assisted procreation techniques in their territories, but also when it comes to their specific regulations and how they strike a balance between the competing interests at stake. This margin of appreciation may well be justified, given the lack of established European consensus in the field of medically assisted procreation and the fact that its use may still raise sensitive moral and ethical issues. The ECtHR however has modulated that margin of appreciation and exercised full jurisdiction in two scenarios: where the rights of children born following a medically assisted procreation treatment were at stake, and where the contested legislation was not consistent and had disproportionate effects vis-à-vis the applicants (as in the case of the Italian ban on pre-implantation genetic diagnosis).

alleged right to donate embryos to scientific research was not one of the core Article 8 rights (see para. 174).

56 *Parrillo, supra*, paras. 194–5.

57 *Parrillo, supra*, para. 215.

The European being a "living instrument", the ECtHR has also said that this area, in which the law appears to be continuously evolving and which is subject to dynamic developments in science, should be kept under review by the Contracting States. Measures or restrictions that once fell within the acceptable margin of appreciation of States may in the future be considered by the ECtHR as contrary to the Convention, especially in the light of the evolution of European consensus. While the ECtHR will certainly be faced with new challenges, it should be attentive to developments in Europe and worldwide, so as to reflect under the ECHR the new standards being required in the fast-moving area of medically assisted procreation.

References

Gallus, N. (2012). La procréation médicalement assistée et la jurisprudence de la Cour européenne des droits de l'homme. *Droit des familles, genre et sexualité Actes du colloque organisé par l'Unité du droit familial du Centre de Droit privé de l'ULB, 9 mars 2012,* Anthemis :Limal, pp. 222–3.

Gentile-Brown, I. (2013). Procréation médicalement assistée et diagnostic génétique préimplantatoire: des interrogations délicates à l'examen de la Cour européenne des droits de l'homme. *Cohérence et impact de la jurisprudence de la Cour européenne des droits de l'homme.* Oisterwijk: Wolf Legal Publishers, pp. 189–200.

Puppinck, G. (2013). L'arrêt *Costa-Pavan c/ Italie* et la convergence des droits de l'homme et des biotechnologies. *Revue générale de droit médical,* (49), pp. 223–45.

Puppinck, G. (2014). ECHR: Towards the Liberalisation of Surrogacy. Regarding the Mennesson v. France and Labassee v. France cases. *Revue Lamy de Droit Civil,* (118), pp. 78–95.

Vaquero López, C. (2015). La paternidad de las parejas del mismo sexo a través de la gestación por sustitución: problemas jurídicos. *La diversidad afectivo-sexual y los mecanismos establecidos por el Derecho internacional para su protección. Anuario de los Cursos de Derechos Humanos de Donostia-San Sebastián, Volumen XIV,* Thomson Reuters Aranzadi, pp. 201–325.

7 Biology-based systems of parentage and safety valves protecting social parenting

Esther Farnós Amorós[*]

I Introduction

Biological truth and family life are two values that frequently come into conflict in parentage claims. This tension, which the ECtHR has had to deal with when ruling on cases originating in paternity claims, has created a body of case law in which the Court has generally respected the varying approaches to the issue taken by different states. This analysis focuses on how the ECtHR resolves the dilemma between the two values when the action claiming paternity brought by the putative father threatens the paternity established in favour of another man, the legal and social father of the child in question. None of the cases settled by the CJEU to have had an impact on the notion of "family life" has actually focused on a child's parentage. The fact that so few of these cases have reached the CJEU can be explained by the ECHR's recognition of the fundamental rights and guarantees linked to protecting the family and family life over more than 60 years, together with the scant practical relevance of family issues in EU policy (Stein, 2012, p. 1388 et seq.)[1]. In this context, parentage has been approached only indirectly, in two recent disputes over whether the respective Member States should guarantee maternity leave to two female employees, one British and one Irish, who had become mothers by means of surrogacy.[2] For this reason, the chapter focuses on the case law created by

* Ester Farnós is Law Professor at Pompeu Fabra University, Barcelona. This chapter forms part of a research project being carried out by the author at the Universitat Pompeu Fabra and directed by Prof. Josep Ferrer Riba ("Libertad reproductiva y formación de relaciones familiares" DER2014-55573-R). The author wishes to thank Prof. Ferrer for his thought-provoking comments following a preliminary reading of the manuscript, as well as for his suggestions for the title.

1 See Section II of this chapter. For more information, see Iglesias Sánchez and Karr in this book.

2 See Case C-167/12 *C.D. v S.T.* EU:C:2014:169 and Case C-363/12 *Z. v A Government Department and The Board of Management of a Community School* EU:C:2014:159. The Court stated in the preliminary rulings that failing to grant the employees the maternity leave they had requested did not constitute discriminatory treatment. It should be noted that while the applicant in the English case had had the child's parentage established by means of a parental order, since surrogacy is legal in the United Kingdom if it is not for commercial gain,

the ECtHR, beginning with an analysis of the same and continuing with an examination of recent trends concerning parentage in some national laws. The overall aim is to frame proposals for regulation that take into account as far as possible the different conflicting interests in parentage claims (chiefly biological truth and family life), acknowledge in each element's respective value in establishing the child's best interests and the shaping of her personal identity. When genetic, biological, and social parenthood are not united in one and the same person, it is the law's task to decide which of these particular attributes shall be construed as constituting parentage. The law must also determine the position of an individual who has genetic or social ties to the child but does not have the status of his or her legal parent (Büchler 2016, p. 35). When the law is not clear or models for attributing parentage diverge significantly, the task falls to the courts, and the ECtHR is no exception.

II Biological truth and family life in the European Convention on Human Rights

The basis of legal protection for biological truth and family life lies in Article 8 ECHR, which recognises the "Right to respect for private and family life".[3] As CJEU decisions on family matters frequently refer to ECtHR case law,[4] the concept of "family life" in EU law is intimately related to the notion that the ECtHR has constructed over time with regard to this Article.[5] This is shown by the Charter's official explanations, according to which, "The rights guaranteed in Article 7 correspond to those guaranteed by Article 8 ECHR. . . . In accordance with Article 52(3), the meaning and scope of this right are the same as those of the corresponding article of the ECHR. Consequently, the limitations which may legitimately be imposed on this right are the same as those allowed by Article 8 ECHR."[6]

in the Irish case the woman was the child's legal guardian and was only considered the legal mother under Californian law. In spite of the CJEU's declarations, the British government approved granting leave and benefits similar to those provided for adoptive parents to intended parents: see s. 122 and Schedule 7 of the Children and Families Act (2014).

3 According to this article, "1. Everyone has the right to respect for his private and family life, his home and his correspondence.

2. There shall be no interference by a public authority with the exercise of this right except such as is in accordance with the law and is necessary in a democratic society in the interests of national security, public safety or the economic well-being of the country, for the prevention of disorder or crime, for the protection of health or morals, or for the protection of the rights and freedoms of others."

4 On the "dialogue" between the two courts and the need to guarantee the coherent development of their case law in the fundamental rights sphere, see Oliveira Pais (2013, pp. 102–3).

5 On this topic, see the chapter in this book entitled "European Convention of Human Rights and Family Life".

6 2007/C 303/02, Official Journal of the European Union 14 December 2007, C 303/17.

In accordance with the broad definition arising from Article 8,[7] the ECtHR has identified "family life" with the existence of close family ties,[8] which can cover *de facto* family bonds between persons who live together outside marriage and extends beyond the nuclear family to include direct dependent relatives and even persons with whom there is no family life. In any event, the cohabitation must involve certain stability,[9] and when the relationship is analogous to marriage, this is independent of the cohabiting couple's sex.[10] The benchmarks of the existence of family life are the fact of living under the same roof, the nature and duration of the relationship and the parties' degree of commitment and common interests. The concept "family life" thus encompasses not only the ties between married couples and their children but also those between couples living together out of wedlock and the children who are either their natural offspring or otherwise in their care, irrespective of the legal status of the parents.[11] The ECtHR has also stipulated that the mother–child relationship at the child's birth[12] and the relationship between a foster family and a child when the child was in their care also constitute family life.[13] Consequently, the confirmation that certain individuals can be said to have "family life" in the ECHR sense is primarily a question of fact that depends on the real and effective existence of close personal relationships, over and above biological reality or the fact of living together (Choudhry and Herring 2010, pp. 170–1; Casadevall 2012, pp. 339–41, and Grabenwarter 2014, pp. 193–6).

Article 8 ECHR also covers respect for biological truth, although in this case the precept contains no explicit reference to the term. Biological truth is protected in the sense that legal actions seeking either to contest

7 Cf. *supra* n. 3 with the narrower notion, centred on the marital family, in Article 12 ECHR: "Men and women of marriageable age have the right to marry and to found a family, according to the national laws governing the exercise of this right."

8 *K and T v Finland* App. No. 25702/94 (ECtHR, 12 July 2001).

9 *Elsholz v Germany* App. No. 25735/94 (ECtHR, 13 July 2000) and *Lebbink v the Netherlands* App. No. 45582/99 (ECtHR, 1 June 2004). The stability requirement is considered decisive for family life to be protected under Article 8 ECHR: see Stein, 2012, pp. 1386–7.

10 *Abdulaziz, Cabales and Balkandali v UK* App. No. 9214/80, 9473/81 and 9474/81 (ECtHR, 28 May 1985). With regard to registered partnerships, in Case C-267/06 *Maruko* EU:C:2008:179 and in Case C-174/08 *Jürgen Römer*. EU:C:2009:669, the CJEU recognized the surviving partner's right to the same state pension provided for survivor spouses, irrespective of sexual orientation. Case C-66/08, *Kozłowski*, EU:C:2008:437.

11 See *Kroon and others v the Netherlands* App. No. 18535/91 (ECtHR, 27 October 1994), in which the ECtHR declared that a child living with the mother and her partner from the moment of its birth, whatever the partner's contribution to his child's care and upbringing, is part of the "family unit" (para. 30). In the case, as a result of the paternity presumption the child's paternity had been attributed to the mother's ex-husband, who had disappeared before the mother became pregnant.

12 *Gül v Switzerland* App. No. 23218/94 (ECtHR, 19 February 1996).

13 *Moretti and Benedetti v Italy* App. No. 16318/07 (ECtHR, 27 April 2010). In this regard, see also Sales, 2015, pp. 170–1.

or claim parentage concern private life, part of which is formed by biological truth in its facet of personal identity. The ECtHR has frequently recognized this in cases where the right to respect for family life could not be invoked (Büchler 2016, p. 33). In *Kautzor v Germany* the putative father claimed paternity of a child who had already been acknowledged by the mother's cohabiting partner. The Court stated that "the applicant had a protected interest in establishing the truth about an important aspect of his private life, namely the alleged fact of his being M.'s father, and having it recognised in law" (para. 73).[14] In *Ahrens v Germany*, a similar case that will be analyzed in detail in the following section, the court also identified this interest with personal identity, stating that "Article 8 protects not only 'family' but also 'private' life . . . proceedings concerning the establishment of or challenge against paternity concerned that man's private life under Article 8, which encompasses important aspects of one's personal identity" (para. 60).[15] The ECtHR has applied this doctrine in actions claiming paternity brought not just by the putative father, but also by a mother and her daughter[16] or by the child herself.[17]

III Paternity claims before the European Court of Human Rights

The group of cases analyzed in this chapter is just one example of the quantitative prominence of Grand Chamber judgments concerning Article 8 (Keller 2016, pp. 3–28). From among all the parentage claims brought before the ECtHR every year, this chapter focuses on those originating in an appeal filed by the putative father against the decision of a court in a member state preventing him from being legally registered as having a biological link to a child or developing any type of personal relationship with her. The main conflicts in this area arise when paternity has already been established in favour of another man, usually the mother's husband or new partner. This group of cases throws into relief the different approaches that states take towards regulating parentage, which vary depending on the weight given to social or biological parenthood.

The current interest in the harmonizing of family law in Europe does not seem to extend to parentage, an area in which state laws could not

14 App. No. 23338/09 (ECtHR, 21 December 2010). In this case, the man with whom the mother was cohabiting acknowledged paternity of the child 14 months after her birth, and the putative father filed the paternity claim two months later, with no success.

15 App. No. 45071/09 (ECtHR, 22 March 2012). The putative father in this case filed, also with no success, the paternity claim two months after the birth of a child whose paternity had been acknowledged by the mother's partner during the pregnancy.

16 *Mikulić v Croatia* App. No. 53176/99 (ECtHR, 7 February 2002), paras. 53–4.

17 *Jäggi v Switzerland* App. No. 58757/00 (ECtHR, 13 July 2006), para. 37, and *Backlund v Finland* App. No. 36498/05 (ECtHR, 6 July 2010), para. 37.

differ more, and this explains the broad margin of appreciation guaranteed by the ECtHR in these cases (Bainham 2007, pp. 278–82; Scherpe 2016, pp. 85–6).[18] However, the Court tends to be stricter about other related issues, for example, when establishing specific parentage involves discrimination on the basis of sex or sexual orientation, which should be investigated in accordance with Article 14 ECHR. States have a more limited margin of appreciation in these matters, as the Court itself has underlined in cases such as *X and Others v Austria*. In this case the Grand Chamber rejected taking the traditional concept of parentage prevailing in Austria into consideration, understanding as discriminatory the rule allowing the cohabiting partner in different-sex but not same-sex couples to adopt the other partner's child if the existence of family life with the child was proved and the other parent did not specify reasons for opposing the adoption.[19]

Beyond specific cases that have come before the ECtHR, the broad references to comparative law in the Court's decisions on parentage display

18 See para. 68 of *A.L. v Poland* App. No. 28609/08 (ECtHR, 18 February 2014), a case where the man who recognized the paternity of a child being aware that he might not be the child's biological father, tried unsuccessfully to contest paternity beyond the one-year time-limit allowed by the Polish law, when the child was 12 years old: "the Court has acknowledged that the margin of appreciation enjoyed by the Member States in respect of the determination of a child's legal status must be a wider one than that enjoyed by the States regarding questions of contact and information rights". As Keller notes (2016, p. 8), the margin of appreciation doctrine has become an indispensable part of ECtHR jurisprudence and has been subjected to serious criticism, particularly from those who consider it a gateway to "cultural relativism", *per se* incompatible with the universal nature of the rights enshrined in the ECHR. The Court has also used this approach with regard to access to assisted reproductive technologies: in this field, see Scherpe (2016, pp. 89–101), who is especially worried for the ECtHR tendency to validate the choice of the persons concerned to deliberately circumvent the rules and therefore render the national public policy underlying the prohibition somewhat meaningless, with dangerous effects such as social injustice. See also Farnós (2016).

19 App. No. 19010/07 (ECtHR, 19 February 2013). The case is therefore to be distinguished from *Gas and Dubois v France* App. No. 25951/07 (ECtHR, 15 March 2012), in which the Court found that there was no difference of treatment based on sexual orientation between an unmarried different-sex couple and a same-sex couple, as second-parent adoption was not open to either of them according to French law. In *X and Others v Austria* the Grand Chamber considered that there had been a violation of Article 14 ECHR, coupled with Article 8. Furthermore, Austrian legislation appears to lack coherence on this point: adoption by one person, including homosexuals, is allowed, therefore the legislature accepts that a child may grow up in a family based on a same-sex couple, thus it also accepts that this is not detrimental to the child – yet insists that a child cannot have two mothers or two fathers. In addition, the case contains an interesting dissenting opinion voiced by seven of the 17 members of the Grand Chamber, according to whom, the fact that the child also had family life with the biological father had to be taken into account: "the child cannot be adopted without the express consent of the father or mother with whom the parental tie remains. Accordingly, whether the person seeking to adopt is a man or a woman, heterosexual or homosexual, the adoption will be impossible as a matter of principle in each case" (para. 6, dissenting opinion).

two fundamental opposing lines with respect to the ways Member States approach the issue of whether the determining elements in the legal configuration of parentage should be biological truth or family life. This is clearly shown in *Schneider v Germany*,[20] where the ECtHR considered that a man's right to private life had been violated in spite of the fact that he had not been proved to be the child's biological father. In this case, paternity had been assumed by the mother's husband, who had agreed with the mother not to have the paternity of the child verified. However, shortly after the child was born the putative father applied to the German authorities for contact and information rights about the child's development. It emerged from the facts of the case that the applicant and the mother had begun a relationship while she was married to a man who lived in the United Kingdom, with whom she had a child. The woman returned to her husband after discovering that she was pregnant and the husband acknowledged paternity prior to the child's birth. According to the ECtHR, the national authorities had failed to take into account both the applicant's efforts to establish a personal and family relationship with the child (paras. 90–1) or whether his petition served the child's best interests (para. 105). The case followed the precedent set by *Anayo v Germany*[21] and is interesting for reasons that go beyond the ECtHR's declaration. It differentiated between legal systems that give preference to knowing the biological truth and consequently enable a putative father to contest paternity (normally within a fixed time period) and to establish his own, and more family life-focused systems that prevent the putative father from contesting legal paternity under any circumstances, or at least while paternity has been established in favour of another man who exercises parental responsibilities. Actually, it was the lack of consensus among Member States regarding the issue at stake that enabled the Court to declare that states have a wider margin of appreciation as to whether the putative father should be permitted to contest paternity.

20 App. No. 17080/07 (ECtHR, 15 September 2011).

21 App. No. 20578/07 (ECtHR, 21 December 2010). In this case the ECtHR recognized the relevance of the socio-legal and biological parenthood, on guaranteeing that the applicant, who was indisputably the biological father, could establish a personal relationship with the children. The German authorities had prevented him from having a personal relationship with his biological children, twins born just after his relationship with the mother ended. The mother then returned to her husband, the father of her other three children, who was also held to be the twin's father on the basis of the marital paternity presumption of §1592 of the German Civil Code. The ECtHR considered that although the applicant could not be declared the legal father because of the restriction in §1600(2) German Civil Code (see *infra* n. 23), his biological paternity was indisputable and so he could therefore have a personal relationship with the children in accordance with §1600(2) German Civil Code (paras. 60–2) (see *infra* n. 23). In reaching this decision the ECtHR took due account of the applicant's efforts to establish contact with the children, both before and after their birth, as well as their best interests (paras. 67–71).

The putative father's position in this group of cases has been debated before the ECtHR on various occasions, as the procedures to contest another man's paternity and then establish his own affect private life, part of which is formed by biological truth in its facet of personal identity. The German cases analyzed in this and the former sections are good examples of the tension between private life in its aspect of biological truth and family life in these claims. All these cases concerned parentage claims brought by putative fathers regarding children acknowledged by the mothers' new partners. In all of them the applicants' paternity claims failed because of the existence of family relationship between the children whose paternity was contested and the men legally registered as their fathers.[22] The ECtHR justified the national authorities' decision in *Kautzorv Germany* because it "was aimed at complying with the legislature's will to give an existing family relationship between the child and her legal father, who was actually living together with the child's mother and provided parental care on a daily basis, precedence over the relationship between an alleged biological father and child" (para. 74). The Court's decision in *Kautzor* was based on §1600(2) of the German Civil Code which only allows the putative father to contest paternity if *there is no social and family relationship between the child and the person registered as the father*.[23] The precept identifies the child's interests with family life, which is associated with a certain ideal of stability, legal certainty and family peace, closer to social parenting than to biological truth. These regulations have now shifted from protecting the "legitimate" or marriage-based family to protecting *de facto* families and those based on emotional and social ties.[24] This position, also endorsed by other jurisdictions like

22 However, the same conflict could also take place if the putative father claimed paternity beyond the time-limits established by law. Although the establishment of a time-limit for the exercise of parentage claims is not a common trend and it varies depending on the states, according to Principle 8, para. 3, of the *Report on Principles concerning the establishment and legal consequences of parentage*, drafted by the Committee of Experts on Family Law of the European Council (2006), "States may specify time limits to institute legal proceedings aiming to establish paternal affiliation.": http://www.coe.int/t/dghl/ standardsetting/ family/ CJ-FA_2006_4e%20Revised%20White%20Paper.pdf (last accessed: 20 May 2016).

23 Emphasis added. Among the especially interesting precepts in this section, which is called "Persons entitled to contest", are these:

"(1) The following are entitled to contest the paternity:

1 the man whose paternity exists under section 1592 nos. 1 and 2 and section 1593,

2 the man who declares in lieu of an oath that he had sexual intercourse with the mother of the child during the period of conception, (. . .)

(2) The contestation under subsection (1) no. 2 requires that there be no social and family relationship between the child and its father in the meaning of subsection (1) no. 1, nor was there a social and family relationship at the date of his death, and that the person contesting is the natural father of the child.". Translation provided by the German Federal Ministry of Justice and Consumer Protection: http://www.gesetze-im-internet.de/englisch_bgb/englisch_bgb.html#p5362 (last accessed: 25 November 2015).

24 Although the marital paternity presumption is still the most common mechanism for establishing legal paternity in many legal systems, it is becoming less relevant. The main

Greece, is in tension with the one followed in England and Wales where it is generally deemed to be most beneficial for the child to know "the truth" and thus DNA tests usually are permitted and ordered by the courts (Scherpe 2016, pp. 85–6).

The mentioned cases *Kautzor, Anayo, Schneider* and *Ahrens v Germany* are in contrast to *Różański v Poland.*[25] In this case, the putative father had not only started the legal procedures to have his paternity recognized, but he had also lived with the child before she was acknowledged by the mother's new partner. This was the decisive factor in the authorities' decision to allow biological reality to prevail over legal paternity, following an assessment of the interests of the child and her new family. It follows from this judgment that where a family relationship has existed between biological father and child, states have a positive obligation to act to enable a pre-existing family tie to develop. However, the mere fact of biological fatherhood does not automatically result in family life being proved, and when father and child have never lived together the question is dependent upon the existence of certain other factors (Choudhry and Herring 2010, p. 173). The acknowledgement of paternity by a man other than the mother's husband must therefore be examined together with the facts of the specific case. Thus, the putative father is not completely deprived of the possibility of establishing his paternity unless there are relevant reasons related to the child's best interests that make this advisable. It emerges from reading the *Kautzor, Anayo, Schneider* and *Ahrens* cases together that one of these reasons could be the absence of a family relationship between a child and her biological father, particularly if the child and the legal father already have a relationship of this kind when the putative father claims paternity. However, this conclusion should not be interpreted in absolute "all or nothing" terms: as *Anayo* and *Schneider* cases showed, even though the putative father's cannot establish paternity of the child, the courts may still take into account his efforts and diligence to keep contact with her shortly after the birth to set some type of measure in his favour. As the cases analyzed prove, Article 8 ECHR requires the contracting states to examine the question of whether maintaining contact with the child is in the child's best interests on a case-by-case basis (Büchler 2016, pp. 57–8).

The broad margin of appreciation that the ECtHR grants Member States in parentage matters, to be respected when it protects values such as family life and, as far as possible, grants a certain relevance to biological truth, can lead to questionable outcomes. This is thrown into relief by *Chavdarov v Bulgaria,*[26] in which the ECtHR relied on the doctrine of the margin of

contributory factors have undoubtedly been scientific advances, especially the biological tests which enable the presumption to be destroyed: (Freeman and Richards, 2006, pp. 72–3, and Bainham, 2008, p. 324).

25 App. No. 55339/00 (ECtHR, 18 May 2006).

26 App. No. 3465/03 (ECtHR, 21 December 2010).

appreciation to prevent the paternity of three children being awarded to the applicant, who was their biological father. The children's paternity had been established in favour of their mother's husband, as she was still married to him when she began living with the applicant. In fact, the applicant had not only lived with the mother for 13 years, in the course of which the children were born, but had also looked after them after the mother left the family home to live with a third man. The applicant then tried unsuccessfully to have his paternity recognized by the Bulgarian authorities. On the basis of the lack of consensus between Member States over the possibility of the biological father contesting the presumption of the mother's husband's paternity, the ECtHR confirmed the Bulgarian authorities' decision and considered that the applicant could have adopted the children or applied to social services to have them placed in his care. The decision has been aptly criticized because "it is somewhat difficult to follow the Chamber's reasoning" (Büchler 2016, p. 38).

IV Biological or social parenthood? Two concepts that can perhaps exist side by side

Analysis of ECtHR case law in parentage matters allows legal systems giving decisive weight to biology or "parenting by being"to be distinguished from others that are closer to the idea of social parenthood or "parenting by doing" (Masson 2006, pp. 131–55).[27] As the German cases analyzed above show, the latter systems prevent the putative father from contesting legally established paternity when there is a family relationship between the child and the person who is registered as the father. However, they leave the way open for contact rights to be set when the putative father has made considerable efforts to have his paternity recognized, and so the time lapse between the child's birth and the filing of the claim has to be taken into account.

This case law essentially recognizes that parentage is determined by various elements and that there is no reason why these should concur as they are independent spheres and each has its own weight in the child's best interests and personal identity. It should be possible to strike a balance between these elements by allowing all types of parentage claims, as more biology-based systems do, while in turn introducing clauses that allow the rigidity of the rules for establishing paternity to be curtailed in certain circumstances and thereby reconciling the respect that social parenthood deserves with the identity-based interests frequently invoked by putative fathers. These clauses allow the attribution of contact rights with

27 Or "parentage", referred to the genetic parent; "parenthood", used for the person who legally is the parent of a child, and "parental responsibility", used for what in many jurisdictions is still called "custody" or "parental authority", as already suggested by Bainham (1999, pp. 25–46, 2005, pp. 88–90) and endorsed recently by Scherpe (2016, p. 84).

no establishment of parentage if the putative father is able to prove the existence of prior family ties, a close personal relationship with the child or his considerable efforts to build this relationship. If the former cannot be proved, these clauses could also refer to the mere establishment of paternity, at least with declaratory effects.[28]

The attribution of parental responsibility or certain parental rights to persons other than legal parents is not an original proposal (Singer 2014, p. 149; Scherpe 2016, pp. 107–10)[29] and makes special sense when the applicant is the biological father who cannot be legally considered the "father" but who has put all his efforts in being considered so. The possibility of admitting claims seeking to merely ascertain or declare biological parentage is nothing new either. In the context of parentage resulting from the use of assisted reproductive technologies, several regulations have thus opted to forgo gamete donor anonymity. Children conceived in this way

28 Some of these ideas underlie the regulation of parentage in Book II of the Catalan Civil Code passed by Act 25/2010 of 29 July (Official Gazette of the Catalan Government No. 5686, 5 August 2010). Although traditionally inspired in a biology-based system that in principle allows all types of parentage claims, subjecting contestation claims to certain time-limits, it aims to protect family life by the use of different safeguards. A successful parentage claim does not therefore mean that the impact of the changes to the child's legal status cannot be limited should circumstances require, when some of the circumstances in Article 235–14.1 Catalan Civil Code concur:

"a) If the parent has been convicted by final judgement in criminal proceedings because of the relationships that have brought about the parentage.

b) If the parentage claimed has been legally declared with the opposition of the defendant parent.

c) If the recognition has been carried out in bad faith or with abuse of rights."

In these cases, the effects of the declaration of parentage are limited to "the mere establishing of this state" (Article 235–14.1 Catalan Civil Code) which, moreover, "produces no civil consequences in the favour of the parent, who is always obliged to look after and maintain the child" (Article 235–14.2 Catalan Civil Code) (Translated by the author from the original). These limits can also operate when a claim contesting parentage is brought precisely because extra-judicial recognition has not been possible, in the absence of one or more of the legal requirements (Article 235–12, Nos. 2–4, Catalan Civil Code). Parentage is established in all these circumstances, but does not produce the legal effects that would generally result. According to Article 235–2.2, these effects are "parental authority, family names, maintenance and inheritance rights, and entail the assuming of parental responsibilities towards minor children and the other effects established by the law" (Author translation).

29 Quoting the Model Family Code which includes these proposals: Schwenzer, 2006, pp. 143–4. In England and Wales, the Children Act 1989, s. 2(5) and (6), already broke away from the two-parent paradigm with regard to parental responsibility and allowed more than two persons to have full parental responsibility for a child: Scherpe, 2016, p. 109. From a different approach, some legal systems already recognize that the person acting as the social father (i.e. the step-father) has contact rights or even custody rights after separation or divorce of the parties or the death of the legal parent: see Budzikiewicz, 2014, pp. 160–1. In Catalonia this question was addressed in 2011 by Article 236–14 and 236–15 Catalan Civil Code.

can identify the donors when they are sufficiently mature and this does not mean that a legal parent–child relationship is established between them.[30] The same happens in the context of adoption, in which the possibility of adoptees to identify their biological parents involves no change to the parentage established by the adoption.[31]

Beyond these specific examples of parentage dissociation, the German legal system provides another good example of the possibility of decoupling the different spheres of parentage by recognizing the role of biological parentage. This is to be found in the Act of 26 March 2008 enabling paternity to be ascertained regardless of any contestation claim. This Act amended §1598a German Civil Code[32] and was a response to the German Federal Constitutional Court judgment of 13 February 2007 that sought to adapt positive law to the issues raised by genetic tests that were carried out clandestinely, that is, either without the knowledge or the consent of one or more of the interested parties (Lamarca 2008, pp. 1–14). Since the right to know one's origins is given increasing weight in the jurisprudence of the ECtHR, there is likely to be some development on declaratory claims in the future.

30 In Europe alone we find numerous examples: Article 4 of the Swedish Act No. 1140 (1984), replaced by Act No. 351 (2006); §20(2) of Austria's Act 275/1992; Article 27 of Switzerland's Act RS 810.11 (1998); §2–7 of Norway's Act No. 100 (2003); Holland's *Wet donorgegevens kunstmatige bevruchting* (2004); the UK's Statutory Instruments 2004 No. 1511, and s. 23 of Finland's Lag om assisterad befruktning (2006). In Spain, where the general rule still is the anonymity of the donor, in the exceptional cases when his identity can be disclosed, parentage neither can be established: see Article 5.5 and 8.3 of Spain's Act 14/2006 of 26 May on Human Assisted Reproductive Technologies (Official Gazette, *BOE*, No. 126, 27 May 2006).

31 See, among others, Article 180, ss. 4 and 6, of the Spanish Civil Code and Article 235–49.2 Catalan Civil Code.

32 According to this section, entitled "Claim to consent to a genetic examination to ascertain natural parentage":

"(1) To clarify the natural parentage of the child,
1 the father may require mother and child,
2 the mother may require father and child, and
3 the child may require both parents
to consent to a genetic paternity test and to acquiesce in the taking of a genetic sample appropriate for the test. The sample must be taken in compliance with the recognised principles of science.

(2) On the application of a person entitled to clarify, the family court must substitute consent that has not been given and order acquiescence in the taking of a sample.

(3) The court suspends the proceeds if and as long as the clarification of the natural parentage would result in a considerable adverse effect on the best interests of the minor child which would be unreasonable for the child even taking into account the concerns of the person entitled to clarify.

(4) "A person who has consented to a genetic paternity test and has given a genetic sample may require the person entitled to clarify who has had a paternity test made to permit inspection of the genetic paternity test report or to provide a copy. The family court decides disputes arising from the claim under sentence 1." Source: n. 23.

V Closing remarks: The need to accommodate biological, social and legal parenthood

The parentage claims that have reached the ECtHR show that traditional systems for establishing paternity have been rendered obsolete by new family models. These cases confirm that parentage is not and cannot be a straightforward concept, as all its spheres can play a role in the child's best interests. In the current context, the role of legislation is to accommodate as far as possible the biological, legal and social spheres of parentage. Acknowledging that biological fathers whose paternity cannot be legally established can have parental responsibility or contact rights with regard to their children or recognizing declaratory claims that merely seek to ascertain parentage are both moves in this direction. If parentage is approached as a complex institution, prejudices that hold that the child's best interests are always and only ever in line with the matching of legal parentage and biological truth can be overcome, as well as others that, in contrast, assume that the marital paternity presumption is always made in the child's best interests, regardless of biological truth.[33]

These proposals are more coherent and more respectful of greater heterogeneity among families and are in contrast to those that necessarily assign the same legal status to three or more parental figures, irrespective of their roles vis-à-vis the child and their contribution (genetic, gestational or simply intentional) to her birth. Although the vast majority of legal systems restrict the number of legal parent–child relationships to two, outside of Europe the possible existence of multiple parent–child relationships has already been adopted by some legislatures based on child's best interest[34] or on parent's intention,[35] or raised before the courts with regard to female same-sex couples using non-anonymous sperm donors (Vonk 2004; Jacobs 2007, and Dimsey 2008, pp. 101–11). In *AA. v B.B.* [2007] ONCA 2, an appeal court in the province of Ontario (Canada) established the parentage of a five-year-old child with respect to three persons: the two women that had used artificial insemination (one was the genetic, gestational and legal mother from birth and the other was her partner) and a male friend who had provided the sperm and was frequently present in the child's environment. Although the legislation applicable to the case was based on the idea of a sole mother and a sole father, the court recognized the claim on the basis of an interpretation which was considered compatible with social

33 It has been said that case law in the United Kingdom has endorsed the former position, which is exemplified by the strong association between paternity and financial responsibility enshrined in the Child Support Act (1991): (Freeman and Richards, 2006, p. 75). Critical of this position in Spain (Barber, 2006, p. 129; Quicios 2014, p. 33, and Díaz, 2015, p. 6). To quote Quicios, "Biological truth, yes, but only when it is backed by an interest worthy of protecting, not biological truth for its own sake" (Author translation).

34 See s. 7612(c) of the California Family Code.

35 See s. 30 of the Family Law Act of British Columbia, only referred to cases of ART.

reality (paras. 20–1).[36] *AA. v B.B.* is not an isolated case: on 22 April 2015 an administrative authority, the registry of persons in the province of Buenos Aires (Argentina), agreed to the paternal recognition applied for by a sperm donor and family friend concerning a child whose double maternity had already been established in favour of a married couple consisting of two women. The provincial director of the register of persons argued that this neither removed nor contradicted any existing parentage but instead incorporated the father figure, which had the mothers' express agreement (Disposition No. 20 62). Among other arguments the disposition alluded to the child's right to her identity, which it related to her best interests, and to the non-existence of a *numerus clausus* concerning the number of persons in a parent–child relationship.[37] In spite of the proposal's indisputable originality, multiple legal parentage has received serious critiques, mainly based on the reasons for fearing that as the number of legal parents increases, so do potential conflicts (Budzikiewicz 2014, pp. 164–5). However, the former assumption is not necessarily correct, since the number of options regarding decisions taken in the child's benefit does not necessarily increase with the number of holders of parental responsibility. There are situations where having more than two persons in a parental capacity indeed will be in the best interest of the child, and also in the best interest of the adults concerned. Assuming that multiple parenting will, while not the norm, become increasingly more common (Scherpe 2016, pp. 110–12 and 118), maybe the success of future proposals raises in attributing to each parental figure a different legal status, depending on the roles developed in effect regarding the child.

What is clear from ECtHR case law is that the Court's concern for child's best interests and her social and biological reality may explain why no

36 The case originated in an application from the partner that was the "social mother", who had lived with the legal mother for over ten years. She rejected the option of adopting the child because if this came to fruition the man would lose his status as the child's father, and none of the three parent figures envisaged the actual outcome. An institution supporting the traditional family appealed against the judgment in the Supreme Court of Canada, but the appeal was denied for procedural reasons: see *Alliance for Marriage and Family v A.A.* [2007] SCC 40, 3 SCR 124. For comments on the case, see Laviolette, 2007, pp. 665–89. Until then the only question raised had been whether a third party, who was not strictly a "donor" and who could not therefore be considered the legal father, could have contact rights regarding the child. That did not involve a triple parentage, as this had not been established with respect to the gestational mother's partner, who was acting as the *de facto* mother: see *J. McD. v P.L. and B.M.* [2009] IESC 81, in which the Irish Supreme Court recognized this right for the male homosexual friend of a lesbian couple, even though the parties had signed an agreement before the conception in which the man had committed himself to donating sperm and then behaving as the baby's uncle ("favourite uncle", according to the judgment).

37 The former Argentinian Civil Code, which was applicable to the case, did not contain a provision similar to Article 558.II of the Civil and Commercial Code approved by Law 26.994 of 1 October 2014 and in force since 1 August 2015, which states that "No person can have more than two parents, whatever the nature of the parentage may be."

absolute right to determine paternity has been established yet (Choudhry and Herring 2010, pp. 182–5). Therefore, the case law analyzed in this chapter grants Member States a wide margin of appreciation with the aim of respecting the more biological or social conceptions on which the legal establishment of parentage is based. Far from propagating a straightforward, exclusive and excluding concept of parentage at a time when biology has become further evidence of something for which there may already be some proof, using the margin of appreciation can give biological and social elements their respective importance. Enabling the persons who are the biological but not the legal parents to build personal relationships with their children through transfer of parental responsibility, custody or contact rights, as well as allowing parentage claims aimed exclusively at declaring biological origins, are all proposals for national legislators to bear in mind (Schwenzer 2007, p. 11; Singer 2007, p. 148, and 2014, pp. 148–9; Budzikiewicz 2014, pp. 162–3, and Scherpe 2016, pp. 107–19).[38] The today's hybrid nature of parentage can be useful in other fields where parentage is discussed, such as complex cases of the mixing up or transfer of switched embryos in the context of access to assisted reproductive technologies,[39] as well as in cases of "deceived fathers" resulting from paternity misattribution.[40]

VI References

Bainham, A. (1999). Parentage, Parenthood and Parental Responsibility: Subtle, Elusive Yet Important Distinctions. In: Bainham, A., Day Sclater, S. and Richards, M. (eds.). *What is a Parent? A Socio-Legal Analysis.* Oxford: Hart, pp. 25–46.

Bainham, A. (2005). *Children. The Modern Law.* Bristol: Jordan.

Bainham, A. (2007). "Truth will out": Paternity in Europe. *The Cambridge Law Journal*, 66 (2), pp. 278–82.

Bainham, A. (2008). Arguments about parentage. *The Cambridge Law Journal*, 67(2), pp. 322–51.

Barber Cárcamo, R. (2006). La jurisprudencia del Tribunal Europeo de Derechos Humanos sobre acciones de filiación: análisis y prospectiva. *Derecho Privado y Constitución*, 20, pp. 105–51.

38 In favour of retaining a less strict parentage system in Spain, (Ferrer, 2006, pp. 109–36, and Quicios, 2015, pp. 270 and 288–90).

39 *Leeds Teaching Hospital NHS Trust v A.* [2003] 1 FCR 599.

40 A recent and somewhat extreme Spanish judgment upheld a child's custody in favour of the man who successfully contested his paternity when the child was three years old, two years after the couple's divorce and custody allocation in favour of the man: see Supreme Court judgment of 20 November 2013 (ECLI:ES:TS:2013:5713), according to which "The child's best interests in a real and not simply abstract sense, cannot be interpreted solely from the point of view of her biological family, but the linchpin must be located in her personal interest (. . .) And the fact is that the child has lived with the applicant for a long time" (para. 3, translated by the author from the original). The child had been under the applicant custody for ten years.

Büchler, A. (2016). The Right to Respect for Private and Family Life. In: Büchler, A. and Keller, H. (eds.). *Family Forms and Parenthood*. Antwerp: Intersentia, pp. 29–58.

Budzikiewicz, C. (2014). Contracting on Parentage. In: Boele-Woelki, K, Dethloff, N and Gephart, W. (eds.). *Family Law and Culture in Europe*. Cambridge: Intersentia, pp. 15–168.

Casadevall, J. (2012). *El Convenio Europeo de Derechos Humanos, el Tribunal de Estrasburgo y su jurisprudencia*, Valencia: Tirant lo Blanch.

Choudhry, S. and Herring, J. (2010). *European Human Rights and Family Law*. Oxford: Hart.

Díaz Martínez, A. (2015). Buena fe, retraso desleal y actos propios en el ejercicio de acciones de filiación. *Revista Doctrinal Aranzadi Civil-Mercantil*, 4, pp. 1–9.

Dimsey, M. (2008). Multi-parent Families in the 21st Century. In: Boele-Woelki and Sverdrup (eds.). *European Challenges in Contemporary Family Law*. Antwerp: Intersentia, pp. 101–12.

Farnós Amorós, E. (2016). La reproducción asistida ante el Tribunal Europeo de Derechos Humanos: de Evans c. Reino Unido a Parrillo c. Italia *Revista de Bioética y Derecho*, 36, pp. 105–23. Available online at http://revistes.ub.edu/index.php/RBD/ article/ view/15381 (Accessed: 8 April 2016).

Ferrer Riba, J. (2006). Paternidad genética y paz familiar: los límites a la impugnación y a la reclamación de la paternidad. *Revista Jurídica de Catalunya*, 3, pp. 109–36.

Freeman, T. and Richards, M. (2006). DNA Testing and Kinship: Paternity, Genealogy and the Search for the 'Truth' of our Genetic Origins. In: Ebtehaj, F., Lindley, B. and Richards, M. (eds.). *Kinship Matters*, Oxford: Hart.

Grabenwarter, C. (2014). *European Convention on Human Rights. Commentary*. München: Beck, pp. 67–95.

Jacobs, M. B. (2007). Why Just Two? Disaggregating Traditional Parental Rights and Responsibilities to Recognize Multiple Parents. *Journal of Law and Family Studies*, 9, pp. 309–39.

Keller, H. (2016). Article 8 in the system of the convention. In: Büchler A. and Keller, H. (eds.). *Family Forms and Parenthood. Theory and Practice of Article 8 ECHR in Europe*. Antwerp: Intersentia, pp. 1–28.

Lamarca i Marquès, A. (2008). Autonomía privada e intervención pública en las acciones de filiación. La reforma del BGB. *InDret*, 3, pp. 1–14. Available online at http://www.indret.com/pdf/561_es.pdf. (Accessed: 25 November 2015).

Laviolette, N. (2007). Dad, Mom and Mom: The Ontario Court of Appeal's Decision in A.A. v. B.B. *La Revue du Barreau Canadien*, 86, pp. 665–89.

Masson, J. (2006). Parenting by Being; Parenting by Doing – In Search of Principles for Founding Families. In: Spencer, J. R. and Du Bois-Pedain, A. (eds.). *Freedom and Responsibility in Reproductive Choice*. Oxford, Oregon: Hart, pp. 131–55.

Oliveira Pais, S. (2013). The Protection of Fundamental Rights in Europe before and after the Accession of the European Union to the European Convention on Human Rights. In: Iliopoulos-Strangas, J., Pereira da Silva, V. and Potacs, M. (eds.). *The Accession of the European Union to the ECHR. The impact on the protection of fundamental rights in Europe*. Baden-Baden: Nomos, pp. 95–106.

Quicios Molina, S. (2014). *Determinación e impugnación de la filiación*. Navarra: Aranzadi.

Quicios Molina, S. (2015). Casos recientes que plantean el difícil equilibrio entre la búsqueda de la verdad biológica y la estabilidad del estado civil de filiación. *Derecho Privado y Constitución*, 29, pp. 263–303.

Sales i Jardí, M. (2015). *La vida familiar en la jurisprudencia del Tribunal Europeo de Derechos Humanos: una interpretación constructiva.* Barcelona: Bosch.

Scherpe, J. (2016). *European Family Law. The Present and Future of European Family Law,* Vol. IV. Cheltenham: Elgar.

Schwenzer, I. (2006). *Model Family Code – From a Global Perspective.* Antwerpen: Intersentia.

Schwenzer, I. (2007). *Tensions between legal, biological and social conceptions of parentage.* Antwerpen: Intersentia.

Singer, A. (2007). Between genetic and social parenthood – a legal dilemma: Establishment of legal parenthood in Sweden. In: Von Spickhoff, A. et al. (eds.). *Streit um die Abstammung:ein europäischer Vergleich.* Gieseking: Bielefeld, 2007, pp. 139–48.

Singer, A. (2014). The Right of the Child to Parents. In: Boele-Woelki, K., Dethloff, N. and Gephart, W. (eds.). *Family Law and Culture in Europe.* Antwerp: Intersentia, pp. 135–50.

Stein, T. (2012). The notion of the term family on European level with a focus on the case law of the European Court of Human Rights and the European Court of Justice. In: Verbeke, A.L. et al. (eds.). *Confronting the frontiers of family and succession law. Liber Amicorum Walter Pintens.* Antwerp: Intersentia, pp. 1375–92.

Vonk, M. (2004). One, two or three parents? Lesbian co-mothers and a known donor with family life under Dutch law. *International Journal of Law, Policy and the Family,* 18(1), pp. 103–17.

Part III

The right to family life in immigration law

8 Family reunification

A tool to shape the concept of EU citizenship

Kristine Kruma[*]

I Introduction

EU citizenship has evolved over the years. At the beginning of the 1990s, the Advocate General in *Micheletti* stated that "at the present stage of development of Community law an independent definition of Community citizenship does not exist".[1] One can argue that there have not been major changes and an independent definition of EU citizenship still does not exist. However, the treatment of EU citizens in certain respects is no longer the reserved domain of the Member States. The CJEU has incrementally strengthened the status of EU citizenship on the basis of Articles 20 and 21 TFEU. By arguing that EU citizenship has over the years obtained fundamental status of EU law, the Court has opened further debate over the concept of EU citizenship and the functions attached to it. In addition, specific secondary legislation has evolved over time to codify the judgements of the CJEU.

The stronger the status of EU citizenship, the better the rights protection available to individuals. The hypothesis behind this affirmation is that the concept of EU citizenship itself might offer different insights on the rights to be claimed by individuals. This is especially relevant in cases of family or private life in so-called "purely internal situations". It is in this context that the EU can offer better treatment to individuals in comparison with human rights mechanisms. At the same time, some challenges remain regarding concepts such as reverse discrimination and the notion of "substance of rights".

* Pro-rector of the Riga Graduate School of Law and former Judge of the Constitutional Court of Latvia and Judge ad hoc of the European Court of Human Rights. Kristine Kruma sadly passed away on 4 July 2016.

1 Opinion of Advocate General Tesauro in Case C-369/90 *Mario Vicente Micheletti and others v Delegacion del Gobierno en Cantabria* EU:C:1992:47. It should be noted that the European Commission does not make such comparisons between national and Union citizenship, see Third Commission Report on Citizenship of the Union COM (2001) 506 final, 9.

This chapter aims to illuminate current tendencies in regulating family reunification issues.[2] It will start by outlining the concept of EU citizenship. Next follows a discussion of recent case law on family reunification contributing to the concept of EU citizenship. Finally, possible avenues for further development either at the CJEU or Member States will be explored.

II The concept of EU citizenship

Nationality originated with the development of the modern nation-State. According to Article 2 of the European Convention on Nationality, "nationality" refers to the legal bond between a person and a State without any indication of the person's ethnic origin. However, growing global migration and travelling have led to situations where there might be legal bonds with several States, e.g., one's country of origin and the country of domicile. These developments have facilitated the emergence of EU citizenship and its gradual strengthening.

The concept of EU citizenship is unfamiliar to the international community and is as yet treated with caution. It differs from both the concept of national citizenship and the regulation of nationality in international law. After almost ten years since the introduction of the concept in the Treaty, the CJEU arrived at the conclusion that EU citizenship affords important status: "Under Article 17 (1) EC, every person holding the nationality of a Member State is to be a citizen of the Union. Union citizenship is destined to be the fundamental status of nationals of the Member States."[3]

This proclamation, in turn, fundamentally affects how citizenship is positioned in the general Treaty system. If EU citizenship is deemed fundamental, then it cannot be interpreted as *lex generalis* that is subject to change or modifications by some *lex specialis* (La Torre 1998, p. 436). This is in line with the argument put forward by Advocate General La Pergola, who, already in *Martinez Sala*, insisted that the right to move and reside is not created by directives and that the directives only concern the actual exercise, not the existence, of the citizen's right.[4] Moreover, if the status of EU citizen is "destined" to be fundamental, the implication is that the construction of that status and the rights attached to it has not been completed. Fundamentality of EU citizenship is of direct relevance for the rights of individuals to move and reside freely in the European Union without necessarily being active economically or having complied with all necessary formalities. In

2 In this chapter, the notion of "family reunification" is used broadly to refer to the living together of family members, regardless of whether they are EU citizens or TCNs. Therefore, it is not reduced to the notion of family reunification according to Council Directive 2003/86/EC of 22 September 2003 on the right to family reunification [2003] OJ L251/12.

3 Case C-184/99 *Grzelczyk* EU:C:2001:458, para. 31.

4 Case C-85/96 *Martinez Sala v Freistaat Bayern* EU:C:1998:217, para. 18.

Baumbast, which also concerned aspects of family reunification, the Court held:

> Moreover, the Treaty on European Union does not require that citizens of the Union pursue a professional or trade activity, whether as an employed or self-employed person, in order to enjoy the rights provided in Part Two of the EC Treaty, on citizenship of the Union. Furthermore, there is nothing in the text of that Treaty to permit the conclusion that citizens of the Union who have established themselves in another Member State in order to carry on an activity as an employed person there are deprived, where that activity comes to an end, of the rights which are conferred on them by the EC Treaty by virtue of citizenship.[5]

The emphasis in *Baumbast* was on the presence of a cross-border element, which remained important for the applicability of EU law. At the same time, scope is left for further development, especially in the context of the principle of non-discrimination. As noted by Advocate General Geelhoed in *Bidar*:

> with respect to matters coming within the scope ratione materiae of the Treaty, citizenship itself may provide a basis for bringing certain matters within that scope where the objectives pursued by the national measure correspond with those pursued by the Treaty or secondary legislation.[6]

Indeed, the approach suggested has allowed the Court to introduce new tests to the advantage of EU citizens. In this context three closely interrelated issues arise: First is the possibility of extending EU competencies related to family reunification cases. In this context, the tests developed by the Court are of importance; i.e., a test of "substantive core rights"[7] of EU citizens, to which Member States are obliged to pay "due regard to EU law". Second, related to the foregoing, is the role of secondary legislation and the scope of application of the Charter. The third issue is a more recent phenomenon regarding reverse discrimination. Not only have national courts been approached with questions on reverse discrimination, but the CJEU has as well. The CJEU has argued that its jurisdiction is limited to cases that are purely internal but in which the genuine enjoyment of the substance of citizenship rights is in jeopardy.[8] Otherwise, the ECHR should apply.[9]

5 Case C-413/99 *Baumbast and R* EU:C:2002:493, para. 83. One can note that the radical shift in the Court's approach coincides with release of the proposal for Directive 2004/38 by the Commission. See COM (2001) 257 final.

6 Case C-209/03 *The Queen ex parte Dany Bidar v London Borough of Ealing, Secretary of State for Education* EU:C:2005:169, para. 52.

7 Case C-34/00 *Ruiz Zambrano* EU:C:2011:124, para. 42.

8 Case C-256/11 *Dereci and Others* EU:C:2011:734, paras 63–9.

9 Ibid. para. 72.

III The right of family reunification of EU citizens

Although the definition of "family" does not fall within the competence of the EU, free movement of EU citizens does. Therefore, the Court has been asked to resolve different cases in which denial of family reunification might infringe the rights of EU citizens on the basis of the Treaties or the rights of family members grounded on Directive 2004/38.[10] These concern the right of entry and residence, as well as the prohibition of expulsion.

Article 3(1) establishes that the Directive applies to all EU citizens who move to or reside in a Member State and to their family members. In addition, and according to their national legislation, Member States should facilitate entry and residence of certain groups of persons:

(a) any other family members, irrespective of their nationality, not falling under the definition in point 2 of Article 2 who, in the country from which they have come, are dependants or members of the household of the Union citizen having the primary right of residence, or where serious health grounds strictly require the personal care of the family member by the Union citizen;
(b) the partner with whom the Union citizen has a durable relationship duly attested.

Although Member States are under an obligation to facilitate family reunification according to Directive 2004/38, the rather narrow definition of the family in the Directive could create problematic situations in the future. The question remains as to how far the Court will go in interpreting the scope of the obligation to facilitate family reunification. In any case, it should be stressed that this is exactly the context in which the EU standards might become higher compared to the standards established by the ECtHR because, according to the ECHR regime, Member States are not under an obligation to facilitate family reunification, but rather only to fulfil the standards established by the Convention and ECtHR case law.

For instance, the common household requirement must be met at the time of application for family reunification. The Court dealt with such a situation in *Diatta*,[11] long before the adoption of the Directive, where the question was whether one Mrs Diatta could request an extension of her residence permit if she was no longer living with her husband. The Court ruled that "[T]he marital relationship cannot be regarded as dissolved so long as it has not been terminated by the competent authority. It is not

10 European Parliament and Council Directive 2004/38/EC of 29 April 2004 on the right of citizens of the Union and their family members to move and reside freely within the territory of the Member States [2004] OJ L158/77.

11 Case 267/83 *Aissatou Diatta v Land Berlin* EU:C:1985:67, para. 20.

dissolved merely because the spouses live separately, even where they intend to divorce at a later date."[12]

Directive 2004/38 follows a similar rationale to that of conclusions drawn from CJEU case law, including *MRAX*.[13] In this case, the Court was confronted with the situation in which EU legislation did not specify the measures that a Member State may take should a TCN married to an EU citizen wish to enter the EU without possession of a valid identity card, passport or visa. The Court ruled that a visa must be issued without delay at the border.[14] A different interpretation would be contrary to the importance the legislature has attached to protection of family life. Therefore, the Court placed spouses of EU citizens, even when they are TCNs, on equal footing with EU citizens.[15] By adopting this approach EU law goes beyond standards accepted under human rights law, which does not provide for an obligation to facilitate a right to enter for TCNs.

In *Akrich*[16] the CJEU came to the conclusion that when an EU citizen returns to the Member State of nationality in order to work and that person's spouse does not enjoy rights provided in EU legislation because the spouse has not previously resided lawfully within the territory of that Member State, the authorities must, in assessing the spouse's application, display

12 Ibid. para. 20.

13 Case C-459/99 *MRAX* EU:C:2002:461. The MRAX case involved the annulment of a Belgian circular from the Ministries of Interior and Justice concerning the procedure for publication of banns of marriage and the documents which must be produced in order to obtain a visa for the purpose of contracting a marriage in Belgium or to obtain a visa for the purpose of reuniting a family on the basis of a marriage contracted abroad. The circular was contested on three main grounds: (1) whether a Member State can send back foreigners at the border, subject to a visa requirement if they are married to a Community national and attempt to enter without being in possession of an identity document or visa; (2) whether a Member State may refuse to issue a residence permit to the spouse of a Community national who has entered their territory unlawfully and expel him; (3) whether a Member State may neither withhold a residence permit nor expel the foreign spouse of a Community national who has entered national territory lawfully but whose visa has expired when application was made for that permit. The applicants claimed that these regulations are contrary to relevant provisions of Directive 68/360, Directive 73/148, Directive 64/221 and Regulation No. 2317/95. The CJEU confirmed their position that an expulsion order cannot be issued on the sole ground that a visa has expired.

14 Ibid. para. 60.

15 See also Case C-503/03 *Commission v Spain* EU:C:2006:74. The CJEU had to balance the effectiveness and the very idea of Schengen Information System against the right to family reunification.

16 Case C-109/01 *Akrich* EU:C:2003:491. The case concerned a Moroccan citizen. He was refused permission to remain in the UK and was subsequently deported on several occasions as a result of criminal offences committed. Whilst residing unlawfully in the UK he married a British citizen. In accordance with his wishes he was finally deported from the UK to Ireland, where his spouse had been established. After half a year they both intended to return to the UK. The authorities refused Mr Akrich the right to enter the UK on the grounds that he had entered into a marriage of convenience in order to circumvent the provisions for entry and residence of nationals of non-EU Member States.

regard to the right to respect for family life under Article 8 of the ECHR, provided the marriage is genuine.[17]

A similar approach was adopted by the CJEU in *Eind*, where no reference to the ECHR was even necessary.[18] The CJEU noted that the approach by the Netherlands led to a situation where a national of a Member State could be deterred from leaving the respective Member State to take up employment in the territory of another Member State if they were not certain of being able to return to the State of origin, irrespective of whether they were going to engage in economic activity there. That deterrent effect would also derive from not being able, on returning to the Member State of origin, to continue living together with close relatives. Thus, a person in the situation of Ms Eind enjoys the right to reside with her father as long as she has not reached the age of 21 years or remains dependent on him. The fact that a TCN who is a member of an EU citizen's family did not, before residing in the Member State where the worker was employed, have a right under national law to reside in the Member State of which the worker is a national has no bearing on the determination of that national's right to reside in the latter State. The important fact in this case was that the father used his free movement rights in the EU. Therefore, there was no need to apply the ECHR because (1) the cross-border test was satisfied (2) family reunification is seen as a cornerstone for the facilitation of free movement of EU citizens (or workers as in *Eind*).

Although the case was not decided as a "citizenship" case but rather as a "worker" case, the principles outlined are also important for current citizenship-related family reunion cases. It is interesting to compare the Court's approach in this case to the provisions of the ECHR. The question arises whether the outcome of the case would have been different if the Charter had been binding when the case was decided. Would a Member State have been invited to apply the Charter Article 7 or would the Court rather have referred to the "substance of rights" concept and concluded that EU citizens' rights were not endangered?

Metock is important for the interpretation of Article 3(1) of Directive 2004/38. Article 3(1) of the Directive stipulates that the Directive is applicable to all EU citizens who move to or reside in a Member State other than that of their nationality and to their family members who accompany or

17 Ibid. para. 60.

18 Case C-291/05 *Eind* EU:C:2007:771. The case concerned Mr Eind, a Dutch national who went to work in the UK. He was joined there by his daughter arriving directly from Surinam. She was granted residence rights as a family member of an EU citizen. Upon return to the Netherlands, Mr Eind was no longer economically active due to a health condition. He applied for a residence permit on behalf of his daughter as a family member of an EU citizen, but the Dutch authorities refused his application. The reasoning for that decision was that despite the fact that Mr Eind worked in the UK, he was not economically active upon return to the Netherlands. Therefore, he no longer qualified as a Community national according to law.

join them. The case concerned a number of non-EU Member State nationals who petitioned the Court for the right to family reunion with spouses who were EU citizens. The question arose whether spouses should be entitled to reunification if they have not previously lawfully resided in another EU Member State.[19]

According to the interpretation given by the CJEU, Directive 2004/38 does not require that the EU citizen must have already founded a family at the time of moving to the host Member State. The CJEU noted that Article 3(1) shall be interpreted to encompass family members who entered the host Member State with the EU citizen and to those who reside with the EU citizen in that Member State. It is not necessary to distinguish between nationals of non-EU Member States who entered that Member State before or after the EU citizen or who became family members before or after the citizen moved. Moreover, the Directive does not include conditions regarding the place where the marriage of the EU citizen and non-EU Member State citizen took place. This significantly expands the scope of application of the Directive. The requirement of the Directive "to accompany or join them" does not require a marriage to be registered before an EU citizen arrives in the host Member State, for example. It also does not require legal residence before marriage in another Member State. Although *Metock* concerned TCNs, it allows one to conclude that even in the case of an EU citizen who has not moved in the EU but is married to another EU citizen who did so, the couple can rely on EU law. This construction would lead to a situation when EU law could be invoked in so-called "purely internal situations". This bolsters the category of EU citizenship as a fundamental status in one sense, but it also increases the number of situations in which the existing "cross-border test" becomes artificial and needless. Apart from that, national courts would have to be particularly cautious to ensure that cases of marriages of convenience are effectively identified.

19 Case C-127/08 *Metock* EU:C:2008:449. Ms N. Ikeng had acquired UK nationality and in 2006 was joined by Mr Metock in Ireland where he was refused asylum in 2007. They had had a relationship in Cameroon since 1994. They had two children. The couple married in Ireland in 2006. Mr. Ikogho arrived in Ireland in 2004 and was refused asylum in 2005. His wife, a UK national, had resided in Ireland since 1996. They met in 2004 and married in 2006. Mr Chinedu arrived in Ireland in 2005 and was refused asylum in 2006. Ms Babucke, a German national, resided in Ireland. They married in 2006. Mr Igboanuse arrived in Ireland in 2004 and was refused asylum in 2005. Ms Batkowska, a Polish national, had worked in Ireland since April 2006. They married in 2006.The Court also noted that if Member States were to retain exclusive competence to regulate first access to EU territory of family members from a non-EU Member State this would lead to a paradoxical outcome if compared to Directive 2003/86. The latter Directive authorizes entry and residence of the spouse of a non-EU Member State national who has not been resident in the EU. Therefore, family reunification of non-EU Member State couples would be treated better than in cases of EU citizens. See also Case C-1/05 *Yunying Jia v Migrationsverket* EU:C:2016:381.

However, in cases of divorce the situation is different, especially if the TCN has not sought free movement rights. Even if parents have joint custody over children, that factor would not be helpful to seek residence rights on the basis of EU law.[20]

IV Applying new tests

A Cases of dual citizens

There are several groups of persons in relation to whom application of EU law is still developing. For instance, this is the case of dual nationals (Kruma 2005, p. 364). The application of the substance of rights test has been acknowledged as relevant. The approach in this regard of the CJEU crystallised in *McCarthy*.[21] In this case the Court was confronted with the question of whether a dual Irish and English national who had never exercised free movement rights could rely on EU law against the State of nationality, the UK, in order to request permission for her husband to remain in the country.[22] Since Directive 2004/38 requires a cross-border element, the CJEU held that it was not applicable to the case, and focused on the interpretation of Article 21 TFEU. The Court noted that just because a person has not made use of the right to freedom of movement does not mean, for that reason alone, that such situations are necessarily purely internal. The Court applied the test of "deprivation of genuine enjoyment of the substance of the rights" conferred on EU citizens, which had been upheld in *Ruiz Zambrano*.[23] The Court concluded, however, that, in the case of Mrs McCarthy, no measure at issue had the effect of depriving her of genuine enjoyment of the substance of the rights associated with her status as a Union citizen,

20 Case C-40/11 *Iida* EU:C:2012:691, where the CJEU found decisive lack of co-habitation rather than the fact that the spouses' marriage was not dissolved and both parents had contact with the child. The CJEU interpreted Article 2(2)(a) of Directive 2004/38 and Article 3(1) of Directive 2003/109 requiring family members of a Union citizen moving to or residing in a Member State other than that of which he is a national should accompany or join him. See para. 61. See also paras. 55–6 in relation to dependence of a child as a basis for family reunification. Compare this approach to *Baumbast supra* n. 5, in relation to residence rights of R.

21 Case C-434/09 *McCarthy* EU:C:2011:277. For comparison see Case C-456/12 *O. and B.* ECLI:EU:C:2014:135, para. 46.

22 *McCarthy supra* n. 21. The case concerned Mrs McCarthy, a British and Irish national who had always resided in England. Her husband was a Jamaican national who had no right to reside in England. The applicant invoked her EU citizenship and Irish nationality to obtain residence rights for herself and her husband. She applied for Irish nationality only after marriage to get a passport. In this context the case concerns family unification that is intended to be achieved circuitously via EU law because domestic law in the UK does not permit unification. The important factor was that Mrs McCarthy did not cross the border at any time.

23 *Ruiz Zambrano supra* n. 7.

or of impeding the exercise of her right to move and reside freely within the territory of other Member States, in accordance with Article 21 TFEU.[24] The Court argued that if the genuine enjoyment of the substance of the rights conferred is not affected or impeded, EU law cannot be invoked (Kruma 2014, pp. 150–1).[25]

Later on, in *Dereci*,[26] the CJEU considerably limited the application of Article 20 TFEU. The Court noted that:

> It follows that the criterion relating to the denial of the genuine enjoyment of the substance of the rights conferred by virtue of European Union citizen status refers to situations in which the Union citizen has, in fact, to leave not only the territory of the Member State of which he is a national but also the territory of the Union as a whole.[27]

This means, as the Court further explained, that the criterion is specific if it relates to situations in which the right of residence may not be refused to a TCN who is a family member of a Member State national, as otherwise the effectiveness of EU citizenship enjoyed by that national would be undermined.[28] Therefore, the Court looks at the facts of the case in great detail and only in very exceptional cases invokes the "substance of rights" rule. One can argue that the Court's ruling might have been different, at least on several factual situations, if it had been argued that the EU citizens were financially dependent on TCNs. Should financial dependence be established, then the possibility that expulsion of a TCN would indirectly lead to forcing EU citizens to leave the EU becomes relevant. Although the children of the first applicant were at risk of being separated from their father, this was insufficient to invoke EU law. Alternatively, the ruling might have also been different if families had crossed the border and then returned to Austria.

The approach of the Court, however, is not to exclude application of the provisions of the Charter or the provisions of the ECHR that form part of the general principles of law. However, the CJEU refused to apply them in the present case by reference to Article 51 of the Charter. Since the situation of Mr Dereci et al. was qualified as purely internal and did not come within the scope of application of EU law, the rules of the Charter did not apply. The Court advised the national court itself to take into consideration the obligations on it that derive from Article 8 ECHR. This, in a way, represents a departure from the Court's approach in *Carpenter*, where it relied on Article 8 of the ECHR itself.[29]

24 *McCarthy supra* n. 21, para. 49.
25 See also the next section.
26 Dereci *supra* n. 8.
27 Ibid. para. 66.
28 Ibid. para. 67.
29 Case C-60/00 *Carpenter* EU:C:2002:434.

It can be argued that situations involving TCNs are more complex because they involve application of not only EU Treaty rights but also rights arising from agreements with third countries. Just such a situation arose in *Mesbah*.[30] The case brought to the CJEU concerned a Moroccan national who was the mother-in-law of a worker originally from Morocco living in Belgium. He had acquired dual Belgian–Moroccan nationality. His mother-in-law applied for social security support but was denied on the grounds that only family members who are Belgian nationals can have access to social security. However, according to the Moroccan–EC Cooperation Agreement, workers of Moroccan nationality and the members of their families who live with them enjoy the same treatment as nationals with regards social security in the Member State where they are employed. This meant that their family members could have access to social security on the basis of Article 41 of the Agreement. Belgium did not dispute the existence of dual nationality but denied a Moroccan national from deriving benefits from both nationalities. The Belgian authorities argued that a claimant who could derive benefits from both nationalities would enjoy more rights than EU citizens who did not qualify for social security benefits and Moroccan citizens who did not enjoy the benefits of Belgian nationality.

Therefore, in a situation where a dual national having the nationality of a Member State and a non-Member State resides in the EU, both nationalities must be taken into account or the Court must invoke the principle of dominant nationality. According to the Court, Belgium is entitled to refuse to pay social security if, in accordance with national law, a person is considered only a Belgian citizen. However, the interpretation of the Court is not convincing. The issue cannot be resolved on the basis of Belgian law alone because the rights of Moroccan nationals are granted at the EU level.

The *Mesbah* case is exceptional if compared to other cases of dual nationality. The Court will certainly have the occasion to reformulate its position in cases of dual nationals if one of the nationalities is that of a non-EU Member State.[31] All in all, dual nationals trigger EU rights more often, even

30 Case C-179/98 *Belgian State v Fatna Mesbah* EU:C:1999:549. See also Joined Cases C-7/10 and 9/10 *Staatssecretaris van Justitie v Tayfun Kahveci, Osman Inan* EU:C:2012:180. The latter case concerned Turkish nationals who were naturalized in the Netherlands but retained their Turkish nationality. They were joined by family members who subsequently faced deportation orders due to criminal convictions in the Netherlands. They relied on Article 7 of Decision No. 1/80 of the EEC–Turkey Association Council providing for the right of the members of the family of a Turkish worker to join him. The question to the CJEU was whether Turkish nationals, who are at the same time nationals of the Netherlands, are entitled to invoke their rights as Turkish nationals according to Decision No. 1/80. The Court gave a positive answer and in its judgment differentiated the case from the situation in *Mesbah*. See in particular para. 37 and Case C-416/96 *Nour Eddline El-Yassini* EU:C:1999:107, paras. 49–62.

31 *Staatssecretaris van Justitie supra* n. 30. According to the Opinion of Advocate General Sharpston, delivered on 20 October 2011, Decision No 1/80 of the EEC–Turkey Association

when the claims are addressed to the country of nationality. Therefore, it can be argued that both international law and EU law tolerate dual nationality as a relevant phenomenon. Yet the approach in each differs. The CJEU does not invoke examination of the dominant nationality and effective link to decide the rights of dual nationals against their State of nationality. However, it will disregard nationality if it has been granted independently of or against a person's will.

B Cases involving children

In cases involving children, the CJEU refers to Article 20 TFEU without inquiring whether there is a cross-border situation. For instance, in *Garcia Avello* the Court referred to both Article 18 and 20 TFEU.[32] The Court's main argument was that there was a link between children and EU law when they lawfully reside in the territory of a Member State other than that of their nationality.

At the same time, the Court took a different approach in *Grunkin Paul*.[33] Here the Court emphasized that Article 18 TFEU was irrelevant because German substantive law on surnames cannot constitute discrimination on grounds of nationality. Therefore, it is rather Article 20 TFEU that would be applicable to clarify the rights of children (Kruma 2014, pp. 49–150). This was confirmed also in case of *Ruiz Zambrano* where the Court stated that: "Article 20 TFEU precludes national measures which have the effect of depriving citizens of the Union of the enjoyment of the substance the rights conferred by virtue of their status as citizens of the Union."[34]

Reference to Article 20 TFEU strengthens the application of EU law to purely internal situations at least in cases of children. Their right to reside and enjoy EU citizen rights is confirmed by their potential exercise free movement rights. It can, however, be argued that the Court's argumentation

---

Council must be interpreted as meaning that the family members of a Turkish worker duly registered in the labour force of a Member State may continue to invoke that provision even after acquiring the nationality of the host Member State while retaining his Turkish nationality.

32 Case C-148/02 *Garcia Avello* ECLI:EU:C:2003:539. The case concerned Mr. Carlos Garcia Avello, a Spanish national, and Ms. Isabelle Weber, a Belgian national, who had two children. Their children had both Spanish and Belgian nationalities. The family resided in Belgium. The case originated from the refusal of the Belgian authorities to register their children with two surnames – the mother's and the father's – in accordance with Spanish law. The Belgian authorities refused to do so because that option was not available in Belgian law.

33 Case C-353/06 *Grunkin* EU:C:2008:559. The case concerned a child born to a German couple while they were residing in Denmark. He was a dual citizen registered in Denmark with a double surname of both of his parents. However, registration of a child with two surnames of both parents was not allowed under German law. The child continued to reside in Denmark.

34 *Ruiz Zambrano supra* n. 7, para. 42.

would have been even stronger if, in these cases, the Court had referred to rights of the child and the obligation to serve children's best interests that is included in Article 24 of the Charter and the CRC. It can also be argued that reference to Article 21 would bring more consistency in applying EU law, at least in cases such as *Garcia Avello* and *Grunkin Paul*. In *Dereci*,[35] however, the situation was different. *Dereci* concerned five family situations where applicants were all TCNs who wished to be with their family members, Austrian citizens residing in Austria.[36] Their applications for residence permits were rejected and four of them were given expulsion orders.[37]

Article 20 TFEU and the concept of substance of rights would remain important when children face expulsion or are otherwise forced to leave the EU because their family members were asked to leave the country. This is the situation in cases similar to *Dereci*, such as *O. and S.*[38] which are quite complex. Ms S., a Ghanaian national and permanent resident of Finland, was married to a Finnish national. After two years she gave birth to a child who had Finnish nationality. The spouses divorced and Ms S. maintained sole custody of the child, whose father also lived in Finland. Ms S. studied in Finland and was gainfully employed. After three years, she married Mr O., a national of Côte d'Ivoire. The child of their marriage, born in Finland, has Ghanaian nationality and both spouses have joint custody. Mr O. was refused a residence permit because he could not prove secure means of subsistence. The CJEU distanced itself from drawing a final conclusion and stated that this is a matter for the national court. Although invocation of EU law would not be applicable to Mr O's case, it would still be relevant in that the family can claim the right of residence considering that the child from the first marriage was an EU citizen and that if one of the parents were expelled, the rights of the child that should be protected under EU law might be affected.

C Reverse discrimination

The cases discussed indicate that family reunification is seen as part of "substance of citizen's rights" to which the Court offers high levels of protection, although in limited fields, i.e., primarily for parents who are care-givers of dependent minors. There are arguments raised in the pertinent doctrine, *inter alia*, for the cases discussed above, that relate to the competence of the CJEU and the "division of labour" between the CJEU, national courts and the ECtHR. The arguments also concern the potential role of the Charter in further developing the concepts of "substance of rights" and "burden to

35 *Dereci supra* n. 8.

36 Their situation differed as to whether they entered lawfully or unlawfully, their place of residence at the time of application, and the type of family relationship with the EU citizen. There were also differences with regards children born in the family relationship.

37 See above section.

38 Joined Cases C-356/11 and C-357/11 *O and S* EU:C:2012:776.

move". According to the Treaties, the CJEU should preserve its role as core guardian so that the rule of law is observed in the EU (Kruma 2015, p. 371). It has been suggested that there are no sound methodological basis or doctrinal justification for the concepts mentioned in the context of Articles 18, 20 or 21 TFEU (Hailbronner and Thym 2011, pp. 1253–70).

The methodological drawbacks have been addressed by Advocate General Sharpston, who has advocated for the application of EU law to purely internal situations on the basis of fundamental rights under certain conditions. In particular she has noted significant drawbacks and the need to deal openly with the issue of reverse discrimination.[39] The current approach does not provide much legal certainty as to when the cross-border element is crucial and when the Court should decline cases for lack of a valid link to EU law. Therefore, in this context, the interpretation of the scope of application of Article 18 TFEU becomes decisive. So far, when dealing with discrimination cases at the EU level, the CJEU has applied a three-step test. First, it considers whether the contested measure falls within the scope of application of EU law. Second, it examines whether the national measure has a discriminatory effect on nationals of other Member States. Third, it determines whether that difference in treatment can be justified. (Lenaerts 2006, p. 289). The first criterion is that which has so far allowed the extension of the application of the EU law to different sectors (Jacobs 2007, p. 593). It is especially important in constructing EU citizenship as a fundamental status in the EU, as it would also include the rights of family members.

Reverting to the constructive suggestion by the Advocate General Sharpston, three conditions would be required for application of Article 18 TFEU:

1 A claim is brought by a citizen of the EU who has not availed of the free movement right but whose situation was comparable to that of other citizens;
2 The complaint of reverse discrimination would have to entail violation of a fundamental right protected under EU law, leaving the rest of the competence to the ECHR;
3 Article 18 TFEU would serve as only a subsidiary remedy, confined to situations in which national law did not afford adequate fundamental rights protection. This condition serves to maintain an appropriate balance between Member State autonomy and the "effet utile" of EU law.[40]

The approach suggested does not open the "Pandora's box" of application of EU law to purely internal situations in all cases. It is well balanced

39 *Ruiz Zambrano supra* n. 7, paras. 138–41.
40 Opinion of Advocate General Sharpston in *Ruiz Zambrano supra* n. 7, paras. 123–50, especially 144–8.

and would be applied only to protect fundamental rights. Moreover, Article 18 TFEU is seen only as a subsidiary remedy. The question that remains is whether this would require or not changing the methodology for how the applicants are considered by national courts. Family reunification claims would now concern EU citizens' rights rather than the rights of their family members. Moreover, in cases of children, Article 20 TFEU might prove more relevant. Therefore, the proposal by the Advocate General should not be seen as revolution but instead merely as the evolution of EU law.

V Conclusions

Although the test for "substance of rights" might seem unclear and its methodology is poorly explained by the Court, it has substantial potential for advancing EU citizenship as a *sui generis* status. When dealing with cases of family reunification, different articles are invoked – Article 18, 20 and 21 TFEU. In addition, Directives form another important part of the Court's argumentation, especially in cases when Article 21 TFEU is invoked.

The test of "substance of rights" falls within the ambit of EU law, and so should be further promoted to benefit EU citizens, while the concept of "reverse discrimination" requires particular consideration. Indeed, in these present times when free mobility across the borders is rather accessible, family reunification cases might offer a means to strengthen the rights of family members beyond the applicable standards of current human rights regimes.

At the same time, there are inherent limits to right to family reunification and an increasing number of internal situations affecting rights of EU citizens (Kruma 2014, pp. 151–2). Furthermore, the "substance of rights" test should not be limited to the scope of application of Charter Article 51(1). The role of the Charter should be increased, particularly because accession to the ECHR remains unclear following the negative Opinion 2/13 of the CJEU.[41]

The possibility of further development for the right to family reunification and the CJEU's approach to it will, of course, depend on political developments. Growing security concerns and talk of revising the Schengen agreement, and the circumstances surrounding "Brexit" might have repercussions for future development. Those, however, fall beyond the scope of this chapter.

References

Hailbronner, K. and Thym, D. (2011). Case C34/09, *Gerardo Ruiz Zambrano v Office national de l'emploi* (ONEm), Judgment of the Court of 8 March 2011. *Common Market Law Review*, 48, pp. 1253–70.

41 Opinion 2/13 *on EU accession to the ECHR* EU:C:2014:2454.

Jacobs, F.G. (2007). Citizenship of the European Union – A Legal Analysis. *European Law Journal*, 13, pp. 591–610.

Lenaerts, K. (2006). Union citizenship and the principle of non-discrimination on grounds of nationality. In: *Festskrift Claus Gulmann – Liber Amicorum*. Copenhagen: Thomson, pp. 289–309.

Kruma, K. (2014). *EU Citizenship, Nationality and Migrant Status. An Ongoing Challenge*. Leiden: Martinus Nijhoff Publishers.

Kruma, K. (2015). A Hopeful Transmission: Searching for Citizenship beyond the State. *European Journal of Migration and Law* 17, pp. 361–93.

La Torre, M. (1998). Citizenship, Constitution, and the European Union. In: M. La Torre, (ed.). *European Citizenship: An Institutional Challenge*. The Hague: Kluwer International Law, pp. 435–57.

9 The right to family life as a bar to the expulsion of third country nationals in the European Union

Aida Torres Pérez[*]

I Introduction

To what extent does the right to family life bar the expulsion of TCNs in the EU? The right to enter and to remain in a country is among the few rights that are still reserved to nationals. Moreover, border control is considered a prerogative of sovereign states. At the same time, the process of EU integration has contributed to restraining the state power over the internal and external borders by upholding the right to free movement and residence across the Member States; and progressively expanding the competences of the Union over immigration policy.

The right to family life is enshrined in Article 7 of the EU Charter of Fundamental Rights. In addition, there is a relevant body of secondary law that contributes to the protection of family life for TCNs. Directive 2004/38, on the right of citizens of the Union and their family members to move and reside freely within the territory of the Member States[1] (Citizenship Directive), applies to EU citizens who move to other Member States and to their families, regardless of whether the family members are EU citizens or not. As such, domestic legislation on immigration and EU legislation on free movement cross-cut each other regarding TCNs who hold family ties with moving EU citizens. Also, Directive 2003/86, on the right to family reunification[2] (Family Reunification Directive), sets the conditions under which the Member States are obliged to allow the entry of relatives of TCNs who are already lawfully residing in the EU.

In addition, Directive 2008/115, on common standards and procedures in Member States for returning illegally staying third-country nationals[3]

* Law Professor at Pompeu Fabra University, I thank Bradley Hayes for all his invaluable help.

1 European Parliament and Council Directive 2004/38/EC of 29 April 2004 on the right of citizens of the Union and their family members to move and reside freely within the territory of the Member States [2004] OJ L158/77.

2 Council Directive 2003/86/EC of 22 September 2003 on the right to family reunification [2003] OJ L251/12.

3 European Parliament and Council Directive 2008/115/EC of 16 December 2008 on common standards and procedures in Member States for returning illegally staying third-country nationals [2008] OJ L348/98.

(Return Directive), indicates that when implementing this Directive, the Member States shall take due account of family life and the best interests of the child.[4] Domestic legislation in this field is thus heavily conditioned by EU law. Since the main inquiry in this chapter regards the right to family life as a potential bar to the expulsion of TCNs who are already in EU territory, rather than the right to entry of TCNs, consideration of the right to family reunification as such will be excluded from the analysis.[5]

Since Charter Article 7 corresponds to Article 8 of the ECHR,[6] the Convention and the ECtHR case law need to be followed for the interpretation of Article 7. Indeed, the ECtHR has already developed significant case law regarding the interpretation of Article 8 as a bar to the expulsion of aliens. According to Charter Article 52(3), the EU has the authority to provide more extensive protection, but may not condone any level of protection that is lower.

In what follows, the ECtHR case law will be analyzed in order to identify the scope of protection available under Convention Article 8 and, in particular, the circumstances under which the expulsion of aliens amounts to an unjustified restriction of the right to family life. Next, I will focus on the role of the right to family life as a bar to the expulsion of TCNs in the EU. While the CJEU initially treated family life as instrumental of the rights to free movement and residence, family life has enabled the protection of TCNs under Article 21(1) TFEU. Moreover, the concern for family life has enhanced a more forceful understanding of citizenship, albeit in limited circumstances.

This chapter will conclude with some remarks arising from the comparison between the rationale of protection under the Convention and the Charter. A reading of the CJEU case law in light of family life contributes to unveiling its actual role and potential and in so doing this chapter calls for a robust understanding of residence that cannot be disentangled from family life.

II The right to family life against expulsion in the Strasbourg case law: A balancing approach

The aim of this section is to explore the extent to which the expulsion of aliens might entail a violation of the right to family life as protected by ECHR Article 8.[7] In the field of immigration, the ECtHR tends to afford a wide margin of appreciation to the states, but the state power over immigration does not go totally unrestrained (Thym 2008). The case law in this area has been evolving over time and a degree of uncertainty remains regarding the criteria formulated by the ECtHR and their application to specific cases. This section intends to systematize the relevant criteria in order to

4 Article 5 of the Return Directive.
5 See Iglesias and Carr in this volume.
6 Explanations Relating to the Charter of Fundamental Rights (2007/C 303/02), OJ C303/17.
7 See López Guerra in this book.

understand the scope of protection of the right to family life granted under Article 8 to block expulsion.

Broadly, the ECtHR acknowledges both that the Convention does not provide aliens a right to enter or reside in a particular country and that states are entitled to control entry to and residence in them.[8] At the same time, the ECtHR has declared that expelling a person from the country where close family members are living may amount to a breach of the right to respect for family life.[9] In this context, there is a need to strike a fair balance between the interests of the state in controlling immigration and the interests of individuals and their families.[10]

For the purposes of our analysis, the judgments will be classified in two main groups: those in which the reason for expulsion is conviction for a criminal offence (criminal conviction cases),[11] and those in which the reason is failure to comply with the administrative requirements for residence (purely immigration cases).[12]

Guiding principles for a balancing analysis have been developed in parallel in these two groups of cases, although there is some overlap. They have also evolved over time. The ECtHR has indicated that these criteria are to be used by domestic courts in expulsion cases, and that the weight attributed to each of them will depend on the circumstances of the case.[13]

For criminal conviction cases, the ECtHR developed a set of criteria in *Boultif*[14] that have been reproduced in later cases,[15] in which other criteria have been added.[16] For immigration cases, the ECtHR established the relevant criteria in *Rodrigues da Silva*,[17] which have also been subsequently com-

8 *Boultif v Switzerland* App. No. 54273/00 (ECtHR, 2 August 2001), para. 30; *Moustaquim v Belgium* App. No. 12313/86 (ECtHR, 18 February 1991), para. 43; *Üner v the Netherlands* App. No. 46410/99 (ECtHR, 18 October 2003), para. 54; *Darren Omoregie and Others v Norway* App. No. 265/07 (ECtHR, 31 July 2008), para. 54.

9 *Boultif supra* n. 8, para. 39.

10 *Darren Omoregie supra* n. 8, para. 57; *Maslov v Austria* App. No. 1638/03 (ECtHR, 23 June 2008), para. 76.

11 *Moustaquim supra* n. 8; *Nasri v France* App. No. 19465/92 (ECtHR, 13 July 1995); *Boujlifa v France* App. No. 122/96 (ECtHR, 21 October 1997); *Baghli v France* App. No. 34374/97 (ECtHR, 30 November 1999); Boultif *supra* n. 8; *Sezen v The Netherlands* App. No. 50252/99 (ECtHR, 31 January 2006); *Üner supra* n. 8; *AA v United Kingdom* App. No. 8000/08 (ECtHR, 20 September 2011).

12 *Berrehab v the Netherlands* App. No. 10730/84 (ECtHR, 21 June 1988); *Rodrigues da Silva and Hoogkamer v The Netherlands* App. No. 50435/99 (ECtHR, 31 January 2006); *Darren Omoregie supra* n. 8; *Nuñez v Norway* App. No. 55597/09 (ECtHR, 28 June 2011); *Jeunesse v the Netherlands* App. No. 12738/10 (ECtHR, 3 October 2014).

13 *AA supra* n. 11, para. 57; *Maslov supra* n. 10, para. 70.

14 *Boultif supra* n. 8, para. 48.

15 *Sezen supra* n. 11, para. 42.

16 *Üner supra* n. 8, para. 58; *AA supra* n. 11, para. 56.

17 *Rodrigues da Silva supra* n. 12, para. 39.

plemented.[18] The criteria can be grouped into four main categories. The first and the second are common to all cases, while the third and fourth are specific of criminal conviction and purely immigration cases respectively.

A Family unit

The ECtHR puts forward some guidelines to identify the type of family relationship that exists in each particular case, including the members that make up the family unit, how strong the family relationship is, and the extent to which it would be affected as a consequence of expulsion. Those criteria are:

- "the applicant's family situation, such as the length of the marriage, and other factors expressing the effectiveness of a couple's family life"[19] and "the extent to which family life is effectively ruptured";[20]
- "whether there are children of the marriage, and if so, their age."[21]

B Ties to the host country and the country of origin

Since according to the Convention there is no such right to choose the country in which the right to family life is to be exercised, the ECtHR considers the ties that exist with the host country and the country of origin and whether there are insurmountable obstacles for one or more of the members of the family to live in the country of origin. The criteria are the following:

- "the length of the applicant's stay in the country from which he or she is to be expelled"[22] and "the solidity of social, cultural and family ties with the host country and with the country of destination"[23]
- "the nationalities of the various persons concerned"[24]
- "the seriousness of the difficulties which the spouse is likely to encounter in the applicant's country of origin"[25]
- "the best interests and well-being of the children, in particular the seriousness of the difficulties that any children of the applicant are likely to encounter in the country to which the applicant is to be expelled".[26]

18 *Jeunesse supra* n. 12, para. 107–9.
19 *Boultif supra* n. 8, para. 48.
20 *Rodrigues da Silva supra* n. 12, para. 39.
21 *Boultif supra* n. 8, para. 48; *Üner supra* n. 8, para. 58.
22 *Boultif supra* n. 8, para. 48.
23 Ibid.
24 Ibid.
25 Ibid.
26 *Üner supra* n. 8, para. 58.

C Criminal offences

In criminal conviction cases, the ECtHR attributes considerable weight to the power of the state to expel aliens convicted of criminal offences in their task of maintaining public order. Yet, the ECtHR has also indicated the need to take into account the following elements:[27]

- "the nature and seriousness of the offence committed by the applicant";
- "the time elapsed since the offence was committed and the applicant's conduct during that period";
- "whether the spouse knew about the offence at the time when he or she entered into a family relationship".

The latter might be questioned, since whether the spouse knew about the criminal record or not does not have any bearing upon the family relationship that is created, or the interest of the state.

D Unlawful immigration situation

Finally, in those cases in which the expulsion stems from a failure to comply with the conditions for lawful stay or residence, the ECtHR will assess the degree of respect and attitude towards immigration rules; and the moment at which the family relationship was established:

- "whether there are factors of immigration control (for example, a history of breaches of immigration law) or considerations of public order weighing in favour of exclusion";[28]
- "whether family life was created at a time when the persons involved were aware that the immigration status of one of them was such that the persistence of that family life within the host State would from the outset be precarious."[29] "Where this is the case, it is likely only to be in exceptional circumstances that the removal of the non-national family member will constitute a violation of Article 8."[30]

In this context, the ECtHR emphasizes that those who are in the country unlawfully and establish a family relationship may not rely on their mere presence as a *fait accompli*, and that they are not entitled to expect to be granted a right of residence on account of their families.[31]

27 *Boultif supra* n. 8, para. 48.
28 *Rodrigues da Silva supra* n. 12, para. 39.
29 Ibid.
30 *Jeunesse supra* n. 12, para. 109.
31 *Rodrigues da Silva supra* n. 12, para. 43; *Jeunesse supra* n. 12, para. 103.

Nonetheless, if a family is genuine, when the family was established and whether those involved were aware of the risk of removal should be irrelevant factors in assessing whether the interference is lawful. Otherwise, it is almost saying that you never have grounds for complaint if the person with whom you fall in love or have kids is expelled for being an irregular immigrant. This is not to deny the states' legitimate authority to sanction that situation, but expulsion might be a disproportionate measure if it restricts family life, regardless of when the family was established. Moreover, the application of this criterion in specific cases might be problematic. For instance, in *Darren*,[32] the ECtHR argued that a married couple, Nigerian and Norwegian nationals, were not entitled to expect a right of residence to be granted to the Nigerian husband. However, as the dissenting opinion emphasized, since they were allowed to marry in Norway, where the man was an irregular immigrant, they might have hoped to be able to regularize his stay. Eventually, the ECtHR held that the obstacles for the Norwegian wife and daughter to settle in Nigeria were not insurmountable, despite the lack of any ties with that country.

At the same time, in subsequent cases, such as *Rodrigues da Silva* and *Nuñez*, in which the applicants, a Brazilian and a Dominican national respectively, never held a valid residence permit, the interests of the children prevailed in the final balancing and the ECtHR found a breach of Article 8 (Thym 2008, p. 102).

From the perspective of the evolution of the case law, the increasing weight attributed to the best interests of children and the situation of settled immigrants[33] needs to be highlighted. We see that, over time, due regard for the best interests of children plays a prominent role in the case law. Regardless of whether the applicants were in the country unlawfully, and even in a case in which the applicant falsified her identity in order to re-enter the country,[34] the best interests of children may well tilt the balance in favour of the right to family life. In *Jeunesse*, the ECtHR devoted specific attention to the impact of expulsion upon the children and emphasized the interests of children as a relevant criterion in the balancing: "Whilst alone they cannot be decisive, such interests certainly must be afforded significant weight. Accordingly, national decision-making bodies should, in principle, advert to and assess evidence in respect of the practicality, feasibility and proportionality of any removal of a non-national parent in order to give effective protection and sufficient weight to the best interests of the children directly affected by it."[35] In that case, the ECtHR took into

32 *Darren Omoregie supra* n. 8.
33 See López Guerra in this book.
34 *Nuñez supra* n. 12. The Court pointed out that the Dominican mother was the primary care person and that her two daughters, born in Norway, were under great stress by the risk of mother being expelled.
35 *Jeunesse supra* n. 12, para. 109.

consideration that the mother was the primary and constant care-giver of the children even though they were economically dependent on the father, and found a breach of Article 8.

Finally, the ECtHR has expressed increasing concern for aliens who were born in or arrived at the country at a very young age (Farahat 2015, p. 310). Usually, the ties with the country of origin are loose, since they left it at such an early age and often do not even know the language. Moreover, the ECtHR has understood that the protection under Article 8 extends to the network of relationships established by settled immigrants as constitutive of private life, beyond the existence of family life (Thym 2008, pp. 90–5),[36] which is particularly relevant for those young adults who have not established a family of their own.[37] This said, the ECtHR has refused to uphold a general ban on the removal of settled immigrants.

In *Üner*, the Grand Chamber devoted special attention to the issue and referred to Recommendation 1504 (2001) on the non-expulsion of long-term immigrants, in which the Parliamentary Assembly recommended that the Committee of Ministers invite the states to "guarantee that long-term migrants who were born or raised in the host country cannot be expelled under any circumstances".[38] However, the ECtHR did not find a violation of Article 8. In a joint dissenting opinion, judges Costa, Zupanic, and Türmen argued that all the *Boultif* criteria tilt the balance in favour of the right to family life. In the end, according to the majority of the Court, the seriousness of his offence prevailed as he had been convicted for killing a person in a gun fight.

Two years later, in *Maslov*, also a Grand Chamber decision, the ECtHR found a breach of Article 8. In that case, the applicant was a Bulgarian national who had entered Austria at the age of six and had received his education there. He had been convicted of numerous offences as a juvenile. The ECtHR claimed that "for a settled migrant who has lawfully spent all or the major part of his or her childhood and youth in the host country very serious reasons are required to justify expulsion".[39]

III European Union: Free movement, citizenship . . . and family life?

The Charter enshrines the right to family life in Article 7. Yet the scope of application of Article 7 is limited by Charter Article 51(1). Thus, with regard to the expulsion of TCNs, the Charter may only provide protection within the field of EU law. In this context, as in many others, the boundaries

36 *Üner supra* n. 8, para. 59.
37 *Maslov supra* n. 10, para. 63.
38 *Üner supra* n. 8, para. 55.
39 *Maslov supra* n. 10, para. 75. See also, *AA supra* n. 11, paras. 46–9.

of the Charter are contested.[40] In the analysis of the role of the right to family life in the EU as a bar to the expulsion of TCNs, we will distinguish two groups of cases: free movement and citizenship.

A Free movement and the right to family life

The right to free movement across Member States is at the core of EU law and it is directly enshrined in Article 21(1) TFEU. The Citizenship Directive, which sets the conditions of free movement and residence for citizens and their families, applies equally to TCNs who are family members of EU citizens. Moreover, the protection of family life has been pivotal for obtaining residence rights under Article 21(1) TFEU when the conditions set by the Citizenship Directive are not fulfilled or the Directive is not applicable.

Regarding the scope of protection under the Citizenship Directive, *Metock*[41] represented a turning point from the perspective of family life and the restriction of the state sovereign power over immigration control (Costello 2009). The case concerned several couples between a EU citizen and a TCN. The applications for a residence permit as spouses of Union citizens working and residing in a host Member State were refused due to the lack of prior lawful residence in another Member State. The CJEU was asked to clarify the compatibility between the Citizenship Directive and the requirement of "prior lawful residence in another Member State" laid down in domestic legislation.

The CJEU grounded its interpretation of the Directive on the need to protect the right to family life[42] and explicitly overruled *Akrich*, in which the condition of prior lawful residence had been upheld.[43] In *Metock*, the CJEU confronted the objection of several governments that sought to retain the power over immigration control. First, the CJEU emphasized the competence of the EU for the regulation of free movement and approached family life in a rather instrumental manner: "if Union citizens were not allowed to lead a normal family life in the host Member State, the exercise of the freedoms they are guaranteed by the Treaty would be seriously obstructed".[44]

Moreover, the CJEU ruled that TCNs are entitled to a right of residence as the spouses of EU moving citizens regardless of when and where the marriage took place, whether the Union citizen became established in the host Member State before or after funding a family, or whether the TCN entered the host Member State before or after becoming the spouse of a Union citizen.

40 See de Witte in this volume.
41 Case C-127/08 *Metock* EU:C:2008:449.
42 Ibid. para. 56.
43 For an analysis of the evolution of the case law, see Kruma in this book.
44 Ibid. para. 62.

In this judgment, the main concern for the CJEU was ensuring the right to free movement, while family life was rather instrumental in reaching that end. And yet, the protection of family life enabled the CJEU to strengthen free movement and reject the condition of prior lawful residence for TCNs.

More recently, however, in cases of divorce,[45] the CJEU has made a restrictive reading of the Citizenship Directive and ruled that a TCN cannot retain a right of residence in the host Member State if the departure of the EU citizen predates the commencement of divorce proceedings, even in a case in which the TCN was the victim of domestic violence.[46] Such a formalistic reading leaves the TCNs who are the family members of EU citizens in a situation of vulnerability.

Next, in cases in which the Citizenship Directive is not applicable or does not grant protection, the combination of Article 21(1) TFEU and the protection of family life has provided protection to TCNs who are family members of EU citizens. The case of *O and others* involved a Nigerian national married to a Dutch national who were established in Spain. When the Dutch wife returned to the Netherlands, Mr O was denied a residence permit there. The CJEU acknowledged that TCNs may not derive a right of residence from the Citizenship Directive in the Member State of which their sponsors were nationals.[47] Nonetheless, the CJEU held that the TCNs could derive a right of residence from Article 21(1) TFEU when an EU citizen returns to the state of nationality if family life had been created or strengthened in the host country. Otherwise, the effectiveness of the right to free movement would be undermined since EU citizens would be discouraged from leaving their countries.[48]

Therefore, even though the Directive was not applicable, Article 21(1) TFEU was activated due to the existence of a family relationship that had been created or strengthened in the host country. The right to family life was still instrumental to free movement, but at the same time family life was the trigger to generate a right of residence for the TCN in the country of nationality of the EU citizen under Article 21(1) TFEU.

In addition, there have been other situations in which even though the connection with free movement was tenuous or non-existent, the Treaty right to free movement and residence, in combination with the respect

45 Case C-218/14 *Singh and Others* EU:C:2015:476; Case C-115/15 *NA* EU:C:2016:487.

46 *NA supra* n. 45, paras. 50–1. Eventually, since the couple had two children of German nationality, but who had been born in the UK and always lived there, the CJEU ruled that Ms. NA, as the primary carer, qualified for a right of residence under Regulation (EEC) No 1612/68 of the Council of 15 October 1968 on freedom of movement for workers within the Community, for the children to be able to continue with their education in the UK (para. 68).

47 Case C-356/11 and C-357/11 *O and Others* EU:C:2012:776, para. 37.

48 Ibid. paras. 54–5.

of family life, provided protection to TCNs, such as in *Carpenter*[49] and *Zhu and Chen*.[50] The fact that Mr Carpenter provided services in Member States other than his State of nationality was considered enough to bring the case within the scope of EU law, even though Ms Carpenter, who was a Philippine national, remained in her husband's state of nationality. The CJEU held that in case of expelling Mrs Carpenter, who played an important role in the upbringing Mr Carpenter's children, "the separation of Mr. and Mrs. Carpenter would be detrimental to their family life and, therefore, to the conditions under which Mr. Carpenter exercises a fundamental freedom."[51]

Finally, the case of *Zhu and Chen* concerned an EU citizen who had never moved from the country of residence, but who held the nationality of a different Member State. Kunqian Catherine Zhu was a minor who had acquired Irish nationality by virtue of being born in Northern Ireland, but she had never left the UK, where she resided with her mother, a Chinese national. As an EU citizen in a host Member State, she could turn to former Article 18(1) EC and Directive 90/364, which granted her the right to reside for an indefinite period of time, since she was covered by sickness insurance and had sufficient resources by way of her mother. Mrs Chen, however, could not claim to be a "dependent" relative in the ascending line of daughter Catherine within the meaning of Directive 90/364 in order to claim a right of residence in the UK. Yet the CJEU relied on the "useful effect of the right of residence" to uphold a derivative right of residence for the mother as the carer of a minor EU citizen.[52]

The right to family life as such was absent in the decision. Still, the CJEU reaffirmed the existing family relationship as essential in ensuring the useful effect of residence and held that: "It is clear that enjoyment by a young child of a right of residence necessarily implies that the child is entitled to be accompanied by the person who is his or her primary carer and accordingly that the carer must be in a position to reside with the child in the host Member State for the duration of such residence."[53]

In this case, hence, the CJEU detached the right of residence enshrined in Article 18(1) EC (now Article 21(1) TFEU) from free movement and emphasized the effectiveness of the right of residence, encompassing the enjoyment of family life, in the host member state as the reason to confer a derivative right of residence to the TCN mother. Family life clearly gave weight to the right of residence outside a freedom of movement scenario.[54]

49 Case C-60/00 *Carpenter* EU:C:2002:434.
50 Case C-200/02 *Zhu and Chen* EU:C:2004:639.
51 Ibid. para. 39.
52 *Zhu and Chen supra* n. 50, para. 45.
53 Ibid.
54 The same reasoning has been followed in NA *supra* n. 45, paras. 75–80, regarding the Citizenship Directive and Article 21(1) TFEU.

To conclude, when the Citizenship Directive applies, the Directive usually specifies the content and limits of Article 21(1) TFEU. Family life contributed to an interpretation of the Directive that was beneficial for the spouses of EU citizens who had no prior lawful residence in the EU. Moreover, the protection under Article 21(1) TFEU may go beyond the Directive when combined with the right to family life. On grounds of the right to free movement, TCNs can claim a right of residence before the country of nationality of their EU relatives when those citizens return to the country, or when the EU citizens move to other Member States while the TCNs stay. Also, the parents of minor EU citizens can claim a derivative right of residence in the host Member State, even if the EU citizen never exercised the right to free movement, on grounds of the useful effect of the right of residence.

Hence, in the end, in cases such as *Metock, O and others, Carpenter, Zhu and Chen*, the protection of family life enhanced a fundamental rights-based interpretation of free movement and residence to the benefit of TCNs; and even contributed to disentangle residence from free movement. In recent judgments, however, the CJEU has adopted a more nuanced and formalistic approach to the Citizenship Directive.[55] And yet, to the extent that EU law applies, the Charter also applies and the CJEU ought to interpret EU law in light of the protection afforded by the Charter also to TCNs.

B Citizenship: **Ruiz Zambrano** *and its progeny*

Apparently, the situation of EU citizens (and their TCN relatives) who have never moved from the state of nationality falls outside the scope of application of EU law.[56] *Ruiz Zambrano* was a ground-breaking decision in that the CJEU acknowledged the claim for protection under Article 20 TFEU against the state of nationality with the effect of granting a derivative right of residence for a TCN in what seemed to be a purely internal situation (Kaesling 2014).

This case involved the Colombian father of two minor Belgian citizens who had never moved from their state of nationality. The father was about to be expelled from the country. The Citizenship Directive was not applicable, but the CJEU reached out to Article 20 TFEU, holding that the Article

55 Thym (2016, pp. 22–3) has observed a shift in recent case-law towards a strict interpretation of the rules at stake, such as in Case C-218/14 *Singh and Others* EU:C:2015:476, and Case C-40/11 *Iida* EU:C:2012:691.

56 Indeed, in *Metock supra* n. 41, paras. 76–80, several state governments argued that the CJEU's interpretation would lead to unjustified reverse discrimination regarding the nationals of the host member state who had never exercised free movement rights. The CJEU responded that that situation was not within the scope of EU law and recalled that all Member States were parties to the ECHR, which afforded protection to the right to family life under Article 8. Regarding the issue of reverse discrimination, see Kruma in this volume.

"precludes national measures which have the effect of depriving citizens of the Union of the genuine enjoyment of the substance of the rights conferred by virtue of their status as citizens of the Union".[57]

In a rather sparse judgment, the CJEU argued that the refusal to grant the father a residence and working permit would have the effect of depriving the children from the genuine enjoyment of their rights as EU citizens since they would be forced to leave the territory of the Union and follow his father in case of deportation. *Ruiz Zambrano* was full of promises from the perspective of a rights-based citizenship. Indeed, the potential reach of the decision was enormous. Yet it was too soon to predict how generously the CJEU would apply it and how the "genuine enjoyment" test would be interpreted. What is "genuine" in legal terms? What are the rights attached to the status of EU citizenship? And what is their "substance"? In the end, how intense must the restriction of a citizenship right be to trigger protection under Article 20 TFEU?

In subsequent cases, the CJEU severely cut back the reach of *Ruiz Zambrano*. In *Dereci*, the CJEU explicitly reduced the "genuine enjoyment" formula to "being forced to leave the territory of the Union".[58] The right of residence seems to be the only right protected under this formula, and the threshold is set very high. This restrictive reading has been confirmed in cases such as *Iida*,[59] *Ymeraga*,[60] *Alokpa*,[61] and *O and S*.[62]

When does the CJEU consider that an EU citizen might be "forced to leave" the territory of the Union if one of their family members is expelled? Even this formula is understood restrictively, and so far only minors who are economically dependent and under the care of a TCN are considered to be compelled to leave the Union if the TCN were expelled. In *O and S*, the CJEU emphasized that "it is the relationship of dependency between the Union citizen who is a minor and the third country national who is refused a right of residence that is liable to jeopardise the effectiveness of Union citizenship".[63] At the same time, in *O and S*, the CJEU acknowledged that the application of *Ruiz Zambrano* was not confined to blood relationships.

As such, if one of the parents has his or her residence secured in the EU and is capable of providing for the children, the CJEU will refrain from concluding that Article 20 TFEU is infringed in case of expulsion. For instance, in the case of *Dereci*, as opposed to *Ruiz Zambrano*, the CJEU did not find that the expulsion of the Turkish father would deprive his minor children of the genuine enjoyment of citizenship rights. The only difference with *Ruiz Zambrano*

57 Case C-34/00 *Ruiz Zambrano* EU:C:2011:124, para. 42.
58 Case C-256/11 *Dereci and Others* EU:C:2011:734, para. 66.
59 Case C-40/11 *Iida* EU:C:2012:691.
60 Case C-87/12 *Ymeraga and Others* EU:C:2013:291.
61 Case C-86/12 *Alokpa and Moudoulou* EU:C:2013:645.
62 Joined Cases C-356/11 and C-357/11 *O and S* EU:C:2012:776.
63 Ibid. para. 56.

was that the mother was Austrian and thus the children may have stayed with her. Still, the CJEU did not seem to give any relevance to the fact that Mr Dereci had claimed that he was maintaining the children.[64] Indeed, the CJEU held that even if it might be desirable for economic reasons or in order to preserve the family unit together for the TCN to stay, this desirability does not sufficiently support the conclusion that the EU citizen would be forced to leave the territory of the Union, were the TCN expelled[65] (Thym 2016, p. 26).

Moreover, in order to conclude that a right of residence may be derived from Article 20 TFEU, EU citizens must be forced to leave not only the Member State in which they reside, but the territory of the Union as a whole. The case of *Alokpa* concerned two children born in Luxembourg who acquired French nationality on account of their father. The mother was a citizen of Togo and the sole carer of the children, who had never moved away from Luxembourg. The CJEU held that expelling the mother from Luxembourg did not necessarily mean that the children would be forced to leave the territory of the Union as a whole, since they could move to France with their mother, where she could apply for a derivative right of residence on the basis of *Ruiz Zambrano*.[66]

In *NA*, Advocate General Wathelet argued for a more nuanced approach and emphasized that the possibility of moving to the Member State of nationality cannot exist only in the abstract and that a factual evaluation of the circumstances of the case needs to be performed.[67] *NA* involved two minors of German nationality who were born in the UK, where they had always lived and gone to school. The Advocate General pointed out that they lacked any connection with the state of nationality and that the UK was the place in which they had constructed their citizenship.[68] Thus, even if on paper the children could remain in the EU by moving to Germany, where the mother could claim a derivative right of residence, they could still be considered to be deprived of the genuine enjoyment of their rights if their mother was expelled from the UK.[69]

Next, the CJEU's approach to family life as a fundamental right in this line of cases will be examined. Even though family life is at the core of all

64 *Dereci supra* n. 58, para. 42.

65 Ibid. para. 68; *O and S supra* n. 62, para. 52.

66 *Ruiz Zambrano supra* n. 57, para. 34.

67 Opinion of Advocate General Wathelet in Case C-115/15 *NA* EU:C:2016:259, para. 114.

68 Ibid. para. 115.

69 However, the CJEU *supra* n. 45, did not echo the Opinion of the Advocate General in that regard. Actually, the CJEU did not even discuss whether the children might be forced to leave the territory of the Union in terms of Article 20, since the CJEU held that the possibility of claiming a right of residence in the host Member State under Article 20 was conditional upon not qualifying for a right of residence under secondary EU law (paras. 72, 74). Since Ms. NA could benefit from a right of residence under Regulation No. 1612/68 on account of the right of her children to receive education in the host country, that condition was not met.

these cases, the CJEU refrained from evaluating the impact of the expulsion of TCNs upon this right, or the rights of the child enshrined in Article 24 of the Charter. The limited scope of the Charter according to Article 51(1) might explain the absence of fundamental rights in these cases. Several Advocates General, however, have already voiced concerns regarding the CJEU's approach.[70] I argue that the dividing line between the effectiveness or genuine enjoyment of residence and family life is artificial and needs to be overcome. Once family life is brought to the forefront, the protection for TCNs with relatives residing in the EU may well be put on much firmer footing.

While the CJEU in *Ruiz Zambrano* and *McCarthy*[71] did not bring up the Charter, in *Dereci, Iida,* and *Ymeraga,* the Court confronted the issue regarding the scope of application of the Charter in a rather intriguing way. In *Dereci,*[72] the Court reasserted the limit that Article 51(1) imposes on the scope of the application of the Charter and the referring court's jurisdiction to decide whether the situation of the applicants was covered by EU law.[73] In this vein, only if the EU citizens involved were deprived of the genuine enjoyment of citizenship, in the sense of being forced to leave the territory of the Union, would Charter Article 7 apply. Thus, the "genuine enjoyment" test, became also the test for the application of the Charter, in a way turning the protection under Article 7 redundant.

In *Iida*[74] and *Ymeraga,*[75] the CJEU adopted a different approach and made use of a set of criteria involving the intention of national legislatures, the character of the law, the objectives of the legislation, and other specific rules of EU law on the matter in order to ascertain the proper scope of application of the Charter. This test, however, was abandoned in later cases.

The "genuine enjoyment" test thus becomes the sole criterion in the CJEU's approach to decide the proper scope of the Charter in this type of cases (Choudhry 2014, 214–5). This approach to the scope of the Charter and the role of the right to family life, however, is flawed. First, the effectiveness (*Zhu and Chen*) or genuine enjoyment (*Ruiz Zambrano*) of the right of residence, be it under Article 20 or 21 TFEU, necessarily involves the respect for family life. Indeed, the structure of *Zhu and Chen* and *Ruiz Zambrano* is the same from the perspective of family life. For the children to be able to enjoy residence in the EU, they must be accompanied by their parents. If

70 Advocate General Sharpston in *O and Others supra* n. 47; Advocate General Wathelet in *NA supra* n. 67.

71 Case C-434/09 *McCarthy* EU:C:2011:277.

72 *Dereci supra* n. 58.

73 Ibid. para. 72. The reasoning of the CJEU was qualified as puzzling by Advocate General Sharpston in *O and Others supra* n. 47, para. 57; and as striking by Advocate General Wathelet in *NA supra* n. 67, para. 121.

74 *Iida supra* n. 59, para. 79.

75 *Ymeraga supra* n. 60, para. 41.

the concern was merely over financial support of the children, the parents could still be expelled as long as the state assumed responsibility for the care of the minor EU citizens, for instance by placing them in foster homes. If this solution is rejected, it is out of respect for the value of family life and the best interests of the children. The right of residence cannot be effective if stripped from the right to family life (Kaesling 2014, p. 302). As Advocate General Sharpston argued in *O and Others*: "a provision such as Article 20 or 21 TFEU is not simply a basis for residence status separate from Article 7 of the Charter. Rather, considerations regarding the exercise of the right to a family life permeate the substance of EU citizenship rights. Citizenship rights under Article 20 or 21 TFEU must thus be interpreted in a way that ensures that their substantive content is 'Charter-compliant' ".[76]

Second, in determining whether protection against a national measure can be claimed under Article 20(1) TFEU, EU law already governs the case. This is not to say that protection shall be granted under EU law, but the scope of application can be distinguished from the scope of protection. The fact that Article 20(1) TFEU applies does not necessarily mean that the national measure under review will be regarded as depriving the genuine enjoyment of citizenship rights. Similarly, the fact that the Citizenship Directive applies to a moving citizen does not necessarily mean that right of residence will be granted, unless the conditions set out in the Directive are met.

In determining whether a national measure deprives EU citizens of the genuine enjoyment of their rights on the basis of Article 20(1), the situation already falls within the scope of EU law.[77] Indeed, the CJEU declared that the situation of a Union citizen "who has not made use of the right to freedom of movement cannot, for that reason alone, be assimilated to a purely internal situation".[78] Then, it argued that the nationals of Member States "enjoy the status of Union citizens under Article 20(1) TFEU and may therefore rely on the rights pertaining to that status, including against their Member State of origin".[79] This is not to say that any citizen can claim protection of any Charter right before the state of nationality irrespective of Article 51(1), but rather that, in determining whether the genuine enjoyment of the right of residence is undermined, the respect of family

76 Opinion of Advocate General Sharpston in *O and Others supra* n. 47, para. 62.

77 Opinion of Advocate General Wathelet in *NA supra* n. 67, para. 122: "If a Treaty provision does not preclude a Member State from refusing a right of residence subject to compliance with certain conditions, it follows by definition that the situation in question falls within the scope of that provision. If that were not the case, the Court would have to decline jurisdiction to answer the question referred."

78 *Dereci supra* n. 58, para. 61; *O and S supra* n. 62, para. 43. This formula had already been used in *Zhu and Chen*, in a situation in which the EU citizen had the nationality of a different state from the state of residence, but had never moved.

79 *Dereci supra* n. 58, para. 63.

life needs to be taken into account. A severe interference with citizenship status might still be required for protection to be granted (Kaesling 2014, p. 304),[80] but the impact upon the right to family life ought to be expressly assessed. For instance, even if one of the parents is an EU citizen and the children can stay in the EU, the expulsion of the other parent might undermine the genuine enjoyment of the right of residence in light of family life. In a way, what triggers the application of the Charter is Article 20(1) TFEU. Whether the conditions to derive a right of residence for TCNs are met is a further question.

In addition, the Return Directive might also provide another trigger for the application of the Charter, since domestic legislation on expulsion can be regarded as falling within the field of application of EU law. As mentioned above, the Return Directive explicitly indicates that the right to family life must be taken into account when implementing the Directive.[81]

Finally, in this context, the recent Opinion of Advocate General Szpunar in *Rendón Marín* deserves special attention.[82] Mr Rendón Marín, a Colombian national, was the father of two minor children born in Málaga, a Polish daughter and a Spanish son who had both spent their whole lives in Spain. Mr Rendón Marín had sole care and custody of the children, and the whereabouts of the mother, a Polish national, were unknown. He lodged an application for a temporary residence permit, but it was rejected on the ground of his prior criminal record. He had been sentenced in Spain to a term of nine months' imprisonment, although the sentence had been suspended. The Spanish Supreme Court submitted a preliminary reference regarding the compatibility between EU law and the statutory prohibition of granting a residence permit when the applicant had a criminal record.

The Advocate General analyzed the situation of the Polish daughter and the Spanish son separately and acknowledged that Mr Rendón Marín was entitled to a derivative right of residence on account of his Polish daughter on the basis of the Citizenship Directive and Article 21(1), following *Zhu and Chen*,[83] and on account of his Spanish son on the basis of Article 20(1), following *Ruiz Zambrano*, since the children would be compelled to leave the country, were he expelled.[84] According to the order for reference, the children were receiving proper care and schooling, and their father was supporting them appropriately.

80 See, more generally, Iglesias 2014; von Bogdandy 2012.

81 Note that in *O and S supra* n. 62 the fact that the Family Reunification Directive was applicable was enough for the CJEU to rule the need to take into account Charter Articles 7 and 24 for the interpretation of EU law and the implementing domestic legislation.

82 Opinion of Advocate General Szpunar in Joined Cases C-165/14 and C-304/14 *Rendón Marín and CS* EU:C:2016:75.

83 Ibid. paras. 86–92.

84 Ibid. para. 121.

Subsequently, the Advocate General analyzed whether the derivative right of residence may be restricted pursuant to a national provision which makes the grant of a residence permit *automatically* subject to the condition of having no criminal record in Spain or any other country. The Advocate General acknowledged that according to the Citizenship Directive, the Member States may restrict the freedom of movement and residence of Union citizens and their family members on grounds of public policy and public security. At the same time, any restrictions must observe the principle of proportionality and be based exclusively on the personal conduct of the individual.[85]

As such, Advocate General Szpunar maintained that the mere existence of a previous criminal conviction did not necessarily justify in itself the refusal to grant a residence permit, regardless of the consequences for the minor dependent children and explicitly asserted the obligation of taking into account the right to family life as protected by Article 7 Charter and 8 ECHR in that assessment.[86] Moreover, he referred to the case law of the ECtHR and the prominent place that ought to be given to the best interests of children.[87] He concluded that national legislation that required automatic refusal of a residence permit in those circumstances was precluded by EU law.

In any event, if a TCN holds a derivative right of residence under the restrictive interpretation of the "genuine enjoyment" test, it means that were the TCN expelled, the children would be compelled to leave the Union. This outcome should be enough to ban expulsion, even in the case of parents with criminal records, for otherwise it would amount to punishing the children for their parents' crimes; and a sort of "double punishment" for the parents.

IV Final remarks

The right to respect of family life may well restrain the States' power to expel aliens. The approaches of the ECtHR and CJEU to family life in this context diverge. The ECtHR, as a human rights court, has focused on the right to family life as such and the extent to which a restriction on that right as a consequence of the expulsion of a member of the family may be justified under the Convention. The final decision is the outcome of balancing the interests at stake. In the CJEU case law, the protection of family life has been achieved through the right to free movement and the notion of citizenship (Thym 2016). Instead of balancing, the CJEU looks into whether the situation fulfils the criteria to be covered by free movement (Article 21

85 Ibid. para. 96.

86 Ibid. paras. 101, 172.

87 Ibid. para. 174, quoting *Jeunesse v The Netherlands*.

TFEU) or citizenship (Article 20 TFEU). Indeed, the protection afforded to EU citizens has indirectly benefited TCNs (Iglesias 2013, pp. 140–1). Still, the focus on EU citizens is wanting for TCN lawful residents whose TCN family members face expulsion.[88]

The differing approach has resulted in diverging levels of protection. While in free movement cases the protection under EU law may well go further than the protection under the Convention, the balancing approach of the ECtHR might result in better protection before the state of nationality when the *Ruiz Zambrano* threshold is not met.

When aliens facing expulsion as a consequence of the failure to comply with immigration law are concerned, the ECtHR will balance the interests in conflict under the criteria specified above. The ECtHR gives special relevance to the prior knowledge of the unlawful immigration situation and to the moment when family life was created, claiming that only in exceptional circumstances will the expulsion be found to breach Convention Article 8. The CJEU, for its part, assesses the impact of expulsion upon the rights to free movement and residence of the EU citizens involved. Despite being EU-citizen-centred, the CJEU case law might eventually improve the protection of TCNs. For instance, in *Metock*, the CJEU held that the infringement of national immigration law did not deprive the TCNs spouses of EU citizens from a right of residence (Costello 2009, p. 605), regardless of when and where the family relationship was established. When the ECtHR has granted protection in "purely immigration cases", the wellbeing of children has been pivotal. Recent CJEU case law also shows that the CJEU might only be willing to extend the protection under EU law to TCNs in order to safeguard the best interests of children, rather than family life as such.[89]

The variable of free movement is not relevant for the ECtHR, while it becomes a trigger for the protection of family life under EU law. On account of the right to free movement and residence, the CJEU has given protection against expulsion for TCNs who have family ties with EU citizens in various situations: before the host Member State when the EU citizens move there, but also before the state of nationality when the EU citizens return or while they are exercising their right to free movement and the TCN stays. In addition, even if EU citizens never exercised the right to free movement, but reside in a state different from the state of nationality, the TCN parents of minor dependent children can claim a derivative right of residence in the host Member State.

88 Indeed, in *O and S supra* n. 62, paras. 68–80, the CJEU, after analyzing the situation from the standpoint of the EU minor children, also examined the case from the perspective of the relationship between the spouses, who were both TCNs. The CJEU held that in determining whether a right of residence could be derived from the Family Reunification Directive, the assessment of whether the sponsor had stable and regular resources had to be conducted in light of Charter Articles 7 and 24(2) and (3).

89 See *Ruiz Zambrano supra* n. 57; and *NA supra* n. 45.

Regarding citizenship, *Ruiz Zambrano* was ground breaking in that the CJEU made use of the notion of citizenship to provide protection under EU law before the state of nationality. However, the threshold was set quite high as the "genuine enjoyment" test requires that EU citizens be compelled to leave the territory of the Union to reach the conclusion that the expulsion order clashes with Article 20 TFEU. At the same time, if that test is fulfilled, then no further consideration need be developed regarding, for instance, the family ties with the host country and the country of origin. The balancing approach of the ECtHR might result in better protection when the "genuine enjoyment" test is not met, but the outcome of the balancing analysis is not guaranteed, since all the circumstances will be taken into account. In cases such as *Rodrigues da Silva*, or *Jeunesse*, in which the ECtHR found a breach of Convention Article 8, the TCNs would not have probably been granted a derivative right of residence under EU law since the other parent was an EU citizen and the children could have stayed in the country, even if their mothers were expelled.

The approach of the CJEU to citizenship cases is very narrow, which might be understood as reflecting the thinness of the CJEU's jurisdiction in such cases, which in the past were regarded as purely internal. Yet once the CJEU took a significant step in *Ruiz Zambrano*, and coupled with *Zhu and Chen*, the right of residence in Articles 20 and 21 TFEU can no longer be detached from the right to family life. The right of residence does not only protect one's physical location in a given country, but also includes the possibility of developing one's personal and social life within a family and the broader community in that place. A robust notion of residence should include a multifaceted individual-social-political dimension. In this vein, the right of residence becomes meaningless if it is detached from the right to live together with close family members.

To conclude, the protection of family life is not just a by-product of the CJEU case law on free movement and citizenship, but is rather the driving force undergirding the judgments under analysis. Over time, the right to family life has gained autonomy from free movement and has furthered an innovative notion of citizenship. Still, the resistance of the CJEU to uphold the right to family life as such undermines its effective protection. The acknowledgment of the family as part of a robust notion of residence offers the CJEU an avenue to give a more prominent role and better protection to the right to family life. In the end, the substance of the right of residence of EU citizens and TCNs alike requires ensuring the enjoyment of family life.

References

von Bogdandy, A., Kottmann, M., Antpöhler, C., Dickschen, J., Hentrei, S. and Smrkolj, M. (2012). Reverse Solange – Protecting the Essence of Fundamental Rights against EU Member States. *Common Market Law Review*, 49(2), pp. 489–519.

Choudhry, S. (2014). Article 7 – Right to Respect for Private and Family Life (Family Life Aspects). In: S. Peers, T. Hervey, J. Kenner and A. Ward (eds.). *The EU Charter of Fundamental Rights. A commentary.* Oxford: Hart Publishing, pp. 183–221.

Costello, C. (2009). Metock: Free Movement and "Normal Family Life" in the Union. *Common Market Law Review,* 46(2), pp. 587–662.

Farahat, A. (2015). Enhancing Constitutional Justice by Using External References: The European Court of Human Rights' Reasoning on the Protection against Expulsion. *Leiden Journal of International Law,* 28(2), pp. 303–22.

Hinarejos, A. (2012). Citizenship of the EU: Clarifying "Genuine Enjoyment of the Substance" of Citizenship Rights. *Cambridge Law Journal,* 71(2), pp. 279–82.

Iglesias Sánchez, S. (2013). Fundamental Rights Protection for Third Country Nationals and Citizens of the Union: Principles for Enhancing Coherence. *European Journal of Migration and Law,* 15, pp. 137–53.

Iglesias Sánchez, S. (2014). Fundamental Rights and Citizenship of the Union at Crossroads: A Promising Alliance or a Dangerous Liaison? *European Law Journal,* 20, pp. 464–81.

Kaesling, K. (2014). Family Life and EU Citizenship. The Discovery of the Substance of the EU Citizen's Rights and its Genuine Enjoyment. In: K. Boele-Woelki, N. Detholff and W. Gephart (eds.). *Family Law and Culture in Europe. Developments, Challenges and Opportunities.* Antwerp: Intersentia, pp. 293–304.

Kochenov, D. (2011). A Real European Citizenship: A New Jurisdiction Test: A Novel Chapter in the Development of the Union in Europe. *Columbia Journal of European Law,* 18, pp. 55–106.

Thym, D. (2008). Respect for private and family life under Article 8 ECHR in immigration cases: a human right to regularize illegal stay? *International and Comparative Law Quarterly,* 57(1), pp. 87–112.

Thym, D. (2016). Family as Link. Explaining the Judicial Change of Direction on Residence Rights of Family Members from Third States. In: H. Verschueren (ed.). *Residence, Employment and Social Rights of Mobile Persons. On How EU Law Defines Where They Belong.* Antwerp: Intersentia, pp. 11–38.

Van Elsuwege, P. and Kochenov, D. (2011). On the Limits of Judicial Intervention: EU Citizenship and Family Reunification Rights. *European Journal of Migration and Law,* 13, pp. 443–6.

Wiesbrock, A. (2011a). Union Citizenship and the Redefinition of the 'Internal Situations' Rule: The Implications of Zambrano. *German Law Journal,* 12(11), pp. 2077–94.

Wiesbrock, A. (2011b). Disentangling the 'Union Citizenship Puzzle'? The *McCarthy* Case. *European Law Review,* 36, pp. 861–73.

Wiesbrock, A. (2012). Granting Citizenship-related Rights to Third-Country Nationals: An Alternative to the Full Extension of European Union Citizenship? *European Journal of Migration and Law,* 14, pp. 63–94.

10 When there is no family

Unaccompanied minors in the EU

*Lucía Alonso Sanz**

I Introduction

The present chapter addresses the legal approach granted by the EU to unaccompanied minors, being this category integrated by the "third-country nationals below the age of eighteen, who arrive on the territory of the Member States unaccompanied by an adult responsible for them whether by law or custom, and for as long as they are not effectively in the care of such a person", and by those "who are left unaccompanied after they have entered the territory of the Member States."[1]

Regardless of the highest peaks reached in cases of severe humanitarian crises, international displacement of unaccompanied minors has become a chronic and timeless feature of the migration phenomenon. And not only within the EU,[2] but also on a global scale, as illustrated by the almost 70,000 minors in that situation intercepted on the United States border in 2014.[3]

Statistics of people pertaining to this group in the EU are uncertain due to the lack of reliable data, especially regarding unaccompanied minors that arrive as immigrants, meaning that they do not apply for international protection (asylum or subsidiary protection). As an illustrative reference, it may be useful to bear in mind that 24,000 unaccompanied minors applied for asylum in Europe in 2014, while at least 8,500 arrived in Europe during the previous year as immigrants.[4]

* Lucía Alonso Sanz, Lecturer in Constitutional Law, Universidad Loyola de Andalucía. lalonso@uloyola.es.

1 Council Resolution on unaccompanied minors who are nationals of third countries [1997], OJ C 221/23, Article 1.

2 European Commission mid-term report to the Council and the European Parliament on the implementation of the Action Plan on Unaccompanied Minors [2012], p. 2.

3 Park, H. (2014). Children at the border. *The New York Times*, [online]. Available at, http://www.nytimes.com/interactive/2014/07/15/us/questions-about-the-border-kids.html?_r=0 [Accessed 30 November 2015].

4 European Migration Network (2015), *Policies, practices and data on unaccompanied minors in the EU Member States and Norway Synthesis Report*, p. 5.

The problem with the legal treatment of unaccompanied minors in the EU is that migration laws are often applied without taking into account the special protection these subjects deserve as minors as well as being a particularly vulnerable group. In this study, the legal obligations derived from such a particular protection will be firstly addressed (II), followed by an identification of the competence-related obstacles leading to compliance problems (III). Lastly, an analysis of the extent to which those legal obligations are met within EU law will be attempted (IV).

II Unaccompanied minor legal status: First child, then migrant

The main premise of the legal treatment of the unaccompanied minors is the prevalence of the condition of "minor" over the condition of "migrant". This is mainly a consequence of the hermeneutical effect of the principle of the best interests of the child, being a rule that, besides representing the core of the Convention on the Rights of the Child,[5] is endowed with the highest legal efficacy within the EU territory due to its inclusion in the Charter.[6]

Nevertheless, in spite of this inclusion and in spite of the principle being invoked as a mantra in most European rules affecting children, especially in those recently passed, its real meaning is still far from being certain.

According to the interpretation provided by the Committee on the Rights of the Child, as well as the application developed by the ECtHR, the main hermeneutical consequence derived from the principle, especially from its claimed priority over other competing interests,[7] is the difficulty that these other principles cause legitimate restrictions on the interest of the child. This means that, when the principle concurs with other principles, rights

5 Article 3(1) CRC: "In all actions concerning children, whether undertaken by public or private social welfare institutions, courts of law, administrative authorities or legislative bodies, the best interests of the child shall be a primary consideration." Besides having been ratified by all EU Member States, the CRC is among the international treaties on Human Rights that CJEU takes into consideration when applying General Principles of Community Law, as can be seen in the following resolutions: Case C-540/03 *Parliament v Council* EU:C:2006:429, para. 37; Case C-244/06 *Dynamic MedienVertriebs GmbH* EU:C:2008:85, paras. 39–40; Case C-348/09 *P.I. v Oberbürgermeisterin der Stadt Remscheid* EU:C:2012:300, paras. 3, 5, 26.

6 Article 24(2) Charter: "In all actions relating to children, whether taken by public authorities or private institutions, the child's best interests must be a primary consideration." Article 6(1) TEU: "The Union recognizes the rights, freedoms and principles set out in the Charter of Fundamental Rights of the European Union . . . which shall have the same legal value as the Treaties."

7 E.g. European Parliament Resolution of 12 September 2013 on the situation of unaccompanied minors in the EU (2012/2263(INI): General Recommendation no. 2: "Recalls also that the best interests of the child, as enshrined in provisions and case-law, must take priority over any other consideration in any act taken with regard to them. . . ."

or interests, the interpretative standards stand as a major obstacle for the legitimation of the limitation of rights pertaining to the minor involved.[8]

On the other hand, the fact that a measure restricting concurring rights or interests favours the interests of the child does not make it automatically legitimate since the interests of the minor prevail upon other interests but do not override them. Thus, in order for a restrictive measure to be deemed legitimate, besides aiming at protecting the child, it must pass the proportionality test.[9]

According to the ECtHR and CJEU case law, the prevalence of the best interests of the child needs to be explicitly included in the reasoning of resolutions affecting minors. This relates to the consideration of the notion by the Committee on the Rights of the Child, not only as a principle for legal interpretation, but also as a right, and as a procedural guarantee.[10] From this perspective, the child has the right "to have his or her best interests assessed and taken as a primary consideration when different interests are being considered in order to reach a decision on the issue at stake". Consequently, "the justification of a decision must show . . . how the child's interests have been weighed against other considerations".[11]

The application of this exegesis of the principle of the best interests of the child to the legal treatment of unaccompanied minors raises the difficulty (or impossibility, according to the Committee on the Rights of the Child) that his or her rights may legitimately be restricted on the basis of

8 UN Committee on the Rights of the Children General Comment No. 14 (2013) on the right of the child to have his or her best interests taken as a primary consideration (Article 3, para. 1), para. 39: "If harmonization is not possible, authorities and decision-makers will have to analyse and weigh the rights of all those concerned, bearing in mind that the right of the child to have his or her best interests taken as a primary consideration means that the child's interests have high priority and not just one of several considerations. Therefore, a larger weight must be attached to what serves the child best". As an example, we could mention the well-settled case law in which the ECtHR protects the best interests of the child related to his or her identity before the alleged father who refuses the request for paternity tests: *Mikulić v Croatia* App. no. 53176/99 (ECtHR, 7 February 2002); *A.M.M. v Romania* App. No. 2151/10 (ECtHR, 14 February 2012).

9 Regarding the limitation of the right to family life in favour of the protection of minors, in which case Article8 ECHR explicitly requires the restrictive measure to possess legal cover and be deemed necessary in a democratic society in order to obtain such a protection, see *Hoffmann v Austria* App. No. 12875/87 (ECtHR, 23 June 1993); *Bronda v Italy* App. No. 22430/93 (ECtHR, 9 June 1998) and *Ageyevy v Russia* App. No. 7075/10 (ECtHR, 18 April 2013). Regarding the limitation of other rights, in case *Vronchenko v Estonia* App. No. 59632/09 (ECtHR, 18 July 2013), for example, the right to a fair trial is declared breached in a case of child sexual abuse. The appellant had been condemned for sexually abusing a minor, who could not be interrogated, her testimony being the only evidence that supported the conviction. Even if the measure was adopted in the best interests of the child, its need was not proved, which ended in the ECtHR in considering it disproportionate.

10 Committee on the Rights of the Children General comment No. 14, *supra* n. 8.

11 Ibid.

immigration management criteria.[12] However, according to the case law of the Strasbourg Court and of the CJEU (although less so since it has issued fewer judgements), when the principle is applied to such a thorny subject as immigration, a distortion of the usual interpretative effects might be observed.[13] This is consistent with the traditional deference that these courts confer to State sovereignty in matters linked to migration, but also with the fact that in that field it is less easy to connect the interests of the child to substantive rights legally recognized (Smyth 2015). So, while the prevalence of such interests as an interpretative principle is peacefully accepted as part of the domain of what is legally possible,[14] its efficacy remains uncertain beyond that comfort zone. But the obstacle is theoretically bridgeable, not just because the problems of migrant minors often relate to rights that, even though not granted at the legal level, possess either constitutional or supranational projection, but also because the duty to take first and foremost into account the best interests of the child also binds lawmakers.[15] This means that the most favourable solution for the minor is also supposed to be legally possible.

Besides the principle of the best interests of the child, other arguments strengthen the protection of the unaccompanied minor before potential restrictions of rights based upon his status as alien, migrant, or other reasons. These arguments are built upon the situation of special vulnerability in which he or she is found because of the intersection of the circumstances of being under-age, migrant and neglected (that is, without his/her parents' or legal guardians' assistance).[16] Following the well-settled ECtHR case

12 Committee on the Rights of the Children General Comment no. 6 on treatment of unaccompanied and separated children outside their country of origin [2005], para. 86: "[n] on-rights-based arguments such as those relating to general migration control, cannot override best interests considerations."

13 Smyth (2015) studies this topic in relationship to the ECtHR. Regarding the CJEU, as an evidence of this dichotomy, see, on the one hand, the case *Dynamic Medien, supra* n. 5, paras. 41–9, in which the Court declares that "protection of the child is a legitimate interest which, in principle, justifies a restriction on a fundamental freedom guaranteed by the EC Treaty, such as the free movement of goods" as long as those restrictions are "suitable to guarantee or securing the attainment of the objective pursued and do not go beyond what is necessary in order to attain it." An example of the distortion of the principle in the field of migration is the case *Parliament v Council, supra* n. 5, in which the Court justifies a restriction of the right to family life regarding certain minors (those over 12 or over 15 years old), with the aim of enabling the integration of residents in the Union.

14 For instance, in case C-648/11 *MA, BT, DA* EU:C:2013:367, the CJEU establishes, among the possible *a priori* interpretations of a section in Council Regulation (EC) 343/2003 establishing the criteria and mechanisms for determining the Member State responsible for examining an asylum application lodged in one of the Member States by a third-country national [2003] OJ L50/1, the most suitable according to the best interests of the child.

15 Article 3 Convention on the Rights of the Child; Article 24 Charter.

16 The so-called *intersectionality* or "multiple discrimination" (the most common term in the context of the EU) appears as a scholarly creation in the works of some Afro-American feminist authors in the 80s (Crenshaw 1989). The notion defends that the interaction of

law, the conditioning of fundamental rights of vulnerable groups, among which unaccompanied minors are included, or differences of treatment affecting them, must undergo a strict proportionality test.[17] Moreover, the Strasbourg Court defends an intensification of the positive obligations of the State when these are applied to vulnerable individuals,[18] as well as the duty to consider the peculiar situation and need of these people as an interpretative criterion when adopting decisions affecting them.[19]

Therefore, in the case of the unaccompanied minor, the condition of immigrant implies the concurrence of opposed legal forces. On one hand, it would be possible to justify the conditioning of his or her rights based upon immigration policy interests, such as the orderly management of migratory flows, or public safety, public order or national security. But on the other hand, when it – the condition of immigrant – overlaps the status of minority and that of neglect, it has the opposite effect, rendering the restriction of rights especially difficult.

In conclusion, the special protection that unaccompanied minors deserve as a vulnerable group reinforces the protecting effect of the best interests of the child, thus neutralizing the restrictive influence – regarding the exercise of rights – derived from their immigrant status.

In what follows, the degree of respect of the prevalence of the status of minor over the status of immigrant, which should inspire the legal treatment of the studied group and which would disallow any conditioning

---

gender and race produces peculiar discrimination results that differ from the addition of effects that both factors produce separately.

17 The Court has declared the breach of certain rights of unaccompanied minors due to acts that, if infringed upon adults, would not entail such a violation. For example, regarding Article 3 ECHR: *A. v United Kingdom* App. No. 25599/94 [ECtHR, 23 September 1998]; *MubilanzilaMayeka and KanikiMitunga v Belgium* App. No. 13178/03 [ECtHR, 12 October 2006]; *Muskhadzhiyeva and others v Belgium*, App. No. 41442/07 [ECtHR,19 January 2010]. Claire Breen 2002 studies the evolution of the consideration of the "underage" factor in the application of this Article by the ECtHR. Some examples of the difficulty of limiting rights of vulnerable groups: *Alajos Kiss v Hungary* App. No. 38832/06 [ECtHR, 20 May 2010], *Horvath and Kiss v Hungary* App. No. 11146/11 [ECtHR, 29 January 2013]; *Plesó v Hungary* App. No. 41242/08 [ECtHR, 2 September 2012], paras. 65–6; *Mihailovs v Letonia* App. No. 35939/10 [ECtHR 22, January 2013], para. 149.

18 Regarding minors: *Durdevic v Croatia* App. No. 52442/09 [ECtHR, 19 July 2011], para. 102; *Z. and others v United Kingdom* App. No. 29392/95 [ECtHR, 10 May 2001] (para. 73: "Article 3 requires States to take measures designed to ensure that individuals within their jurisdiction are not subjected to torture or inhuman or degrading treatment, including such ill-treatment administered by private individuals. . . . These measures should provide effective protection, in particular, of children and other vulnerable persons and include reasonable steps to prevent ill-treatment of which the authorities had or ought to have had knowledge.") Regarding Roma people: *Oršuš and others v Croatia* App. No. 15766/03 [ECtHR, 16 March 2012], paras. 147–148. Regarding asylum seekers: *M.S.S. v Belgium and Greece* App. No. 30696/09 [ECtHR 21 January 2011].

19 E.g. *Stochlak v Poland* App. No. 38273/02 [ECtHR, 22 September 2009].

of their rights based upon immigration management motivations, will be addressed within EU law.

III Consequences of the lack of competence of the EU over children

Regarding the legal treatment of unaccompanied minors, the first challenge that the EU faces in order to guarantee the prevalence of the status as a minor over the status as immigrant is actually the lack of competence in the subject of minors. This circumstance, along with the existence of EU competence shared with the Member States in the field of immigration and asylum, has meant that European regulations affecting the studied group have been developed within the arena of Migration Law, which has an impact on the spirit and content thereof.

The lack of EU competences on the subject of minors is partly a legacy of the traditional lack of interest of the EU on them. For years, children remained away from the construction process of the Union, focused on the creation of the single market (Poillot 2004, pp. 33–4). However, the inexorable impact of European policies on the legal sphere of minors, albeit in an indirect fashion (Pringle 1998), has meant that finally the EU has had to face their needs and interests.

On the other hand, the Charter enshrines the specific fundamental rights of the children,[20] so they stand up as an insurmountable limit for the action of the EU and its Member States when applying or transposing EU law. In addition, due to the double nature of fundamental rights, positive obligations regarding the promotion of these rights arise from the Charter. In the case of children's rights, such obligation is reinforced by the fact of its promotion being also an explicit goal of the EU[21] (Stalford and Schuurman 2011, p. 400).

The tightrope-walking exercise that EU institutions have to do in order to promote the rights of minors without counting with legal competence in the area of protection of minors[22] has found support in the technique

20 Mainly in Article 24: "1. Children shall have the right to such protection and care as is necessary for their well-being. They may express their views freely. Such views shall be taken into consideration on matters which concern them in accordance with their age and maturity. 2. In all actions relating to children, whether taken by public authorities or private institutions, the child's best interests must be a primary consideration. 3. Every child shall have the right to maintain on a regular basis a personal relationship and direct contact with both his or her parents, unless that is contrary to his or her interests."

21 Article 3(3)TEU: "[. . . The EU] shall combat social exclusion and discrimination, and shall promote social justice and protection, equality between women and men, solidarity between generations and protection of the rights of the child."

22 Article 6(1) Charter: "[. . .] The provisions of the Charter shall not extend in any way the competences of the Union as defined in the Treaties."

of mainstreaming.[23] When applied to the protection of children, it entails "the incorporation of children's rights, needs, and welfare, according to the principles of the CRC, at all stages and at all levels of EU law and policy-making" (Stalford and Drywood 2009, p. 163).[24] This means that the EU, in order to comply with the obligation to promote the rights of minors, resorts to competences on other subjects, thus dodging, at least partially, the lack of legitimacy to act directly in the protection of those specific rights.

In the case of unaccompanied minors, the most favourable jurisdiction for the EU to mainstream their rights is immigration and asylum, since it contains the rules that have the most direct impact on the legal sphere of the group (Drywood 2011, p. 411). Yet, this has shown to be problematic, given that the underlying rationale of European Migration Law, based upon utilitarian and safety criteria (Cholewinski 2000), is radically different to that inspiring the protection of minors, guided by the prevalence of their interests. This explains why European migration regulations often surpass the protection tenets granted to minors by the States.[25] This occurs even in the case of provisions specifically aimed at unaccompanied minors, which often represent a softening of the general regime, which nevertheless preserves its *telos* and essence.

The integration of the best interests of the child principle within European Migration Law therefore entails a clash of values demanding European lawmakers to resort to schizophrenic reasoning. This has proved to be a tough task, especially considering that the aforementioned lawmakers do not possess the appropriate jurisdiction over minors within the EU and hence are not ultimately responsible. In what follows, the repercussion of this difficulty on European provisions dealing specifically with unaccompanied minors will be analyzed.

IV Specific provisions on the topic

Though there has been an increase of *soft law* provisions dealing with unaccompanied minors during the last years, specific legally binding rules are still scarce and they mainly focus on aspects of international protection,

23 The technique consists of the integration of a determined perspective or angle for the elaboration and execution of European policies. Regarding the rights of minors, it was established for the first time at: European Commission Communication of 4 July 2006 — Towards an EU strategy on the rights of the child [COM (2006) 367].

24 With such an aim, the European Commission has created an inter-service group as well as a coordinator for the rights of the child as part of its Directorate-General for Justice. Furthermore, the European Agency of Fundamental Rights issued the following report encouraging the creation of indicators that measure the impact of different Community policies on the rights of the child: FRA, *Developing indicators for the protection, respect and promotion of the rights of the child in the European Union, Summary Report* (2009).

25 As explained by Sandra Lavenex 2006, p. 1285, the incomplete form of government of the EU allows "escape routes" for measures that go beyond domestic jurisdictions. However, according to this scholar, those measures may be gradually "attained" in the process of constitutionalization of the Union.

thus circumventing, in some aspects, children who fall within the category of irregular immigrants.

Among the particular guarantees granted specifically to unaccompanied minors who apply for international protection or benefit from it (and not to irregular immigrants), we find the right to legal representation,[26] psychological assistance,[27] early identification of their status as minors and as unaccompanied,[28] research and localization of their families,[29] and appropriate accommodation.[30] The right to reunify parents or legal guardians is only recognized to beneficiaries of international protection.[31]

In addition, while applicants and beneficiaries of international protection are granted the right to education on the same terms as national citizens,[32] irregular immigrants are only conferred a basic modality of this right, which is also modelled according to the duration of their stay.[33]

Specific guarantees granted to every unaccompanied minor regardless of his or her status are quite few. These include those relating to detention, which is to be applied as a measure of last resort, for the shortest possible time, in a facility that is appropriate for the needs of the minors and granting their leisure activities.[34] EU border guards are also required to follow

26 European Parliament and Council Directive 2013/33/EU of 26 June 2013 laying down standards for the reception of applicants for international protection [2013] OJ L180 (Reception Conditions Directive recast), Article 24; European Parliament and Council Directive 2013/32/EU of 26 June 2013 on common procedures for granting and withdrawing international protection (recast) [2013] OJ L180/60 (Asylum Procedures Directive recast), Article 25(1); European Parliament and Council Directive 2011/95/EU of 31 December 2011 on standards for the qualification of third-country nationals or stateless persons as beneficiaries of international protection, for a uniform status for refugees or for persons eligible for subsidiary protection, and for the content of the protection granted (recast) [2011] OJ L337/9 (Qualifications Directive recast), Article 31.

27 Qualifications Directive recast, Article 30(2); Reception Conditions Directive recast, Article 23(4).

28 Reception Conditions Directive recast, Article 22.

29 Ibid, Article 24(3); Asylum Procedures Directive recast, Article 25(5); Qualifications Directive recast, Article 31(5). According to European Parliament and Council Regulation (EU) 604/2013 of 26 June 2013 establishing the criteria and mechanisms for determining the Member State responsible for examining an application for international protection lodged in one of the Member States by a third-country national or a stateless person (recast) [2013] OJ L180/31; Article 8(1), unaccompanied minors seeking asylum are also granted that their applications be processed by the State where their families lawfully reside.

30 Reception Conditions Directive recast, Article 24.

31 Council Directive 2003/86/EC of 22 September 2003 on the Right to Family Reunification [2003] OJ L 251/12, Article 10(3).

32 Reception Conditions Directive recast, Article 14; Qualifications Directive recast, Article 27.

33 Parliament and Council Directive 2008/115/EC of 16 December 2008 on common standards and procedures in Member States for returning illegally staying third-country nationals [2008] OJ L348/98 (Return Directive), Article 14 and 17.

34 Return Directive, Article 17; Reception Conditions Directive recast, Article 11(2); Asylum Procedures Directive recast, Article 26.

special border control procedures, having been specifically trained for the detention and treatment of minors.[35] Moreover, regulations on this subject usually include a generic clause taking into account their special needs as vulnerable people.[36]

Lastly, there are two exclusive guarantees regarding the return of unaccompanied minors with irregular immigrant profiles. First, before the State decides to issue a return decision, they must be granted with "assistance by appropriate bodies other than the authorities enforcing return . . . with due consideration being given to the best interests of the child".[37] Second, they just "will be returned to a member of his or her family, a nominated guardian or adequate reception facilities in the State of return".[38]

The aforementioned guarantees are deemed clearly insufficient by the European Parliament. In its 2013 Resolution on unaccompanied minors, the institution "strongly condemns" the exiting lacunae in this field, as well as "the numerous breaches of their fundamental rights in certain Member States".[39] It also insists upon the notion that the guiding principle of public agency on this subject, including the search for durable solutions for these children, must be the protection of minors, not immigration-related objectives.[40]

It is therefore important to acknowledge that, even though the specific guarantees mentioned may soften or smooth the general status of the immigrant or applicant/beneficiary of international protection based upon the special vulnerability of unaccompanied minors, the *ratio essendi* of the regime being applied remains the same, that is, an efficacious management of migratory flows that safeguards the commitments acquired on international protection. This means that the international protection/return dichotomy, which is the backbone of migration law, also regulates the legal treatment of unaccompanied minors and the search for a durable solution for their life project. Thus, this leaves no space for the best interests of the minor.

In this regard, the Return Directive is particularly illustrative.[41] It establishes that unaccompanied minors in an irregular administrative situation must be returned to their countries. In order to fulfil this mandate, they

35 European Parliament and Council Regulation (EC) 562/2006 of 15 March 2006 establishing a Community Code on the rules governing the movement of persons across borders [2006] OJ L105/1, Annex VII, section 6.

36 E.g.: Return Directive, Article 14.

37 Return Directive, Article 10.

38 Ibid, Article 10.

39 European Parliament Resolution of 12 September 2013 on the situation of unaccompanied minors in the EU, *supra* n. 7, Recommendations 3 and 4.

40 Ibid.

41 For criticism regarding the enactment of this norm see, among others: Baldaccini 2009, Acosta 2009.

may be under detention for a period up to 18 months.[42] After the expulsion or return, a prohibition of entry into EU territory of up to five years may be issued in certain cases.[43]

The aforementioned guarantees relating to the return of the unaccompanied minors with the status of irregular migrants, despite tempering the application of the rules of the Directive, do not mutate its *telos*, which is still the fight against irregular immigration and not the protection of children. Though there have been some non-binding attempts to undertake an interpretation according to the Charter (Article 24) of the regulations on the return of unaccompanied minors and turn it into one durable solution that would be chosen whenever it was in the best interests of the child,[44] such a conforming interpretation would not be possible in the case of measures of detention and entry bans.

On the other hand, the existence of subterfuges that allow states to avoid the application of the Directive to unaccompanied minors (by granting them a residence permit[45]) is not enough to prevent the breach of their rights by the European norm, since according to the CJEU, "a provision of a Community act could, in itself, not respect fundamental rights if it required, or expressly or impliedly authorised, the Member States to adopt or retain national legislation not respecting those rights".[46]

The Return Directive clearly breaches the requirements derived from the principle of the best interests of the child when allowing solutions that may not be the most suitable for his or her future. Solutions that might entail restrictions of the rights of the child (as the right to development,[47] or economic, social and cultural rights, among others) drawing from criteria related to immigration management, which is incompatible, as defended above, with the principle at stake.

The scope of the principle of the best interests of the child in the adoption of a durable solution regarding the unaccompanied minor with status of irregular immigrant in turn becomes the epicentre of the legal treatment of the studied group. This is where the prevalence of either the status of minor or of immigrant is to be proved, since that is where the

42 Return Directive, Article 15.

43 Ibid, Article 11.

44 Commission Recommendation of 1 October 2015 establishing a common "Return Handbook" to be used by Member States' competent authorities when carrying out return related tasks (C(2015) 6250 final), annex, pp. 50–1. Accordingly, the return of an unaccompanied minor is only one option for a durable solution for unaccompanied minors and any Member State action must take into account as key consideration the "best interests of the child".

45 Return Directive, Article 6(4).

46 *Parliament v Council, supra* n. 5, paras. 22 and 23.

47 Article 6 of the Convention: "1. States Parties recognize that every child has the inherent right to life. 2. States Parties shall ensure to the maximum extent possible the survival and development of the child."

main difference of treatment would lie. This explains its consideration as the major cause of friction among the different European institutions. In this regard, *soft law* instruments adopted in the field of migration after the enactment of the Return Directive[48] show an enduring confrontation between the more guarantee-based position of the Commission and, above all, the Parliament, on one side, and that of the Council (and of the European Council), much more pragmatic and closer to the international protection/return dichotomy, on the other.

For example, when the Stockholm programme asks the Commission to undertake an Action Plan on unaccompanied minors, stress is put upon measures to facilitate "the return of the high number of unaccompanied minors that do not require international protection", since "best interests for many may be the reunion with their families and development in their own social and cultural environment".[49] In the Action Plan, the Commission expressly answers the European Council request, alleging that return is just one of the possible durable solutions, and the choice of one of them should rest on an individualized assessment of the interest of the child.[50] In its response to the Commission, the Council reminds that the Return Directive "constitutes the EU-wide legal framework for the return of UAMs [unaccompanied minors] who are not eligible for international protection or other forms of protection and who are illegally staying on the territories of Member States".[51] In 2013, the Parliament took part in the confrontation with the mentioned Resolution, where it "reiterates in the strongest terms that no decision to return a minor may be taken if it is not in the child's best interests".[52]

Lastly, the Union's action on unaccompanied minors is currently based upon a double collaboration – *ad extra*, with third countries and *ad intra*, within the EU. Within this last frame, amongst multiple proposals, those not implying legislative action but rather study, research and exchange of good practice between States have specially succeeded. These actions, promoted

48 Committee of the Regions Opinion 51/2007 on the situation of unaccompanied minors in the migration process – the role and suggestions of regional and local authorities [2007] OJ C51; Commission Communication to the European Parliament and the Council on an Action Plan on Unaccompanied Minors (2010–2014) [2010] SEC(2010)534; Justice and Home Affairs Council Conclusions on unaccompanied minors, 3 June 2010; Commission mid-term Report to the Council and the European Parliament on the implementation of the Action Plan on Unaccompanied Minors [2012] COM(2012) 554 final; European Parliament Resolution on the situation of unaccompanied minors in the EU, *supra* n. 7.

49 European Council, The Stockholm Programme - an open and secure Europe serving and protecting citizens [2010] OJ C115/1, 6.1.7.

50 Commission Action Plan on Unaccompanied Minors, *supra* n. 48, s. 5.

51 Justice and Home Affairs Council Conclusions on unaccompanied minors, *supra* n. 48.

52 European Parliament Resolution on the situation of unaccompanied minors in the EU, *supra* n. 7, para. 25.

by the Commission, have addressed topics such as age determination[53] or guardianship of minors[54] and, above all, the return.[55]

In this way, the Union seems to find itself in a reflection phase, in some sort of embryonic stage, as if preparing for the search for right answers to complex questions, which have revealed to be particularly sensitive since they affect both children and the public purse.

V Conclusions

Due to the magnitude and persistence of immigration of unaccompanied minors in the last decades, the EU, as a competent body along with the Member States in the field of immigration and asylum, has had to deal with unaccompanied minors as a spin-off.

Both within domestic and European jurisdiction, unaccompanied minors constitute a challenge to both the consistence and robustness of the postulates of the rule of law and the Social State. Its legal treatment entails a prickly tension between the sovereign power to decide who enters and resides in the territory as to establish priorities in terms of public expenditure on the one hand, and the protection of minors and their rights, on the other.

Within the EU, this tension may be detected in the lack of consensus of the European institutions, which has resulted in erratic actions. Opposing the position that defends the application to the group at stake of migration rules that, even if tempered due to vulnerability reasons, still keep their underlying rationale (utilitarianism, safety, the international protection/return binomial), we find the view that sustains the abandonment of that logic in favour of a rationale embedded in the principle of the best interests of the child. So far, and leaving *soft law* instruments aside, European Law has favoured the first option.

Considering the mobility of unaccompanied minors within the AFSJ, subsidiarity seems to justify EU action on this field. The requirement that the status as minor prevails over the status as migrant in the legal treatment of this group – derived from the principle of the best interests of the child – entails the convenience of placing the actions in the area of protection of minors rather than in the area of immigration. Yet, for this to happen,

53 European Asylum Support Office (2013). *Age assessment practice in Europe.* [online] Available at: http://www.refworld.org/pdfid/532191894.pdf [Accessed 8 December 2015].

54 European Network of Guardianships Institutions (2011). *Towards a European Network of Guardianship Institutions.* [online] Available at: http://www.epim.info/wp-content/uploads/2011/02/ENGI-Report-Towards-a-European-Network-of-Guardianship-Institutions.pdf [Accessed 8 December 2015].

55 ECRE and Save the Children-European Commission Directorate (2011). *Comparative Study on practices in the field of return of Minors.* [online] Available at: http://ec.europa.eu/home-affairs/doc_centre/immigration/docs/studies/Return_of_children-final.pdf [Accessed 8 December 2015].

competence in this issue needs to be attributed to the EU. Nevertheless, the existing friction among European institutions regarding this topic poses the question of the extent to which the EU legal system is sufficiently mature to regulate such a sensitive matter.

While the constitutional heritage of the Union becomes strengthened so that it is ready to assume a shared competence in the field of protection of children, the Union must take the rights of minors seriously. It must therefore incorporate the principle of the best interest of the child into the treatment of unaccompanied minors, displacing the logic that rules immigration and its softer versions. Human rights, far from acting as exceptional patches, must illuminate the whole system from its very core.

References

Acosta, D. (2009). The Good, the Bad and the Ugly in the EU Migration Law: Is the European Parliament becoming Bad and Ugly? (The adoption of the Directive 2008/15: The Returns Directive). *European Journal of Migration and Law*, 11, pp. 19–39.

Baldaccini, A. (2009). The return and removal of irregular migrants under EU Law: an analysis of the Returns Directive. *European Journal of Migration and Law*, 11, pp. 1–17.

Breen, C. (2002). *The standard of the best interest of the child. A western tradition in International and Comparative Law.* The Hague: Martinus Nijhoff Publishers.

Cholewinski, R. (2000). The EU *Acquis* on Irregular Migration: Reinforcing Security at the Expense of Rights, *European Journal of Migration and Law*, 2, pp. 361–405.

Crenshaw, K. (1989). Demargenalizing the Intersection of Race and Sex: A Black Feminist Critic of Antidiscrimination Doctrine, Feminist Theory and Antiracist Politics. *University of Chicago Legal Forum*, 1989(1), pp. 139–67.

Drywood, E. (2011). "Child proofing" EU and policy: interrogating the law-making processes behind European asylum and immigration provision. *International Journal of Children Rights*, 19, pp. 405–28.

Lavenex, S. (2006). Towards the constitutionalization of aliens' rights in the European Union? *Journal of European Public Policy*, 13(8), pp. 1284–301.

Lenaerts, K. (2013). The best interest of the child always come first: the Brussels II bis Regulation and the European Court of Justice. *Jurisprudence-Court of Justice of the European Union*, 20(4), pp. 1302–28.

Poillot Peruzzetto, S. (2004). Les droits de l'enfant dans l'ordre communautaire. In: D. Gadbin and F. Kernaleguen (eds.). *Le statut de l'enfant dans l'espace européen.* Brussels: Bruylant.

Pringle, K. (1998). *Children and social welfare in Europe.* Buckingham: Open University Press.

Smyth, C. (2015). The Best Interests of the Child in the Expulsion and First-entry Jurisprudence of the European Court of Human Rights: How Principled is the Court's Use of the Principle? *European Journal of Migration and Law*, 17, pp.70–103.

Stalford, H. and Drywood, E. (2009). Coming of age? Children Rights in the European Unión. *Common Market Law Review*, 46, pp. 143–72.

Stalford, H. and Schuurman, M. (2011). Are we there yet?: the impact of the Lisbon Treaty on the EU Children's Rights Agenda. *International Journal of Children´s Rights*, 19, pp. 381–403.

11 The protection of family life in the EU common policy on asylum

*Sílvia Morgades-Gil**

I Introduction

After the Treaty of Lisbon, the need for European asylum policy to respect fundamental rights, including the right to family life, was acknowledged in Article 6 of the TEU in general terms. This article states that the Charter is legally binding, and Article 78(1) of the TFEU specifically states that treaties on the refugee status and on human rights are binding as regards measures on asylum.[1] The right to family life is provided for in Article 17 of the ICCPR; in Article 8 of the ECHR;[2] and in Article 7 of the Charter,[3] and has been recognized by the CJEU as part of the common constitutional traditions of the Member States.[4]

* Lecturer in Public International Law and International Relations, Pompeu Fabra University, http://orcid.org/0000–0003–1255–9285 Member of the Research Group on Public International Law and International Relations <www.upf.edu/orbis> and the Interdisciplinary Research Group on Immigration (GRITIM-UPF) <www.upf.edu/gritim>.

1 Article 78(1) TFEU, OJ L C83/76: "The Union shall develop a common policy on asylum, subsidiary protection and temporary protection with a view to offering appropriate status to any third-country national requiring international protection and ensuring compliance with the principle of *non-refoulement*. This policy must be in accordance with the Geneva Convention of 28 July 1951 and the Protocol of 31 January 1967 relating to the status of refugees, and other relevant treaties."

2 One of the most recent interpretations of the possible justifications for interference with the right to private and family life can be found in the judgment *Udeh v Switzerland* App. No. 12020/09 (ECtHR, 16 April 2013). The right to enjoy family life recognized in Article 8 of the ECHR does not directly involve the right to enter or the right to stay in a country and not be expelled. However, states must exercise their jurisdiction over the control of immigration in a manner consistent with the rights and guarantees of the Convention. For this reason, the right to recover family life could entail a right to entrance, or the right to maintain family life might entail the right to remain in a country. However, there has been no case where an asylum seeker has cited the right to enter a country for asylum recognized in Article 8; and in the event of a right to remain being cited, the situation of an asylum seeker would not differ from that of other foreigners, apart from their greater vulnerability (FRA, Council of Europe and ECtHR 2013, pp. 125–51).

3 See Martín y Pérez de Nanclares 2008, pp. 209–22; Alonso García and Sarmiento 2006, pp. 113–19.

4 For example, Case C-540/03 *European Parliament v Council of the EU* EU:C:2006:429.

In the past five years, the EU has entered what has become known as the second phase of the implementation of a Common European Asylum Policy or System (CEAS). The final approval by the European Parliament of three of the four main legal instruments that make up this policy on 12 June 2013 finally lead to its effective renewal. The targets set for the creation of a CEAS, i.e. a common asylum procedure and a uniform stature, will not be met during this phase. However, the changes will entail some improvements in the protection of those seeking international protection in the common European area, and greater harmonization of the regulations in that respect.

The mechanisms for the protection of family life specifically established in the main instruments that comprise the CEAS are analyzed herein, together with some jurisprudential interpretations made by the European courts. The instruments of the second phase of the realization of the CEAS that will be analyzed are: First, the Dublin III system for determining the Member State responsible for examining an application for asylum lodged in the area of free movement;[5] second, the Directive on standards for qualification as a refugee or beneficiary of a right to subsidiary protection and its statutes;[6] and, third, the Directive on minimum standards for the reception of asylum seekers.[7] The Directive on minimum standards for asylum procedures, the fourth most important instrument in European asylum policy, does not contain any specific provision that is relevant to the protection of the family unit, which has not been discussed during the analysis of other rules.[8]

II The protection of family life in regulatory instruments of the common European asylum policy

The protection of family life has gradually become a part of the regulatory instruments that make up the common European asylum policy, albeit on a

5 European Parliament and Council Regulation (EU) 604/2013 of 26 June 2013 establishing the criteria and mechanisms for determining the Member State responsible for examining an application for international protection lodged in one of the Member States by a third-country national or a stateless person (recast) [2013] OJ L180/31–59 (Dublin III Regulation).

6 European Parliament and Council Directive 2011/95/EU of 13 Decmber 2011 on standards for the qualification of third-country nationals or stateless persons as beneficiaries of international protection, for a uniform status for refugees or for persons eligible for subsidiary protection, and for the content of the protection granted [2011] OJ L 337/9–26.

7 European Parliament and Council Directive 2013/33/EU of 26 June 2013 laying down standards for the reception of applicants for international protection (recast) [2013] OJ L180/96–116.

8 The family of the asylum seeker is only considered as a possible source of information to examine the dangerous situation in which the asylum seeker is in; and the interviews would in principle take place individually, without the other members of the applicant's family. European Parliament and Council Directive 2013/32/EU of 26 June 2013 on common procedures for granting and withdrawing international protection (recast) OJ L180/60–95.

limited basis. The first instrument is the most interesting as regards to the protection of family life.

A The protection of family life in the Dublin III regulation

The Dublin III Regulation, establishes criteria and mechanisms for determining which Member State will be responsible for examining an application for asylum lodged in the common area, based on the idea that each application should be examined by only one of the participating states, and the others will reject any application filed with them by the same person. The Dublin III Regulation replaces the Dublin II 343/2003 Regulation, which was adopted after the European Community got competence to adopt EU secondary law in the field of asylum in the Treaty of Amsterdam. Despite the new Regulation introducing some improvements, it is based on the same principles and mechanisms as the Dublin [I] Convention of 1991 and the Dublin II Regulation.[9]

The criteria for assigning responsibility for examining an asylum application are objective and hierarchical, and closely linked with the general idea that Member States are responsible for their actions as regards the entry and residence of foreigners in the EU. These criteria therefore aim to determine which state has contributed to the greatest extent to the applicant's entry or residence in the territories of the Member States, either by granting a visa or residence permit, or due to not being sufficiently diligent in controlling its borders.

Nevertheless, the first criterion for determining the Member State responsible for examining an application for asylum lodged in the territory of one of the states participating in the system does not comply with this general idea, but instead consists of applying the principle of the preservation of the family unit (Hurwitz, 2009, p. 96–111).[10] As a result, by virtue of this principle, the first four articles discussing the applicable criteria state that:

a Concerning the protection of the family life of minors: "Where the applicant is an unaccompanied minor, the Member State responsible shall be that where a family member or a sibling of the unaccompanied minor is legally present, provided that it is in the best interests of the minor"; and "Where the applicant is an unaccompanied minor who has

9 For a review of the protection of the family unit in the first phase of the Dublin system, see Maiani 2006.

10 Paragraphs 14–15 of the Preamble of the Dublin III Regulation recognize that the principle of the preservation of family unity should be a "primary consideration of Member States when applying" the Regulation. The Dublin III Regulation added to the Preamble the recognition of "the best interests of the child" (para. 13) and that some relationship of dependency "should become a binding responsibility criterion" (para. 16).

a relative who is legally present in another Member State and where it is established, based on an individual examination, that the relative can take care of him or her, that Member State shall unite the minor with his or her relative and shall be the Member State responsible, provided that it is in the best interests of the minor."[11]

b As a general criterion, the protection of the family unit entails:

i First, that: "Where the applicant has a family member, regardless of whether the family was previously formed in the country of origin, who has been allowed to reside as a beneficiary of international protection in a Member State, that Member State shall be responsible for examining the application for international protection, provided that the persons concerned expressed their desire in writing."[12]

ii Second, that: "If the applicant has a family member in a Member State whose application for international protection in that Member State has not yet been the subject of a first decision regarding the substance, that Member State shall be responsible for examining the application for international protection, provided that the persons concerned expressed their desire in writing." [13]

The principle of the family unit is also recognized in the final section of the criteria, in the so-called *tie-break* (Peers 2013) clause. Article 11 therefore recognizes the principle of the family unit by stipulating that in case of asylum applications presented simultaneously by different members of a family, responsibility for examining the applications of all the members "shall lie with the Member State which the criteria indicate is responsible for taking charge of the largest number of family members" or, failing this "with the Member State which the criteria indicate is responsible for examining the application of the oldest of them".[14]

The protection of the right to family life is also included in the systems' two final clauses of the Fourth Chapter of the Regulation, the clause for dependent persons, and the discretionary clause.[15]

In the Dublin II Regulation, the case for dependent persons was included in the "humanitarian clause",[16] which was conceived, in principle, as a dis-

11 Article 8 of the Dublin III Regulation.

12 Article 9 of the Dublin III Regulation.

13 Article 10 of the Dublin III Regulation.

14 Article 11 of the Dublin III Regulation.

15 The CJEU held that the use of the sovereignty clause in Article 3(2) does not depend on the concurrence in the case of circumstances allowing the humanitarian clause in Article 15 to be used: Case C-528/11 *Zuheyr Frayeh Halaf* EU:C:2013:342, para. 39.

16 Article 15(2) of the Dublin II Regulation: "In cases in which the person concerned is dependent on the assistance of the other on account of pregnancy or a newborn child, serious illness, severe handicap or old age, Member States shall normally keep or bring

cretionary clause. In the Dublin III Regulation, the former "humanitarian clause" as such disappears but the provisions for dependent persons remain in a separate article confirming his non-discretionary character (the rest of the humanitarian clause can be considered as included in the discretionary clause[17]): Article 16 of the Dublin III Regulation establishes now that:

> Where, on account of pregnancy, a new-born child, serious illness, severe disability or old age, an applicant is dependent on the assistance of his or her child, sibling or parent legally resident in one of the Member States, or his or her child, sibling or parent legally resident in one of the Member States is dependent on the assistance of the applicant, Member States shall normally keep or bring together the applicant with that child, sibling or parent.

In this new rule, dependency is recognized in both senses (from the asylum seeker in respect to one relative, and from one relative in respect to the asylum seeker). Nevertheless, the scope of application is restricted by establishing that relatives must be "legally resident" in one of the Member States, and dependency is only recognized for a limited number of reasons, and for a limited number of relatives.[18]

In a judgment of 6 November 2012, the CJEU interpreted how the "humanitarian clause" of the Dublin II Regulation should be applied in situations of dependence of relatives who are not "family members"[19] in the strictest sense and therefore ruled: First, that to ensure the effectiveness of

---

together the asylum seeker with another relative present in the territory of one of the Member States, provided that family ties existed in the country of origin".

17 The first part of the "humanitarian clause" (Article 15 of the Dublin II Regulation) held that: "Any Member State, even where it is not responsible under the criteria set out in this Regulation, may bring together family members, as well as other dependent relatives, on humanitarian grounds based in particular on family or cultural considerations." According to the Commission, this humanitarian and discretionary clause aimed to strengthen the protection of the family unit in general terms, because although there were other provisions in the regulations with the same objective, "the situations that may arise are so diverse that they cannot all be regulated by individual provisions": Proposal for a Regulation of the European Parliament and of the Council establishing the criteria and mechanisms for determining the Member State responsible for examining an application for international protection lodged in one of the Member States by a third-country national, COM (2001) 447 final, Brussels, 26.7.2001, p. 16. Other humanitarian considerations than dependency can be subsumed now in the discretionary clause even when nothing is said concerning those considerations.

18 The Commission's first proposal was more protective as it transferred part of the humanitarian clause to the criteria for determining responsibility: COM (2008) 820 final, 3.12.2008, pp. 8–10.

19 Spouse or unmarried partner in a stable relationship; minor children of couples or of the applicant; or the father, mother, or another adult responsible of the applicant or beneficiary of international protection if he/she is a minor: Article 2(i) of the Dublin II Regulation; Article 2(f) of Dublin III Regulation.

Article 15(2), the term "shall normally keep or bring together the asylum seeker with another relative" must be understood as limiting the discretion of the states, so that in a situation of dependence "a Member State may derogate from that obligation to keep the persons concerned together only if such a derogation is justified because an exceptional situation has arisen".[20] And, second, that Article 15(2) is applicable to both cases of dependence by the asylum seeker with a relative present in the territory of one of the Member States, and in cases in which the person dependent on the assistance of the asylum seeker is the relative who is present in the common area of freedom of movement.[21]

In this judgment, the CJEU did not consider it necessary to examine the argument based on the possibility that the "power" to bring together members of a family or other dependent members in Article 15(1) of the Dublin II Regulation would become an "obligation" because of the risk that, otherwise, there would be a violation of the right to freedom from inhuman or degrading treatment (stipulated in Article 3 ECHR and Article 4 of the Charter) or of the right to respect for family life (Article 8 ECHR and Article 7 of the Charter). In this regard, the Advocate General Verika Trnstenjak concluded that it was possible to apply to this case the same reasoning used in the *N.S.* on the possibility that the power contained in the sovereignty clause of Article 3(2) would become an obligation for states in cases of a risk of violation of fundamental rights. Furthermore, she maintained that "in exceptional circumstances the Member States can be obliged to exercise their right to examine an asylum application on humanitarian grounds in accordance with the

20 "And it should, however, be noted that, in its reference for a preliminary ruling, the referring court did not refer to any such exceptional situation" Case C-245/11 *K* EU:C:2012:685 para. 46. This interpretation is consistent with the decision taken by the Dublin Convention Committee which considered that in cases now covered by para. 2 of Article 15, family reunification should *normally* take place: Decision No 1/2000 of 31 October 2000 of the Committee set up by Article 18 of the Dublin Convention concerning the transfer of responsibility for family members in accordance with Article 3(4) and Article 9 of that Convention, OJ L281/1–2.

21 The case dealt with a woman who had irregularly entered Poland and applied for asylum in Austria, where her son, his wife and three grandchildren had refugee status. According to the national court, the daughter-in-law's dependence on the applicant (her mother-in-law), was accredited due to the recent birth of a child, a serious illness and major disability that prevented her from taking day-to-day care of their children, and a traumatic event occurring in a third country which, if known, could lead to situations of violence due to cultural traditions that seek to restore family honour. Strictly interpreted, the new Article 16 in the Dublin III Regulation, even if specifically recognizes dependency as a criterion for determining one state responsible, would not encompass the factual situation of this case, because it limits the personal scope of dependency between relatives to the "child, sibling or parent" of the applicant for asylum. The assumption of responsibility in these kind of cases of dependency not covered by the article 16 of the Dublin III Regulation would depend on the triggering of the new humanitarian clause or of the sovereignty clause by the Member State.

requirements of Article 15 of Regulation No 343/2003 if otherwise there would be a serious risk of an unjustified interference with the asylum seeker's rights enshrined in the Charter".[22] Even though the former humanitarian clause has disappeared in the new Dublin III Regulation, this reasoning must be considered applicable throughout the remaining flexibility clause held in Article 17, that is in principle considered "discretionary". In the second phase Dublin III Regulation, the rest of the "humanitarian clause" consists in the paragraph 2 of Article 17, which establishes that any responsible state or "which is carrying out the process of determining the Member State responsible" may "request another Member State to take charge of an applicant in order to bring together any family relations, on humanitarian grounds based in particular on family or cultural considerations".

As regards the flexibility clause, I believe that the protection of the right to family life also falls within the scope of issues that must be taken into account by states in order to trigger it following the reasoning in the judgment in *M.S.S v Belgium and Greece* held by the ECtHR on 29 of January 2011. The first part of the flexibility clause, the so-called *sovereignty clause* was enshrined in Article 3(2) of the Dublin II Regulation, and nowadays it is encapsulated in Article 17(1) of the Dublin III Regulation.[23] This clause allows any state to examine any application for asylum presented to it, even when it is not responsible for it according to the criteria of the system. In the *M.S.S.* judgment, the ECtHR established that the applicant's transfer from Belgium to Greece under the Dublin criteria had entailed a violation of Article 3 of the ECHR because of the situation of inhuman and degrading treatment that he suffered as an asylum seeker in the latter country (due to both the conditions under which he was detained on two occasions, and the state of extreme poverty in which he had lived, having failed to receive any official support). For this reason (and others) the Court ruled against Greece and Belgium. Belgium was ultimately condemned for having implemented the Dublin system and having transferred the applicant to Greece, despite the situation for asylum seekers in that country being absolutely deplorable when the events took place, and the extensive deficiencies in the asylum procedures there (as had been pointed out repeatedly by reliable NGOs).[24] The UNHCR had asked Belgium to suspend the transfers, and this measure had already been adopted by other states. The ECHR

22 Opinion of Advocate General Trstenjak Case C-245/11 *K* EU:C:2012:389, para. 77.

23 "(E)ach Member State may examine an application for asylum lodged with it by a third-country national, even if such examination is not its responsibility under the criteria laid down in this Regulation. In such an event, that Member State shall become the Member State responsible within the meaning of this Regulation and shall assume the obligations associated with that responsibility."

24 *M.S.S. v Belgium and Greece* [GC] App. No. 30696/09 (ECtHR, 21 January 2011), paras. 344–61.

ruled that, in this case, the state should have used the sovereignty clause to prevent the transfer and take responsibility for the applicant's reception and the processing of his application for asylum.[25] What is interesting about this ruling as regards the protection of family life is that according to its reasoning, a high risk of violation of other rights in the ECHR, such as the right to family life in Article 8, may also preclude the transfer of an asylum seeker under the Dublin system, and oblige the member state in which the applicant is located to trigger the sovereignty clause to take responsibility for the application for protection.[26]

The new Dublin III Regulation for the second phase of the CEAS is still based on the incorrect assumption that the asylum systems of the States parties are comparable in terms of access to protection and the content thereof. Nevertheless, some improvements have been made as regards the protection of family life for cases of unaccompanied minors and dependent individuals: First, it expands the definition of "family members" to include minor children even if they are not dependent on their parents. Besides the spouse or partner and dependent unmarried children, the Dublin II system already included parents or guardians of unaccompanied minors as members of the family (this is new in the other EU asylum policy instruments). In the case of the Dublin II system, the modification in practice of the responsibility criteria is due not so much to the expansion of the concept of the family, but instead to the fact that the system will now apply both to refugees and beneficiaries of subsidiary protection and applicants for either status and, family reunification will therefore also take place in the case of beneficiaries of subsidiary protection and applicants for that protection, when it was previously only applicable to the former category.

Second, regarding unaccompanied minors, the best interest of the child is included as a general principle in the Preamble,[27] and references are introduced to members of the extended family to facilitate the reunification of unaccompanied minors with "any other relative".[28] In particular, unconditional reunification of siblings of any age or legal status is guaranteed in

25 Ibid. para. 340. On this judgment, *see* Morgades-Gil 2012.

26 The judgment of the CJEU in Cases C-411/10 and C-493/10 *N.S and M.E. and others* EU:C:2011:865, para. 94, admitted this possibility only when the risk was related to the right to freedom from inhuman or degrading treatment, which is also provided for in the Charter.

27 As regards the preservation of the best interests of the child, the CJEU also established in *MA* that in cases of multiple asylum applications in different Member States, Article 6 of the Dublin II Regulation should be interpreted as attributing responsibility for examining the application for asylum to the state where the applicant is located if he/she submitted the application for protection there (and not the first state in which the application was filed). Case C-648/11 *MA* EU:C:2013:367, paras. 56–61.

28 In principle, a "family member" is a child, spouse or parent, and a "relative" is an adult aunt, uncle or grandparent, following the Article 2(g) and (h) of the Dublin III Regulation.

the tie-break clause, and the need to preserve the best interests of the child is introduced on a generic basis. In addition, married minors are therefore included in the definition of unaccompanied minors (and their reunification with their family and siblings when not accompanied by their spouse is permitted); and the obligation of states to act proactively and begin the search for family members of unaccompanied minors is suggested.[29]

Member States have also the obligation to preserve the protection of the family life in the concrete application of the Dublin system following the standards set up by the ECtHR. In this sense, the judgement in the *Tarakhel* case, given in November 2014, requires to the states to examine "the applicant's individual situation in the light of the overall situation prevailing in (a country) at the relevant time".[30] The Tarakhel's family were composed of a couple and six minor children and following the Dublin criteria would have to be transferred from Switzerland to Italy. Taking into account both the extreme vulnerability of the minors, the importance of preserving the unity of the family in the receiving country, and the doubts concerning the adequacy of the reception conditions in the destination country, the ECtHR issued a ruling of conditional violation against Switzerland: "were the applicants to be returned to Italy without the Swiss authorities having first obtained individual guarantees from the Italian authorities that the applicants would be taken charge of in a manner adapted to the age of the children and that the family would be kept together, there would be a violation of Article 3 of the Convention".[31]

B The protection of family life in the "qualification" directive

Improving the protection of family life was also one of the aspects in the review of this instrument, as well as the clarification of some legal concepts; the improvement and harmonization of the two statutes (for refugees and for beneficiaries of subsidiary protection); and the improvement of the standards of treatment of vulnerable people.

The European Commission proposed to expand the definition of family members to include cases where the beneficiary of protection was a minor, and the wide variety of situations in which a minor may be dependent, ensuring that the decisive criterion was the best interests of the minor.

29 See Article 8(5)–(6) of the Dublin III Regulation that establishes powers of the European Commission in order to adopt delegated acts and implementing acts concerning the identification of family members, siblings or relatives of the unaccompanied minor.

30 *Tarakhel v Switzerland* [GC] App. No. 29217/12 (ECtHR, 4 November 2014), para. 101.

31 Ibid. para. 122. Considering the special vulnerability of the victims, the ECtHR established there to have been a violation of the right not to suffer inhuman or degrading treatment in the case of a family with five children (one of whom with cerebral paralysis died afterwards) expulsed from the reception system and exposed to conditions of "dénuement extrême" for four weeks: *V.M. et autres c. Belgique* App. No. 60125/11 (ECtHR, 7 July 2015).

The other family members already recognized as such by the former first phase Directive (2004/83/CE) are the spouse or partner of the applicant (if the country treats unmarried couples in a way comparable to married couples); and the unmarried children of either partner, without discrimination ("regardless of whether they were born in or out of wedlock or adopted as defined under national law") if the family already existed in the country of origin.[32]

There were discrepancies among the Member States as regards expanding the concept of family members, which led to the Commission's proposal on this point not being adopted in its entirety. Finally, in the second phase Directive the expansion of the definition of family members to include "the father, mother or another adult responsible for the beneficiary of international protection whether by law or by the practice of the Member State concerned, when that beneficiary is a minor and unmarried" was accepted.[33]

The extension of the concept of the family to "the minor unmarried siblings of the beneficiary of international protection, when the latter is a minor and unmarried, or when the beneficiary of international protection or his/her siblings are minors and married but it is in the best interests of one or more of them that they reside in the same country" was not accepted.[34] This means that the right to family life is not accepted in the case of siblings who are minors, or single, or married in this Directive, nor in the rest of the directives adopted for the second phase of the CEAS (reception; procedures), that take the same definition of "family members".

This reluctance to expand the concept of the family is explained by the Directive's recognition that "Family members, merely due to their relation to the refugee, will normally be vulnerable to acts of persecution in such a manner that could be the basis for refugee status."[35] Although it could strengthen the protection of the best interests of the child[36] and the principle of family unity, this directive's recognition of more people as family members of a refugee or beneficiary of temporary protection would also mean that the states would have to accept recognition of autonomous protection statutes sometimes almost automatically for the family members defined as such in the Directive who are present in the territory of states

32 Article 2(j) Directive 2011/95.

33 Ibid.

34 Proposal for a Directive of the European Parliament and of the Council on minimum standards for the qualification and status of third country nationals or stateless persons as beneficiaries of international protection and the content of the protection granted, Brussels, 21.10.2009, COM(2009) 551 final, 2009/0164 (COD), p. 23.

35 Preamble para. 27 of Directive 2004/83; and para. 36 of Directive 2011/95.

36 The notion of the family would comply to a greater extent with the international obligations under the United Nations Convention on the Rights of the Child, as well as the ECHR, as interpreted by the ECtHR (Ippolito and Velluto 2011, p. 45).

parties. Another aspect that could be improved in the Qualification Directive's definition of the family is that it maintains the criteria of the need for the family to effectively exist in the country of origin, and excludes relations that may have arisen during the migratory journey or in the host country (ECRE, 2011, p. 4).

The text of the Directive also recognizes the right to the maintenance of the family unit in cases where family members of the beneficiary of international protection do not themselves meet the conditions to qualify for this protection.[37] According to Article 23 of Directive 2011/95, states "shall ensure" the maintenance of the family unit and that the family members of the protected person may apply for the appropriate benefits (residence permits, travel documents, access to employment, education, healthcare, social protection, etc.). The final paragraph of this article also establishes a flexibility clause similar to the humanitarian clause in the Dublin system, under the terms of which "Member States may decide that this Article also applies to other close relatives who lived together as part of the family at the time of leaving the country of origin, and who were wholly or mainly dependent on the beneficiary of international protection at that time".[38] In this case, words seem to indicate that states are completely free to decide, whereas in the Dublin system this was not the case, as the CJEU said in the *K* judgement.[39]

C The protection of family life in the "reception conditions" directive

The Directive 2013/33/UE on minimum standards for the reception of applicants for international protection in Member States aims to ensure that in all states, people seeking protection will have "a dignified standard of living and comparable living conditions in all Member States".[40] Secondary movements of asylum seekers in the area of free movement are anticipated to decline as a result of the disappearance of the incentive for better reception conditions in some states than in others.

This directive includes a general recognition of the protection of family life in the area of reception in Article 12, which states that: "Member States shall take appropriate measures to maintain as far as possible family unity as present within their territory, if applicants are provided with housing by the Member State concerned. . . ."

37 The preamble to Directive 2011/95 also recognizes the need to pay attention to the best interests of the child and to the respect of the right to family unity (Preamble, para. 18).

38 Article 23(5), Directive 2011/95.

39 *Supra* n. 20.

40 Preamble para. 11, European Parliament and Council Directive 2013/33/EU of 26 June 2013 laying down standards for the reception of applicants for international protection (recast), OJ L180/96–116 (Preamble para. 7 of the CEAS's first phase Council Directive 2003/9/EC, OJ L31/18).

The protection of family life is included in several further provisions. The first one describes the types of accommodation, and recognizes the right of family members to be housed together. It states that:

> in relation to housing . . . Member States shall ensure that:
> (a) applicants are guaranteed protection of their family life;
> (b) applicants have the possibility of communicating with relatives, legal advisers or counsellors (. . .);
> (c) family members, legal advisers or counsellors (. . .), are granted access in order to assist the applicants. Limits on such access may be imposed only on grounds relating to the security of the premises and of the applicants.

The protection of family life is also recognized in the context of the protection of minors in an improved way than in the previous directive on the same field. The main principle to be considered, according to Directive 2013/33/EU, is the best interests of the child and this must guide the duty of states to "ensure a standard of living adequate for the minor's physical, mental, spiritual, moral and social development".[41] In assessing the "best interests of the child" Member States have to take into account, among others, "family reunification possibilities". In addition, it is relevant for the protection of the family life of minors the provision stipulating that "Member States shall ensure that minor children of applicants or applicants who are minors are lodged with their parents, their unmarried minor siblings or with the adult responsible for them whether by law or by the practice of the Member State concerned, provided it is in the best interests of the minors concerned." [42] In case of unaccompanied minors, Member States shall also "as far as possible" assure that "siblings shall be kept together, taking into account the best interests of the minor concerned and, in particular, his or her age and degree of maturity"; and that "Member States shall start tracing the members of the unaccompanied minor's family."[43]

The new Directive for the reception of applicants for international protection in Member States does not significantly expand the definition of the family since it only adds one new paragraph (concerning unmarried unaccompanied minors) to bring the definition of this regulation in line with the definition in the new "qualification" Directive.[44]

The Directive adopted for the second phase of the European asylum policy is thus more restrictive in this regard than the Commission's proposal, which expanded the definition of family members in relation to minors. The Commission included the married minor children of the applicant,

41 Article 23(1) of Directive 2013/33/EU.
42 Article 23(5) of Directive 2013/33/EU.
43 Article 24(2)(a) and 24(3) of Directive 2013/33/EU.
44 Article 2(c) of Directive 2013/33/EU.

the underage siblings of the applicant minor, and, in addition to the parents, other adults responsible for the child.[45]

III Final thoughts

First None of the new regulations in the second phase of the establishment of a CEAS or policy in the European Union generally expand the concept of the family to include siblings in the case of minors, or uncles, aunts or grandparents as family members, as the Commission proposed. The family staying together in these cases if there is a relationship of dependency could only be interpreted as an obligation of states within the Dublin Regulation. In other cases, the most that is established is that the states will or shall "ensure" that minors are housed with an adult family member responsible for them in accordance with law, custom or usage provided it is in the best interests of the minors concerned.[46] In spite of this those people are not recognized as members of the family of the minor, which remains a restricted concept (Chetail and Bauloz 2011, pp. 11–12). For this reason, the application of the European regulations on asylum must additionally respect the right to protection of family life enshrined in Article 7 of the Charter, and in Article 8 of the ECHR. The standard of protection of this right cannot be lower than the standard recognized in the jurisprudence of the ECtHR, but can only be ensured indirectly, by monitoring the application of the European regulations. The second phase of the implementation of the CEAS has thus lost an opportunity to strengthen the protection of family life in this area and thereby to avoid monitoring of the enforcement of its rules by the ECtHR.

In this regard, it could be said that the principle of family unity is a factor that regulates European asylum policy to a greater extent as it is linked with elements of vulnerability: unaccompanied minors, dependent persons, etc. Vulnerability is a factor linked to protection by the EU.

Second Although there have been some improvements in this second phase of the establishment of a CEAS, there is still a great deal of work to be done to fully adapt the underlying instruments to the European standards for protection of human rights. This work is already partially underway by means of the evolutionary interpretation of both the ECtHR and the CJEU, as in the case of the interpretation of the flexibility clauses of the Dublin system to protect the right to freedom from inhuman treatment and the right to enjoy family life. However, this adaptation to human rights protection

45 Proposal for a Directive of the European Parliament and of the Council laying down minimum standards for the reception of asylum seekers, Brussels, 3 December 2008, COM(2008) 815 final, 2008/0244 (COD); and Modified Proposal, Brussels, 1 June 2011, COM (2011) 320 final, 2008/0244 (COD).

46 Article 23(5) of Directive 2013/33/UE.

standards cannot solve some of the problems arising from the very conception behind some instruments. For example, the Dublin system is an administrative instrument linking border control to responsibility for examining applications for asylum, rather than a real burden-sharing instrument for the protection of refugees and asylum seekers in the EU based on solidarity (Ippolito and Velluto 2011, p. 61; Thielemann 2005).

Third In some areas of European policy relating to foreigners who are not EU citizens, the interpretation of the right to family reunification is part of a trend towards standardizing the rights of citizens and the rights of foreigners in terms of the recognition and enjoyment of certain fundamental rights that are not absolute, such as the right to enjoy family life. This trend excludes asylum seekers and some beneficiaries of international protection (but not refugees), which is an unjustified reduction of the benefit from a fundamental right. The sensitivity of European asylum policy to states' security concerns constitutes a threat to the enjoyment of fundamental rights, including the right to family life.

Finally, the interpretation of the concepts of the right to asylum and refugees by the ECtHR and the CJEU entails "the end of a national exclusivity" (Sauvé 2012, p. 4) and the development of a European right to asylum, which, although it is sometimes too sensitive, ultimately tends towards the reinforcement of guarantees for asylum seekers.

References

Alonso García, R. and Sarmiento, D. (2006). *La Carta de los derechos fundamentales de la Unión Europea. Explicaciones, concordancias, jurisprudencia.* Madrid: Civitas.

Chetail, V. and Bauloz, C. (2011). *The European Union and the Challenges of Forced Migration: From Economic Crisis to protection Crisis?* Research Report EU–US Immigration systems 2011/07. Robert Schuman Centre for Advanced Studies. San Domenico di Fiesole: European University Institute.

European Council on Refugees and Exiles (2011). *ECRE Information Note on the Directive 2011/95/EU of the European Parliament and of the Council of 13 December 2011 on standards for the qualification of third-country nationals or stateless persons as beneficiaries of international protection, for a uniform status for refugees or for persons eligible for subsidiary protection, and for the content of the protection granted (recast).* [online] Available at: http://www.ecre.org/component/downloads/downloads/805.html (Accessed: 15 November 2015).

FRA, Council of Europe and ECtHR (2013). *Manuel de droit européen en matière d'asile, de frontières et d'immigration.* Luxembourg: Office des Publications de l'UE.

Hurwitz, A. (2009). *The Collective Responsibility of States to Protect Refugees.* Oxford: OUP.

Ippolito, F. and Velluti, S. (2011). The recast process of the EU Asylum system: A balancing act between efficiency and fairness. *Refugee Survey Quarterly,* 30 (3), pp. 24–62.

Maiani, F. (2006). *L'unité familiale et le système de Dublin: entre gestión des flux migratoires et respect des droits fondamentaux.* Basel: Helbing and Lichtenhahn.

Martín y Pérez de Nanclares, J. (2008). Artículo 7. Respeto de la vida privada y familiar. In: A. Mangas Martín, dir., *Carta de los derechos fundamentales de la Unión Europea. Comentario artículo por artículo.* Bilbao: Fundación BBVA, pp. 209–22.

Morgades-Gil, S. (2012). El funcionamiento efectivo de la política europea de asilo ante la garantia del derecho a no sufrir tratos inhumanos o degradantes del CEDH. TEDH-Sentencia de 201.01.2011 (Gran Sala), *M.S.S. v Belgium and Greece*, 30696/09. *Revista de Derecho Comunitario Europeo*, 41 (1), pp. 183–204.

Peers, S. (2013). The second phase of the Common European Asylum System: A brave new world – or lipstick on a pig? *Statewatch analysis*, 8 April. [online] Available at: http://www.statewatch.org/analyses/no-220-ceas-second-phase.pdf (Accessed: 15 November 2015).

Sauve, Jean-Marc (2012). Les affaires de principe en matière de droit d'asile. *International Association of refugee law judges.* Strasbourg, 9.11.2012, p. 4. [online]. Available at: http://www.conseil-etat.fr/content/download/3217/9679/version/1/file/asile-strasbourg.pdf (Accessed: 15 November 2015).

Thielemann, E. (2005). Symbolic Politics or Effective Burden-Sharing? Redistribution, Side-payments and the European Refugee Fund. *Journal of Common Market* Studies. 43 (4), pp. 807–24.

Part IV

Social rights and family life

12 Moving patients and families and the social right to cross-border healthcare

Lucia Busatta[*]

I Healthcare as a multifaceted right and the role of the EU

The definition of the right to healthcare is a highly complex issue, as it can be analyzed from several different perspectives: from the viewpoint of the subjects involved, of health needs and of the nature of public obligations to substantiate that right. A brief outline of the three main constitutional dimensions of the right serves as a starting point to better face the emerging concept of an EU understanding of the right to healthcare that is currently taking shape along with the long-established national competences in organizing medical services and providing health treatments.

Against this background, the first facet of the right to healthcare consists in its "negative" dimension and has to be intended as freedom from unwanted interference in the personal sphere concerning health. It entails the right to choose or refuse medical treatment without undue interposition by public powers or private subjects; it is strictly and definitively related to the right to physical and psychological integrity (Goldworth 2008, p. 54).

The second understanding concerns health as a social right and will be the main focus of this chapter: it relates to public powers' obligation to grant health treatments and healthcare structures and set up a healthcare service that satisfies the population's needs. It encompasses the choices concerning treatments to be granted within the healthcare service; it also requires healthcare bodies to set priorities and to foresee legal, economic and medical conditions in order to efficiently allocate scarce resources and to treat the widest possible number of patients (Cappelletti 2015).

A third dimension of the right to health can be singled out, which is the individual demand for unusual treatments or medications that are still under trial and not yet approved for prescription. This perspective goes beyond the "social dimension" of the right to health and it is rather connected to the freedom of scientific research and to the right of the individual to take advantage of scientific progress (Tomossy 2008; Bin, Lorenzo & Lucchi 2012). The possibility of authorization for the off-label use of drugs

* Assistant Law Professor at the University of Trento.

or for a medical treatment not yet approved could serve as a good example of limits and problems connected to this dimension of the right.

Focusing on the right to access to health services (which is the aspect of the right to healthcare that is most consistent with the general definition of social rights), it is important to note that this right is encountering a particularly high level of attention from EU institutions, although it is not formally included within EU competencies (Busse 2011, p. 48). As is well known, Article 35 of the Charter expressly states that: "Everyone has the right of access to preventive health care and the right to benefit from medical treatment under the conditions established by national laws and practices. A high level of human health protection shall be ensured in the definition and implementation of all Union policies and activities." Even though all EU policies shall pursue the objective of obtaining a high level of health protection and quality of services, not just in the field of healthcare services, but also in all of its spheres of intervention (i.e. the so-called "Health in all policies" approach), the competencies regarding healthcare services and their organization rests with Member States.[1]

The EU commitment regarding individual access to healthcare services has recently found new relevance as an outcome of the adoption of the Directive concerning patients' rights in cross-border healthcare,[2] which aims to bring legal certainty following several interventions by the CJEU "that, whilst safeguarding the internal market principles of the Treaty . . . , seemed to restrict national policy makers in organising their healthcare systems" (Peeters 2012, p. 31).

The CJEU case law as well as the new Directive have, therefore, significantly affected the field of healthcare, in particular with reference to the right of EU citizens to move throughout the Union to get medical treatment. The spectrum of EU interventions and competences, moreover, is also interesting if we consider patients not as mere individuals but as persons connected to others, integrated into a group and related to the most basic form of social aggregation, the family. In this context, the circulation of individuals, groups and families across Europe is, nowadays, a hugely developed phenomenon.

Individuals, often with their families, move across Europe and their reasons for travelling might be very different in nature (pleasure, work, the presence of relatives in other countries or even health), as well as the duration of their stay abroad (undetermined, very long or very short). Besides, the families moving throughout Europe can be varied, e.g. composed of European citizens, mixed or composed of nationals of third countries. In particular, factors that drive families to move across Europe for healthcare

1 See Article 168 TFEU and foreword no. 7 of the Directive.

2 Directive 2011/24/EU of the European Parliament and of the Council of 9 March 2011 on the application of patients' rights in cross-border healthcare, [2011] OJ L 88/45, hereinafter "the Directive".

might depend on the ban of a specific treatment in the home State and its availability in another one (i.e. abortion or assisted reproduction); another reason might be an interest in getting the required treatment more quickly; finally, some patients go abroad in order to receive better quality treatment or highly specialized healthcare (Palm and Glinos 2010, p. 530; Baeten 2014, p. 195).

This chapter focuses on the rights of individuals and families travelling across the EU for healthcare reasons; it is aimed at highlighting the most critical aspects of this phenomenon and proposing feasible solutions.

II Definitions and boundaries

The phenomenon of cross-border healthcare involves patients who travel from their home State to another country to receive medical treatment. As we have seen, reasons that force patients to move for healthcare might be very different in nature, which has quite a significant impact on the variability of the phenomenon. Depending on the kind of healthcare required and on state legal frameworks, the conditions under which patients can access treatments abroad and the possibility of obtaining a reimbursement of medical expenses can differ considerably from case to case. Therefore, a brief definition of the main legal concepts that are relevant in this matter might help to better draw the boundaries of the issue and highlight the most salient legal points regarding patients and families who cross national borders for healthcare.

First of all, it is not a matter of migration law: patients go abroad only in order to get the medical treatment they need, with the purpose of returning home afterwards. Under EU law, the phenomenon falls under the principles of free movement of persons and services and does not concern freedom of establishment (with the exception of healthcare professionals) or residence permits.

Secondly, the approval of Directive 2011/24/EU has finally given a comprehensive and systematic legal framework to the phenomenon of "cross-border healthcare" within the EU. The act "provides rules for facilitating the access to safe and high-quality cross-border healthcare . . . in full respect of national competencies in organising and delivering healthcare" (Article 1(1)). Crossing borders for healthcare, for the purposes of the Directive, is related to the possibility of having access to healthcare services in a different country from the one of residence without discrimination.

Within this concept, moreover, a further distinction is necessary. Patients might travel to another Member State to obtain a treatment that is regulated and provided for by their home healthcare institution. In this case, the Directive's provisions (especially those on prior authorization and on reimbursement eligibility of medical expenses) are applicable.[3] Alternatively,

3 See Articles 7, 8 and 9 of the Directive.

patients could also travel to another Member State to get a medical treatment that is strictly limited or prohibited by the home healthcare institution (for example, for ethical or moral reasons). In this case, Member States cannot prevent their citizens or residents from travelling to another country for a treatment that is banned within the territory of the State. In this event, however, patients could not claim reimbursement of medical expenses incurred abroad, as the treatment they sought is not included within the list of benefits that the home healthcare institution grants to its patients.

This profile is particularly relevant in the context of family life, as limited or prohibited treatments are often connected with reproductive rights (i.e. medically assisted reproduction) or, more generally, with the most intimate dimension of individual lives (e.g. end-of-life choices). In this sense, conceiving, bearing a pregnancy and dying are definitively the moments of life – connected to healthcare – in which the individual dimension of rights tends to merge into the concept of family life, for two reasons. Firstly, because often these decisions are taken together with loved ones; secondly, because in this context the notion of family life includes a set of rights connected to self-determination and to individual choices in ethically difficult matters (Council of Europe 2015).

Furthermore, it has to be considered that, at a European level, the framing and organization of healthcare services might fundamentally vary from one State to another: each State has its own healthcare service, which might be publicly funded or based on an insurance system. For the purposes of EU law, however, healthcare systems might be regarded under the same definition, irrespective of the kind of financial support and institutional organization that each Member State has chosen to grant medical services. Healthcare systems could be considered as "The collection of policies and programmes, constituting the manifestation of the specificities and legacies of a particular nation-state, that are used by that nation-state to meet its healthcare obligations to those resident on its territory, usually its own nationals, on its own territory" (Flear 2007, p. 244).

From a subjective viewpoint, the phenomenon of cross-border healthcare affects patients who are registered within a Member State's insurance or healthcare system. Addressees of these provisions are "those persons who . . . are therefore authorized to receive treatment paid for and provided by that system" (Flear 2007, p. 245). For the purposes of the present analysis, the term "patients" will be preferred to the expression "insured persons" which is, nevertheless, used throughout the whole text of the directive.[4] EU law provisions, finally, are addressed to both insured persons

4 Directive 2011/24/EU, Article 3(1)(b) defines "insured persons" as "persons, including members of their families and their survivors, who are covered by Article 2 of Regulation (EC) No. 883/2004 and who are insured persons within the meaning of Article 1(c) of that Regulation" and "nationals of a third country who are covered by Regulation (EC)

and their family members, in compliance with the definition provided by Article 2 of Regulation No. 883/2004 on the coordination of social security systems.[5]

III Cross-border healthcare: Case law and legislation

European citizens' right to travel to another Member State for medical care is deeply entrenched in EU law, and EU institutions have had to deal with it several times.

From the statutory viewpoint, one of the first sources of law that addressed this specific delineation of free movement is Regulation no. 1408/71/EC, which was replaced by Regulation no. 883/2004 on the coordination of social security systems. Under its provisions, an insured person who travels to another Member State with the purpose of receiving benefits shall seek an authorization from the competent institution and, if authorized, receive the benefits provided as though she were insured there (Regulation No. 883/2004, Article 20). A prior authorization shall be accorded by the competent authority if the required treatment (i) is among those provided by the legislation of the home State and (ii) cannot be granted within a timeframe that is medically justifiable, taking into account the patient's illness, the probable course of the disease and their state of health.

Besides these rules, over the years, a second way of access to healthcare has been taking shape in EU law, through the direct application of Treaty provisions concerning free movement of services and the case law of the CJEU. The principles thereby established have finally found a normative settlement with the enactment of the Directive on cross-border healthcare and its implementation at a state level: if conditions of the abovementioned Regulation are not satisfied, an EU citizen who has undergone a medical treatment in another Member State is entitled to receive reimbursement from the home institution for medical expenses for care obtained abroad.[6]

The CJEU developed a system of legal guarantees and procedural rights connected to cross-border healthcare in Europe, reconfirming, at the same time, the principle that competencies on the creation and management

No. 859/2003 or Regulation (EU) No. 1231/2010, or who satisfy the conditions of the legislation of the Member State of affiliation for entitlement to benefits."

5 Regulation (EC) No. 883/2004 of the European Parliament and of the Council of 29 April 2004 on the coordination of social security systems, [2004] OJ L200/1 Article 2: "This Regulation shall apply to nationals of a Member State, stateless persons and refugees residing in a Member State who are or have been subject to the legislation of one or more Member States, as well as to the members of their families and to their survivors." This Regulation replaced the provisions already established by Regulation (EEC) No. 1408/1971 of the Council of 14 June 1971 on the application of social security schemes to employed persons and their families moving within the Community.

6 See Article 7(1) of the Directive. This rule applies if "the healthcare in question is among the benefits to which the insured person is entitled in the Member State of affiliation".

of national healthcare systems belong to Member States and that the EU cannot deprive them of this power.[7] In other words, through progressive interventions, European judges have contributed to more precisely define patients' rights when seeking healthcare abroad. Authorization requirements have been further specified, possibilities for authorization denial have been restricted and the CJEU has also intervened on reimbursement procedures, thereby restricting the discretionary power of state administrations.

Since its first decision on the matter in 1984,[8] the CJEU has stated that healthcare must be considered a service under the Treaties' provisions, imposing the application of the principles on free movement. For these reasons, according to EU judges, the scheme of prior authorization, required by some Member States' healthcare systems for the reimbursement of medical expenses obtained abroad, represents a restriction on the freedom to provide services. Nevertheless, the aim of maintaining a balanced medical service, open to all, could be regarded as a general objective that justifies, on the grounds of public health, such a restriction.[9]

Regarding concrete cases from which these decisions arose, the CJEU has progressively specified whether the restriction could be objectively justifiable under the Treaty, by verifying if the risk of distortion of economic equilibrium of the national healthcare system was real, in respect to the specific medical treatment sought by the patient.

Interestingly enough, the CJEU has excluded the reimbursement of complementary expenses, in addition to the cost of the treatment obtained, such as travel, accommodation and subsistence costs that the patient or any person accompanying her incurred.[10] Once again, the principles established by EU case law found a normative settlement in the Directive, as Article 7 provides that the insured person shall receive a reimbursement of medical expenses "up to the level of costs that would have been assumed by the Member State of affiliation, had this healthcare been provided in its territory". Therefore, no further expenses shall be reimbursed, unless specific provisions adopted at a national level expressly recognize this possibility (see Article 7(4) of the Directive).

Moreover, the CJEU has gradually developed some procedural requirements that must be followed by State authorities during the evaluation of

7 The main decisions of the CJEU in this matter are: Case C-158/96 *Kohll*: EU:C:1998:171; Case C-120/95 *Decker* EU:C:1998:167; Case C-368/98 *Vanbraekel*: EU:C:2001:400; Case C-157/99 *Smits* and *Peerbooms*:EU:C:2001:404; Case C-385/99 *Müller-Fauréevan Riet* EU:C:2003:270; Case C-56/01 *Inizan* EU:C:2003:578; Case C-8/02 *Leichtle*:EU:C:2004:161;Case C-145/03 *Keller*:EU:C:2005:211; Case C-372/04 *Watts* EU:C:2006:325; Case C-444/05 *Stamatelaki*: EU:C:2007:231;Case C-211/08 *Commission v Spain*:EU:C:2010:340;Case C-173/09 *Elchinov*:EU:C:2010:581; Case C-430/12 *Luca*:EU:C:2013:467; Case C-268/13 *Petru*:EU:C:2014:2271.

8 Case C-286/82 and C-26/83, *Luisi and Carbone*:EU:C:1984:35.

9 *Kohll*, para. 50 and more recently *Watts supra* n. 7, para 104.

10 Case C-466/04 *Acereda Herrera* EU:C:2006:405, para. 39.

patients' authorization. The conditions for granting authorization must be justified under imperative criteria and must not exceed what is objectively necessary and proportionate; the issue of an authorization must be funded on objective and non-discriminatory parameters known in advance, so that the exercise of discretionary power by State authorities is limited.[11] Furthermore, refusals to grant authorization shall be changeable in judicial or quasi-judicial proceedings.[12] Under the Directive's provision, a system of prior authorization could be allowed at a State level only in the case of hospitalization of the patient (either for overnight accommodation or if highly specialized and cost-intensive medical infrastructures are necessary), or if the healthcare required involves a risk for the patients or for the general population, or if it is provided by a subject that raises serious concerns regarding quality and safety of care.[13]

IV The directive and the right to reimbursement: Enforcing social rights through EU law

The Directive has finally given a comprehensive normative shape to patients' rights in cross-border healthcare, by harmonizing national disciplines on access to healthcare abroad: the main goal of the act is to create a shared ground of guarantees for patients and to remove undue barriers to freedom of movement imposed by national legislations. The Directive, which was discussed for a long time before its final approval in March 2011 (the first bill proposed was dated 5 July 2008; De La Rosa 2012, p. 26.), points at the creation of a common European standard for the right to access to healthcare abroad. It pursues three main objectives, which consist of (i) the recognition of some general principles shared by all national healthcare systems in the EU, (ii) the development of a framework for cooperation and coordination among Member States to guarantee mutual acknowledgement of medical and pharmaceutical prescriptions among States and to create a European network for health technology assessment, and (iii) the clarification of principles established by the CJEU with regard to access to healthcare and reimbursement of medical expenses.[14]

The legal framework resulting from the Directive does not substitute Regulation no. 883/2004: two distinct and parallel tracks for cross-border healthcare have been established. The first one, settled by the Regulation, is still based on the regime of prior authorizations, under which a patient can obtain medical treatment in another Member State under the conditions that the receiving country grants to its insured persons. A patient

11 *Smits e Peerbooms*, para. 90; *Müller-Fauré e van Riet*, para. 85; *Watts*, para. 116; *Elchinov*, para. 44, *supra* n. 7.

12 *Watts*, *supra* n. 7, para. 116.

13 Article 8(2), *sub* a, b and c of the Directive.

14 See foreword of the Directive nos. 10–13.

can seek authorization from her home institution to receive abroad the medical treatment that is appropriate to her condition; as provided by the Regulation, the authorization shall be accorded where the person cannot obtain such treatment "within a time-limit which is medically justifiable, taking into account his current state of health and the probable course of his illness".[15] The patient therefore receives healthcare from the host institution as if she were insured there; there is no reimbursement, as expenses are paid directly by the home health authority to the host one.

The second track, namely the regime created by the Directive, applies to both hospital and non-hospital care and requires a prior authorization only in exceptional circumstances. In this system, the patient receives healthcare abroad and, once back home, can claim reimbursement from the competent health authority. Patients are entitled to reimbursement of medical expenses (Article 7(4) of the Directive); the decision concerning reimbursement of further expenses is up to Member States' legislations (such as those for travel or accommodation or costs for caregivers and accompanying family members).

For reimbursement eligibility, it is necessary that the medical treatment undergone abroad already be included within the package of benefits provided by the healthcare service of the State of affiliation.[16] This limitation finds its rationale in the acknowledgement by the EU institutions of the centrality of States' competencies in decisions regarding healthcare and in the willingness not to interfere with complex ethical and moral decisions concerning some specific treatments (such as those connected to reproductive rights), which are still highly controversial at a national level. Nevertheless, in addition to reimbursement eligibility requirements, it should be pointed out that the Directive imposes some important targets on Member States regarding the raising of healthcare standards at a national level and boosts the circulation of information on healthcare services and treatments available throughout the EU.

V The enforcement of the social right to health beyond EU competencies

The Directive's provisions concerning patients' right to obtain reimbursement of medical expenses incurred abroad might be viewed as an interesting measure that has permitted EU institutions to indirectly affect an area that is strictly dependent on national states' competencies. In this perspective, the very nature of the right to healthcare as a social right (see *supra*,

15 Regulation no. 883/2004, Article 20.

16 See foreword of the Directive no.33: "This Directive does not aim to create an entitlement to reimbursement of the costs of healthcare provided in another Member State, if such healthcare is not among the benefits provided for by the legislation of the Member State of affiliation of the insured person."

para. I) concerns States' obligation to grant medical services, by providing health structures and professionals, allocating resources to ensure an adequate level of health protection, identifying health needs of the population and satisfying them through available benefits. Within the complex relationship between State competencies and EU powers – as already noted – decisions concerning healthcare are a matter that remains with States. Nevertheless, Article 35 of the Charter and the abovementioned legal interventions reveal that a European path towards the elaboration of – at least – a common standard of health protection in the Union and a set of common rights for European patients has already been paved.

In particular, the EU's indirect intervention in decisions concerning healthcare services is utterly clear if we consider the legal interpretation of provisions concerning reimbursement eligibility. As it is quite obvious, healthcare standards and available treatments differ widely from one Member State to another and this variability has significantly increased after the accession of new Member States in 2004 and in 2007 and as a consequence of the financial crisis (Frishhut and Fahy 2016, p. 41).

The Directive expressly addresses the problem of different levels and standards of healthcare within the EU, by boosting the exchange of best practices and by requiring cooperation among Member States for the achievement of a common standard of healthcare delivery, especially in the field of health technologies and for highly specialized treatments.[17]

Furthermore, several decisions by the CJEU – quite interestingly, the most recent ones[18] – dealt with the definition of "availability" of medical treatments. In particular, European judges have been called to resolve requests for a preliminary ruling related to the interpretation of the Regulation provision concerning cross-border healthcare. The solutions they provided will also be crucial in the concrete application of the Directive itself.

In 2010, the CJEU had to intervene in a case concerning a Bulgarian national, Mr Elchinov, who went to Germany for a highly specialized medical treatment that was not provided in his home State. Before leaving, he applied for prior authorization by his home healthcare institution, under the Regulation provisions. The authorization was refused and, after the treatment, he started a legal proceeding against the Bulgarian health institution to obtain the reimbursement for his medical expenses. In *Elchinov*, the crucial point was that the treatment he received in Germany was not included within the package of benefits available for Bulgarian insured persons. In this respect, the CJEU held that, taking into account all the relevant medical factors and the available scientific data, it should be established whether the healthcare received abroad could be considered as included within the types of reimbursable treatments, even if "the list of

17 This is particularly evident in the area of rare diseases. See Articles 10, 12, 13 and 15.
18 In particular in *Elchinov* and *Petru*, *supra* n. 7.

benefits for which the national legislation provides does not expressly and precisely specify the treatment method applied but defines types of treatment reimbursed".[19]

In other words, in the event that the list of benefits available to patients is not updated to include the most appropriate medical interventions that, in accordance with scientific evidence, should be considered adequate for a certain disease, the interpretation of national legislation could be extended to the inclusion of a therapy that is not explicitly contemplated within this list.

The concept of adequacy of medical care available at a national level was further specified in *Petru*, the first CJEU decision after the Directive's approval. Even though the concrete case was not focused on the Directive interpretation (it actually dealt with the Regulation provisions), the principles established by the Court will definitely impact upon both normative acts.

Ms Petru is a Romanian citizen who had been suffering from a serious cardiovascular disease. After a significant deterioration in her health, medical examinations suggested proceeding with open heart surgery to replace the mitral valve and insert two stents.[20] The woman decided to undergo this intervention in a German clinic, believing that Romanian hospitals were not adequate for her condition. Before leaving, she applied for costs recovery (under the Regulation provisions) before the competent health administration in her home country. Her request was refused, on the basis that there was no evidence that "the healthcare service sought, which qualified as basic healthcare, could not be provided in a medical establishment in Romania within a reasonable length of time in the light of Ms. Petru's current state of health and the course of the disease".[21]

Once back, she claimed for the refund of medical expenses, alleging that healthcare structures and services in Romania were not adequate for her condition, being generally scarce and rather insufficient for the treatment of her illness.

The legal proceeding went up to the CJEU for a preliminary reference ruling concerning the correct interpretation of the concept of "undue delay" as a general condition to recognize the right of patients to obtain medical treatments abroad at the expense of the home healthcare institution. The core of the issue focuses on the reasons that could lead to an "undue delay", which might include medical and scientific criteria, beyond administrative standards, in setting priorities and waiting lists.

In the opinion of the Court, the lack of medication, basic medical supplies and infrastructure has to be taken into account by the competent institutions when deciding on authorizations to cross-border healthcare.

19 *Elchinov, supra* n. 7, para. 73.
20 *Petru, supra* n. 7, para. 9.
21 Ibid, para. 11.

The time factor that, under the Regulation provisions, permits patients to obtain healthcare abroad at the expense of the home health institution, has to be considered *per se*, without drawing a distinction between the different reasons that can contribute to the delay: "such a lack of medication and of medical supplies and infrastructure can, in the same way as the lack of specific equipment or particular expertise, make it impossible for the same or equally effective treatment to be provided in good time in the Member State of residence".[22]

The concept of "undue delay" found a subjective interpretation, based on the individual patient's medical condition, firstly in 2003 in *Inizan* and – more precisely and with specific reference to the related organization of healthcare services – later in 2006 in *Watts*.[23] In the latter, the Court directly faced the issue of waiting lists as organizational criteria that regulate access to healthcare for patients and that, if badly managed, could cause an undue delay in obtaining a medical service. To determine whether the time factor has been improperly managed by the home healthcare institutions, an objective medical assessment of the clinical needs of the person concerned, in the light of her medical condition and history and probable course of her illness, the degree of pain she suffers and the nature of her disability at the time when the authorization is sought, must be given due consideration.[24]

As these few examples clearly demonstrate, the CJEU intervention in cross-border healthcare case law is decisive even in the internal organization of healthcare services. In the event that the package of benefits has not been properly updated (as in *Elchinov*), or medical supplies are inadequate (as in *Petru*), or even when waiting lists are not appropriately organized to satisfy individual patients' needs, then the person is entitled to receive the medical treatment she needs in another Member State, at the expense of the home healthcare institution.

As a result of the combination of these principles, "health systems with lower levels of financing would be faced with outflows of patients that would be potentially both large and, by definition, more expensive than provided for domestically" (Frishhut and Fahy 2016, p. 48). In order to prevent systematic patient migration and try to maintain "a balanced medical and hospital service open to all"[25] national healthcare services should try to implement the list of benefits and the general medical and administrative organization in order to better satisfy patients' needs and to adapt internal services to a general and rather conceptual European healthcare standard.

22 *Petru*, *supra* n. 7, para. 33.

23 Before *Inizan* (para. 46), the CJEU dealt with the meaning of "undue delay" in *Smits and Peerbooms* (para. 104) and in *Müller-Fauré and van Riet* (para. 90); the concept was further specified in *Watts* (para 79), *supra* n. 7.

24 *Watts*, *supra* n. 7, para. 79.

25 As stated by the CJEU in *Watts*, para. 104, *supra* n. 7.

Therefore, even beyond its competencies, the EU is playing a pivotal role in influencing Member States' healthcare policies and, above all, it could be argued that it will increasingly determine decisions on resource allocation in medical services (McHale 2007, p. 284). As a consequence, the positive dimension of the right to healthcare, traditionally strictly dependent upon States legislations – is moving towards a "Europeanization" through the pursuit of common European standards of healthcare delivery across Member States.

VI Reproductive rights

There is one last aspect of cross-border healthcare that deserves due consideration with reference to states' decisions on social rights and to moving patients and their families.

As we have seen, States are responsible for healthcare choices, including both decisions on the affordability of medical services and the ethical dimensions of some specific treatments. This latter profile leads us to address the issue of treatments that are strictly limited or even prohibited in some Member States, whereas they remain available and openly legislated in other ones. The legal framework concerning medically assisted reproduction techniques serves as a good example of the phenomenon of European patients who cross national borders to get treatments that are banned in their country of origin. It is also relevant because it often involves families and not only individual patients.

Over the years, EU fundamental freedoms and EU law have played an important role in the definition and extension of reproductive rights, especially with reference to the right to information and the right to movement for reproductive services. The first aftermath of these principles dates back to the 1990s, when the CJEU was called to give its opinion on an "abortion information case", contributing to the framing of a European standard for access to cross-border information and services.[26] In *Grogan*, the Court stated that abortion must indeed be considered a service under EU law and, therefore, providing information on a service legally available abroad was theoretically compatible with the Treaties' provisions. This case still represents a very important step in the definition of EU rights and freedoms, even beyond national decisions concerning ethically sensitive matters, such as those on reproductive rights.

With specific regard to cross-border reproductive rights and access to medically assisted reproduction techniques abroad, the first important aspect to consider is that neither the Regulation nor the Directive provisions could find application, with reference to the reimbursement of healthcare expenses and the system of prior authorization. In general terms, patients

26 Case C-159/90 *Grogan* EU:C:1991:378.

are free to travel to another Member State to get a treatment limited or prohibited by their home institution, but they cannot claim costs upon their return. Nevertheless, there are some goals pursued by the Directive that are relevant even in this controversial matter, such as the objective to achieve a common basis of access to information on medical services available abroad, also in order to fill linguistic and cultural gaps. For this purpose, the Directive provides for the institution of National Contact Points, which shall facilitate the exchange of information "concerning healthcare providers, including, on request, information on a specific provider's right to provide services or any restrictions on its practice . . . , information on patients' rights, complaints procedures and mechanisms for seeking remedies, according to the legislation of that Member State, as well as the legal and administrative options available to settle disputes".[27]

Finally, even beyond the political or ethical decision to forbid a specific medical treatment, Member States should respect their obligations under EU law. Among these, the task of ensuring the safety of European citizens when going abroad for matters related to their health assumes a central role in the cross-border healthcare framework and should characterize, at least, national regulations concerning the dissemination of information on services legally available abroad.

VII Concluding remarks

The analysis developed in the previous paragraphs has shown an intense connection between States' choices on medical treatments to be granted and EU interventions in the field of health and, ultimately, on Member States' competencies on the organization of their own healthcare systems.

In this context, it is worth making some further considerations regarding the essence of social rights. As is well known, social rights found a wide constitutional recognition in Europe after the Second World War and require a positive and concrete implementation by lawmakers (Cappelletti 2015). In other words, it is not enough that social rights (and among them, the right to healthcare) are included in the "Bill of Rights" of the constitution. For their effectiveness, a legislative intervention is required, together with the assumption of positive obligations by public powers in order to provide means, structures and resources to make these rights concretely accessible for individuals.

With particular reference to cross-border healthcare, the tension between individual freedom and affordability of social rights is particularly evident. On the one hand, EU institutions boosted the liberal dimension of individual rights, applying the principle of free movement also to services related to healthcare and forcing national legal orders and healthcare systems to

27 Directive 2011/24/EU, Article 6.

adopt the necessary measures to grant this freedom. On the other hand, by interfering with the social dimension of the right to healthcare (namely, with resource allocation decisions and with the instruments adopted at a national level for the rationing of scarce resources), cross-border healthcare also impacts upon states' financial interests connected to the field of health. In order to try to reconcile these opposite trends, the Directive attempts to safeguard Member States' autonomy concerning the affordability of the right to health (De La Rosa 2012, p. 31).[28]

As we have briefly noted, this could be connected to the preservation of state autonomy in decisions on ethically sensitive matters (such as those on reproductive rights). Nevertheless, this principle also has highly remarkable importance, if related to rationing choices: "in the event that treatment provided in another State is not specifically mentioned in the list of reimbursable care, the competent institution in the State of affiliation must determine whether this treatment constitutes a benefit under its legislation, and authorisation should not be refused on the grounds that a treatment method of this type is not available within its territory".[29]

Once again, the principle established at an EU level demonstrates that, beyond a declared willingness to safeguard Member States' autonomy in decisions on healthcare treatments, the general tendency is moving towards the elaboration of a common European standard of healthcare accessibility, justified on the basis of Article 168 TFUE and Article 35 of the Charter. The elaboration of this common standard, obviously, could not pass directly through the essence of decision-making mechanisms concerning the social right to healthcare; it should rather indirectly influence Member States' deliberations by requiring the respect of EU law obligations.

Finally, it is worth developing some further considerations regarding the relationship between the right to travel for healthcare services and family life. In this respect, we saw that the EU legal framework on cross-border healthcare does not expressly address the issue of family life, but it rather gives prevalence to the individual dimension of the right to health; nevertheless, the increasing challenges brought by the biotechnological development are significantly impacting on the field of reproductive rights at a European level. In this perspective, national bans or limitations on access to reproductive services (especially those for medically assisted reproduction) do not prevent individuals and families from travelling abroad to get a treatment they could not have access to in their State of residence. EU law, in this context, is contributing to the creation of a common standard of rights connected to reproductive technologies and is therefore progressively influencing States' choices (Busatta and Penasa 2015). In conclusion,

28 For example, art. 7(3) makes it clear that the determination of the "package" of treatments eligible for reimbursement stands within states competencies.

29 Ibid. See also the principles established in *Elchinov* and Petru (*supra*, para. V).

we cannot rule out the possibility that a future development in the interpretation of these set of rights could more significantly affect also family life, for example through the direct application of the principles established by the Charter.

References

Baeten, R. (2014). Cross-border patient mobility in the European Union: in search of benefits from the new legal framework. *Journal of Health Services Research and Policy*, 19(4), pp.195–7.

Bin, R. Lorenzon, S. and Lucchi, N. (2012). *Biotech innovations and fundamental rights*. Milan: Springer.

Busatta, L. and Penasa, S. (2015). The Italian perspective on cross-border assisted reproduction: the law no. 40/04 in action. In: Kaiafa-Gbanti, M., Kounougeri-Manoledaki, E. and Symeonidou-Kastanidou, E. (eds.). *Assisted Reproduction in Europe: Social, Ethical and Legal Issues*, Athens-Thessaloniki: Sakkoulas Publications. pp. 435–53.

Busse, R. et al. (2011). Access to health care services within and between countries of the European Union. In: Wismar, M. et al. (eds.). *Health care in the European Union*. Copenhagen, Denmark: European Observatory on Health Systems and Policies, 2011, pp. 47–90.

Cappelletti, M. (2015). Healthcare Tight and Principle of "Minimum Standards". The interpretation of the Judiciary in a Comparative Perspective. In: Pineschi, L. (ed.). *General Principles of Law – The Role of the Judiciary*. Cham: Springer. pp. 243–61.

Council of Europe (2015). Thematic report, Health-related issues in the case-law of the European Court of Human Rights, June 2015. Available at http://www.echr.coe.int/Documents/Research _report_health.pdf.

De La Rosa, S. (2012). The Directive on Cross-border Healthcare or the Art of Codifying Complex Case Law. *Common Market Law Review*, 49, pp. 15–46.

Flear, M. (2007). Developing Euro-Biocitizens through Migration for Healthcare Services. *Maastricht Journal of European and Comparative Law*, 14(3), pp. 239–61.

Frishhut, M and Fahy, N. (2016). Patient Mobility in Times of Austerity: A Legal and Policy Analysis of the *Petru* Case. *European Journal of Health Law*, 23, pp. 36–60.

Goldworth, A. (2008). Human Rights and the Right to Health Care. In: Weisstub, D.N. and Díaz Pintos, G. (eds.). *Autonomy and human rights in health care an international perspective*. Dordrecht: Springer. pp. 45–54.

McHale, J.V. (2007). Framing a Right to Treatment in English Law? Watts in Retrospective, *Maastricht Journal of European and Comparative Law*, 14(3), pp. 263–85.

Palm, W. and Glinos, I.A. (2010). Enabling patient mobility in the EU: between free movement and coordination. In Mossialos, E. et al. (eds.). *Health systems governance in Europe*. Cambridge: Cambridge University Press, pp. 509–60.

Peeters, M. (2012). Free Movement of Patients: Directive 2011/24 on the Application of Patients' Rights in Cross-Border Healthcare. *European Journal of Health Law*, 19, pp. 29–60.

Tomossy, G.F. (2008). Human Rights, Health Care and Biomedical Innovation: Confronting the Research Imperative? In: Weisstub, D.N. and Díaz Pintos, G. (eds.). *Autonomy and human rights in health care an international perspective*. Dordrecht: Springer, pp. 341–52.

13 The right to housing and the protection of family life and vulnerable groups

European judicial activism

*Joan Solanes Mullor**

I Introduction

In Europe, legal developments with regard to the right to housing have always been arduous, largely due to the conservative theoretical framework and economic *status quo* that have long prevented its categorization as a genuine right. The European legal framework in which the right to housing is recognized – within the so-called economic, social and cultural rights – presents textual limitations and non-justiciability claims that shove this right into the background. These shortfalls are found both in national constitutional structures and in the European instruments for the protection of human rights (the Council of Europe and the EU).

The economic and financial crisis, however, seems paradoxically to have represented a turning point for the right to housing. The massive loss of homes as a result of evictions has put a significant percentage of the population in social risk, with deeper impact felt in southern European countries such as Spain.[1] Social exclusion and poverty have become real threats for entire families – often with children in their care – whose adult members have lost their jobs.[2] In most of the cases, the loss of a home is the beginning of the path to poverty and social exclusion and, especially in the case of children, the entrance to an unstable environment which jeopardizes their physical and psychological development.

* Law Professor at Pompeu Fabra University.Supported by the Spanish Ministry of Economy and Competitiveness (Grant DER2014-57116P). Special thanks to Maribel González Pascual, Aida Torres Pérez and Cristina Vila Gisbert for their support and help with the drafting of this chapter.

1 In 2012, one of the most severe years of the economic crisis in Spain, the courts ruled on 43,858 evictions derived from foreclosure proceedings and 54,718 evictions derived from non-payments of house rental contracts (Consejo General del Poder Judicial 2013, p. 8). According to publicly available information, 74.76% of the foreclosure proceedings initiated in 2012 corresponded to the habitual residence of individuals or families (Colegio de Registradores de la Propiedad, Bienes Muebles y Mercantiles de España 2013, pp. 7–8).

2 In 2012, 1,737,900 of Spanish families had all their members without a job (Instituto Nacional de Estadística 2012, p. 7).

In this context, the protection of the home and the right to housing has gained relevance. Social pressure from individuals and families in need, as well as NGOs and even new political parties, have turned to courts seeking protection and have pushed the battle to the political arena (see, in relation to Spain, González Pascual 2014, pp. 125–6). This chapter shows that European courts – the ECtHR and CJEU – have been sensitive to the social pressure and have revised the appropriate level of scrutiny when the right to housing is at stake. The reaction of European courts shows increasing interest in the need to protect families and vulnerable groups. It remains a timid development, but represents a step forward vis-à-vis the *status quo.* It is also surprising that this change has come from the European level while the highest national courts have remained inactive in countries where the loss of homes has been a social tragedy. In Spain, the inactivity of the highest courts, bearing in mind that the lower courts have taken part in a fluid collaboration with the CJEU that has derived in a greater level of protection for consumers when facing evictions, is particularly shocking (Gómez Pomar and Lyczkowska 2014, pp. 7–10).

These judicial developments, which could be defined as a manifestation of European judicial activism, reinforce the claims of some scholars who have traditionally argued in favour of the indivisibility and judicial enforceability of social rights, including the right to housing. Contrariwise, such judicial activism weakens the arguments of other legal schools, such as critical legal studies, that are sceptical of the language of rights and the judicial avenue as effective tools for advancing the left-wing agenda.

Part II of this chapter briefly describes the *status quo* and the European framework in which the right to housing should be understood. Part III analyzes the standard response provided by European courts on the basis of the existing legal framework. It shows that courts have adopted, until now, a kind of soft judicial review focused on procedural grounds. Part IV explores the importance of the protection of families and vulnerable groups as a key element in raising the judicial scrutiny when the right to housing is at stake. Finally, Part V concludes that, contrary to the position of certain legal schools, the discourse of rights still matters for the right to housing and judicial activism can lead to tangible outcomes and improvements against the *status quo.*

II The *status quo*: The weakness of the right to housing as a social right

The right to housing has traditionally been classified as a social right. This classification implies that the right to housing faces both textual limitations and theoretical constraints that hinder its effective realization as a right. National constitutions and European human rights protection mechanisms, together with scholarship that brings out the shortfalls of positive law, have hobbled aspirations to make the right to housing fully operative.

In western European countries, the constitutional language has been ambiguous regarding the true nature of social rights. It is common to distinguish social rights from civil and political rights and define them as mere "principles" or "matters of concern" for national authorities, to leave their concretization to ordinary legislation or barely codify them in constitutional texts (Fabre 2005, pp. 17–21). In this context, carrying out a full comparative analysis of social rights in western European constitutionalism is very difficult. The lack of safe textual grounds, always present with regard civil and political rights, is a common feature to social rights. In most cases, this characterization implies that social rights, including the right to housing, are not directly enforceable before courts and that the legislator and government enjoy much greater discretion in their regulation.

The Council of Europe framework seems to incorporate this constitutional trend. This legal system has drawn a line that puts civil and political rights on one side and economic, social and cultural rights on the other, with important implications for the protection mechanisms available for each type of right.[3] This textual division is also relevant for the right to housing. The ECHR denominates this right the "right to home",[4] putting value on the civil dimension of the right – or, as it is described in scholarly literature, the "obligation to respect and protect" – and in the ESC it is termed the "right to housing"[5] – or the "obligation to fulfil" – i.e., emphasizing the social dimension of the right.[6]

In EU law, the Charter also distinguishes between the right to a home,[7] as an individual right, and the "right to housing assistance", which,[8] lacking guidance by the CJEU, shall be considered a "principle" operating as an interpretation canon.[9] It is important to recall that the Charter is only applicable when a substantive EU law provision is relevant for the case and, therefore, without this connection, it is not possible to extend the scope of application of the Charter.[10] In this regard, the possibilities of the Charter,

3 Civil and political rights are recognized in the ECHR and a judicial body, the ECtHR, is in charge of their protection. However, almost all economic, social and cultural rights are recognized by a web of treaties that include the European Social Charter of 1961 and the Revised European Social Charter of 1996 with additional and amending protocols. The European Committee, a quasi-judicial body, is in charge of the protection of economic, social and cultural rights enshrined in these international treaties. Only a few social rights, like the right to education, are directly protected by the ECHR.

4 Article 8 ECHR.

5 Article 31 ESC.

6 The obligation to respect prohibits infringements by state authorities, the obligation to protect mandates the state to protect citizens from private third parties' interferences and the obligation to fulfil implies positive obligations to furnish and make the right to housing effective (Riedel, Giacca and Golay 2014, pp. 18–21).

7 Article 7 Charter.

8 Article 34(3) Charter.

9 Article 52(5) Charter in connection with the Explanatory Note on Article 52.

10 Article 51(1) Charter and Article 6(1) TEU.

possibly one of the most advanced declarations of rights in the field of social rights, are rather limited.

On the basis of these textual foundations, a theoretical legal framework has been built on the premise that social rights are different in nature than civil and political rights and that they are non-justiciable (Nolan 2011, pp. 21–32). These differences lie in the positive obligations for the state, the higher costs and the textual indeterminacy of social rights. These characteristics make social rights non-justiciable because the enforcement by courts entails technical, democratic legitimacy and separation-of-powers issues.

In this setting, critical legal studies has comprised one of the most belligerent legal schools since the 1980s in opposing the use of the rights discourse to improve the living conditions of people in need and the left-wing agenda. The movement's most powerful critique focuses on the abstraction, indeterminacy, and vagueness of the rights discourse and, therefore, the risk of manipulation of rights by powerful members of the society who are capable of blocking social redistribution using the ambiguity of rights as an excuse (Tushnet 1984, p. 1363; Gabel and Kennedy 1984, pp. 33–7; Horwitz 1988, pp. 405–6; West 2001, pp. 1904–7). Boiled down, the basic charge of critical legal studies is that the rights discourse is useless for social progress and that it should be replaced by social, political struggle and, ultimately, effective remedies that tackle social needs (Tushnet 1984, p. 1394). This concern may apply to all rights in general, but it is even more powerful in the context of social rights: human rights texts, the scholarship and the courts have recognized even higher degrees of indeterminacy and unjusticiable claims in the realm of social rights, making them more ineffective than civil and political rights (Pieterse 2007, pp. 800–4).The legal construction of social rights as second-class rights preserves the right-wing *status quo*, which advances neoliberal policies whose aims shun social policies in favour of the persons in need.

Some scholars, however, have argued for rethinking social rights and overcoming the shortfalls impeding their legal protection. They claim that the division between social rights and civil and political rights can be validly and effectively tackled through the use of rights in the courts (Nolan 2011, pp. 21–32). The indivisibility and dependency of all human rights could lead to defend the same level of justiciability for all of them (Scott 1989, pp. 832–41). The task, they hold, is concretizing the content of social rights – like has been done in the scholarship and courts for civil and political rights – reducing their indeterminacy and converting them into specific legal claims enforceable before courts (Pieterse 2007, pp. 819–22).

This middle-ground position has been reinforced by contemporaneous developments. Specifically, human rights law has evolved through new treaties protecting vulnerable groups[11] and has added a quasi-jurisdictional

11 Some recent examples are the Convention on the Rights of Persons with Disabilities of 2006, the soft law Declaration on the Rights of Indigenous Peoples of 2007 and the Brasilia

protection mechanism in the framework of the ICESCR.[12] In this regard, the textual foundations of social rights are improving and are on the path to concretization and justiciability. In addition, Latin-American constitutionalism – the so-called neoconstitutionalism – has also increased the attention and the protection – both at the textual and jurisdictional levels – of social rights: new constitutions with highly-developed declarations of social rights have emerged[13] and some high courts have shown great commitment in enforcing social rights.[14] Nor should experiences of South African and Indian constitutionalism in the field of social rights be underestimated (Sunstein 2001, pp. 123–32, and Khosla 2010, pp. 739–65).

After all, the destructive approach by critical legal studies and the response of some scholars against the traditional understanding of social rights reveal the persistence of the *status quo*. Textual limitations and a theoretical framework that still differentiate social rights from civil and political rights distance the realization of the indivisibility ideal of human rights. In the words of Jääskinen (2014, p. 1703), a "veil of doubt permanently shadows the debate on fundamental social right". European courts – the ECtHR and the CJEU – cannot escape from these shadows and they approach social rights with tools different from those applied to civil and political rights and, therefore, have difficulty granting the same level of protection. The right to housing is no exception and the following section examines the traditional response – based on procedural grounds – of the European courts in this field.

III The standard response: A soft judicial review on the right to housing

Once one's "home" is at stake,[15] Article 8 ECHR provides protection against disproportionate interference from national authorities. On the one hand, the right to respect one's home implies negative obligations for the state, which include, in the most extreme cases, the prohibition of the deliberate

Regulations regarding Access to Justice to Vulnerable People of 2008. These texts should be added to the more consolidated texts on vulnerable groups such as the Convention relating to the Status of Refugees of 1951; the CRC, the Convention on the Elimination of All Forms of Discrimination Against Women of 1989, the Convention n°169 on Indigenous and Tribal Peoples of 1989 or the International Convention on the Protection of the Rights of All Migrant Workers and Members of Their Families of 1990.

12 This is the individual complaint procedure (Optional Protocol to the ICESCR of 2008, which entered into force in 5 May 2013).

13 See for instance the constitutions of Venezuela (1999); Ecuador (2008) and Bolivia (2009).

14 The Constitutional Court of Colombia is the emblematic case.

15 What constitutes a "home" to the effect of Article 8 ECHR depends on the factual circumstances of each case. Special and continuous links with the place is normally a relevant indicator. See *Prokopovich v Russia* App. No. 58255/00 (ECtHR, 18 November 2004), para. 36.

destruction of homes[16] or the obligation to only carry out reasonable and limited searches.[17] On the other hand, the right to protect one's home also entails positive obligations for the state, such as actions to prevent interference from noise or pollution.[18] This is a well-known path of the ECtHR rooted in the civil dimension of the right to housing.

This path also leads to a sort of protection against interference from individuals. The case law of the ECtHR on evictions – in the context of a conflict either between the state and individuals or between individuals – is clear in determining that an eviction interferes with the right to a home.[19] Thus, when an individual is facing an eviction, the ECtHR requires, firstly, a fair balance between all the interests at stake – the general interests pursued by the state or the interest of the creditor against the interests safeguarded by Article 8.[20] In this line, the mere loss of a legal basis for occupying the home – an automatic eviction after a formalistic legal analysis according to national law – is not enough and the proportionality test cannot be avoided.[21] Secondly, this balancing test must be applied under the observance of a minimum set of procedural guarantees, i.e. "the decision-making process leading to the measures of interference must also have been fair" and adopted by an "independent tribunal".[22] Significantly, these procedural guarantees must include an adversarial–contentious type of judicial process – a "regular civil proceeding" – as enforcement proceedings without an adversarial nature are deemed particularly unfit for assessing the interests at stake.[23] The ECtHR is displaying a kind of soft judicial review, calling national authorities to apply a proportionality test and to enforce procedural guarantees in eviction procedures. In this sense, Article 8 ECHR gains a procedural dimension and acts similar to Article 6 ECHR in the field of evictions procedures.

However, the social dimension of the right to housing – the right to fulfill – has not met the same fate. The ECtHR has been emphatic in stating that neither Article 8 ECHR nor its case law recognizes "a right to be

16 In these cases, the ECtHR has gone beyond Article 8 ECHR and has determined the destruction of homes as "inhuman or degrading treatment" according to Article 3 ECHR. See the cases regarding Turkey: *Selçuk and Asker v Turkey* App. 23184/94, (ECtHR, 24 April 1998); *Bilgin v Turkey* App. No. 25659/94 (ECtHR, 17 July 2001) *Dulas v Turkey* App. No. 25801/94 (ECtHR, 30 January 2001).

17 For all, see *Funke v France* App. No.10828/84 (ECtHR 25 February 1993).

18 See, *inter alia*, *Powell and Rayner v the United Kingdom* App. No.9310/81 (ECtHR, 21 February 1990) and *López Ostra v Spain* App no16798/90 (ECtHR, 9 December 1994).

19 *Orlić v Croatia* App. No. 48833/07 (ECtHR, 21 September 2011), para. 56.

20 *Ćosić v Croatia* App. No. 28261/06 (ECtHR 15 January 2009), para. 21; *Gladysheva v Russia* App. No. 7097/10 (ECtHR, 6 March 2012), para. 94.

21 Ibid.

22 *Brežec v Croatia* App. No. 7177/10 (ECtHR, 18 October 2013), para. 44; *Rousk v Sweden* App. No. 27183/04 (EctHR, 25 October 2013), para. 137.

23 *Paulić v Croatia* App. No. 3572/06 (ECtHR, 1 March 2010), para. 44.

provided with a home".[24] The ECtHR seems to acknowledge all the textual limitations and the non-justiciability claims of social rights and clearly states that this is a question for "political not judicial decision".[25] Only in two cases has the ECtHR left the door half-open, though in very ambiguous terms, to recognize a positive obligation on the state to provide a home to a person in need.[26] Nonetheless, even in these cases, the ECtHR did not expressly condemn the state. The different treatment of the civil and social dimensions of the right to housing moves away the ECtHR from its enthusiastic declaration in favour of the indivisibility of human rights in *Airey*.[27]

A similar pattern emerges in the attitude of the CJEU. In a series of cases on consumer law, the CJEU has used Article 47 of the Charter as a powerful tool to protect individuals' homes in mortgage foreclosure proceedings in the aftermath of the severe economic crisis in Spain. Like the ECtHR, in these cases the CJEU has strengthened the judicial guarantees allowing, in the context of mortgage enforcement proceedings, claims for the existence of an unfair term;[28] interim measures or stays on the procedure;[29] and appeals against the decision of the judge of first instance dismissing an objection to the enforcement.[30] Prior to these pronouncements, Spanish mortgage legislation precluded these judicial guarantees to the debtor. The Spanish legislator has subsequently amended the mortgage legislation according to the findings of the CJEU. In addition, after the amendment of the legislation, the CJEU has declared incompatible with EU law the design of a transitory system that only allows one month to claim the existence of an unfair term in proceedings launched before the amendment of the legislation (without communicating personally to the affected the start of it, the term begins the day after the publication of the law).[31] However, in the context of these cases on consumer law, when the CJEU faced the social dimension of the right to housing in Article 34(3) of the Charter, it declared that "this provision does not guarantee the right to housing, but rather 'the right to social and housing assistance' in social policies based on Article 153 TFEU" and, therefore, it was not relevant for the outcome of the case.[32]

This cautious and procedural approach of the ECtHR and the CJEU contrasts with the substantive review carried out by the ECSR under Article 31

24 *Chapman v the United Kingdom App. No.27238/95* (ECtHR 18 January 2001), para. 99.
25 Ibid.
26 *Marzari v Italy* App, 36448/97(ECtHR 4 May 1999); *Peter O'Rourke v the United Kingdom* App. No. 39022/97 (ECtHR Decision, 26 June 2001).
27 *Airey v Ireland App. No.6289/73* (ECtHR 9 October 1979), para. 26.
28 Case C-415/11 *Aziz* EU:C:2013:164.
29 Ibid.
30 Case C-169/14 *Sánchez Morcillo* EU:C:2014:2099.
31 Case C-8/14 *BBVA, S.A.*:EU:C:2015:731.
32 Case C-539/14 *Sánchez Morcillo* Order EU:C:2015:508, para. 49.

ESC. The European Committee, through the so-called collective complaint mechanism, has reviewed the housing policies of the states in depth and has not hesitated to establish positive obligations – to fulfill – upon national authorities.[33] In this line, the ECSR follows the example of the Committee on Economic, Social, and Cultural Rights, also very active in carrying out a substantive review of national housing policies under the ICESCR.[34] However, as the experience of the latter suggests, when a more judicial procedure is adopted, even a non-judicial body, like a committee, turns to a softer procedural review, centred on procedural guarantees.[35] Again, the theoretical framework of social rights and the non-justiciability claims encourages committees, as European courts, to move to a safer avenue for a judicial or quasi-judicial body: a soft judicial review that is procedural in nature.

IV Family life and vulnerable groups: A new avenue for a stricter scrutiny

Notwithstanding this state of affairs, the recent case law of European courts is showing unfamiliar sensitivity to housing issues in Europe. This new attitude is related, in some cases, to the new challenges that the economic crisis entails for housing issues in several European countries. Thus, the relationship between home and the protection of family life – i.e., the belief that a family needs a home – is now gaining prominence in cases where the economic crisis has occasioned the loss of a home, particularly when these involve families with children. In other cases, the new approach means the continuation of the path the courts have already started to take, especially

33 The ECSR carried out an exhaustive review of facts, domestic law and measures to reduce homelessness in France and condemned the state for these measures being insufficient (*Feantsa v France*, Complaint No. 39/2006, Decision on the merits of 5 December 2007). It also analyzed domestic immigration law of The Netherlands and concluded that it did not provide sufficient housing protection to children that were in the country illegally (*DCI v the Netherlands*, Complaint No. 47/2008, Decision on the merits of 20 October 2009). Despite the initial caveats of the ECSR declaring that the state enjoys deference in the field of the right to housing, in fact, it adopts a strong review analyzing all the facts, arguments, domestic legislation and practical measures and substitutes the assessment of the state for its own.

34 For their relevance, see General Comment No. 4, *The Right to Adequate Housing (Art. 11.1 of the Covenant)*, 13 December 1991, U.N. Doc. E/1992/23 and General Comment No. 7, *The Right to Adequate Housing (Art. 11.1 of the Covenant): Forced Evictions*, 14 May 1997, U.N. Doc. E/1998/22. However, national reports have also been relevant for assessing national housing policies in relation to countries like Kosovo, Mexico, Spain or the United Kingdom (Chapman and Carbonetti 2011, pp. 709, 712, 713 and 714).

35 In the first decision taken under the individual communication mechanism provided by the Optional Protocol, the Committee concluded that Spain violated the right to housing because its courts failed to take all reasonable measures to adequately notify Ms. I.D.G that the lending institution had filed a mortgage foreclosure procedure against her. See Decision n° 2/2014, of 17 June 2015, E/C.12/55/D/2/2014.

the ECtHR, in protecting so-called vulnerable groups or individuals. In this regard, the concept of vulnerability is becoming increasingly important in the case law of the ECtHR and its interaction with the right to housing has led to the adoption of stricter scrutiny, in eviction procedures, in favour of persons in need.

This scenario could be defined as a case of clear judicial activism in which courts increase the level of protection of families and vulnerable groups despite the fact that the right to housing is limited by its textual and theoretical framework as a social right. Likewise, such a judicial response must be also interpreted in the context of national legal frameworks that are highly reluctant – even regressive – when it comes to the protection of social rights in the context of economic crisis.

A Family life, children and the home

Several scholars have pointed out the interrelationship and dependence of family life with and on the home. At the extreme, some understand housing as an indispensable condition, not only for developing any kind of family life, but also for developing all the basic needs of human life (Waldron 1993, pp. 309–38 and Nussbaum 2000, pp. 231–2 and 238–9). Housing in that sense is a freedom right – and a foundation for the exercise of other rights – rather than a socio-economic claim (King 2003, pp. 665). In a more specific approach to family life, scholars have argued that a home is necessary for the well-being of the family in, at least, three ways (Bratt 2002, pp. 14–16), for it: (1) makes family life possible, providing a safe and quality place for developing it, i.e. it is related to the physical integrity or even the existence of family life; (2) creates a positive sense of self-empowerment and stability to the members of the family; and (3) impacts directly – in connection with the conditions of the neighbourhood – to the education and employment opportunities of the members of the family.

European courts have scarcely recognized such tight bounds between family life and the home. In the aftermath of the economic crisis, the CJEU, however, has timidly begun acknowledging this close interrelationship in cases relating to eviction procedures. In *Sánchez Morcillo*, the CJEU granted the defendant the expedited procedure because "the risk, for the owner, of losing his main dwelling puts him and his family in a particularly fragile situation".[36] These cases show some sensitivity by the CJEU with regard to the effects of the economic crisis on individuals in debt and families that are in danger of losing their homes.[37] More significantly, in *Kušionová* the CJEU appeals directly to Article 7 of the Charter and the case law of the ECtHR and emphasizes that the loss of the family home "places the

36 Case C-169/14 *Sánchez Morcillo* Order EU:C:2014:1388, para. 11.
37 Ibid. paras. 10–11.

family of the consumer concerned in a particularly vulnerable position".[38] *Kušionová* was a case involving the extrajudicial enforcement of a family's home, which had been provided as security for a loan of 10,000 Euros. The CJEU declared that the proportionality of the eviction should "give particular attention" to the fact that the property constituted the consumer's family home.[39] Ultimately, in *Kušionová* the CJEU considered that the possibility of adopting interim measures for staying evictions under national legislation was a sufficient guarantee. In reaching this conclusion, the CJEU offered a solution based on a soft judicial review that was procedural in nature. In *Sánchez Morcillo* the consequences were limited to granting the expedited procedure for the preliminary ruling, providing once again a procedural advantage. The language used by the CJEU, however, should not be underestimated and the references to Article 7 of the Charter and the connection between family and home are significant.

This procedural and cautious approach by the CJEU varies when children are part of the family. In an important judgment on this matter, *Saciri*, the CJEU, interpreting EU law on reception of asylum seekers, declared that the State could not deny social assistance – including housing – to asylum seekers on the basis of allegations that the special reception centres were overpopulated.[40] If such were the case, the State was obliged to find other alternatives, *inter alia*, the granting of financial allowances in an amount sufficient to cover a "dignified standard of living"; paying special attention to housing needs; and enabling the family, if necessary, to obtain housing on the private rental market.[41] For our purposes, the relevance of this case relies on the fact that the CJEU emphasizes that social services should pay special attention to the housing needs for preserving the family unit, taking always into account the best interest of the child.[42] Children are considered – in a similar approach to the category of vulnerable group used by the ECtHR – as "persons having special needs".[43] In *Saciri*, the presence of children in the family was determinant for the CJEU to raise the standard of protection and impose clear and precise positive obligations on the state, coming closer to more substantial, less procedural judicial review.

Saciri also opens a new path to a more substantive review in housing policies. The CJEU makes a direct link between the minimum standards for reception of asylum seekers provided by EU law and human dignity recognized in Article 1 of the Charter.[44] Housing accommodation is included by

38 Case C-34/13 *Smart Capital* EU:C:2014:2189, para. 63.
39 Ibid. para. 62.
40 Case C-79/13 *Saciri* EU:C:2014:103.
41 Ibid. para. 42.
42 Ibid. para. 46.
43 Ibid.
44 Ibid. para. 35.

the CJEU, without hesitation, at the core of these minimum standards.[45] This is a striking move by the CJEU which may be developed further in the future. In this regard, the coupling of human dignity and social rights could potentially lead to increased judicial scrutiny, especially in cases where vulnerable groups and individuals are involved. Only time will tell whether this initial move of the CJEU will be successful and spread to other fields of EU law, or even to national and European conventional law through the case law of the highest national courts and the ECtHR.

On the other hand, the ECtHR recognizes that all the concepts included in Article 8 ECHR – private life, family life, home and correspondence – are not mutually exclusive and are interrelated.[46] Until now, the ECtHR case law has not provided a clear link between the protection of family life and the home. The economic crisis seems to have pushed the ECtHR to clarify this link and adopt interim measures staying forced evictions to protect families.[47] In granting these measures, the ECtHR analyzed whether national authorities offered alternative or temporary accommodation for the families, and, therefore, the right to fulfill – the social dimension of the right to housing which entails positive obligations – seems to emerge in the context of families in need.[48] In addition, similarly to the approach of the CJEU in *Saciri*, in these cases before the ECtHR, the families in danger of losing their homes had children at their care.[49] This confirms that the connection between family life and the protection of children appears determinant to raise the level of judicial scrutiny and, in these cases, for the ECtHR to grant interim measures.

In short, both the CJEU and the ECtHR seem willing to raise the level of protection in the context of economic crisis when families may lose their home and especially in cases involving children. In all cases neither court undertakes a deep analysis between the connections of family life, children and home. However, European courts are increasingly recognizing that the vulnerability of children is intrinsically connected to the well-being of the family (Ippolito 2015, pp. 23–49). The reasoning of both courts implies that the preservation of the family unit, as a general principle, is determinant for

45 Ibid. para. 38.

46 See *López Ostra supra* n. 18.

47 *A.M.B and others v Spain* App. No. 77842/12 (ECtHR Decision, 28 January 2014); *Mohamed Raji and others v Spain* App. No. 3537/13 (ECtHR Decision, 16 December 2014). However, the ECtHR has not decided on the merits of either case. In *A.M.B.* the ECtHR lifted the interim measures and declared inadmissible the complaint because of the non-exhaustion of domestic remedies; in *Mohamed Raji* the ECtHR struck the application from its list of cases because the Madrid city council decided not to enforce the demolition and suspended eviction proceedings.

48 See *A.M.B. supra* n. 47, para. 11 and *Mohamed Raji supra* n. 47, para. 15.

49 In *A.M.B.* the applicants were a married couple of Moroccan nationals and their daughter, who had Spanish nationality. In *Mohamed Raji* the applicant was a mother – with Spanish nationality – with two minors.

the best interests of children who at the same time are qualified as persons with special needs because of their lack of autonomy and their dependence on their families. *Saciri*, in particular, shows the relevance of a home for protecting these linked interests: without a home, family life and the well-being of children are jeopardized. These cases are an example that protecting a home constitutes a necessary measure for the protection of, simultaneously, family life and children under their care: when the three factors are combined, European courts may offer a stricter scrutiny.

B Vulnerability and the home: The stricter scrutiny of the ECtHR

Over the years, the relevance of the concept of vulnerability has grown in the field of international human rights law (Chapman and Carbonetti 2011, pp. 683–7). Although some scholars have argued that its vagueness and ambiguity dull its potentiality,[50] new treaties and soft law have relied on the concept.[51] Even the Inter-American Court of Human Rights uses the concept of vulnerability quite regularly.[52] Despite the blurred contours of the concept, a group or individual could be qualified as vulnerable because certain personal, social, cultural or economic circumstances place them in a disadvantaged situation at risk of potential harm (García Roca 2013, pp. 302–3; Ippolito and Iglesias Sánchez 2015, p. 1). The ECtHR has not adopted a holistic or systematic approach to vulnerability, but its case law shows the use of the category – explicitly or implicitly – in protecting some groups such as children, the elderly, the disabled, women, national minorities or the non-nationals (Ippolito and Iglesias 2015, pp. 5–20; Anagnostou 2010, pp. 16–20).

This section is focused on the more mature case law of the ECtHR on vulnerability and the home, rather than the experience of the CJEU. The use of the concept in EU law should be highlighted, however, particularly in the field of asylum seekers (Ippolito and Iglesias 2015, pp. 5–6). In fact, *Saciri* is a case that could be read both from the perspective of family life/children and from that of the protection of a vulnerable group, that is, asylum seekers. The cross-references of the CJEU to the case law of the ECtHR in *Saciri* show the close relationship between both courts in these matters and, in some way, the alignment of their case law. Moreover, the link between human dignity and social rights in *Saciri*, although limited and very premature, places the CJEU at the forefront and could become a reference for the ECtHR in future cases in this field.

50 See Chapman and Carbonetti (2011, pp. 722–8), criticizing the approach of the Committee on the Economic, Social and Cultural Rights to the concept of vulnerability and the necessity to adopt a more conceptually robust and integrated perspective.

51 See *supra* n. 11.

52 The Inter-American Court has developed the so-called "test of vulnerability" (García Ramírez 2013, pp. 493–502).

In connection with the right to housing, the ECtHR has used the tool of vulnerability to protect the home and the way of living of the Roma community. In a number of well-known cases, the ECtHR has qualified the Roma community as a vulnerable minority and, when housing policies are applied, the characteristics of its home lifestyle should be "specially" considered.[53] These cases are one of the first examples in which the vulnerability tool has had repercussions for the interpretation of the right to housing. This stricter scrutiny requires national authorities to take into account the special needs of a vulnerable group or individual when balancing the interests at stake.

This is a significant development that moves the ECtHR away from the soft judicial review described above (see *supra* section III). In its general approach, the ECtHR only requires procedural guarantees in the eviction procedures; i.e. it is enough under the procedural dimension of Article 8 that the decision be taken by an independent tribunal, in a fair process and applying a general balancing test taking into account the interests at stake without any special qualification. When a vulnerable group – such as the Roma community – is concerned, the balancing test requires a qualification. The case law of the ECtHR now requires that, when applying the balancing test, national authorities – including courts – weigh the special interests of the vulnerable group against the other interests at stake.

This reinforced balancing or proportionality test is not confined to the Roma cases. In *McCann*, the ECtHR has explicitly stated that its reasoning is applicable beyond the eviction of the Roma community from their homes.[54] More significantly, in *Yordanova*, although a case involving the Roma, the ECtHR displays a more holistic approach and uses the expressions of "outcast community", "socially disadvantaged groups" or "underprivileged status of the applicants' group" to refer to a situation that must be taken into account in the balancing or proportionality test.[55] Although *Yordanova* is a Roma case, the language of the ECtHR reveals a universal application of the reasoning of the court: "In general, the underprivileged status of the applicant's group must be a weighty factor in considering approaches to dealing with their unlawful settlement and, if their removal is necessary, in deciding on its timing, modalities and, if possible, arrangements for alternative shelter."[56] *Yordanova*, as well as other recent case law, highlights the importance of offering social assistance as an alternative to the eviction – e.g.

53 *Chapman supra* n. 24, para. 96; *Connors v the United Kingdom* App. No.66746/01 (ECtHR 27 May 2004), para. 84.

54 *McCann v the United Kingdom* App. No.19009/04 (ECtHR, 13 May 2008), para. 50.

55 *Yordanova and others v Bulgaria*, App. No. 25446/06 (ECtHR, 24 September 2012), paras. 129 and 133.

56 Ibid. para. 133.

providing social housing – for assessing the proportionality of the measure.[57] In this sense, the proportionality test is strengthened even more.

This universal application of the reinforced balancing or proportionality test, which gives special weight to the vulnerability condition, was ratified in *Zehentner*.[58] This case involved the eviction of a woman – who was not Roma – who lacked legal capacity at the moment in which a court order for the sale of her house was issued. This condition had undermined the capacity of the applicant "to participate effectively in the proceedings and without having any possibility to have the proportionality of the measure determined by the court."[59] Even the ECtHR emphasized that the principles of *bona fide* purchaser and legal certainty did not countervail the vulnerable condition of the applicant.[60] This case is particularly relevant because it did not involve a conflict between public authorities and a private individual but a conflict between two private individuals. The eviction was a consequence of non-payment to a private individual for the cost of plumbing work carried out in the applicant's home. However, in the end this case was related to the lack of legal capacity, an issue well settled and covered by substantive civil law and civil procedural law. In this regard, the activism of the ECtHR was easier. In *Bjedov*, similar reasoning led the ECtHR to declare a violation of Article 8 ECHR for the eviction of the applicant, an elderly person in poor health, for breach of the rules of special protected tenancy.[61] The vulnerability of the applicant was one of the factors that the ECtHR highlighted in determining the lack of reasonableness or proportionality of the measure.[62]

These cases show great commitment by the ECtHR to include vulnerability conditions in the core of the decisions taken by national authorities on the right to housing. This inclusion qualifies the balancing or proportionality test as follows: national authorities should identify vulnerable conditions – physically or mentally impaired groups mostly recognized and protected by substantive and procedural civil law as well as social disadvantaged groups that are less recognizable under current national legislations – and, if found, these conditions would have to be taken into consideration when applying the balancing test or proportionality test in eviction procedures. *Yordanova* is clearly the leading case on the development of this new reinforced balancing test,[63] but *Zehentner* is also crucial, as it applies this reinforced test to conflicts between private individuals (private creditors

57 Ibid. para. 132; *Stolyarova v Russia* App. No. 15711/13 (ECtHR, 29 April 2015), para. 62.

58 *Zehentner v Austria* Application no.20082/02 (ECtHR 16 July 2009).

59 Ibid. para. 65.

60 Ibid.

61 *Bjedov v Croatia* App. No. 42150/09 (ECtHR, 29 August 2012).

62 Ibid. para. 68.

63 For further references to the proportionality test developed in *Yordanova*, see Peroni and Timmer 2013, pp. 1079–80 and Remiche 2012, pp. 787–800.

and debtors). According to the ruling in *Zehentner*, national courts should also take into account vulnerability conditions in assessing the proportionality/balance of the measure in eviction procedures, even if public authorities are not involved.

The potential of the qualified proportionality test at the national level is far-reaching. In Spain, an assessment of the legislation on mortgage foreclosure proceedings and rent evictions leads to the conclusion that the qualified proportionality test is not entrenched at the legislative level. These legislative texts only allow the evicted defendant to rely on formalistic legal grounds to oppose evictions, but not on vulnerability conditions.[64] However, recent legislative developments, qualified as extraordinary measures, have provided courts with some tools that allow them to take into account and weigh vulnerability.[65] Nevertheless, the overall procedural legislation on evictions remains untouched and maintains the same grounds for objection of which vulnerability is not included. The situation in Spain shows that the qualified proportionality test developed by the ECtHR still lacks safe textual grounds at the national level and depends almost entirely on the will of the national judiciary for implementation.

V Conclusions

Contrary to the combative criticism of the acolytes of critical legal studies, rights still matter and are useful for improving the conditions of persons in need. They matter because judicial activism is transforming them into effective tools for disadvantaged groups and individuals. Critical legal studies' sharp critique is quite accurate in identifying the risk of manipulation that rights, as well as judicial reasoning, are subject to, and that the direction of judicial activism might easily shift, becoming more progressive or more conservative. The image of elites equipped with the resources to maintain the *status quo* and influence and align judicial activism with their interests

64 Under Law 1/2000, of 7 January, on Civil Procedure, in mortgage foreclosure proceedings, the only objections that the defendant could raise against the eviction are (1) the extinction of the debt or the guarantee; (2) the error in the quantification of the debt; and (3) the existence of an unfair term according to consumer protection laws (Article 696). In rent evictions due to the non-payment of the rent, phrased in very ambiguous terms, the defendant can object to the eviction on the grounds that the due payment had already been satisfied and "circumstances related to the requirements of the eviction" (Article 444).

65 See Law 1/2013, of 14 May, against evictions and Law 25/2015, of 28 July, on second opportunity, reduction of the financial burden and other social measures. These laws provide the suspension of home evictions in favour of specific vulnerable groups for a period of four years after the entrance into force of the law in 2013 (the suspension will elapse in May 2017). However, the ECtHR has stated that the proportionality test requires a resolution on the substance, weighting the interests at stake: to suspend and postpone the decision does not satisfy by itself the procedural guarantees of Article 8 ECHR (See *Bjedov supra* n. 61, para. 71).

is also powerful, almost convincing (Hirschl 2004, pp. 43–7). However, human rights law and recent developments in Europe demonstrate how persons in need can and do rely on courts, make rights claims before them and, in the end, they win battles (Anagnostou 2010, pp. 1–4). The right to housing and recent case law of the ECtHR and the CJEU are illustrative of this successful empowerment of the interests of persons in need.

European judicial activism has thus led to the strengthening of judicial guarantees of the right to home. In the aftermath of the economic crisis, the CJEU has not hesitated to interpret EU consumer law in a way that reinforces the position of the debtor in eviction procedures. This soft judicial review is still procedural in nature, but it has led to important changes in mortgage legislation in a country, like Spain, where evictions became and continue to be a social trauma. The alliance between ordinary Spanish judges and the CJEU against unfair provisions in national legislation on mortgage foreclosure proceedings represents a tale of judicial activism with tangible results: the law has changed and the debt or under risk of eviction now has greater chance of success in judicial proceedings.

This path could be expected. The long-standing textual limitations and the theoretical framework of social rights made the courts' pro-procedural review reaction predictable. What was unexpected was the courageous response that moves European courts close to adopting full substantive review of the right to housing. Courts are exploring the interconnections between the home, family life, children and vulnerability and they are raising the level of protection. The qualified proportionality test in eviction procedures, which specially weighs vulnerability conditions, is an important development of the ECtHR, while the reference to human dignity in housing affairs by the CJEU could lead to further developments in this field. Moreover, the obligation to consider housing alternatives in cases of evicted families in need and, accordingly, to provide social assistance when the case requires it, blurs the separation of the civil from the social dimensions of the right to housing. Courts are beginning to face such cases in three dimensions.

Much more remains to refine these techniques. Indeed, the full implementation of the qualified proportionality test at the national level may lead to striking developments in favour of disadvantaged groups and individuals regarding the right to housing. In addition, it seems that courts are prepared to recognize the importance of a safe home for a family when children are involved. However, the protection of the home for safeguarding the family interest itself, in the absence of children's interests, is still unclear. Finally, the vulnerability concept remains vague. Again, courts are prepared to protect vulnerable groups such as national minorities, children, women, the elderly or asylum seekers, even the unwell. However, the level of protection of the vulnerable because of economic circumstances – the poor or transient poor – is still uncertain. In the end, the connection between vulnerability and structural inequality requires further developments and closer attention by courts.

In any event, the incremental approach of judicial activism is one of its characteristics and some courts are currently more sensitive to the claims of persons in need than governments or legislators. Law is evolving through case law rather than formal changes in positive law. The *status quo* is being threatened in a way that the critical legal studies movement did not anticipate – through courts, not politics. Social rights are slowly shedding their label of "constitutional lyrics" that characterizes them as vague, imprecise and ineffective (Pawel Karolewski 2010, p. 139) and becoming genuine tools that are enforced by courts and responsive to persons in need and the left-wing agenda.

References

Anagnostou, D. (2010). The Strasbourg Court, Democracy and the Protection of Marginalised Individuals and Minorities. In: Anagnostou, D. and Psychogiopoulou, E. (eds.). *The European Court of Human rights and the Rights of Marginalised Individuals and Minorities in National Context.* Leiden and Boston: Martinus Nijhoff Publishers, pp 1–26.

Bratt, R. (2002). Housing and Family Well-Being. *Housing Studies*, 17 (1), pp. 13–26.

Chapman, A. and Carbonetti, B. (2011). Human Rights Protection for Vulnerable and Disadvantaged Groups: The Contributions of the UN Committee on Economic, Social and Cultural Rights. *Human Rights Quarterly*, 33, pp. 682–732.

Colegio de Registradores de la Propiedad, Bienes Muebles y Mercantiles de España. (2013). *Panorama registral. Impagos hipotecarios de vivienda 2012.* Madrid: Colegio de Registradores.

Consejo General del Poder Judicial. (2013). *Conciliación de datos sobre ejecuciones hipotecarias y desahucios.* Madrid: Consejo General del Poder Judicial.

Fabre, C. (2005). Social Rights in European Constitutions. In: De Búrca, G. and Witte, B (eds.). *Social Rights in Europe.* New York: Oxford University Press, pp. 15–28.

Gabel, P. and Kennedy, D. (1984). Roll Over Beethoven. *Stanford Law Review*, 36(1), pp. 26–41.

García Ramírez, S. (2013). Las afectaciones a los derechos humanos de las personas vulnerables y las minorías. El papel de la Corte Interamericana de Derechos Humanos. In: Henao, J.C. (ed.). *Diálogos constitucionales de Colombia con el mundo. VII encuentro de la Jurisdicción constitucional.* Bogotá: Universidad Externado, pp. 493–503.

Roca Martínez, J.M. (2013). Tutela jurisdiccional de los derechos de las personas y grupos vulnerables en los órdenes civil y laboral. In: Presno Linera, M. (coord.). *Protección jurídica de las personas y grupos vulnerables.* Oviedo: Universidad de Oviedo, pp. 299–354.

Gómez Pomar, F., Lyczkowska, K. (2014). Spanish Courts, the Court of Justice of the European Union, and Consumer Law. *Indret, Revista para el Análisis del Derecho*, 4, pp. 1–34.

González Pascual, M. (2014). Austerity Measures and Welfare Rights: The Spanish Constitutional System under Stress. *European Journal of Social Law*, 1–2, pp. 116–27.

Hirschl, R. (2004). *Towards Juristocracy. The origins and consequences of the new constitutionalism.* Cambridge: Harvard University Press.
Horwitz, M. (1988). Rights. *Harvard Civil Rights-Civil Liberties,* 23, pp. 393–406.
Instituto Nacional de Estadística, (2012). *Encuesta de Población Activa (EPA). Tercer Trimestre de 2012.* Nota de prensa de 26 de octubre.
Ippolito, F. and Iglesias Sánchez, S. (2015). Introduction. In: Ippolito, F. and Iglesias Sánchez, S. *Protecting Vulnerable Groups. The European Human Rights Framework.* Oxford: Hart Publishing, pp. 1–18.
Ippolito, F. (2015). (De) Constructing Children's Vulnerability under European Law. In: Ippolito, F. and Iglesias Sánchez, S. *Protecting Vulnerable Groups. The European Human Rights Framework.* Oxford: Hart Publishing, pp. 23–48.
Jääskinen, N. (2014). Fundamental Social Rights in the Charter–Are They Rights? In Peers, S., Hervery, T., Kenner, J., Ward, A. (eds.). *The EU Charter of Fundamental Rights. A Commentary.* Oxford: Hart Publishing, pp 1746–57.
Khosla, M. (2010). Making social rights conditional: lessons from India. *International Journal of Constitutional Law,* 8(4) pp. 739–65.
King, P. (2003). Housing as a Freedom Right. *Housing Studies,* 18(5), pp. 661–72.
Nolan, A. (2011). *Children's Socio-Economic rights, Democracy and the Courts.* Oxford: Hart Publishing.
Nussbaum, M. (2000). Women's Capabilities and Social Justice. *Journal of Human Development,* 1(2), pp. 219–47.
Pawel Karolewski, I. (2010). *Citizenship and Collective Identity in Europe.* London: Routledge.
Peroni, L. and Timmer, A. (2013). Vulnerable Groups: The promise of an emerging concept in European Human Rights Convention Law. *International Journal of Constitutional Law,* 11(4) pp. 1056–85.
Pieterse, M. (2007). Eating Socioeconomic Rights: The Usefulness of Rights Talk in Alleviating Social Hardship. *Human Rights Quarterly* 29, pp. 796–822.
Remiche, A. (2012). *Yordanova and Others v Bulgaria*: The Influence of the Social Right to Adequate Housing on the Interpretation of the Civil Right to Respect for One's Home. *Human Rights Law Review,* 12 (4), pp. 787–800.
Riedel, E., Giacca, G. and Golay, C. (2014). The Development of Economic, Social and Cultural Rights in International Law. In: Riedel, E. Giacca, G. and Golay, C. (eds.). *Economic, Social and Cultural Rights in International Law: Contemporary Issues and Challenges.* Oxford: Oxford University Press.
Scott, C. (1989). Interdependence and Permeability of Human Rights Norms: Towards a Partial Fusion of the International Covenants on Human Rights. *Osgoode Hall Law Journal,* 27(4), pp. 769–878.
Sunstein, C. (2001). Social and Economic Rights? Lessons from South Africa. *Constitutional Forum* 11(4), pp. 123–32.
Tushnet, M. (1984). An Essay on rights. *Texas Law Review* 62. pp. 1363–403.
Waldron, J. (1993). Homeless and the issue of freedom. In: Waldron, J. *Liberal Rights: Collected Papers, 1981–1991.* Cambridge: Cambridge University Press, pp. 309–38.
West, R. (2001). Rights, Capabilities and the Good Society. *Fordham Law Review* 69. pp. 1901–32.

14 Unjoined-up policy making and patchy promotion of gender equality

Free movement and reconciliation of work and family life in the EU

Samantha Currie[*]

I Introduction

The way in which citizens of the EU experience day-to-day family life may, at first consideration, seem quite far removed from the interest of the Union, with its historically-entrenched preoccupation with economic objectives and supranational structure. Of course, as the contributions to this volume demonstrate, EU law and policy in actual fact impact on family life in a myriad of ways and have implications for a number of different policy areas that can help shape family experiences. This chapter considers two such significant areas of EU law and policy: reconciliation of work and family life and free movement of persons. These areas have the potential to impact in a grounded, practical sense on the lives of Union citizens. To this extent, whilst family members of EU migrant workers have traditionally been afforded important entitlements under Union secondary legislation, and the CJEU has further enhanced the available protection through its interpretive role, there has also been developed a distinct body of law and policy that endeavours to facilitate a better balance between work and family life within the EU.

It will be demonstrated here that, in spite of the *existence* of these two family-implicated policy areas, there is little synergy between them and they have developed in the absence of cross-consideration. The agenda for reconciliation of work and family life fails to take into account the importance of balancing work and family life for migrant workers and, by corollary, the law on free movement fails to appreciate the need to embrace an approach that respects the particular family circumstances of many migrants. The focus of this contribution is, therefore, on family life of migrant workers on the basis that the experience of this group, when seeking to work and enjoy family life, stands as a particularly illuminating

* Samantha Currie is a Lecturer at the University of Liverpool.

case study. Such mobile EU citizens essentially find themselves occupying the site at which the policy areas of free movement and reconciliation of work and family life meet. Migration poses particular challenges for family life, not least that migrant families are less likely to have access to wider family support networks to provide informal childcare. Taking this into account, the main contention of the chapter is that the failure of the two policy areas to have a meaningful impact on this group, who operate at the point of tension between the two, undermines the value of them in a discrete, individual sense.

Central to the analysis is examination of the extent to which the two policy areas presently engage with, and acknowledge, the long-standing trend of women having responsibility for the majority of care carried out within family units, which remains relevant today (see, e.g. Pickard 2008, Equality and Human Rights Commission 2013 and European Commission 2015). Not only do women continue to spend more time than men carrying out domestic tasks and care work but, in many instances, obligations relating to care (often but not always relating to children) necessitate a break from employment (maternity leave is the most obvious example) and/or a change in, or even cessation of, working patterns (European Commission 2014). This chapter will demonstrate that such breaks can pose problems for the continuance of protection under the free movement of persons provisions. It will also illustrate that the reconciliation of work and family life agenda – despite expressly recognizing the particular circumstances of many women with caring obligations – does not presently extend the sort of sufficiently robust male-focused entitlement to reconciliation-related rights that would be necessary to engender a shift in the gendered patterns of care within families.

The first section will examine the reconciliation of work and family life agenda from the perspective of whether it truly incorporates a commitment to gender equality and can have implications beyond the static context for mobile workers. The section that follows will pick up on the free movement context to consider how far it engages with pregnancy-related leave and the caring commitments that follow, as well as with gender equality more broadly. Overall the chapter will demonstrate the lack of synergy between the two areas of EU law and policy and the current stagnation of any efforts to promote progression and crossover between the two. It addresses a lacuna in the literature in that, although both policy areas have attracted a wealth of research in their own right, there has been little consideration of the potential overlap between the spheres or acknowledgement of the lack of joined-up policy making. Ultimately, analysis across both policy areas through the lens of family life leads to articulation of a broader argument that the EU institutions are presently unable, or perhaps unwilling, to embody in their actions or judgments a genuine commitment to gender equality.

II EU policy on reconciling work and family life: How (ir)relevant is it to modern family life and mobile workers?

A Current position and future directions

The reconciliation of work and family life is consistently portrayed as a priority on the agenda of the EU institutions, as is demonstrated by the launch of a European Commission Roadmap in August 2015 entitled "New start to address the challenges of work-life balance faced by working families" (European Commission 2015). This initiative, rather than setting out a distinct plan of action for the EU in the area, maps different options (encompassing a combination of legislative, non-legislative and policy-based activity) to move law and policy on work–life balance in the Union forward. Reconciliation of work and family life is not, of course, unfamiliar territory for the Commission or the EU more broadly, as various Union policy initiatives and legal measures have, over the years, been designed, implemented and promoted under the headline of helping workers to better ensure that both work (professional responsibilities) and family (care responsibilities) can be accommodated within increasingly busy schedules. Indeed, the 1974 Social Action Programme[1] requested implementation of measures to help achieve gender equality in the workplace, with particular emphasis on ensuring reconciliation of family and professional responsibilities (for more detailed discussion of EU law and policy in this area see Caracciolo di Torella 2011, Masselot and Caracciolo di Torella 2010, Busby and James 2015, Golynker 2015). From a hard law point of view, obvious examples include the directives on pregnant workers (maternity leave),[2] parental leave,[3] working time[4] and part-time work.[5] Given the lack of clear competence in the area, the Union has tended to use a combination of health and safety[6] and equality[7] as legal bases for action in the area. Amongst the plethora of "softer" initiatives, the Council Recommendation on childcare, which encouraged initiatives to enable women and men to

1 EC Bulletin Supplement 2/74.

2 Directive 92/85/EEC of 19 February 1992 on the introduction of measures to encourage improvements in the safety and health at work of pregnant workers and workers who have recently given birth or are breastfeeding [1992] OJ L348/1.

3 Directive 2010/18/EEC of 8 March 2010 implementing the revised Framework Agreement on parental leave concluded by BUSINESSEUROPE, UEAPME, CEEP and ETUC and repealing Directive 96/34/EC [2010] OJ L68/13.

4 Directive 93/104 of 23 November 1993 concerning certain aspects of the organization of working time [1993] O.J. L307/18.

5 Directive 97/81/EC of 15 December 1997 concerning the Framework Agreement on part-time work concluded by UNICE, CEEP and the ETUC – Annex: Framework agreement on part-time work [1998] OJ L14/19.

6 Article 137 TFEU.

7 Article 141(3) TFEU.

reconcile their occupational, family and child-raising responsibilities[8] and a later Resolution on balanced participation of women and men in family and working life,[9] provide noteworthy examples.

Throughout its history, EU law and policy on reconciling work and family life has been framed very much within the ambit of the broader goal of achieving gender equality (Busby and James 2015, p. 297). In the early stages of its development, the emphasis was on enabling women to combine their traditional (and often considerable) responsibility for childcare and domestic tasks with the more contemporary propensity (in many instances financial necessity) for families to be dual-earning. More recently, there has been growing recognition that reconciliation is viewed as a fundamental right with the potential to enhance both women and men's lives. The reference to it in Article 33 of the Charter supports this perception of reconciliation as a notion that holds such resonance (see Masselot and Caracciolo Di Torella 2010, pp. 39–48, James 2012, p. 364). The case law of the CJEU has also reinforced the status of reconciliation as a principle protected by Union law.[10]

It would be short-sighted (and naïve), however, to consider only equality and fundamental rights concerns as having shaped the development of law and policy on reconciliation of work and family life. Economic objectives have also played a major influencing role, and the Commission has linked reconciliation particularly with a desire for as many individuals as possible to be economically active in order to enhance the competitiveness of the EU (Masselot and Caracciolo Di Torella 2010, p.3).[11] The 2015 "New Start" Roadmap highlights as the main issue the need to "address the low participation of women in the labour market by modernising and adapting the current EU legal and policy framework to today's labour market to allow for parents with children or those with dependent relatives to better balance caring and professional responsibilities" (European Commission 2015, p.1).

The undeniable undercurrent in this latest initiative is that the approach the EU has taken in previous years when seeking to advance the reconciliation agenda has failed to deliver, largely due to the lack of success in meeting the targets for women's employment as set out in strategies such as the Lisbon Agenda and Europe 2020.[12] That such employment targets have shaped the approach taken to achieving better reconciliation, however, is

8 Recommendation 92/241/EEC [1992] OJ L123/16.

9 [2000] OJ C218.

10 See, for example, Case C-1/95 *Gerster*:EU:C:1997:452; Case C-243/95 *Hill* EU:C:1998:298; Case C-104/09 *Roca Alvarez* EU:C:2010:561; Case C-222/14 *Maïstrellis* EU:C:2015:473.

11 *Europe 2020: A Strategy for Smart, Sustainable and Inclusive Growth* COM(2010) 2020.

12 In 2000, the Lisbon Agenda set a target of 70% full employment. In 2020, the Europe 2020 target was set at 75% full employment. According to the European Commission (2015), in

itself open to criticism. Lewis (2000, p.13), for example, has been critical of how reconciliation has been instrumentally used as a tool to raise employment rates and has proliferated a concentration on economic aspects, at the expense of attention being given to non-economic considerations, such as the conditions of work experienced by individuals. Busby and James (2015, p. 296) also lament the entrenched economic focus of reconciliation policies and express particular disappointment in the presently stagnated position of Union-level policies in the area.

Of course, reconciliation of work and family life is not the only "social" policy area in a state of listlessness. The recession, combined with austerity policies at the national level in a number of Member States, and the practical difficulties of decision-making on sensitive issues in an EU of 28, have impacted on social law and policy more broadly. For example, in so far as equality law is concerned, there is little appetite for fresh action on the part of the Union in this area (at least so far as hard law is concerned). The lack of agreement regarding the Commission's 2008 proposal for a new Equality directive,[13] and continued slow progress of the discussions in Council, is indicative of the disinclination to genuinely reopen or update the secondary legislation in this area.[14]

From one perspective, the existence of the Roadmap, and the linked consultations (with social partners and the public) about the future direction of EU action on work–life balance (launched in November 2015), are indicative of a vibrant policy area. From another angle, it is very telling that the launch of the Roadmap followed on quickly from the withdrawal of the Commission's 2008 proposal to amend the directive on pregnant workers.[15] This contained provision to extend the minimum level of maternity leave from 14 weeks to 18 weeks and to introduce the principle of full pay during maternity leave, subject to a ceiling that Member States could enforce. The failure of this proposal demonstrates the present inability, and unwillingness, of the EU (or at least many of its Member States) to take even fairly limited legislative action at the current time. Therefore, in reality, the Roadmap is representative of an attempt by the Commission to at least keep the issues on the agenda, and to reignite discussion about the significance of the issues.

2014, the percentage of women in employment was 63.5%, whereas the percentage of men in employment was 75%.

13 Proposal for a Council Directive on implementing the principle of equal treatment between persons irrespective of religion or belief, disability, age or sexual orientation COM/2008/0426 final.

14 See Council of the European Union, Proposal for a Council Directive on implementing the principle of equal treatment between persons irrespective of religion or belief, disability, age or sexual orientation – Progress Report, 16 November 2015 (2008/0140).

15 COM (2008) 600/4).

B Recognition that women face particular challenges in reconciling work and family life . . . but what about male-focused initiatives?

There is a definite acceptance that women continue to face particular challenges linked to reconciliation, frequently as a consequence of child-bearing and being primarily responsible for the child-rearing, within the Roadmap: "[t]here is strong evidence that after having children many women drop out of the labour market entirely and those who continue to work often do so in part time although they would like to work full time or they work in jobs below their level of qualification" (European Commission 2015, p. 1). Furthermore, it expressly states that "female labour market participation remains below its potential due to a lack of possibilities to balance work and family responsibilities, including lack of affordable childcare, rigid working arrangements or absence of incentives for men to take more care responsibilities in their families" (European Commission 2015, p. 1). It ultimately frames the desire to increase women's economic independence as necessary to avoid wasting the EU's resources and to reverse the current "sub-optimal allocation of skills and competences acquired through education by women" (European Commission 2015, p. 1).

The recognition of the particular challenges faced by women is welcome but it is striking that the Commission's concern for the experience of women extends only in so far as they wish to be economic actors. The message continues to be that women (and men) should be supported in their ability to provide care for their families – whether that be for children or for other dependent family members, including elderly parents – so long as they remain part of the labour market. Caring of itself is not valued, and this is a theme that will be returned to later in the context of the free movement framework. Moreover, in no way should appreciation of the recognition that women continue to be primarily responsible for care within families be misinterpreted as a suggestion that reconciliation policies do not also need to focus on men. Quite to the contrary, the burdens experienced most acutely by women in seeking to incorporate within their lives a better balance between professional and family life render it even more important that men can enforce accessible reconciliation-based rights. Not only is this significant for men's own personal experience of family life and fatherhood, which men today are expected to embrace in a more active manner than was the case for previous generations (Collier 2009), it is only through the greater participation of men in activities connected to caring that women will ever be alleviated of some of the expectation of responsibility.

This does appear to have been recognized by the Commission in the latest Roadmap. Indeed, various policy documents and soft law produced by the political institutions over the years have been keen to promote the value of reconciliation for women *and* men.[16] In contrast, the CJEU has not always been as keen to encapsulate within its reconciliation-related judgments the notion that men too should derive such protection. For example, the case of *Hofmann* is frequently cited as an example of the Court being reluctant to get involved in decisions capable of being perceived as an attempt to alter the balance of responsibilities between parents in the private sphere.[17] This case concerned a father, the primary carer of the child, whose attempt to access a German benefit available to mothers was refused. The CJEU was not convinced of his argument that this ran contrary to Equal Treatment Directive.[18]

In the later case of *Roca Alvarez*, however, the CJEU did "endorse a model of (more) equal parenting" (James 2012, p. 371). Here a father's claim that the restriction of a right to take leave in the first nine months of a child's life to employed *mothers* was contrary to the Equal Treatment Directive was upheld. The Court explicitly referred to the ramifications of the national rule as perpetuating men and women's traditional roles.[19] *Maïstrellis*[20] provides a further example of the Court supporting a man's claim to protection under EU reconciliation of work and family life legislation, this time in respect of parental leave. This case concerned a Greek judge (classified as a civil servant under Greek law) who challenged Greek legislation that provided that male civil servants were not entitled to access paid parental leave if their wife did not work or exercise any profession, unless it was considered that the wife was unable to meet the needs related to the upbringing of the child due to serious illness or injury. The Court found this to be direct discrimination on grounds of sex, contrary to the Recast Equal Treatment Directive 2006/54, pointing out that "the mere fact of being a parent is not sufficient for male civil servants to gain entitlement to that leave, whereas it is for women with an identical status".[21] This provides an example therefore of the Court applying the Equal Treatment Directive to find that men are placed in a more disadvantageous position than women by virtue of the national law. The Court in *Maïstrellis* did not go so far as placing the decision within the broader equality context, for example by explicitly recognizing the link between the enhancement of men's access to reconciliation as a means of also increasing women's experience of managing work

16 See, for example, the Council Resolution on the Balanced Participation of Women and Men in Family Life [2000] O.J. C218/5.

17 Case C-184/83 *Hofmann* EU:C:1984:273.

18 Directive 76/207 [1976] O.J. L39/40, as later amended by Directive 2002/73 [2002] O.J. L269/15. See also Case 163/82 *Commission v Italy* EU:C:1983:295, and Case C-476/99 *Lommers* EU:C:2002:183. The case law is discussed in more detail in James (2012), and also in Masselot and Caracciolo Di Torella 2010.

19 Case C-104/09 *Roca Alvarez* EU:C:2010:561 para. 36.

20 *Maïstrellis, supra* 11.

21 Ibid, para. 49.

and family life.[22] It did again, though, make reference to the desire to avoid perpetuating traditional distributions of gender roles.[23]

The discussion in this section so far has demonstrated an awareness on the part of the political institutions and the Court of the need for women and men alike to be able to access reconciliation-related rights. This is undermined, however, by certain aspects of the EU's legislative framework on reconciliation and the Commission has acknowledged that the "current policy and legislative framework tends to discourage men to take family-related leave" (European Commission 2015, p. 2). Commentators such as Masselot and Caracciolo Di Torella (2010) (see also Caracciolo Di Torella 2007), for example, have pointed to the stark differences between women and men's entitlement to leave following the birth of a child. The right to take a period of maternity leave is considerably more developed and protected than the male equivalent right to take paternity leave. Article 8 Directive 92/85 on Pregnancy specifies that paid maternity leave should be granted for a minimum of 14 weeks. In contrast, EU law does not expressly set out any right to a period of paternity leave; rather, Member States are *encouraged* to provide such entitlement by the Council Resolution on the Balanced Participation of Women and Men in Family Life. Here, the use of soft law in respect of the fathers' rights, compared to the hard law-protected rights of mothers, most likely signifies that the reconciliation of men's work and family life is a goal less able to attract a level of agreement amongst the 28 Member States. In other words, this remains a more politically sensitive issue than the more readily culturally accepted notion that women should be able to combine paid work with family life.

The Parental Leave Directive 2010/18 is acknowledged as a measure that treats mothers and fathers on equal terms by providing both parents with a right to leave in respect of their family obligations. However, the effectiveness of this Directive has also been questioned on the basis of the lack of any guaranteed entitlement to pay. Masselot and Hadj Ayed (2004, p. 333) point out that because fathers "generally generate the highest income in families they are reluctant to exercise their right to leave. Accordingly, it is more likely that the partner with the lowest income (usually women) will take unpaid leave". Consequently, the usefulness of this Directive in truly facilitating reconciliation for fathers is uncertain. In reality the apparently "preferential" treatment given to mothers by certain of the reconciliation measures only serves to reinforce the traditional stereotype of women as holding primary responsibility for caring and domestic tasks and to, ultimately, undermine the ability for families as a whole to reconcile work and

22 The CJEU was, of course, applying the provisions of the Equal Treatment Directive on direct discrimination on grounds of sex. It is perhaps not surprising that the emphasis in the judgment is on the "subsidiary" position of the man in contrast to the female comparator (para. 50).

23 Ibid, *supra* 11, para. 50.

family life (Caracciolo Di Torella 2007, p. 322). Taking such considerations into account, it would seem that, in spite of rhetoric about reconciliation being relevant to both women and men, and a shift by the CJEU to recognize a more equal model of parenting, the body of hard law that incorporates reconciliation-related rights remains inaccessible to many men in practice. Women undoubtedly face greater challenges in respect of reconciliation, but if progress is to be made in addressing such challenges, the law and policy agenda should take seriously (as the Roadmap suggests) the need to incorporate men in the reconciliation discourse and, more concretely, ensure that men can enforce reconciliation-related rights.

C Promulgation of a static worker model

In addition to the criticism that the reconciliation agenda has not gone far enough in creating male-focused rights and entitlements, this policy area can also be challenged on the basis that it has not taken into account the position of migrant workers. The reconciliation agenda is premised on the basis of a static workforce operating in a single national jurisdiction and does not make any provisions for those exercising EU-facilitated rights of mobility to work and reside across national borders. This brings to the fore a number of issues. First, it is at odds with the trajectory and life–work course of many mobile citizens in the EU (Currie 2013), and ignores research that explicitly recognizes the need to consider mobility, work and family life in conjunction as part of a coherent policy strategy (Ackers and Stalford 2004). Moreover, the very reason people often make the decision to migrate is to try and enhance the living standards and life chances available to themselves and their family members alike (Boyd 1989). Thus, migration may be a household/family strategy for achieving a better quality of family life.

Secondly, the very premise upon which Union law initially extended residence and equal treatment rights to family members under the free movement provisions was to encourage workers, as factors of production, to exercise their economic right to free movement. The CJEU has also consistently extended benefits to the immediate family members of workers on the basis that such assistance has an indirect benefit for the worker him or herself; the Court asserted that such an approach was necessary in order to "facilitate the migrant workers' migration to and integration in the host Member State".[24] Given this apparent understanding of the link between mobility and family life, evidenced both in the secondary legislation and in the Court's case law on free movement, it is unfortunate that reconciliation initiatives have not, at any point, sought to acknowledge the particular situation of migrant workers.

24 E.g. Case C-32/75 *Cristini* EU:C:1975:120; Case C-63/76 *Inzirillo* EU:C:1976:192; Case C-207/78 *Even* EU:C:1979:144.

Of course, this argument could be challenged by the contention that, in fact, there is no need for the reconciliation agenda to acknowledge the particular position of mobile citizens because, as has been pointed out already, the free movement provisions (and the Court) have addressed this by including family entitlements within the free movement provisions. While it is true that valuable family-related entitlements have been extended to migrant citizens (workers in particular) when residing in Member States other than that of their nationality – including educational rights, labour market rights and entitlement to various forms of social assistance – the basis of such rights is "national treatment". In other words, the migrant workers and their families are entitled to receive the same rights as nationals of that Member State.[25] Arguably, such "national treatment", although valuable for extending a core nucleus of key rights, is not far-reaching enough to specifically target the rather particular reconciliation-related family needs of migrants. Mobility in itself raises particular challenges in this regard. For example, migrant families are frequently separated from the extended family unit and, consequently, have less support in terms of *informal* childcare than national workers (Ackers and Stalford 2004). This is particularly pertinent when the often inadequate nature of formal childcare services in Member States – in terms of affordability, availability and accessibility – is taken into account (European Commission 2013).

In addition, migrant workers have often been resident in the host Member State for relatively short periods of time. This can be especially problematic as EU law enables Member States to impose qualifying periods before which workers become entitled to various reconciliation-related rights, such as requesting flexible working or parental leave. For example, Directive 2010/18 states that entitlement to parental leave can be made subject to a period of work qualification of up to one year in duration. While factors such as these can pose difficulties for all migrant families when it comes to seeking to balance work and family life, it is also clear that such challenges will be heightened in the case of poorer migrant families without the resources to, for example, afford formal childcare or take unpaid leave at times of family need.

25 As the section below will demonstrate, the main provisions relating to the residence and equal treatment entitlement of migrant citizens and their family members are primarily set out in the Directive 2004/38/EC of the European Parliament and of the Council of 29 April 2004 on the right of citizens of the Union and their family members to move and reside freely within the territory of the Member States OJ 2004 L158/ p 7, with educational rights of the children of migrant workers addressed in Article 10 of Regulation 492/2011 of the European Parliament and of the Council of 5 April 2011 on freedom of movement for workers within the Union [2011] OJ L141/1. It is important to recognise that practical access to such rights is, of course, dependent on national implementation of the relevant EU law. Research demonstrates that in practice there are significant differences across the Member States in relation to how far EU-based rights are protected. (O'Brien, Spaventa and De Connick 2016).

The failure of the reconciliation initiatives to even give consideration for particular provision to be made addressing the specific situation of mobile citizens, for example by way of exceptions to the standard qualifying periods being introduced to the relevant provisions, demonstrates the dominance of the static worker model within this area of law and policy. This is unfortunate from the point of view of EU migrant families as it leaves them in a position in which it is even more difficult for them to rely on provisions designed to achieve a balance between work and family life than it is for their national counterparts. In the next section the discussion will move on to the free movement of persons provisions in order to consider further the extent to which this area of law is engaging with particular challenges faced by families, especially in relation to the provision of care.

III Migrant worker women and (in)security of status

Free movement as an area of EU law and policy is very distinct from the reconciliation of work and family life agenda. Free movement has historically been inextricably linked to the development of the Single Market and, as a fundamental freedom, has a much more visible place in the treaties than the reconciliation of work and family life agenda. Traditionally, free movement of persons has encompassed free movement of workers, freedom to provide services and the freedom of establishment.[26] Free movement has also been a key element of the status of EU citizenship,[27] which has built on the nucleus of "citizenship" rights (including residence and equal treatment on grounds of nationality) already developed under the free movement of workers, and extended them to cover certain non-economic situations and migrants.[28] Clearly, the EU's claim to competence in the area of free movement also goes beyond that in the area of reconciliation.[29]

It has already been pointed out that, despite the original economic preoccupation of the Union and free movement policy more generally, there was early recognition of the necessity for workers' family members to be extended rights in order to render free movement a more realistic and attractive option for the EU's working age population.[30] This section will consider the extent to which elements of free movement law and policy are currently engaging with concerns relevant to the discussion above as

26 Articles 45, 56 and 49 respectively.

27 Article 20 TFEU.

28 Article 21 TFEU sets out the "general" right of free movement for Union citizens, with further elaboration of the conditions relating to different categories of migrants set out in Directive 2004/38. (See, further, Currie 2009, Dougan 2013 and Thym 2015).

29 For a contemporary discussion of the position of EU law on free movement see Shaw 2015.

30 E.g. the original free movement regulation, Regulation 1612/68 of 15 October 1968 on freedom of movement for workers within the Community [1968] OJ L257/ 2, included family rights.

regards to the reconciliation of work and family life. It builds on the premise of the previous section, that reconciliation policy has not incorporated an understanding of the lives of mobile citizens, to argue that, similarly, free movement law is not encompassing a genuine commitment to ensuring that migrant workers can manage family and caring responsibilities. In essence, free movement law continues to operate in a gender-discrete way, and can have particular implications for the experience of female migrants, especially those with caring responsibilities, exercising their EU rights to mobility. The focus of this analysis is primarily on the "case study group" of those exercising rights to move as workers pursuant to Article 45 TFEU.[31] Specifically, it considers the potential for the status of worker to have continuing effects once employment has stopped as a result of pregnancy, care responsibilities, or the temporary or insecure nature of the work carried out.

A *Incorporation of pregnancy-related employment breaks into the free movement framework: Time-limited protection*

The starting point when considering whether a migrant can retain the status of migrant worker under EU law, and continue to enjoy the benefits that attach to it, is Article 7(3) of Directive 2004/38. This provision provides a number of circumstances in which a migrant who has been a worker pursuant to Article 45 TFEU can retain the status despite no longer being in the labour market. These include: (a) being temporarily unable to work as the result of an illness or accident; (b) being involuntarily unemployed after one year of employment and registering as a job-seeker; (c) being involuntarily unemployed before having completed a year of employment and registering as a job-seeker, or completing a fixed-term employment contract of less than a year (in these instances the status of worker shall be retained for no less than six months), and (d) embarking on vocational training relating to the former work. Conspicuously absent from this list is any mention of pregnancy or maternity leave. The CJEU had the opportunity to consider the relevance of the provision, however, to pregnancy-related leave in *Jessy Saint Prix.*[32]

Ms Saint Prix was a French national who arrived in the UK in July 2006. She worked as a teaching assistant before enrolling on a Post Graduate Certificate in Education course. In February 2008 she withdrew from the course as she was pregnant, the baby being due in early June 2008. Ms Saint Prix then sought employment in a secondary school (registering with an employment agency to assist her). As no positions at secondary

31 In practice, migrants will often have a shifting status over time and derive rights of residence from different sites of the Treaty (e.g. as workers under Article 45 TFEU and economically inactive migrants under Art 21 TFEU).

32 Case C-507/12 *Saint Prix* EU:C:2014:2007. On *Saint Prix* see Currie 2016.

school level were available, she instead worked in a series of nursery school roles. When she was almost six months' pregnant the demands of caring for pre-school children had become too strenuous and Ms Saint Prix stopped this work. She initially searched for lighter work but, when none was available, made a claim for Income Support. Ms Saint Prix's claim was refused by the UK authorities, ultimately because she was not considered to have continuing status of a migrant worker under EU law (and, consequently, could not be considered as having a right to reside in the territory).

The CJEU in its judgment made the clear statement that a woman should not, in principle, be deprived of the status of worker within the meaning of Article 45 TFEU by virtue of being required to give up work due to the constraints of the late stages of pregnancy and immediate aftermath of childbirth.[33] The outcome of this case was therefore positive in so far as the Court accepted that female migrant workers who temporarily give up work because of the physical constraints of the late stages of pregnancy and the aftermath of childbirth are entitled to continue to hold the status of migrant worker pursuant to Article 45 TFEU. Significantly, this in turn can provide access to valuable entitlements in the host Member State, such as Income Support and other benefits available to nationals in analogous circumstances.

However, the Court in *Saint Prix* also limited the time period that a woman could be expected to be absent from the labour market: "the fact that she was not actually available on the employment market . . . for a few months does not mean that she has ceased to belong to that market during the period, *provided she returns to work or finds another job within a reasonable period after confinement*".[34] Those that do not return to work within a reasonable time will, presumably, revert to the status of "initial" work seekers. Although Article 45 TFEU continues to govern the situation of such "initial" work seekers, the scope of their right to reside and, particularly, their stake to equal treatment-derived, social protection-related (social assistance) rights, is more curtailed and unclear than those with the retained status.[35] It will be

33 Para. 40.

34 Para. 41 (emphasis added).

35 Work seekers have a right to reside under Article 45 TFEU in order to enhance the potential of work being secured. Under Directive 2004/38, there is an initial right to reside for three months (Article 6) and they cannot be expelled by the Member State providing they can provide evidence they are continuing to look for work and have genuine chances of being engaged (Article 14(4)(b)). In terms of work seekers' broader equal treatment rights, Article 24(2) of the Directive allows Member States to derogate from the equal treatment principle in so far as social assistance rights for work seekers are concerned. Case C-67/14 *Alimanovic* EU:C:2015:597 is one of the more recent judgments of the CJEU relevant to the scope of work seekers' equal treatment rights. See also Case C-138/02 *Collins* EU:C:2004:172and Cases C-22/08 and C-23/08 *Vatsouras* EU:C:2009:344.

the role of national courts, taking into account national rules on maternity leave to make the determination on reasonableness.[36]

At this point, there may well be more of a tangible overlap between EU free movement and reconciliation policies in that the national law the court engages with is likely to be shaped, at least partially, by policies and commitments contained in reconciliation-related initiatives at EU level (most notably the Pregnancy Directive). This raises a number of issues. First, it creates some uncertainty for women who rely on their retained worker status for a period but then struggle to find employment upon their return to the labour market, either because their employer has gone out of business or due to difficulties finding work that can accommodate the changed family circumstances. It is also not clear whether a woman who does have difficulty in securing employment beyond the "reasonable time" would be required to pay back money received as a benefit. This could potentially be a very stressful experience for the migrant and her family members. Secondly, the need to return to work in a "reasonable" time poses particular difficulties for women with ill babies or babies that have additional needs and for whom a prompt return to work is simply not feasible (or desirable, from their point of view).[37]

This also links to a wider consideration about how EU free movement law fails to value unpaid care work, despite the often significant nature of the work involved, in terms of time and resource (O'Brien 2013 and Busby 2011). The CJEU has been consistent in its refusal to include unpaid care work within the scope of economic activity in the free movement context.[38] This reinforces the view that a woman unable to return to work in a "reasonable" time, even when this is due to having to care for her ill baby, would be unable to demonstrate fulfillment of the conditions needed to qualify as a worker with retained status. Indeed, the case of *Dias* involved a woman who did not work while she was caring for her ill child. Here, the woman was not treated as a worker with retained status, although this was not directly considered by the CJEU in that case. Advocate General Wahl in *Saint Prix*, however, did pick up on *Dias* and distinguished it from *Saint Prix* on the basis that "the mother's absence from work extended beyond the time when there was a medical reason for her not to return to work".[39] This illustrates quite starkly the reluctance to even give serious consideration to the potential to recognise that pregnancy and childbirth at times may necessitate flexibility with regards to the ability of women to return to the labour market as promptly as seems to be expected. If there is a failure

36 Para. 42.

37 Ms Saint Prix herself, even though she returned to work after only three months' absence, delayed her return as a consequence of her baby being seriously ill with a heart condition. Her baby died at only one-year-old as a result of this condition.

38 Case C-77/95 *Zuchner* EU:C:1996:425; Case C-325/09 *Dias* EU:C:1992:327.

39 AG Wahl Opinion, *Saint Prix*, para. 24.

to acknowledge this socially and politically, the legal framework governing the rights of migrant workers, including (and perhaps especially) those that apply when the worker leaves the labour market, is at present also failing to incorporate or promote any such flexibility.

The analysis here highlights how the free movement framework fails to value care-giving and, in extending protection only to those women who can be categorized as still being part of the labour market, is preoccupied – like the reconciliation agenda – with women (and men) being economically active.

B Slipping through the net of Article 7(3): Migrant women in short-term and insecure work

The preceding discussion pointed out the problematic nature of the time-limited protection extended to those on pregnancy-related breaks from employment. However, for those unable to retain worker status in the Article 7(3) sense *at all*, the situation is perhaps even more precarious. Those who do not fall within the scope of the provision must immediately navigate the process essentially as an "initial" work seeker, without any recognition being given to any time already built up in the labour market.

This precariousness of this position is illustrated by the case of *Alimanovic*.[40] This concerned a Swedish woman, and one of her adult daughters, both of whom had been in (temporary) work in Germany, but for 11 months, and not within the previous year. The Court in this case was quick to apply Article 7(3) in a rather literal sense, stressing that the claimant had been unemployed for longer than the six months specified in the provision (Article 7(3)(c)), and therefore could not rely on a retained status to secure continuing entitlement to benefits, including family allowances. This approach actually stands in contrast to that adopted in *Saint Prix*, where the Court was keen to emphasize, when considering the non-exhaustive nature of the provision, how the status of worker stems directly from the Treaty as opposed to the secondary legislation (para. 32).[41] Perhaps even more tellingly in *Alimanovic*, the Court did not refer to the supposed "fundamental" nature of the status of Union citizenship, nor did it incorporate proportionality and conduct an "individual assessment" of the claimant's

40 Case C-67/14 *Alimanovic* EU:C:2015:597.

41 The contrasting, more literal approach in the later case of *Alimanovic* can be categorized, along with a line of other cases – notably Case C-333/13 *Dano* EU:C:2014:2358 and Case C-299/14 *Garcia Nieto* EU:C:2016:114 – as indicative of the Court's more restrictive approach towards the free movement rights of economically inactive migrants pursuant to Article 21 TFEU and Directive 2004/38, particularly as regards application of the right to equal treatment in Article 24 (See further Thym 2015 and Dougan 2013). Arguably, the different approach in *Saint Prix* might be accounted for by the Court's realization that a finding *against* Ms Saint Prix, effectively confirming that her situation was outside the scope of Article 7(3) would, quite simply, be unpalatable from a gender equality perspective.

circumstances, both hallmarks of the citizenship free movement case law since *Grzelcyk*.[42] The CJEU stated that no individual assessment was needed because the directive itself "establish[ed] a gradual system as regards the retention of the status of 'worker'. . . [which] itself takes into consideration various factors characterising the individual situation of each applicant in particular, *the duration of the exercise of any economic activity*".[43] The condition of having worked for one year was thus applied strictly.[44]

The Alimanovic family consequently found themselves categorized as work seekers without recourse to the equal treatment principle, in spite of having worked on the territory for almost a year and having spent a considerable amount of time in Germany. Indeed, the three children had been born there. Clearly, the exercise of economic activity for a year or more is deemed as especially worthy of attracting entitlement to rights whereas other indicators of integration, such as time spent on the territory, familial or kinship networks, is seemingly unworthy.

This application of a literal approach to Article 7(3) can be criticized for having gender-specific implications in that women are particularly likely to be in forms of employment that make it more difficult to satisfy the conditions of the provision. While, of course, both women and men occupy positions of temporary and insecure employment, "atypical" work is of particular relevance to women (O'Brien 2013). Furthermore, women are significantly more likely to have their work interrupted by breaks that link directly to family life and caring responsibilities (Waddington 2011). A link can be made here with O'Brien's (2013) work on "rights cliff edges" under the law on free movement of workers. Such cliff edges are frequently faced by women, who are more likely to perform "unpaid work, informal care work, or reproductive work". Such work is deemed to fall outside the scope of the "worker" status in Article 45 TFEU because the Court has insisted on maintaining the requirement that the work be "part of the normal labour market" that excludes (and clearly does not value) those individuals not categorized as carrying out "genuine and effective" work.[45]

Essentially, then, migrant women face particular challenges in gaining access to the all-important status of worker under Article 45 TFEU. Additionally, even for those that do secure the status, the forms of employment they are likely able to access (e.g. temporary or atypical) have the potential to undermine their ability to qualify for retention of that status should difficulties arise down the line.

42 Case C-184/99 *Grzelcyk* EU:C:2001:458.

43 Para. 60, emphasis added. This strict approach has also been taken in Case C-299/14 *Garcia Nieto* EU:C:2016:114.

44 This mirrors the approach taken in Case C-333/13 *Dano* EU:C:2014:2358 to the residence conditions in Article 7 of Directive 2004/38.

45 Case 344/87 *Bettray* EU:C:1989:226; Case 196/87 *Steymann* EU:C:1988:475; Case C-456/02 *Trojani* EU:C:2004:488.

C Gender and family dynamics of free movement law

This analysis of migrant working women has primarily considered two cases: *Saint Prix* and *Alimanovic*. Both judgments have specific implications for female migrants, though it is clearly *Saint Prix* that is more associated with addressing "gender issues" owing to the centrality of pregnancy to the particular factual circumstances. *Alimanovic's* relevance to the issue of how far free movement law incorporates gender dynamics, by contrast, is more subtle. Nevertheless, in spite of the issue of pregnancy being at the forefront of the *Saint Prix* case, and the positive outcome for the applicant in the case, it cannot be justifiably claimed that free movement law genuinely does embody a commitment to gender equality or to enabling women and men to reconcile work (and mobility) with family life. Indeed, there is a more general failing in that there does not appear to be any recognition of how reconciliation of work and family life-related issues directly link to gender equality.

The Court in *Saint Prix* actually spent little time considering the principle of gender equality. Whereas the Advocate General expressed the constitutional significance of both the principles of gender equality and protection from nationality-based discrimination,[46] the Court's response on this issue was more muted. For example, it did not make reference to its back catalogue of case law on pregnancy and discrimination.[47] Substantive equality, previously said by the CJEU to be the basis of the pregnancy rights contained in the Pregnancy Directive,[48] receives no attention and there is no clear declaration that pregnancy and childbirth – necessitating a break in employment – should not result in a woman, effectively, being treated in a disadvantageous way (see also Busby 2015). It is disappointing that the Court did not take the opportunity to re-confirm the principles established in its earlier case law, or to reassert their constitutional nature in the same way as the Advocate General, to send a clear message as regards to their continuing significance.

It is also quite telling that, in contrast to the Advocate General who considered the gender discrimination elements more directly, the Court did not bring the Charter, specifically Article 23 that enshrines the principle of equal treatment between men and women, into its deliberations (and neither the Advocate General nor the Court relied on Article 33 of the Charter on reconciliation). Given the tendency of the Court in its case law on the equality principle to combine the authority of the Charter with that of the general principles (Bell 2013),[49] this is significant. Had the CJEU been

46 AG Wahl Opinion, *Saint Prix*, para. 2.

47 Such as, *inter alia*, Case C-177/88 *Dekker* EU:C:1990:383 and Case C-207/98 *Mahlburg* EU:C:2000:64.

48 E.g. Case C-104/09 *Alvarez* EU:C:2010:561, para. 34.

49 E.g. Case C-555/07 *Kücükdeveci* EU:C:2010:21; Case C-236/09 *Test-Achats ASBL* EU:C:2011:100.

more responsive to the gender equality and family life dimensions of *Saint Prix*, and framed some discussion in the context of the Charter in this way, the constitutional relevance of the issues at stake in *Saint Prix* would have been emphasized to a greater extent. Moreover, more prominence would have perhaps been given to the state of affairs that led to the case in the first place: the gender-disparate way in which the secondary legislation on continuing worker status is framed and phrased. Had the Court given more consideration to the principle of equality and the reconciliation rhetoric in its *Saint Prix* judgment, and considered the challenges that migration can pose for family life, there would have arguably been scope for it to articulate the importance of the connection between these principles and policy areas.

Interestingly, in light of the stronger claim to competence the Union has in relation to free movement, it could be argued that it would actually be possible for a more concrete reconciliation agenda to be pursued in this way, with the free movement provisions providing a legal basis for measures directly addressing migrant workers' potential to access family-related rights. Furthermore, it is conceivable that, just as rights of residence and equal treatment were granted to family members on the basis of facilitating the mobility of workers, barriers to mobility caused by obstructions to enjoyment of family life, or family-related rights, could be could be caught by Article 45 TFEU.[50] While the theoretical possibility of such developments is worth noting, it is highly unlikely that there would be the political desire (at Member State or Union level) or judicial inclination to make them a practical reality.

IV Concluding remarks

This contribution has considered two areas of EU law and policy that can have a very real impact on the way that family life is experienced. The reconciliation agenda has sought to respond to the concerns of many working families in relation to the difficulties of combining work and family life. While the focus here has predominantly been on caring obligations relating to children, there are also very obvious needs for this agenda to address caring obligations relating to older adults (Horton 2015). This policy area currently stands at a juncture in that the Commission appears to recognize the limitations of the previous initiatives and the need to move forward. Whether there will be the political appetite to do so is a consideration outside the realms of this chapter, but it is noteworthy that the Roadmap stresses so vehemently the particular challenges that women continue to face in terms of accommodating care and their professional lives. It is clear,

50 On the basis that they pose obstacles to free movement as opposed to being discriminatory, as per Case C-18/95 *Terhoeve* EU:C:1999:22.

though, that if the law and policy in the area was to genuinely embody a commitment to gender equality in order to seek to overcome some of these challenges, there would need to be a real shift in the rights and entitlements available to men. It is only through the greater legal availability of family/care-related entitlements to men (particularly in a form that does not economically penalize those that seek to rely on them), and crucially in a cultural sense their *take up* by men, that there might be genuine steps towards overcoming the greater burden experienced by women in that regard.

In terms of free movement law and policy, this area has traditionally been posited as a way for individuals in the EU to achieve a better life for themselves and their families. It is also clear, in a practical sense, that mobility is disruptive to family life. While the free movement provisions have extended rights to family members to place them in an analogous *legal* position to nationals, the reconciliation agenda has not sought to include mobile families within its remit so as to address reconciliation concerns specific, or at least of heightened significance, to the "free moving" cohort. Moreover, the framework that governs free movement, as it is interpreted by the CJEU, includes some trends that are concerning from a gender equality and reconciliation perspective. In particular, there is scope for women exercising free movement rights who are unable to return to the labour market in a "reasonable time" following childbirth to find themselves without protection. There is a very evident lack of recognition in the free movement sphere of how caring obligations can impact on people's lives, particularly those of women, and prevent them from falling within the parameters of (often rigid) legal categories.

It has been illustrated that the position of migrant workers effectively "tests" the rhetoric of reconciliation of work and family life. Analysis of this group's situation highlights the shortcomings of both policy areas. This has two important implications: first, the significance of the reconciliation rhetoric is undermined if, at the point at which it meets the free movement provisions, it appears to collapse, or at least have very little visibility. Secondly, if within the EU institutions there was the political appetite to genuinely tackle issues relating to the balance of family and professional responsibilities, the stronger level of competence vis-à-vis the free movement provisions could potentially provide an avenue through which a more concrete family–work reconciliation agenda could be promoted. From this point of view, the lack of a joined-up approach, and the prevalent standalone nature through which these policy areas operate, represents somewhat of a lost opportunity.

Finally, a dominant theme being espoused within both policy spheres, principally by the Commission in relation to reconciliation and the CJEU as regards to free movement, is that individuals are worthy of most protection in so far as they can be described as being economically active. This economic preoccupation is open to criticism on a number of levels, not least in its failure to value care-giving as an activity, and also in its failure to appreciate the saving to the economy as a consequence of carers who, through their actions, save government significant sums of money. From the point of view of the analysis here, it emphasizes clearly (and quite depressingly) the current stance of the EU. With the trend across both policy spheres, and indeed beyond, being one of stagnation and/or restriction, and with the ongoing economic situation of the Member States being utilized as justification for the continuance of austerity policies, there are very real concerns about the extent to which EU law will continue to offer individuals the potential to enhance their experience of family life, or at least offer some protection when their interaction with EU law creates difficulties for their family lives.

References

Ackers, L. and Stalford, H. (2004). *A community for children: children, citizenship and migration in the EU*, Aldershot: Ashgate.

Ackers, L., (1998). *Shifting Spaces: Women, Citizenship and Migration within the European Union*, Bristol: The Policy Press.

Bell, (2013). Constitutionalization and EU Employment Law, University of Leicester, *School of Law Research Paper* 13(05).

Boyd M., (1989). 'Family and Personal Networks in International Migration: Recent Developments and New Agendas', 23(3) *International Migration Review*, 638–70.

Busby N., (2015). 'Crumbs of Comfort: Pregnancy and the Status of 'Worker' under EU Law's Free Movement Provisions' 44(1) *Industrial Law Journal*, pp. 134–45.

Busby N. (2011). *A Right to Care? Unpaid Work in European Employment Law*, Oxford: Oxford University Press.

Busby, N. and James, G. (2015). Regulating working families in the European Union: a history of disjointed strategies. *Journal of Social Welfare and Family Law*, 37(3), 295–308.

Caracciolio Di Torella, E. (2007). New labour, new dads the impact of family friendly legislation on fathers. *Industrial law journal*, 36(3), pp. 318–28.

Caracciolio Di Torella, E. (2011). Is there a fundamental right to reconciling work and family life in the EU? In Busby, N. and James, G *Families, care-giving and paid work: challenging labour law in the 21st century*, Cheltenham: Edward Elgar.

Collier, R. (2009). Father's rights, gender and welfare: some questions for family law. *Journal of social welfare and family law*, 31(4) pp. 357–71.

Currie, S. (2013). Men on the sidelines: the reconciliation of work and family life in the context of cross-border posting. *Journal of Social Welfare and Family law* 35(3), pp. 389–408.

Currie, S. (2016). Pregnancy-related employment breaks, the gender dynamics of free movement law and curtailed citizenship, *Common Market Law Review* 53(2), pp. 543–62.

Dougan, M. (2013). The Bubble that Burst: Exploring the Legitimacy of the Case Law on the Free Movement of Union Citizens. In: Adams, M., de Waele, H., Meeusen, J. and Straetmans, G. (eds.). *Judging Europe's Judges: The Legitimacy of the Case Law of the European Court of Justice.* Oxford: Hart, pp. 127–54.

Equality and Human Rights Commission (2013), *Women, Men and Part-time Work*, Briefing Paper, January Available at http://www.equalityhumanrights.com/about-us/devolved-authorities/commission-scotland/legal-work-scotland/articles/women-men-and-part-timework.

European Commission (2013), *Press Release: Report on childcare provision in the Member States and study on the gender pension gap* (Brussels). Available at http://europa.eu/rapid/ press-release_MEMO-13–490_en.htm.

European Commission (2014), *Tackling the Gender Pay Gap in the European Union* Luxembourg.

European Commission (2015), Roadmap, *New start to address the challenges of work – life balance faced by working families* 2015/JUST/012.

Golynker, O. (2015). Family-friendly reform of employment law in the UK: an over-stretched flexibility. *Journal of Social Welfare and Family Law*, 37(3), pp. 378–92.

Horton, R. (2015). Caring for adults in the EU: Work–life balance and challenges for EU law. *Journal of Social Welfare and Family Law*, 37(3), pp. 356–67.

James, G. (2012). Forgotten children: work-family reconciliation in the EU. *Journal of social welfare and family law*, 34(3), pp. 363–79.

Lewis, J. (2000). *Work-family balance, gender and policy*. Cheltenham: Edward Elgar.

Masselot, A. and Caracciolio Di Torella, E. (2010). *Reconciling work and family life in EU law and policy*, London: Palgrave.

O'Brien, C. (2013). I trade, therefore I am: Legal personhood in the European Union. *Common Market Law Review*, 50, pp. 1643–8.

O'Brien, C. Spaventa, E. and De Connick, J. (2016). The concept of worker under Article 45 TFEU and certain non-standard forms of employment. Brussels: European Commission.

Pickard, L. (2008). Informal care for older people provided by their adult children: Projections of supply and demand to 2041. *Report to the Strategy Unit and Department of Health* London: Personal Social Services Research Unit.

Shaw, J. (2015). Between Law and Political Truth? Member State Preferences, EU Free Movement Rules and National Immigration Law. *Cambridge Yearbook of European Legal Studies*, Available at CJO 2015 doi:10.1017/cel.2015.10.

Spaventa, E. (2015). Family rights for circular migrants and frontier workers: O and B and S and G, *European Law Review* 52, pp. 753–78.

Thym, D. (2015). The Elusive Limits of Solidarity. Residence Rights of and Social Benefits for Economically Inactive Union Citizens, *Common Market Law Review* 52, pp. 17–50.

Waddington, L. (2011). Carers, Gender, and Employment Discrimination – What Does EU Law Offer Europe's Carers? In: Moreau, M. *Before and after the economic crisis: what implications for the EU social model?*, Cheltenham: Edward Elgar, pp. 101–28.

Index

For Product Safety Concerns and Information please contact our EU representative GPSR@taylorandfrancis.com Taylor & Francis Verlag GmbH, Kaufingerstraße 24, 80331 München, Germany

Batch number: 10725973

Printed by Printforce, the Netherlands